I0820584

Discerning Religious Truth
A Didactic Exposition of the Logic and Epistemology of the Islamic Sciences

Islamic Philosophy and Theology Series

The ASIPT Series in Islamic Philosophy and Theology, published by Lockwood Press, is seeking submissions of manuscripts that explore the vibrant contributions and applications of Islamic philosophy and theology from early to contemporary periods of Islamic intellectual history. We aim to develop a shared interdisciplinary publishing space for both academic and confessional approaches in order to publish significant monographs and translations that meet rigorous academic standards. We aim to dissolve unnecessary tensions and divisions between the academic and confessional study of Islamic philosophy and theology and promote greater collaboration and communication.

Editor in Chief

Aaron Spevack

Advisory Board

Macksood Aftab Muhammad Hozien

Editorial Board

Talal Ahdab, Zaytuna College

Asad Q. Ahmed, University of California, Berkeley

Safaruk Chowdhury, Whitethread Institute

Khaled El-Rouayheb, Harvard University

Carl Sharif El-Tobgui, Brandeis University

Najah Nadi, DPhil (Oxon)

Jawad Qureshi, Zaytuna College

Omar Qureshi, Yaqeen Institute

Haroon Sidat, Cardiff University

Himmet Taskomur, Harvard University

See last page for volumes in the series

Discerning Religious Truth

A Didactic Exposition of the Logic and Epistemology of the Islamic Sciences

Based on al-Khabīṣī's Commentary on al-Taftāzānī's *Tahdhīb al-manṭiq* and Its Glosses

by

Hamza Karamali,
Marwan Tayyan, and
Justin Poe

LOCKWOOD PRESS
Columbus, GA · 2025

American Society of Islamic Philosophy and Theology
Islamic Philosophy and Theology Series, volume 1

Copyright © 2025, American Society of Islamic Philosophy and Theology, inc.
Online: https://asipt.org

All rights reserved. No part of this publication may be reproduced, distributed, or transmitted in any form or by any means, including photocopying, recording, or other electronic or mechanical methods, without the prior written permission of the publisher, except in the case of brief quotations embodied in critical reviews and certain other noncommercial uses permitted by copyright law.
First printing, 2025

ISBN: 978-1-957454-78-8
LCCN: 2024950714

This work is copyrighted by it's authors and/or publishers American Society of Islamic Philosophy and Theology (ASIPT)

Published by Lockwood Press on behalf of the
American Society of Islamic Philosophy and Theology

Printed in the United States of America

CONTENTS

SERIES INTRODUCTION

In the Name of Allah, the Compassionate, the Merciful.
All praise is due to Allah. May peace and blessings be upon the Prophet Muhammad, his family, companions, and those who follow him.

The purpose of the **American Society of Islamic Philosophy and Theology**'s series in **Islamic Philosophy and Theology** is to provide a publishing space that welcomes a range of disciplinary approaches to the broadly conceived categories of Islamic theology and philosophy. In particular, we aim to foster engagement between scholars of confessional, academic, and interdisciplinary backgrounds, allowing each to benefit from the approaches and methods of the other's discipline without the typical institutional divisions. This series strives to maintain a consistently high quality of academic excellence, and through an intentionally dialogical review process along with distribution to diverse markets, to spark new channels of rigorous and fruitful scholarly conversation.

Among the varied topical foci of the series is the subject of logic as taught in the classical Islamic seminary tradition. To this end, we bring the post-Avicennian Islamicate tradition into conversation with the Latin and analytical traditions of logic, observing and studying the common historical roots that these traditions share in Aristotle, al-Fārābī, and Ibn Sīnā as well as their divergences in method, focus, and terminology.

The book before you represents a unique effort to translate the Islamic logic tradition into the English language in a dialogical and familiar manner. The reader not only gets a deep look into a tradition that would normally require significant fluency in Arabic and training in the Islamic sciences but also experiences how this tradition engages in practice with logical arguments and relates to discussions in contemporary logic.

The primary author, Hamza Karamali, and his co-authors Marwan Tayyan and Justin Poe, who joined the project as it developed over the years, have produced a volume that we hope will benefit readers for years to come. I thank the authors for their hard work and dedication and thank the anonymous reviewer for a careful and astute reading which has no doubt produced a stronger book. I would also like to thank the Templeton Foundation for providing generous funding to complete this volume, allowing us to devote ample attention to shepherding the manuscript from draft to published book.

Dear reader, we hope that this will be the first of many volumes from the **ASIPT** series on your shelf. We are honored to have your readership and support.

— Aaron Spevack, Series Editor

PREFACE

The spirit of my teachers runs through this book. They taught everyone that Islam is true. And they made that truth the basis of their scholarship in the traditional Islamic sciences.

I have tried to bring their scholarship into the modern academic world. That has been a struggle because the modern academic world believes that religious truth-claims are the fervently held assumptions of religious theologians who are not open-minded enough to entertain the possibility that they might be wrong.

But that's not what my teachers were like. They expected me to challenge them, and to try to prove them wrong. They expected me to realize for myself—based on evidence—that what they were teaching me—whether it be the understanding of a hadith or the exegesis of a Qur'ānic verse or a point of Arabic grammar or anything else—was, in fact, true.

They did this because they had all trained in logic and a sophisticated epistemology. And I found myself using that same logic and epistemology as I taught *kalām*, Qur'ānic exegesis, legal theory—even history—to my own students. Then, for three years, I worked as the Academic Programme Manager for Kalam Research and Media, where I had the opportunity to collaborate as a Muslim theologian with scientists and analytic philosophers. This forced me to express the logic and epistemology that I had learned from my teachers in the language of modern science and analytic philosophy.

It was during this time, about ten years ago, that I began working on this book. I carefully read, annotated, summarized, re-organized, and engaged with four glosses on one of the most influential textbooks of logic in the post-classical Muslim scholarly tradition. And I expressed all of those ideas in the language of modern analytic philosophy in order to bring the logic and epistemology of the Muslim scholarly tradition into conversation with modern philosophy. This wasn't a mere translation. It was a readable explanation that unlocked dozens of cryptic expressions, connected them to modern logic and modern analytic philosophy, and gave a philosophical compass to students of the Islamic sciences.

I almost finished. I just needed two things. I needed to finish some very tedious logical proofs of obscure syllogistic figures and of how to manipulate propositions with complex modalities. And I needed someone who had trained in logic and the Islamic sciences and who was extremely intelligent to patiently and painstakingly review and critically examine everything that I had done, and to challenge me. That is the only way to confirm, correct, and improve any complex work of philosophy.

I left the book unfinished for almost ten years. But I was constantly using it. I spent these years using and applying this research to develop, teach, and disseminate rational arguments for the truth of Islam, first in a course, a textbook, a teacher-certification program, and an iman-protection program for parents called *Why Islam is True* (see: www.WhyIslamIsTrue.com), and then in a comprehensive manual of arguments called *Kalām 3.0: The Muslim Manual of Logical Arguments to Show the Truth of Islam in the 21st Century*.

Last year, Dr. Aaron Spevack took this almost-finished work under the wings of the *American Society of Islamic Philosophy and Theology* (ASIPT). He assigned his researchers Marwan Tayyan and Justin Poe to help me to finally take it to completion. It was a dream come true. Both of them had been traditionally trained in logic and the Islamic sciences and were extremely intelligent. Marwan already understood how I thought because he had formerly been one of my most talented students. They read the book with a fine-toothed comb, challenged my translations, edited its language and presentation, improved its style, and eagerly wrote the remaining tedious logical proofs. We had many exhilarating discussions along the way that have confirmed, corrected, and improved the book. I am grateful to them for their scholarly company. You will feel it as you read this book.

Hamza Karamali
Istanbul, Türkiye
Tuesday, April 30, 2024

INTRODUCTION

Logic as an Islamic Science

Logic today is a discipline that studies the forms of valid inference. An example of a form of valid inference is what logicians call *modus ponens*,[1] which looks like this:

First Premise:	If A, then B.
Second Premise:	A.
Conclusion:	Therefore, B.

Logicians call this a *form* of inference because it is an abstract representation of an unlimited number of particular inferences. We can, for example, replace *A* with the proposition, "It is daytime," and *B* with the proposition, "The sun has risen," which results in this particular inference:

First Premise:	If it is daytime, then the sun has risen.
Second Premise:	It is daytime.
Conclusion:	Therefore, the sun has risen.

This is a *valid* inference because the truth of the two premises entails the truth of the conclusion: the form of a valid inference is such that if its premises are true then the conclusion must also be true.

Validity is different from *soundness*. An inference might be *valid* but nevertheless *unsound*, such as this one:

First Premise:	If science is true, then religion is a myth.
Second Premise:	Science is true.
Conclusion:	Therefore, religion is a myth.

1. *Modus ponens* is Latin for "method of affirming," so called because it infers the truth of the consequent by *affirming* the antecedent. Its counterpart is *modus tollens*, which is Latin for "method of denying," so called because it infers the falsehood of the antecedent by denying the consequent.

This inference is valid because its form is such that if its premises are true then its conclusion must also be true. But the conclusion is not true because the first premise is false. Although this inference is valid, it is not sound. An inference is *sound* when it is both (a) valid and (b) all its premises are true.

Modern logic only studies the validity of inferences; it does not study their soundness. Discerning whether a particular inference is sound requires knowledge of the disciplines that study the kinds of premises that are being used (the example above would require some knowledge of the philosophy of science and the philosophy of religion). It also requires knowledge of certain universal kinds of questions that are indispensable in determining the truth of any particular premise. These include questions of *epistemology* (the study of the nature, origin, and limits of human knowledge), questions of *metaphysics* (the study of everything that exists insofar as it exists), questions of the *philosophy of language* (the study of the nature of language, meaning, and signification), and questions of the *philosophy of mind* (the study of the nature of mental phenomena and the relation of the mind not only to the body but also to the rest of the extramental world).

Modern logic does not study any of these kinds of questions; today they are usually relegated to philosophy. But in traditional Islamic civilization logic *did* study these kinds of questions because they are universal questions that are required for the discovery of truth, particularly religious truth. Making sound (and not merely valid) inferences to discern truth, especially as it pertains to God and His religion, has always been at the very heart of Islamic scholarship, and it has always been the purpose of Islamic logic.

From Aristotle to Modern Logic

Aristotle, the founder of the science of logic, was also concerned about both validity and soundness. The six books of Aristotle that treated questions of logic were called the *"Organon". Organon* means tool, and these books were the tools that Aristotelian philosophers used to prevent themselves from making mistakes as they used inference to discover truths about God, natural philosophy, and ethics. As they did that, they committed themselves to a particular epistemology, a particular metaphysics, a particular philosophy of language, and a particular philosophy of mind. And these philosophical commitments were scattered throughout the books of Aristotle.

Aristotelian logic was carried into antiquity by philosophers such as Galen, Alexander of Aphrodisias, and Porphyry. But after these philosophers, an anti-philosophical Christianity became the official religion of the Roman empire, and the study of ancient Greek philosophy in Europe steadily declined, culminating in Justinian's closure of the School of Athens in 529 AD. Greek philosophy then moved from Europe into North Africa, the Levant, and Persia, which, soon afterwards, fell under the rule of Muslims, who made ancient Greek learning their own.

The translation of ancient Greek learning into Arabic began in Damascus less than a hundred years after the demise of the Prophet (God bless him and give him peace) and reached its peak at the House of Wisdom in Baghdad during the reign of the Abbasid caliph al-Ma'mūn (197/813–218/833). Most of these early translators were Christians who were translating their own heritage from Syriac into the language of their new rulers. But by the time of al-Fārābī (d. 339/950) and then Avicenna (d. 427/1037), Islamic civilization was critiquing and enhancing this once Greek and Christian heritage.

After al-Fārābī and Avicenna, there are two historical paths. The first historical path leads to modern logic; the second historical path leads to Islamic logic. I will describe each one in turn, beginning with the first.

The historical path to modern logic proceeds from al-Fārābī and Avicenna to the Spanish Muslim Averroes (d. 595/1198), the Spanish Jewish Maimonides (d. 1204), and the Italian Christian Aquinas (d. 1274), and then into the revival of Aristotelian philosophy in Christian Europe. At the hands of Aquinas and Bonaventure, Aristotelian philosophy merged with Christian theology in a synthesis that lasted for many centuries until it was famously challenged by Galileo (d. 1642) when he introduced a new and explicitly anti-Aristotelian scientific method into Christian Europe.[2] Galileo's scientific method was vindicated by Isaac Newton (d. 1726) and the Scientific Revolution. The Church was unable to defend Aristotelianism against the rise of the new anti-Aristotelian science. As a result, from the 17th through the 19th centuries, philosophy in the Christian world broke its links with Aristotelianism and fragmented into hundreds of pieces.

The link between sensation and knowledge broke with Descartes; the link between cause and effect broke with Hume; the link between reality and the mind broke with Kant; the link between premise and conclusion broke with Hegel; the link between language and logic broke with Frege; the link between author and reader broke with Derrida; and with these and dozens of other breakages, the notion of a philosophical or intellectual unity was

2. See Ian G. Barbour, *Religion and Science* (New York: HarperCollins, 1997), 9-17.

completely lost. Each philosopher proceeded to chart his own philosophical course, leading to further disagreement and fragmentation. The historical synthesis between Aristotelian philosophy and Christian theology broke into the separate philosophical disciplines of metaphysics, epistemology, philosophy of language, ethics, philosophy of religion, and numerous other modern branches of philosophy, each discipline starting from philosophical disagreements over a collection of questions. These disagreements in turn led to new questions, which led to the further fragmentation of these disciplines into sub-disciplines, and so on.

Modern logic has emerged as one of these philosophical fragments. Historically, it traces itself back to the Aristotelian logic of the scholastic period, which sought inferential soundness in addition to inferential validity and weaved questions of metaphysics, epistemology, and the philosophy of language into the analysis of philosophical truths, all within the unified (but tenuous) philosophical system of medieval Christian Aristotelianism. Now, those questions have become scattered among the various disciplines of modern philosophy, and modern logic has become an isolated discipline concerned merely with validity. Whether an inference tells us truths about the real world is no longer a question of logic, but of metaphysics. Whether it gives us real knowledge is no longer a question of logic, but of epistemology. Whether it has meaning in human language is no longer a question of logic, but of the philosophy of language. And so on.

Modern logic is so severely fragmented that it has even separated itself from natural human language. Instead of natural language, it uses a mathematical formal language composed of logical variables, constants, and functions. These logical variables, constants, and functions are meta-logical concepts, which means that their meanings can be arbitrarily defined, and what it means for an inference to be valid can also be arbitrarily defined. The resulting logical systems can be axiomatized by arbitrarily defining primitive truth statements; and these systems can then be studied for properties such as *completeness* (whether all expressible logical statements can be derived in the system) and *decidability* (whether arbitrary formal-language expressions are valid theorems in the logical system). Although modern philosophers do use modern logic, logic today finds its most sophisticated applications not in philosophy, but in mathematics and computer science, which generate inference-systems that can be used by scientists to study and manipulate the universe. One might even say that Aristotelian logic was optimally designed for human thought and modern logic is optimally designed for machines.

From Aristotle to Islamic Logic

There is another historical path from Aristotle that goes through al-Fārābī and Avicenna. But instead of going West to the Spanish Averroes, it goes East to the Persians Abū Ḥāmid al-Ghazālī (d. 505/1111) and Fakhr al-Dīn al-Rāzī (d. 606/1210).

Al-Ghazālī was the one who facilitated the critical integration of Aristotle into the Muslim scholarly tradition through his seminal *Tahāfut al-falāsifa* (Incoherence of the Falāsifa). The *Tahāfut* is popularly misrepresented as a non-rational religious condemnation of rational inquiry, but nothing could be further from the truth—it is a carefully argued *philosophical* work that develops *philosophical* arguments to demonstrate the rational incoherence of those conclusions of al-Fārābī and Avicenna that conflict with what the genuine revelation of the Prophet Muhammad (God bless him and give him peace). This philosophical critique is accompanied by an acknowledgment of those aspects of their *falsafa* that are correct and useful. Muslim scholars could now use his philosophical analysis as a guide to engage with Aristotelianism and to incorporate its useful aspects into their scholarly tradition.

One of these useful aspects was logic. Al-Ghazālī wrote several textbooks on logic, most notably his *Miʿyār al-ʿilm*, in which he retained Avicenna's formal logic, but instead of illustrating its application with philosophical inferences, he applied it to legal inferences that Muslim scholars were thoroughly familiar with. He employed this logic in his *al-Iqtiṣād fī al-iʿtiqād*, which went on to become a seminal reference-work in the science of rational theology (*kalām*), and in his *al-Mustaṣfā min ʿilm al-uṣūl*, which went on to become a seminal work in the science of legal theory (*uṣūl al-fiqh*). Through al-Ghazālī, logic became a part of the Muslim scholarly tradition.

Al-Ghazālī critiqued *falsafa* and incorporated its useful elements, especially logic, into the Islamic sciences. Al-Rāzī went further. He became a *faylasūf*.[3] But,

3. The most important works in which al-Rāzī gives a comprehensive analysis of *falsafa* are his *al-Mabāḥith al-mashriqiyya fī ʿilm al-ilāhiyyāt wa-l-ṭabīʿiyyāt* (*Eastern Studies in Metaphysics and Natural Philosophy*), his study of the metaphysics of *kalām* in his *al-Maṭālib al-ʿāliya* (*High Issues*), his summary and review of the positions of previous *falāsifa* in his *Muḥaṣṣal afkār al-mutaqaddimīn wa-l-muta'akhkhirīn* (*Summary of the Philosophical Positions of the Early and Late Falāsifa*), his commentary on Avicenna's *al-Ishārāt wa-l-tanbīhāt* (*Signs and Pointers*), and his *falsafa*-and-*kalām*-oriented exegesis *al-Tafsīr al-kabīr* (*The Great Commentary*).

unlike his predecessors al-Fārābī and Avicenna, he was also an accomplished scholar of the traditional Islamic sciences. Like al-Ghazālī, his philosophical acumen, combined with his religious learning, guided him through the alleyways of *falsafa*, protecting him from both philosophical and religious error. He seamlessly weaved a new Islamized *falsafa* first into *kalām* (the Islamic science of rational theology whose scholars are called *mutakallimūn*), and from there into legal theory, Qur'ānic exegesis, and a host of other religious disciplines. At the hands of al-Rāzī, *falsafa* was renewed, corrected, and elaborated, becoming a vibrant discipline whose foremost scholars were the religiously oriented graduates of the madrasa.

Philosophers used Aristotle's *Organon* to protect their minds from mistakes as they sought to discover *philosophical* truths. After al-Ghazālī and al-Rāzī, logic became a tool that religious Muslim scholars used to protect their minds from mistakes as they sought to discover *religious* truths. Al-Ghazālī famously remarked that "Whoever doesn't learn it thoroughly, all of his learning is completely unreliable."[4] The science of logic became an integral part of the madrasa curriculum. And every Islamic science was eventually structured by the science of logic.[5]

As the scholars of the madrasa used logic to discern religious truth, particularly in the science of *kalām*, they had to consider philosophical questions that today belong to the fields of epistemology, metaphysics, philosophy of language, philosophy of mind, etc.—

Do the extramental objects of our knowledge exist?

Yes, they do.

Do they exist in our mind when we know them?

No, they don't.

Then what is the relation between mental concepts and extramental objects?

The concepts represent the objects.

How does this representation arise in our minds?

---

4. Abū Ḥāmid Muḥammad al-Ghazālī, *al-Mustaṣfā min ʿilm al-uṣūl* (Beirut: Dār al-Kutub al-ʿIlmiyya, 1993), 10.

5. This is illustrated in Chapter 11, the final chapter of this book, though to appreciate it requires familiarity with the content of the other chapters. To understand how logic structures the Islamic sciences might be one of the most worthwhile fruits of the study of logic, especially in the contemporary age, characterized as it is by the fragmentation of knowledge.

The mind abstracts the representation from the extramental object. This process, like all physical processes, is a contingent, regular association subject to God's creative agency.

But aren't the associations between natural causes and effects necessary?

No, they are contingent. That being said, they are also continuous, but continuity is a different kind of propositional modality than necessity.

Doesn't that mean that human knowledge is fallible?

Yes, it does.

Doesn't that make knowledge impossible?

No, it doesn't—hypothetical possibilities do not vitiate certainty.

What exactly is human knowledge anyway?

It is a property of the human soul.

But don't I see with my eyes, hear with my ears, and smell with my nose?

Your eyes, ears, and nose are physical means by which you, i.e., your soul, perceives. That is to say, they are regularly associated with your soul or mind knowing them. And physical perceptions aren't real knowledge, anyway, because real knowledge is conceptual knowledge that is abstracted from physical sensations. Everything that I've said here, for example, is conceptual knowledge, not physical sensation.

What exactly does it mean for you to say something?

It means that I use sounds to signify mental concepts.

But doesn't that mean that you only ever talk about mental concepts, never about extramental objects?

No, because the mental concepts refer to extramental objects.

—and so on.

Since, for the religiously oriented scholars of the madrasa, the goal of logic was not merely to analyze the *validity* of their religious inferences but also their *soundness*, these questions and hundreds of others like them were gradually incorporated into the madrasa textbooks of logic, critiqued, analyzed, and elaborated with exacting precision, always subjected to rational inquiry, never accepted on religious authority. Logic became the tool for discerning religious truth, and that is why the title of this book is *Discerning Religious Truth*. This conception of logic, insofar as it reflects the religious importance and function of the science as studied in the madrasas of the Muslim heartlands by the 14th century CE, is what I am calling *Islamic logic*.

This Book

The historical path from Aristotle to modern logic leads to incoherence and fragmentation; the historical path from Aristotle to Islamic logic leads to coherence and unity. The goal of this book is to connect Islamic logic with modern philosophy in a way that suggests how Islamic logic and the traditional Islamic sciences might engage with modern philosophy to create a new synthesis that replaces the fragmentation of modern philosophy and logic with the religious and philosophical coherence and philosophical unity of the Muslim scholarly tradition.

This book is based on one of the most influential logic textbooks of the post-classical madrasa tradition, *Tahdhīb al-manṭiq wa-l-kalām* (*The Refinement of Islamic Logic and Rational Theology*, henceforth, *Tahdhīb*) by the brilliant Persian polymath, Saʿd al-Dīn al-Taftāzānī (d. 792/1390). Al-Taftāzānī was the author of influential madrasa mainstays in Islamic logic, *kalām*, Arabic eloquence (*balāgha*), legal theory, and Qurʾānic exegesis that are taught and regarded as authoritative reference works to this day. The *Tahdhīb* is a carefully organized and precisely worded manual (*matn*) of Islamic logic and *kalām*. Its influence, like the influence of any madrasa manual, can be measured by the dozens of commentaries (*shurūḥ*), glosses (*ḥawāshī*), and notes (*taʿlīqāt*) that madrasa scholars wrote as they taught, critiqued, and debated its questions.[6] This book re-presents the logic portion, with the commentary of the Persian logician ʿUbaydallāh al-Khabīṣī (d. 1050/1640), the glosses of the Egyptian polymaths Muḥammad al-Dasūqī (d. 1230/1815) and Ḥasan al-ʿAṭṭār (d. 1250/1835), and the notes of the recent Egyptian scholar ʿAbd al-Majīd al-Sharnūbī (d. 1348/1929).

The goal of this book is to comprehensively gather all the substantial questions and debates of Islamic logic that are mentioned in these books; to supplement them with a selection of important questions from other important madrasa manuals in Islamic logic, *kalām*, and *falsafa*; to unravel their layered organization into a more readable linear fomat;[7] and to then

6. The commentary and the gloss were the means of scholarly conversations in the madrasa community. For a description of how these conversations happened, see the beginning of Karamali, *Madrasa Curriculum*, as well as Asad Q. Ahmed, "Post-Classical Philosophical Commentaries/Glosses: Innovation in the Margins," *Oriens* 41, no. 3-4 (2013).

7. Discussions in the original manual (*matn*), commentary (*sharḥ*), and gloss (*ḥāshiya*) are

re-express them in an accessible English style and a convenient organization of chapters and sections. Students of the terse manuals of Islamic logic will find that this translation clarifies, explains, and contextualizes dozens of difficult-to-understand expressions. It is much more than a translation. It is also an explanation and a commentary.

But it is even more than that. The questions and debates of traditional Islamic logic have, to date, been translated using the vocabulary of medieval scholasticism. This kind of translation looks at Islamic logic from the perspective of its Aristotelian origins, forgetting that the purpose of Islamic logic was not to uncritically mimic Aristotle, but to use his vocabulary to protect religious scholars from mistakes in their inference of religious truths, and to use that vocabulary to delve into the heritage of the ancient Greeks with the critical eye of reason that was aided by the light of revelation in order to correct and improve the inference of old philosophical truths, and to discover new ones.

The reason why al-Ghazālī, al-Rāzī, and multitudes of religious scholars before and after integrated the learning of the ancient Greeks was that it was,

---

layered and often interspersed with textual debates that are not substantial questions of Islamic logic. The following is an example taken from ʿUbaydallāh b. Faḍl al-Khabīṣī, Muḥammad b. Aḥmad al-Dasūqī, and Ḥasan b. Muḥammad al-ʿAṭṭār, *al-Tadhhīb sharḥ ʿalā Tahdhīb al-manṭiq wa-l-kalām wa-ʿalayhi ḥāshiyatān* (Cairo: Maṭbaʿat Muṣṭafā al-Bābī al-Ḥalabī, 1936) (*TB*), 287:

1. *Al-Taftāzānī* (author of the original manual) defines a *complex proposition* as a proposition in which "one simple predication is judged to be the case based on another simple predication hypothetically being the case."
2. *Al-Khabīṣī* (author of the commentary) then illustrates the definition with the example, "If the sun has risen then it is daytime," explaining that "the existence of daytime" is a simple predication that is judged to be the case based on another simple predication, "the rising of the sun."
3. *Al-Dasūqī* (author of the gloss) examines why, even though simple predications should be illustrated with sentential expressions—such as "Daytime exists"—al-Khabīṣī has yet chosen to illustrate them with phrasal expressions—such as "the existence of daytime." He explains that the reason why he does this is to subtly indicate that what is sought in the definition of the complex proposition is not the mental act of predication, but the occurrence of the predication *in reality*. Whereas the sentential expression does not explicitly indicate the real occurrence of the predication the phrasal expression does. The phrasal expression is hence used *figuratively* to refer to the occurrence of a predication in reality.
4. *Al-Sharnūbī* (author of the super-gloss) uses the science of Arabic eloquence (*balāgha*) to analytically unpack the exact rhetorical structure of the figurative use and illustrates al-Dasūqī's analysis by returning to al-Taftāzānī's original definition in the manual and rewording it to show how, when he says, "simple predication," he actually means "the occurrence of a simple predication."

at that time, the ubiquitous language of philosophy, science, medicine, ethics, politics, *kalām*, logic—everything, and it was not possible to demonstrate the truth of the message of the Prophet Muhammad (God bless him and give him peace) and effectively communicate the knowledge of religious scholarship in that time without using that vocabulary. But that vocabulary is now obsolete. Now, those questions are all expressed in the language of modern science and modern analytic philosophy. Islamic logic, and all the traditional Islamic sciences, now need to be expressed in this vocabulary. That is what this book does. And that is important because it gives a philosophical compass that is grounded in the Muslim scholarly tradition.

The translation-choices in this book carefully extrapolate the discussions of Islamic logic onto problems in modern analytic philosophy. This vividly illustrates the modern philosophical relevance of Islamic logic: it discusses whether the meanings of words are about things in the mind or things in the world (4.2, 6.1); how words that refer to the same object in the real world can have different meanings (4, 6.1); whether representations, objects, or meanings possess reference (2.1.3); internal language and universal grammar (almost the entire book, arguably, is about this); how the meaning of a sentence emerges out of its parts (2.2, 3.4.1); speech acts (i.e., non-propositional statements) (5.1); the truth of statements like, "The present king of France is bald" (5.2); whether definition descriptions are singular or universal terms (2.1.4); the various kinds of extramental reality (5.1, 1.5, 6.6); intension, extension, and the morning-star paradox (6.1 , 6.7.1.1, 6.7.2.1); justification and the production of knowledge (1.1.4, 4.2.1); whether justification necessitates truth (1.1.3.3); foundationalism and the regress problem (1.1.4); the nature of causation (6.7, 7.1.1, 10.2.1.4, 10.2.1.3, as well as 1.1.3.4, 1.1.2, 1.1.3); consciousness, mental events, the mind and soul, and their relation to the physical body (1.1.2, 1.1.4.2, 1.5, and 10.2.1.4); the relationship between the mind and reality (the mind-body problem) (1.1.3.4, 1.1.2, 1.1.3, 6.7); self-knowledge (10.2.1.2); philosophical skepticism (10.2.1.2); the different ways in which things can "exist" and their relation to truth and falsity (3.5, 5.2, 6.6); truth-bearers and truth-makers and the relation between them (5.1, 5.2); the realist correspondence theory of truth (1.1.3.2, 1.2.3, 5.1.1); paradoxes of self-reference and their solutions (5.1.2, 6.6.3); existential import (6.6); the meaning, epistemology, and metaphysics of propositional modality; (6.7); how the world and natural phenomena exist, and how this relates to the analysis of propositional truths (1.1.1, 5.3, 6.7, 7.1.1); the nature of reality (4.2,

5.1.1); abstract and concrete objects (4.2, 5.2, 6.6); the nature of objects and their properties (4.2.1, 6.6); the problem of universals (3.5); whether existence is a property of individuals (4.2.1, 6.6.3); rigid and non-rigid designators (2.1.3); the referents of empty names (6.6.3); nothingness, impossibility, and privation (6.5, 6.6.3); the kinds of necessity (6.7.1.1); possible (and impossible) worlds (6.6, 6.7.1); the difference between material and real conditionals (7.1.1); the problem of induction (10.2.1.3); and inference to the best explanation (10.2.1.4).

But, unlike with modern philosophy, all these discussions coalesce into a coherent, evidence-based, philosophical system embedded in reason, illuminated by divine revelation, and infused with a spirit of godfearingness, which, when grasped, enables a detailed extrapolation onto every important problem in modern analytic philosophy. Such an extrapolation would place modern analytic philosophy neatly into the traditional sciences of the Muslim scholarly tradition, and would give the questions and debates of modern analytic philosophy their most coherent, sensible, and, in fact, correct expression. Philosophical coherence, sensibility, and correctness are not found in the fragmented and argumentative philosophical debates of contemporary academic journals, but they will be found in the coherent, unified, and true scholarly tradition of Islamic logic and *kalām*.

These last sentences are a claim—that the questions and debates of modern metaphysics, epistemology, and philosophy of language find their most coherent, sensible, and, in fact, correct expression in the scholarly tradition of Islamic logic and *kalām*. This book is the first step towards proving it.

The outline of this book is as follows.

Part I: Preliminaries consists of introductory matters to the study of the science of logic. Chapter 1 explains what the science of Islamic logic is, as well as its purpose and subject. In order to do that, it also explains what knowledge is, how it is acquired, and the meaning of truth and falsity. Chapter 2 explains what language is and exactly how it is used to bring about meanings in the mind.

Part II: Conceptual Knowledge, which contains Chapters 3 and 4, examines the various kinds of universals and how to correctly compose them to construct a definition. These chapters also include a number of important discussions about the difference between definitional propositions and the propositions in arguments and the relation between language, the mind, and reality.

Part III: Propositional Knowledge, which contains Chapters 5, 6, 7, 8, and 9, examines the various kinds of propositions, how they are constituted, their modalities, how to transform them, and how to use them to construct a valid argument. Along the way, these chapters discuss in detail what it means for a proposition to be true, the domains of reality that are relevant to the determination of propositional truth, the differences between mental existence and extramental existence, problems of self-reference, the epistemology of *kalām*, the precise meanings of propositional predications, existential import, and modal logic.

Part IV: Supplements, which contains Chapters 10 and 11, examines how to ensure that a valid argument is also sound, and how to use the science of logic to organize the traditional Islamic sciences. It includes discussions about the types of basic noninferential premises to which deductive arguments resolve.

The material of each chapter is logically layered into sections, sub-sections, and sub-sub-sections. Sometimes, however, it has not been possible to fit the complex text-commentary-gloss conversations of the *Tahdhīb* into the logical structure of the chapter, in which case the related discussions are relegated to footnotes. Footnotes are also used at times to point out how various discussions in this book are related to discussions in modern analytic philosophy. At the end is a glossary of technical terms, arranged alphabetically according to the transliterated Arabic, together with English translations and brief explanations of rationale in translation.

I

PRELIMINARIES

1

PROLEGOMENON TO THE SCIENCE OF LOGIC

Scholars of the traditional Islamic sciences[1] customarily begin their teaching manuals with a scholarly *prolegomenon to the science* (*muqaddimat al-ʿilm*)[2] that defines the science, explains why it needs to be studied, and defines the subject of its questions. This prolegomenon makes the student aware of what he is about to study, which makes it possible for him to direct himself toward learning it.

The content and form of this prolegomenon is motivated by the logicians' theory of human knowledge. They observe that we acquire knowledge by reflection and inference, which require that we direct our mind's attention to those definitions and arguments that will lead us to the knowledge that we seek. Before we can learn any science, therefore, we must *conceive* it in some approximate manner; without this approximate conception, the science would be an absolute unknown, and it is impossible for us to direct ourselves to an absolute unknown. The logical role of the scholarly prolegomenon is to provide this approximate conception to enable first-time students

1. For the definition of *science*, see 11.1. For a description of the traditional Islamic sciences, see Karamali, *Madrasa Curriculum.*

2. The Arabic word *muqaddima* literally means "introduction." The logicians (and, by extension, scholars of all the traditional Islamic sciences) distinguish between the *muqaddima* of a *book* (*muqaddimat al-kitāb*) and the *muqaddima* of a *science* (*muqaddimat al-ʿilm*). The *muqaddima* of a book refers to the text of the general introduction that precedes the main subject of the book. The *muqaddima* of a science, however, refers to the concepts at hand in the present chapter.

of logic to direct the attention of their minds to acquiring knowledge of the science's questions.

The logicians describe three levels of conception that a student might have before embarking on the study of a science. The first and lowest level is any conception at all, however vague, such as one's conception that what one is about to study is some unknown science. This vague conception is enough to bring the science out of the absolute unknown, enabling the student to direct his mind's attention to learning its questions, even though he does not clearly know what exactly the science is. In order to be motivated to acquire this conception, the student must also believe that there is some benefit to be gained by acquiring knowledge of the science.

The second level gives clear knowledge of what exactly the science is by *defining* it. This, together with the student's belief in some vague benefit in learning the science, enables him to direct his mind with greater focus and clarity toward its questions.

But the clarity that the student acquires through the science's definition is incomplete without the addition of two other clarifications: (1) the exact *need* that it is the *purpose* of the science to fulfill and (2) the exact *subject* of its *questions*. With the addition of these two clarifications, the conception rises to its third and highest level. At this level, the student understands exactly what he is directing his attention to and exactly why he is doing it (the logicians call this *complete clarity* (*baṣīra tāmma*)), which enables him to direct himself most effectively to learning its questions. It is these three things—the definition, the need, and the subject of the science's questions—that, according to the logicians, must comprise the scholarly prolegomenon to any science, whether logic, *kalām*, Arabic grammar, or any other science.

This chapter is a prolegomenon to the science of logic. It begins by examining human knowledge through a series of four divisions (1.1). The last two of these divisions—the division of knowledge into conception and judgment (1.1.3) and the division of each of these into inferential and noninferential (1.1.4)—are required to understand the need for the science of logic (1.2). Understanding this need allows us to devise a definition for the science (1.2.4). Finally, in light of all of the above, we can precisely determine the subject of the science's questions (1.3). Over time, scholars of the Islamic sciences added seven other elements to the three customarily mentioned in prolegomena to give even greater clarity to the students of a science. These are included for the sake of completeness (1.4). The chapter then concludes with a supplement that describes the logicians' account of knowledge (1.5).

1.1 Knowledge

The Arabic word for knowledge, *ʿilm*, can mean:

1. Rules (*qawāʿid*) and criteria (*ḍawābiṭ*), such as the rule of logic that a positive universally quantified proposition converts to a positive particularly quantified proposition, or the criterion that a genus is a universal that is predicated of many things of different essences.
2. The skill (*malaka*) that comes from experience in the application of those rules, such as the skill of logical reasoning that comes from experience in the application of the rules of logic.
3. Perception (*idrāk*).[3]

The logicians use *knowledge* (*ʿilm*) in this last meaning, namely perception. The knowledge that they study is not perception in its widest sense, but a specific kind of perception. They define this kind of perception by analyzing knowledge (or perception) through a series of four divisions and then using these divisions to identify the kind of knowledge that is their subject of study. This series of four divisions is described below.

1.1.1 *Eternal and Created Knowledge*

The first of the four divisions of knowledge is its division into *eternal knowledge* (*ʿilm qadīm*) and *created knowledge* (*ʿilm ḥādith*).[4] Eternal knowledge belongs to God. It never began to exist, and has, in other words, "always" existed ("always" is figurative because God's eternality is timeless). It is not acquired or learned, nor does it change. Rather, it is perfect and complete since beginningless eternity, timelessly revealing all matters to God as they really are without ever being preceded by ignorance. The knowledge that human beings possess is created knowledge. Unlike divine knowledge, human knowledge comes into existence after its nonexistence. Like every other created thing in the universe, it owes its existence to God's creative act. Logic studies created human knowledge. Its rules and criteria therefore do not

---

3. It can also mean *science*. See 11.1.

4. For simplicity, the Arabic terms *qadīm* and *ḥādith* are here translated "eternal" and "created," respectively, to capture the intended distinction. One could more precisely translate *ʿilm qadīm* as *beginninglessly eternal knowledge* and *ʿilm ḥādith* as *knowledge that began to exist*.

apply to eternal divine knowledge. The study of eternal divine knowledge belongs to *kalām*, not to logic.

1.1.2 *Direct and Indirect Knowledge*

The second of the four divisions of knowledge is the division of *created knowledge* into *direct knowledge* (*ʿilm ḥuḍūrī*) and *indirect knowledge* (*ʿilm ḥuṣūlī*). The locus of each of these kinds of created knowledge is the human soul (*nafs*). All physiological phenomena that are associated with this knowledge (e.g., the firing of neurons in the brain) are not the knowledge-perception itself, but regular causes[5] that God regularly creates when He creates the knowledge-perception in the soul.

Direct knowledge comes from the presence of the object of knowledge in the knower. It refers to self-knowledge, meaning knowledge of one's own soul and its attributes, each of which is actually present in the knower. Indirect knowledge comes from the appearance of the object's *representation* (*ṣūra*) in the knower, either in his soul or in one of its faculties. For example, one's knowledge of a particular tree comes from the appearance of its representation within the soul's faculty of sight, and one's knowledge of the universal concept ‹tree› comes from the appearance of its representation within one's soul (see 1.5).

Direct knowledge is stronger than indirect knowledge because knowledge of something through its presence within oneself is obviously stronger than knowledge of it through the presence of its representation within one. But the scope of direct knowledge is confined to the knower himself whereas the scope of indirect knowledge extends to the external world. Knowledge of the external world requires indirect knowledge. Logic only studies indirect knowledge.

1.1.3 *Conceptual and Propositional Knowledge*

The third of the four divisions of knowledge is the division of indirect knowledge into *conception* (*taṣawwur*) and *judgment* (*taṣdīq*). (Conception is sometimes also called *conceptual knowledge* and judgment is sometimes also called *propositional knowledge*. This is a more accurate translation because it makes

5. A *regular cause* (*sabab ʿādī*) is a created event that God regularly associates with another created event. Our knowledge of the associations between regular causes and effects in the universe enables us to subject the causes to our purposes. The true cause of every event, however, is God's creative act. Ibrāhīm al-Bājūrī, *Ḥāshiyat Ibrāhīm al-Bājūrī ʿalā matn al-Sanūsiyya fī ʿilm al-tawḥīd* (Cairo: Maṭbaʿat Muṣṭafā al-Bābī al-Ḥalabī, 1955), 29-30.

explicit the fact that the conception and judgment are objective and involuntary perceptions rather than subjective and voluntary actions.) This division arises from an analysis of speech as the composition of basic concepts. For example, "God exists," is composed of: (1) the concept ‹God›, (2) the concept ‹existence›, and (3) the concept of the predication of existence to God. Knowledge that God exists comprises the perception of each of these three concepts along with the perception that the third perception corresponds to reality. The first three perceptions are termed *conception* (*taṣawwur*); the latter perception is termed *judgment* (*taṣdīq*).

Knowledge that God exists thus has four elements:

1. Conceiving the meaning denoted by the subject, "God."
2. Conceiving the meaning denoted by the predicate, "existence."
3. Conceiving the meaning of predicatively composing the predicate with the subject, i.e., the meaning of, "God exists."
4. Judging (i.e., perceiving) this latter *predicative composition* to be true.

It is important to note the difference between Element *3* and Element *4*. The difference can be illustrated by someone who understands the expression, "God exists," but is not yet sure whether it is true. This person conceives the meaning of "God," he conceives the meaning of "existence," and he conceives the meaning of the predication of existence to God, but he does not yet perceive whether the latter conception is true. Whenever we consider new propositions to evaluate their truth, we possess conception, but we do not possess judgment until we complete our evaluation by examining whether or not the conceptual predication corresponds to reality.

To put it more precisely, Element *3* is the perception of what it means for a particular predicate to be said of a particular subject without considering whether it is really the case, whereas Element *4* is the perception of whether or not it is really the case—whether or not it corresponds to an extra-propositional reality that is independent of our perception.

Judgment is hence defined as indirect knowledge that comprises perception of whether or not a predicative composition is true independently of our perceiving it, and *conception* is defined as indirect knowledge that does not comprise such perception. Judgment presupposes conception. The logicians disagree, however, whether the three conceptions (the first three elements above) are conditions (*shurūṭ*) of the ensuing judgment or its parts (*arkān*). The *falāsifa* held that they are conditions, not parts. As a result, they held that judgments are basic (*basīṭ*). Prominent theologians, most notably Fakhr al-Dīn al-Rāzī, on the other hand, held that the conceptions are parts, not conditions, of the judgment, which entails that judgments are composite (*murakkab*). Most later logicians preferred the view of the *falāsifa*, while acknowledging that the disagreement has few if any consequences.

The definition of judgment refers to the concepts of *predicative composition* and *truth*. These two concepts are explained in further detail in Subsections 1.1.3.1 and 1.1.3.2 below. Judgments come in different strengths, which are described in Subsection 1.1.3.3. Finally, the distinction between judgment and belief is discussed in Subsection 1.1.3.4.

1.1.3.1 Kinds of Compositions

The composition (*nisba*) whose truth or falsity is perceived in a *judgment* is a particular kind of composition called a *predicative composition* (*nisba khabariyya*). This subsection explains what distinguishes a predicative composition from other kinds of composition.

Both mental thoughts and verbal expressions consist of the composition of basic concepts and words into composite wholes. These compositions are divided into *sentential* (*tāmm*) and *phrasal* or *qualifying* (*ghayr tāmm*) compositions. The difference between the two is that when someone is addressed by a sentential composition, he does not normally expect anything more, whereas when he is addressed by a merely qualifying composition, he perceives that the speech is incomplete and expects something more.

Examples of *qualifying compositions* are (1) the composition of "genuine" with "prophet" in the phrase "genuine prophet," and (2) the composition of ‹destiny› with ‹you› in the composite concept ‹your destiny›. Someone who hears or apprehends either of these compositions will notice that the speech is incomplete and will expect the speaker to continue. These examples illustrate that qualifying compositions are further divided into *adjectival compositions* (*nisba tawṣīfiyya*), e.g., "genuine prophet," and *possessive compositions* (*nisba iḍāfiyya*),[6] e.g., ‹your destiny›.

Examples of *sentential compositions* are (1) the composition of the word "God" with the word "existence" in, "God exists," or (2) the composition of the solicitation of truthful speech with the implicit second person pronoun in,

6. Possessive compositions are not confined to the Arabic grammatical relation of *iḍāfa*, nor are all grammatical *iḍāfa* relations possessive compositions. What is pertinent to the categorization of a composition as possessive is whether the qualification obtains by the meaning of possession, as present for example in the English-language phrase provided.

"Speak truthfully!" Someone who is addressed by either of these compositions will feel that the speech has been completed and will not expect anything more. These examples illustrate that sentential compositions are further divided into *predicative compositions* (*nisba khabariyya*), e.g., "God exists," and *non-predicative compositions* (*nisba inshā'iyya*), e.g., "Speak truthfully!" Predicative compositions are sometimes simply called *predications* (sg. *ḥukm*). The difference between a predication and a non-predicative composition is that the actualization of a predication does not depend on its being stated (a predication refers, in other words, to a reality that is actual even if it is not stated) whereas the actualization of a non-predicative composition does depend on its being stated (a non-predicative composition, in other words, actualizes a reality by its being stated).[7]

For example, the composition in the predication ‹God exists› is actualized regardless of whether it is stated because it corresponds to a reality independently of its being stated. Analogously, the composition in the predication ‹God has a partner in His divinity› is unactualized regardless of whether it is stated because it does not correspond to any reality. These are predicative compositions. On the other hand, a non-predicative composition such as the command, "Speak truthfully!" which composes the solicitation of speaking truthfully with the implicit second person pronoun, is only actualized by being stated; without the expression being uttered, there is no solicitation. Other examples of non-predicative compositions are prohibitions, questions, expressions of praise and blame, wishes, and anticipations, each of which is only realized by its being stated. A consequence of this is that non-predicative compositions cannot be described as being true or false, whereas predicative compositions can.

Logicians do not study non-predicative compositions; the study of non-predicative compositions belongs instead to sciences like the science of Arabic eloquence (*balāgha*). The only type of sentential composition that logicians study is predicative composition. This is the type of composition that distinguishes judgment from conception: if a perception (*idrāk*) is a perception of whether or not a predicative composition is true, then it is judgment; otherwise, it is conception.

7. Predicative and non-predicative compositions may be further composed into conditional and disjunctive compositions, which are described in Chapter 7.

1.1.3.2 Truth and Falsity

Previous sections have defined *judgment* as the perception of the truth or falsity of a *predication*. This section explains the meaning of *truth* (*ṣidq*) and *falsity* (*kadhib*). A predication may either bear a relation of correspondence (*muṭābaqa*) to an extra-propositional reality (*wāqiʿ*), or it may not. For example, the predication in the statement, "God exists," corresponds to an extramental reality because God really does exist. On the other hand, the predication in, "God has a partner in His divinity," does not correspond to an extra-propositional reality because God does not, in fact, have a partner in His divinity. If a predication corresponds to reality, it is *true*. If it does not correspond to reality, it is *false*. Truth and falsity are hence measures of whether a predication corresponds to reality.

Truth and falsity do not apply to *non-predicative sentential compositions*, such as, "Speak truthfully!" because these compositions do not have an extramental reality that is independent of their being stated; their reality is only actualized by their being stated. There is hence nothing beyond the expression for it to correspond to. Truth and falsity also do not apply to *qualifying compositions*, such as the uttered phrases "genuine prophet" and "your destiny," because qualifying compositions only apply to mental concepts.

1.1.3.3 Strength of Perception of Judgment

The strength with which one perceives the truth of a predication is divided into four levels:

1. **Certainty (*jazm*) of truth**, which, expressed in terms of probability, corresponds to a probability of 100 %.
2. **Probabilistic knowledge (*ẓann*)**, which corresponds to a probability greater than 50 %.
3. **Uncertainty (*shakk*)**, which corresponds to a probability of exactly 50 %.
4. **Conjecture (*wahm*)**, which corresponds to a probability below 50 %.

Properly speaking, certainty and probabilistic knowledge are judgments (*taṣdīq*), but uncertainty and conjecture are not, for they do not comprise a mental representation of whether the predication corresponds to reality. This perception of correspondence (or judgment) may thus be *conclusive* (*qaṭʿī*) or it may be *probabilistic* (*ẓannī*). The difference between conclusive and probabilistic perception is one of strength: a perception that is conclusive is so strong that it prevents the perceiver from believing that it is possible for the opposite to be the case, whereas a perception that is probabilistic is not as strong and thus leads the perceiver to believe that it is unlikely, albeit possible, for the opposite to be the case. Both perceptions, however, are judgments that are perceptions of reality, in contradistinction to uncertainty and conjecture. The probabilistic nature of perception does not, in other words, reduce it to uncertainty or conjecture. The difference between conclusive and probabilistic judgment is the difference between certainty and confidence, not, as many modern philosophers might imagine, the difference between knowledge and doubt.

The epistemology of probabilistic knowledge is found in manuals of legal theory (*uṣūl al-fiqh*), which study the methods of acquiring probabilistic knowledge of God's commands as well as the attributes that a qualified scholar (*mujtahid*) must possess in order for his probabilistic knowledge of God's commands to be binding. This reveals that probabilistic knowledge bears the stamp of the knower and part of acquiring it is growing in one's ability to know, whereas conclusive knowledge is independent of that ability.

1.1.3.4 Belief and Authority

Theologians and legal theorists distinguish between *judgment* and *mere belief* (*iʿtiqād*). Whereas judgment is perception that arises from a regular cause (i.e., reflection on evidence), this is not the case with mere belief. That is to say that judgment is a kind of knowledge that comprises a perception of reality based on evidence, while mere belief is not knowledge but a *decision* to affirm something, often by an appeal to authority (*taqlīd*).

Muslim theologians (*mutakallimūn*) establish the science of theology on this distinction between judgment and mere belief. They hold that the first obligation of human beings is to acquire conclusive knowledge of God, His messengers, and the afterlife. Conclusive knowledge only arises from evidence-based judgment, not from mere belief. Mere belief in these matters does not fulfill this first obligation because unlike evidence-based conclusive knowledge, mere belief that is based on an appeal to authority is susceptible to doubts. Even if the religious belief of a Muslim that is based on authority is religiously acceptable in the sense that it leads to salvation in the afterlife, it is still lacking in that it leads a Muslim to sin in virtue of his failure to discharge the obligation of basing his religious belief on evidence. A primary goal of the science of *kalām* is to teach Muslims that evidence in order to help them discharge their first obligation.

After belief in God, His messengers, and the afterlife, the next obligation of human beings is to live according to the sacred law, which places all possible human actions under one of five legal rulings: (1) obligatory, (2) recommended, (3) permissible, (4) offensive, and (5) unlawful. Whereas inferring the tenets of religious belief does not require scholarly expertise, inferring the rulings of sacred law does, and legal theorists therefore divide people into two categories: *qualified scholars* (sg. *mujtahid*) and *laymen* (sg. *muqallid*). Qualified scholars have the capacity to independently infer legal rulings and they are hence obliged to make this inference and act according to it. Laymen do not have this capacity and they are therefore obliged to refer to the authority of a qualified scholar and live according to his interpretation of the sacred law. Most evidence that qualified scholars use is probabilistic and most rulings of sacred law that they infer are therefore probabilistic judgments. It is obligatory to tolerate the disagreement of qualified scholarship. This disagreement has historically been considered a divine mercy because in times of hardship, it gives laymen the flexibility of following a scholarly opinion that is easier than the one that they normally adhere to.

The theological inferences of the theologians and the legal inferences of the jurists are all based on the inference methods of the Muslim logicians. This section is a brief and highly simplified synopsis of how logic is used in some of the important sciences of the Muslim scholarly tradition. Further detail is found in the manuals of those sciences themselves.[8]

1.1.4 *Inferential and Noninferential Knowledge*

The fourth and final division of knowledge is the division of both conceptual knowledge (or conception) and propositional knowledge (or judgment) into *inferential* (*naẓarī*) and *noninferential* (*ḍarūrī*) knowledge.[9] If arriving at a conception or judgment requires inference, it is inferential; otherwise, it is noninferential.

8. For a description of these sciences and their most important manuals, see Karamali, *Madrasa Curriculum*, 19-21; 24-26.

9. The translations *inferential* and *noninferential* have been chosen for their directness. Although the word "inference" normally refers to the drawing of propositional conclusions, it is to be understood that *inference* (*naẓar*) here extends to conceptual as well as propositional reasoning. The precise meaning of *ʿilm naẓarī* is knowledge attained through the medium of deliberate thought, and of *ʿilm ḍarūrī* knowledge possessed without the medium of deliberate thought. The latter might also be rendered *immediate knowledge*.

There are therefore four kinds of knowledge:

1. *Noninferential conception*, e.g., conceiving the concept ‹existence›, which does not require inference from any other conception.[10]
2. *Inferential conception*, e.g., conceiving the concept ‹human being›, which requires inference from the concepts ‹rational› and ‹animal› (see 3.4.2).
3. *Noninferential judgment*, e.g., judging that opposites cannot coexist, which does not require inference from any other judgment.
4. *Inferential judgment*, e.g., judging that the universe requires the existence of a necessary being, which requires inference from the two judgments that (a) the universe exists contingently and that (b) everything that exists contingently requires the existence of a necessary being.

Even though noninferential knowledge does not require any definition (i.e., inference from other concepts) or argument (i.e., inference from other judgments), one might nevertheless not be consciously aware of certain noninferential conceptions or judgments. One becomes consciously aware of these noninferential conceptions or judgments through *reminders* (*tanbīhāt*). Though these reminders are often formulated in the same manner as inferences, they are not truly inferences because the knowledge that they remind one of is noninferential (for an example see 1.1.4.1 below).

Inference (*naẓar*), in general terms, is the arrangement of already-known matters to acquire knowledge of an unknown. This definition is based on the position that the discovery of an unknown is always based on more than one known matter. The early logicians (along with some logicians from the later tradition of logic) held that it is possible to reach knowledge of an unknown with a single known matter, citing as proof incomplete essential and non-essential definitions (see 4.3.1). But most late logicians disagreed, insisting that knowledge of all new matters is based on the knowledge of at least two known matters, and responding that although deficient definitions do not state the genus, they nevertheless imply it, and this implicit genus must be brought to mind in order for the definition to work.

10. See Saʿd al-Dīn Masʿūd b. ʿUmar al-Taftāzānī, *Tahdhīb al-manṭiq wa-l-kalām* (Hawalli: Dār al-Ḍiyāʾ, 2017), 225.

1.1.4.1 The Inferential-Noninferential Division

The *division* (*taqsīm*) of a universal concept into its sub-categories is divided into *essential division* (*taqsīm dhātī*) and *nonessential division* (*taqsīm ʿaraḍī*). Essential division is the division of a *genus* into its *species*. Nonessential division is the division of a *genus* into its *types* (see 3.4.3.2 and 3.4.3.3).

The division of knowledge as discussed above into conceptual and propositional knowledge is an essential division because conception and judgment are two different species of perception (or knowledge). The division of knowledge into inferential and noninferential knowledge, on the other hand, is nonessential because inferential and noninferential knowledge are not different species of perception, but merely mental considerations of perception from the nonessential perspective of how the perception is acquired, regardless of what species (or kind) of perception is being considered. That is why this division applies equally to both conceptual and propositional knowledge.

Every exhaustive division of a universal concept ‹A› into its sub-categories ‹B›, ‹C›, ‹D›, ... is equivalent to a *disjunctive complex proposition* of the form ‹‹A› is either ‹B› or ‹C› or ‹D› or...›. In this case, the division of knowledge into inferential and noninferential knowledge is equivalent to the proposition ‹Knowledge is either inferential or noninferential›. The logicians differ whether the truth of this proposition is inferential or noninferential. Those who hold that it is *inferential* infer its truth as follows.

1. Knowledge is either conceptual or propositional knowledge.
2. Some conceptual knowledge and some propositional knowledge is inferential because we have *direct knowledge* of the process of inferring some conceptual knowledge through *definition* and some propositional knowledge through *argument*.
3. The inference of new knowledge through definition or argument requires inferential starting points.
4. If these inferential starting points were also inferential, knowledge of them would, in turn, require inference from other inferential starting points.
5. It is impossible for this chain of inference to continue *ad infinitum* because we would then never know anything.
6. Therefore, this chain of inference must eventually stop at inferential starting points that are noninferential.
7. Therefore, some conceptual knowledge and some propositional knowledge is noninferential.

On the other hand, those logicians who hold that the division of knowledge into inferential and noninferential knowledge is *noninferential* hold that this line of reasoning is not an argument but a *reminder*, and that it presupposes unstated premises that are equivalent to saying that the division is noninferential.

1.1.4.2 Inference

We acquire knowledge of what we do not know through inference from what we do know. If the unknown matter is conceptual, we acquire knowledge of it through inference from known concepts, and if the unknown matter is propositional, we acquire knowledge of it through inference from known propositions (or judgments).

For example, we acquire conceptual knowledge of *human* through our prior knowledge of *animal* and *rational*, from which we construct the definition, "*Human* is *rational animal*."

Similarly, we acquire propositional knowledge of, "A necessary being exists," through our prior knowledge of the following premises.

Minor Premise:	The universe exists contingently.
Major Premise:	Everything that exists contingently needs a necessary being to exist.

These premises constitute an argument from which we infer that the universe needs a necessary being to exist, which means that a necessary being does, in fact, exist.[11]

Acquiring new conceptual or propositional knowledge does not merely require prior knowledge of any other conceptual or propositional knowledge. Rather, in order for the new conceptual or propositional knowledge to arise, it must be constructed from other conceptual or propositional knowledge that is (1) appropriately selected based on its relation to the knowledge that is sought and (2) appropriately arranged.

For example, acquiring conceptual knowledge of ‹human› is only possible through prior knowledge of ‹animal› and ‹rational›, which then need to be arranged into a *qualifying composition* of the form ‹rational animal› in order to bring about knowledge of ‹human›. The already-known concepts from

11. The scholars of *kalām* hold that the first premise is noninferential and that the second is inferential.

which knowledge of an unknown concept is inferred are called *conceptual starting points* (*mabādiʾ taṣawwuriyya*).

Similarly, acquiring propositional knowledge of ‹A necessary being exists› is only possible through prior knowledge of the propositions ‹Everything that exists contingently needs a necessary being to exist› and ‹The universe exists contingently›, which need to be arranged into a simple syllogism of the form illustrated above in order to bring about knowledge of ‹A necessary being exists›. The already-known propositions from which knowledge of an unknown proposition is inferred are termed *propositional starting points* (*mabādiʾ taṣdīqiyya*).

In order to appropriately select and arrange the inferential starting points of the unknown concept or proposition, the unknown concept or proposition cannot itself be *completely* unknown; rather, some remote conception of it must exist in the mind for that selection and arrangement to take place. Even before knowledge of the unknown concept or proposition is inferred, the unknown concept or proposition must be known in some vague way. Otherwise, its inference would not be possible.

The logicians describe this process of knowledge acquisition as two mental motions (*ḥarakat al-nafs*).[12] The first mental motion is a movement from a remote conception (i.e., a vague consciousness) of the unknown concept or proposition to a mental search in one's memory for those known concepts or propositions (or inferential starting points) that might be arranged to infer the unknown concept or proposition whose knowledge is sought. This is then followed by a second mental motion that actually arranges the inferential starting points in a way that infers the conception or proposition whose knowledge is sought.

The first motion is a movement from a remote conception of the unknown to its inferential starting points and the second motion is a movement from the inferential starting points to knowledge of what was initially conceived remotely. The second motion, in other words, returns to the place from where the first one began, ending in complete knowledge of what was initially conceived vaguely.

The early logical tradition defines *inference* (*naẓar*) as a combination of both mental motions. The later logical tradition (represented by this book)

12. "Mind" here means "soul," and "motion" means "change in a quality (*kayfiyya*) that comes about as a result of a voluntary action." The process of inference, in other words, involves a choice made by the soul to infer, as a result of which it undergoes a qualitative change that corresponds to its actually coming to know the new concept or proposition. *TB*, 56-57.

defines it as the second mental motion only. Both the early and the later traditions hold *inference* to be synonymous with *reflection* (*fikr*).

1.1.4.3 Noninferential Judgments and Self-Evident Judgments

Noninferential judgments (or noninferential propositional knowledge) should not be confused with *self-evident judgments*, sometimes also called *first principles*. A noninferential judgment is any judgment whose knowledge does not require the two mental motions of inference described above. There are six different kinds of noninferential judgments (see 10.2.1). A self-evident judgment is only one kind of noninferential judgment, namely the kind of noninferential judgment that results from merely conceiving the subject and predicate. But there are other kinds of judgments whose knowledge does not require inference, such as *intuited judgments*.

The potential for confusion is greater in Arabic, where the words *ḍarūrī* and *badīhī* are used imprecisely to refer interchangeably to "knowledge that does not require inference," and "knowledge that does not require acquisition." The reason for the confusion is that inference is not the only way to acquire knowledge—observation and empirical testing, for example, are both means to acquire knowledge; yet, the knowledge that is acquired through them is noninferential because although it was acquired, it was not acquired through *inference*. This confusion does not exist in this translation. Knowledge that does not require inference is always translated as *noninferential knowledge*. Knowledge that does not require any means of acquisition at all is translated as a *self-evident judgment*.

1.2 The Need for Logic

The previous section showed that human knowledge is either *conceptual* or *propositional*, that both conceptual and propositional knowledge are either *noninferential* or *inferential*, and finally that inferential conceptual and propositional knowledge are acquired through *inference* from noninferential conceptual or propositional knowledge.

The inference of inferential knowledge from noninferential knowledge is susceptible to error. We observe this error in the fact that intelligent people often come to *contradictory* conclusions. For example, the Sunnis inferred that the universe began to exist, whereas the *falāsifa* inferred that it has always existed without beginning. Since these conclusions are contradictory, one of them must be true and the other one must be false. Since one of them is false, either the Sunnis or the *falāsifa* made a mistake in their inference.

Some logicians objected that our observation of contradictory conclusions among people only leads to *probabilistic knowledge* of the occurrence of inferential error because, in fact, all we observe is their verbal statements of contradictory conclusions. As for the actual inference, it takes place within their souls, which we have no access to. Because of the possibility that the *falāsifa* (the mistaken party in the above example) might be lying, we do not have conclusive knowledge that an inferential error actually occurred, but only probabilistic knowledge.

In response to this objection, the logicians cited the example of different conclusions within ourselves—we have all, at some point in our lives, inferred a conclusion, only to later discover that it was incorrect because we made a mistake in our inference. Whereas some might argue that the previous example only gives probabilistic knowledge, this example gives conclusive knowledge because it is based on *direct knowledge* of the occurrence of an inferential mistake within ourselves.[13]

Since people sometimes fall into error during their inferential acquisition of inferential knowledge, they need a criterion (*qānūn*) by which to distinguish correct inference from incorrect inference. By observing this criterion during their inferences, they can protect themselves from falling into error. The science of logic is just that criterion.

1.2.1 *Logic as Universal Principles*

What it means for logic to be a *criterion* is that it is a collection of universal principles that apply to many specific instances of inference. One of these principles, for example, is that every affirmative universally quantified proposition converts to an existentially quantified affirmative proposition (see 8.2). The application of this universal principle to the specific proposition, "Every *human* is *animal*," correctly converts it to, "Some *animal* is *human*."

The exact way to apply a universal principle to a specific instance is to use both the principle and its specific instance to form a *simple syllogism*. The minor premise of the argument is composed of the specific instance of its subject and the subject of the universal principle as its predicate. The major premise of the argument is the universal principle itself. The conclusion will

13. Many logicians hold that these are not arguments but *reminders* because the fact that inference is susceptible to error is known noninferentially. *TB*, 62.

then be the result of applying the universal rule to the specific instance. The example above will then look like this:

Minor Premise: “Every ‹human› is ‹animal›” is a universally quantified affirmative proposition.

Major Premise: Every universally quantified affirmative proposition converts to an existentially quantified affirmative proposition.

Conclusion: “Every ‹human› is ‹animal›,” converts to an existentially qualified affirmative proposition (i.e., “Some ‹animal› is ‹human›”).

1.2.2 *Logic and the Natural Operation of the Mind*

The collection of universal principles that protects the mind from mistakes in inference merely describes how the mind naturally works. One might inquire why, since the mind naturally works as described by these universal principles, can we not simply rely on the mind’s natural operation (*fiṭra*) rather than on the universal principles of logic? The logicians considered several arguments for relying on the natural operations of the mind rather than on the universal principles of logic. Three of these arguments are described below.[14]

The first argument is an objection to the logicians’ argument for why the science of logic is needed. Recall that they argued from specific instances of mistakes in inference to the need for universal principles to protect the mind from those mistakes. One might object that the fact that mistakes occur in specific instances of inference does not entail that one needs universal rules to prevent them from occurring because it is possible for those mistakes to be prevented by the natural operation of the mind. The logicians answered this objection by saying that the numerous examples of mistakes in inference that actually occur among people obviously show that the natural operation of the mind is insufficient.

The second argument is another objection to the same argument. Like the first argument, it argues that the fact that mistakes occur in specific instances of inference does not entail that one needs universal rules to prevent them from occurring, but instead of arguing that one might rely on the natural operation of the mind, it argues that it might be sufficient to simply learn all the

14. The first two arguments are extremely weak and far-fetched arguments that the logicians themselves contrived and answered in order to strengthen their argument for the need for the science of logic.

specific correct instances instead of learning the universal rule. The logicians answered this objection by saying that the specific correct instances of inference are extremely numerous and, in fact, will continuously increase with the passage of time (and hence be potentially unlimited). Enumerating all the correct instances is therefore practically impossible, and the only way to give a criterion for the correctness of specific inferences is through a universal rule.

Whereas the first two arguments are merely cited and summarily dismissed, the third argument is left unanswered as an indication of its strength. This third argument argues that mastering the universal principles of the science of logic is insufficient to protect the mind from error. Some of the greatest logicians, for example, were the *falāsifa* who mastered the universal principles but nevertheless fell into serious error in their inferences, holding, for example, that the universe always existed, that God's knowledge does not encompass particular instances, and that bodily resurrection is impossible.[15] Indeed, most of their inferential errors were not a result of any failure to observe these universal principles, but rather of mistakenly accepting certain false premises as noninferential (*ḍarūrī*). One such premise, for example, is the premise, "Nothing can proceed from the One except something that is one," which provides the basis for an emanationist theory of the origin of the universe of multiplicity. Beginning from such faulty premises, groups such as the *falāsifa* then used the universal principles of logic to build entire philosophical systems. The point is that they faithfully observed the universal principles of logic, yet, because the principles were applied to false premises, their conclusions were nevertheless erroneous.

Ultimately, the universal principles of logic can only correct mistakes in the *form* of inference, whereas the mistaken inferences of intellectual groups like the *falāsifa* are related to the *matter* of inference (see Chapter 10). Now, the only way to show that these premises are false is to return to the natural operation of the human mind, which reveals that the false premises that provide the basis for such faulty arguments are not noninferential—in fact, they are inferentially known to be false. Thus, it can be said that the natural operation of the human mind is, in a sense, more important for protecting the mind from mistakes in inference than the universal principles of logic, though each has its role.

---

15. These were their three most serious errors in theology according to al-Ghazālī in his *Tahāfut al-falāsifa*. One might add to these errors dozens of other errors in natural science, including, for example, their inference that the universe is geocentric.

1.2.3 *Is Conceptual Knowledge Susceptible to Error?*

The statement made earlier that inference is susceptible to error refers, as it stands, both to the inference of conceptual knowledge and to the inference of propositional knowledge. Most logicians, however, hold that conceptual knowledge is never incorrect (see 4.1). They argue that for knowledge to be incorrect means that it is false, and for it to be false means that it does not correspond to reality. Whether or not some knowledge corresponds to reality, however, is a description that only applies to propositional knowledge, not to conceptual knowledge.

This is the view of the majority of logicians. A minority of logicians, however, have held that it is indeed possible for conceptual knowledge to be incorrect. For example, we might see a vague figure in the distance and conceive of it as a human being even though it is actually just a boulder. In this problem-case, the boulder has been incorrectly conceptually represented in our minds as a human being. Our conceptual knowledge of the boulder is therefore incorrect.

The majority-view logicians respond to this problem-case by saying that the mistake does not lie in our conception of a human being, which, as conceptual knowledge, can neither be true nor false; rather, the mistake lies in our judgment that the mental representation of a human being in our mind represents the figure that we see in the distance. When we later discover that we actually saw a boulder rather than a human being, we discover that this judgment is incorrect. As for the conception of the human being in our minds, it is simply a mental conception of a human being that, inasmuch as it is conceptual knowledge, cannot be evaluated as to its correspondence to reality and hence can neither be true nor false. To further emphasize this point, these logicians point out that we can mentally conceive both of things that exist of things that do not (e.g., unicorns), and even of things whose existence is impossible (e.g., a partner in God's divinity). The fact that these things do not (or cannot) exist does not make our conceptions false; what is false is the judgment that instances of those concepts exist.

The minority-view logicians object that what is incorrect in this problem case is not the mentioned judgment but the original conception. We did not merely conceive of a human being; we conceived of the boulder as a human being, and that conception was incorrect.

The majority-view logicians respond that there is a difference between (1) having knowledge of a conception and (2) having knowledge of something through that conception; the first is conceptual knowledge but the second is propositional knowledge in the manner described above. The minority-view logicians' objection that what is incorrect is not the mentioned judgment but the original conception fails to recognize this distinction and conflates that second kind of knowledge, which is actually propositional, with conceptual knowledge, which is actually restricted to the first kind of knowledge (see 4.2.1).

Since it is not possible for conceptual knowledge to be false, what is actually meant by the statement above that inference is susceptible to error is that one may form incorrect definitions when inferring conceptual knowledge or that one may form incorrect arguments when inferring propositional knowledge. An error with respect to conceptual knowledge, then, lies not in the conception itself, but in *how it was acquired.*

1.2.4 *The Definition of Logic*

A *science* is a collection of noninferential propositions that are called its *questions* (see 11.1). The science of logic, then, is a collection of questions. These questions all take the form of universal principles that can be applied to specific instances of logical inference to protect the mind from error.

One popular *definition* of the *science* of logic is based on the reason why it is needed or, equivalently, on its *goal.*[16] According to this definition, logic is a criterion (or a collection of universal principles) which, if observed, prevents the mind from making mistakes in inference. Definitions of sciences that are based on their goal are *nonessential definitions* because, although they enable one to distinguish one science from another, they do not lead to an *essential conception* of the science.[17] This nonessential type of definition is what is appropriate for the student of logic seeking to direct his studies by understanding the science at the second level discussed above. To construct an essential definition would require knowledge of all the questions of the science, a knowledge the student can possess only after the completion of his studies.

---

16. The terms *need* and *goal* are conceptually distinct but referentially identical. For example, in the case of the science of logic, to protect the mind from errors in inference is both the need and the goal. It is the need when considered from the perspective of our dependence on it, and it is the goal when considered from the perspective of its being the purpose of the science of logic. *TB*, 64.

17. To be more precise, since a science is a collection of questions, nonessential definitions enable one to distinguish the *questions* of one science from the *questions* of another.

1.3 The Subject of Logic

The *subject* of a given science is that which it studies in order to accomplish its goal. Since the goal of logic is to provide universal principles that protect the mind from error in its inferences, its subject is determined by the kinds of inferences to which logic pertains. There are two kinds of inferences—conceptual and propositional. The first kind of inference is made through *definition*; the second kind is made through *argument*. Thus, definitions and arguments are among the subjects of the science of logic.

But in order to construct correct definitions, one needs a collection of concepts called the *five universals*. These concepts, in turn, presuppose the concept of the *universal*. These, too, must therefore be subjects of the science of logic.

Similarly, in order to construct correct arguments, we need to use the concept of the *proposition*. This concept in turn involves the concepts *subject*, *predicate*, *antecedent*, and *consequent*. These, too, must then be subjects of the science of logic.

Therefore, the subject of the science of logic is the following four things: (1) definitions, (2) concepts that are needed to construct definitions, (3) arguments, and (4) concepts that are needed to construct arguments. A definition is conceptual knowledge that *directly* leads to new conceptual knowledge. The concepts that are needed to construct definitions are conceptual knowledge that *indirectly* lead to new conceptual knowledge. An argument is propositional knowledge that *directly* leads to new propositional knowledge. The concepts that are needed to construct arguments are propositional knowledge that *indirectly* lead to new propositional knowledge. Based on this analysis, the logicians defined the subject of logic as follows:

1. Conceptual knowledge that directly leads to new conceptual knowledge, i.e., *definitions*.
2. Conceptual knowledge that indirectly leads to new conceptual knowledge, i.e., *universals* and the *five universals*.
3. Propositional knowledge that directly leads to new propositional knowledge, i.e., *arguments*.
4. Propositional knowledge that indirectly leads to new propositional knowledge, i.e., *propositions* and *propositional reasoning*.

Chapter 11 provides further detail on the structure of a science in terms of its subject and questions. For specific examples of the questions of the science of logic, see 11.5.2.

1.4 The Ten Topics of Scholarly Prolegomena

After al-Taftāzānī, later logicians added seven other topics that have been customarily included in scholarly prolegomena of every one of the traditional Islamic sciences. The three topics mentioned by al-Taftāzānī, along with the seven topics that were added by later logicians are known as *the ten topics of scholarly prolegomena* (*al-mabādi' al-ʿashara*). These ten topics enable students of the traditional Islamic sciences to study a science with even greater clarity. The ten topics for the science of logic are:

1	**Name** (*ism*)	The Arabic name for the science of logic is manṭiq. Linguistically, the word manṭiq can mean (1) perception (i.e., knowledge), (2) the faculty of perception, or (3) speech.[18] This is an appropriate name for the science of logic because it corrects universal perceptions, accounting for the first linguistic meaning; strengthens the faculty of perception, accounting for the second linguistic meaning; and perfects one's ability to verbally express one's knowledge (or perceptions), accounting for the third linguistic meaning.
2	**Definition** (*ḥadd*)	*Essential Definition*: Logic is a science that studies conceptual and propositional knowledge from the perspective of it directly or indirectly leading to new conceptual or propositional knowledge. *Nonessential Definition*: Logic is a collection of universal principles the application of which protects one from mistakes in inference.
3	**Benefit** (*thamara*)	Application of the principles of logic protects one from mistakes in inference.

18. The Greek word for "logic," *logos*, also refers to both the faculty of knowledge and the faculty of speech.

4	**Legal Ruling (*ḥukm*)**	Mastering the science of logic is communally obligatory (*farḍ kifāya*) for every Muslim community. A communal obligation is an action which some people from every community need to undertake in order to serve the rest of the community by protecting it from harm. The science of logic is needed to analyze and respond to religious aspersions. Without anyone to do this, Muslims would fall into religious doubts, which is one of the greatest dangers.
5	**Derivation (*istimdād*)**	The questions of the science of logic are derived using the mind alone. Revelation is not needed to derive them.
6	**Subject (*mawḍūʿ*)**	See 1.3
7	**Questions (*masāʾil*)**	See 1.3 and 11.5.2
8	**Relation to Other Sciences (*nisba*)**	The questions of every science are included in the science of logic because the questions of every science comprise conceptual and propositional knowledge and conceptual and propositional knowledge are the subjects of the science of logic. Another way of saying this is that every science comprises the definitions of concepts, the composition of those concepts into propositions, and the construction of arguments for those propositions, and the rules of the science of logic must be observed throughout in order to ensure that the conclusions of the science are in fact correct. This is why the science of logic has been called "the criterion of every science" (*miʿyār al-ʿulūm*).
9	**Special Merit (*faḍl*)**	Logic is distinguished from other sciences in its general benefit: every other science needs logic, but logic does not need any other science.[19]
10	**Founder (*wāḍiʿ*)**	Aristotle

19. Though, practically speaking, the study of language must inevitably precede the study of logic, since concepts and judgments are conveyed and studied through expressions.

1.5 Supplement: The Metaphysics of Knowledge

Knowledge, in general terms, is that thing within us by virtue of which things are disclosed to us. Yet, due to the historical connection between logic and *falsafa*, the logicians sought a more metaphysically precise definition of knowledge. Like some of the *falāsifa*, they understood knowledge of a thing to be the occurrence of that thing's representation (*ṣūra*) in the soul of the knower.[20]

20. Aristotle famously categorized *being* into ten basic categories. The Muslim theologians (*mutakallimūn*) inherited his categorization from the *falāsifa*; critiqued, modified, and developed it; and then used it extensively in their theologically oriented analyses of the physical universe. These ten basic categories are commonly referenced by the Muslim logicians. The ten basic categories are: (1) object, (2) quantity, (3) property, (4) location, (5) time, (6) position, (7) encompassment, (8) correlation, (9) action, and (10) reaction. The table below lists each category with an example in the context of a sentence.

	Category	Example in a Sentence
1	Object	The car in, "The car is red."
2	Quantity	Five in, "Zayd owns five houses."
3	Quality	Whiteness in, "The chair is white."
4	Location	Being in the mosque in, "Zayd is in the mosque."
5	Time	Being at nine o'clock in, "Work begins at nine o'clock."
6	Position	Lying down in, "Zaynab is lying down."
7	Encompassment	Wearing a turban in, "Omar is wearing a turban."
8	Correlation	Being a father in, "Zayd is Omar's father."
9	Action	Heating in, "The fire is heating the water."
10	Reaction	Being heated in, "The water is being heated by the fire."

The *mutakallimūn* held that the ten categories are first-order mental concepts abstracted from extramentally existing objects (1 above) and from all the ways in which they might exist (2-10 above). This puts the *kalām* tradition somewhere between a kind of realism that gives mental concepts extramental existence, on the one hand, and a kind of conceptualism that makes them mere *a priori* mental concepts without any known relation to extramental reality, on the other hand. For example, ‹car› (1 above) is a universal mental concept that is abstracted from the actual cars in the world that we drive; ‹five houses› is a mental concept that is abstracted from the actual houses that people live in along with a mental multiplication of that concept by five; and ‹fatherhood› is a mental concept that is abstracted from the actual father-child pairs of which each of us is an instance.

The ten categories are an exhaustive list of contingent objects and the various ways in which they might exist. The *mutakallimūn* inferred the exhaustiveness of the ten categories through *inductive generalization* (see 9.2.1). Note that objects are commonly subjects of propositions while the remaining nine categories are commonly predicates. The fact that these are categories of *contingent* things excludes God and His attributes, to which these categories do not apply, and it excludes mental concepts without reference to extramental objects and the ways in which they exist, such as second-order concepts (e.g., ‹universal›

"To which basic category of existent things does knowledge belong?" Some logicians answered that it belongs to the category of *quality* (*kayf*), others that it belongs to the category of *reaction* (*infiʿāl*), and others that it belongs to the category of *correlation* (*iḍāfa*). The difference is ultimately a semantic one. Different answers placed knowledge in different categories because they actually referred to different phenomena, which are different aspects of knowledge. To clarify, our knowledge of something involves three aspects:

1. The occurrence of the object's representation in the soul
2. The soul's receipt of this representation
3. A relation between the soul and the object of knowledge.

The first belongs to the category of *quality*, the second to *reaction*, and the third to *relation*. Those who held that knowledge is a quality referred to the first; those who held that it was a reaction referred to the second; and those who held that it was a relation referred to the third.

The real question, then, is not what category knowledge belongs to, but which one of these three aspects to properly call *knowledge*. The late-period logicians predominantly identified knowledge with the first aspect, namely, the occurrence of the representation, which corresponds to the definition of knowledge given above.[21] Some logicians in fact placed knowledge in a fourth category, namely the category of *action*. The later logicians dismissed this categorization as an obvious mistake because it renders knowledge subjective.[22]

---

and ‹existence›), which refer to mental concepts, not extramental objects. The fact that the categories are an exhaustive inventory also reflects the fact that detailed knowledge of each of the ten categories corresponds to detailed knowledge about the entire contingent universe. The goal of the *mutakallimūn* in their detailed analysis of each category (in which they far exceeded Aristotle's initial treatment) was to demonstrate its contingency in order to develop a detailed understanding of a contingent universe that depended for its existence on its necessarily existing Creator.

21. This mental representation may be the effect of an external thing, in which case it is a *first-order concept*, or it may be the effect of another mental representation, in which case it is a *second-order concept* (see 3.1).

22. This position was held by al-Rāzī and his followers. According to the theologian and metaphysician, ʿAbd al-Ḥakīm al-Siyālkūtī, the reason why these scholars held this position was that humans are morally responsible (*mukallaf*) to have religious belief (*īmān*). Since religious belief is a kind of knowledge and since anything for which humans are morally responsible must be a voluntary action, religious belief, and therefore knowledge, must belong to the category of action. Later theologians confirmed that it was an obvious mistake to put knowledge in the category of action and responded to this line of reasoning by saying that religious belief is *inferential knowledge* and the action for which humans are morally responsible is not religious belief as *knowledge*—which belongs to the category of quality—but rather as the *inference* (*naẓar*) that leads to that knowledge. *TB*, 41. Theological manuals clarify that

This representational account of knowledge was adopted by the Sunni Muslim theologians and became mainstream among Muslim logicians. According to this account, one comes to know an extramental object by means of a mental form or representation (*ṣūra*) that lacks the extramental properties and effects (*āthār*) of the object that it represents. The mode of existence enjoyed by this representation is sometimes termed *mental existence* (*wujūd dhihnī*).[23]

Sources

Section	Sources
1 Prolegomenon to the Science of Logic	*TB*, 21-23, 26-28, 68-69; for further reading, see Tony Street, trans., *Najm al-Dīn al-Kātibī's al-Risālah al-shamsiyya: An Edition and Translation with Commentary* (New York: New York University Press, 2024), 88-96; Asad Q. Ahmed, *Palimpsests of Themselves: Logic and Commentary in Postclassical Muslim South Asia* (Oakland: University of California Press, 2022), 145-47; Khaled El-Rouayheb, *The Development of Arabic Logic (1200-1800)* (Basel: Schwabe Verlag, 2019), 21-27; Allan Bäck, "Islamic Logic?" in *The Unity of Science in the Arabic Tradition: Science, Logic, Epistemology and their Interactions*, eds. Shahid Rahman, et al. (Dordrecht: Springer, 2008), 255-79
1.1 Knowledge	*TB*, 28; for further reading, see Jonathan Jenkins Ichikawa and Matthias Steup, "The Analysis of Knowledge," *Stanford Encyclopedia of Philosophy* (Summer 2018), ed. Edward N. Zalta, https://plato.stanford.edu/archives/sum2018/entries/knowledge-analysis; Mohammed Ardeshir, "Ibn Sīnā's Philosophy of Mathematics" in The Unity of Science, 53-57

religious belief is not knowledge; it is rather the soul's action of accepting that knowledge. Muḥammad al-Dasūqī, *Ḥāshiyat al-Dasūqī ʿalā Umm al-barāhīn* (Cairo: Dār Iḥyāʾ al-Kutub al-ʿIlmiyya, n.d.), 53. This is how it is possible for a disbeliever to have knowledge that what the Prophet (God bless him and give him peace) brought is true, and yet not have religious belief—for the disbeliever has not inwardly accepted that knowledge. See *TB*, 30.

23. Though the term *wujūd dhihnī* is often associated with the doctrine that the extramental thing itself has a kind of existence in the mind, that is not what the theologians mean because they explicitly reject *wujūd dhihnī* in this sense.

Section	Sources
1.1.1 Beginningless and Created Knowledge	*TB*, 28-29; Ibrāhīm al-Bājūrī, *Ḥāshiyat al-imām al-Bājūrī ʿalā Jawharat al-tawḥīd al-musammāh bi-Tuḥfat al-murīd ʿalā Jawharat al-tawḥīd* (Cairo: Dār al-Salām, 2006), 126-28
1.1.2 Direct and Indirect Knowledge	*TB*, 29-30
1.1.3 Conceptual and Propositional Knowledge	*TB*, 28-48
1.1.3.1 Kinds of Compositions	*TB*, 45-46
1.1.3.2 Truth and Falsity	*TB*, 28-32
1.1.3.3 Strength of Perception of Judgment	*TB*, 30
1.1.3.4 Belief and Authority	Ḥasan b. Muḥammad al-ʿAṭṭār, *Ḥāshiyat al-ʿAṭṭār ʿalā Jamʿ al-jawāmiʿ* (repr., Beirut: Dār al-Fikr, n.d.), 1:200; *TB*, 30; al-Bājūrī, *Tuḥfat al-murīd*, 76-80
1.1.4 Inferential and Noninferential Knowledge	*TB*, 49-60
1.1.4.1 The Inferential-Noninferential Division	*TB*, 49-60
1.1.4.2 Reflection and Inference	*TB*, 56
1.1.4.3 Noninferential Judgments and Self-Evident Judgments	*TB*, 52, 56-57
1.2 The Need for Logic	*TB*, 60-69
1.2.1 Logic as Universal Principles	*TB*, 65-67
1.2.2 Logic and the Natural Operation of the Mind	*TB*, 65
1.2.3 Is Conceptual Knowledge Susceptible to Error?	*TB*, 60-61
1.2.4 The Definition of Logic	*TB*, 21-22, 26-27
1.3 The Subject of Logic	*TB*, 64
1.4 The Ten Topics of Scholarly Prolegomena	Muḥammad b. ʿAlī al-Ṣabbān, *Ḥāshiya ʿalā Sharḥ al-Sullam li-l-Mallawī* (Cairo: Maṭbaʿat Muṣṭafā al-Bābī al-Ḥalabī, 1938), 31, 33, 35, 39-42
1.5 Supplement: The Metaphysics of Knowledge	*TB*, 28-33, 40-41

2

EXPRESSIONS AND SIGNIFICATION

Properly speaking, expressions are not the subject of logic. The subjects of logic are mental concepts and mental propositions (sg. *mafhūm*), not uttered expressions (sg. *lafẓ*). But we use expressions to refer to mental concepts and propositions so frequently that our private reflection on our own mental concepts and propositions will introspectively reveal that it is exceedingly difficult to bring concepts or propositions to mind without also bringing to mind the expressions that we conventionally use to signify them.[1] Uttered expressions and mental concepts and propositions are theoretically independent of each other, but their constant conjunction in our minds makes them practically inseparable.

The reason for their constant conjunction is that we are social creatures; we need to communicate our thoughts to the people who we live with, and uttered expressions are the most effective and widespread means for this communication. For example, the way that we communicate the concept ‹human› to someone else is by uttering the expression "human." Note how, even in the previous sentence, in order to refer to the concept that the expression "human" signifies, we were compelled to use the expression itself!

Logicians thus cannot study mental concepts and propositions without using the expressions that signify them. This is why it is the custom of Muslim logicians to preface their study of logic with a study of expressions and their significations. But it is not just logic that benefits from the study of expressions

1. In this book the convention, for instructional purposes, is to distinguish the *expressional* from the *conceptual* by enclosing elements representing the former in double quotation marks (e.g., "example expression"), and enclosing elements representing the latter in single side-pointing quotation marks (e.g., ‹example concept›).

and signification. Since every science studies some particular collection of mental concepts and propositions, the study of expressions undertaken by the logicians is not a prerequisite only for the study of logic, but indeed for the study of every science.

While grammarians, too, study expressions, they do so from a different perspective. Whereas grammarians are concerned with the syntax and semantics of a particular language, logicians are concerned with expressions in general, independent of any particular language. They are concerned with how expressions in any language signify mental representations, or meanings. Thus, logicians preface their study of expressions with the study of signification. This chapter begins with the study of signification in Section 2.1 and follows that with the study of expressions in Section 2.2.

2.1 Signification

A *sign* (*dāll*) is something that is related to its *significate* (*madlūl*) in such a manner that knowledge of the sign along with knowledge of its relation to the significate directs one to knowledge of the significate. For example, the expression "man" is a *sign* because it is related by linguistic convention to the meaning ‹male human being›. Similarly, a gravestone is a *sign* because it is related by convention to the meaning that the person whose name is inscribed on the stone is buried in that location, and so on. The relation that directs one to understand the signified meaning from its sign is called *signification* (*dalāla*).

Signs are divided into (1) *expressional signs* (*alfāẓ*), i.e., uttered expressions, e.g., the expression "man," and (2) *non-expressional signs*, i.e., things other than expressions, e.g., a gravestone. The signification of each of these two kinds of signs is divided into (a) *conventional signification* (*dalāla waḍʿiyya*), (b) *rational signification* (*dalāla ʿaqliyya*), and (c) *natural signification* (*dalāla ṭabīʿiyya*). This amounts to six kinds of signification as follows.

1. *Conventional expressional signification*, e.g., the expression "man" signifying ‹male human being›, by virtue of the conventions of the English language.
2. *Rational expressional signification*, e.g., the expression "man" signifying the existence of its utterer, by virtue of inference from the premise that expressions can only exist if someone utters them.
3. *Natural expressional signification*, e.g., the expression "Aaah!" signifying one's pain, by virtue of the natural regularity that this sound

is uttered by people in extreme pain.

4. *Conventional non-expressional signification*, e.g., a nod signifying one's assent and a headshake signifying one's dissent, by virtue of the conventions of some societies.[2]
5. *Rational non-expressional signification*, e.g., the contingent universe signifying the existence of a necessary being, by virtue of inference from the premise that every contingent thing requires a necessary being to make it the way that it is.
6. *Natural non-expressional signification*, e.g., paleness signifying one's fear and redness signifying one's embarrassment, by virtue of the natural regularities that people turn pale when afraid and red when embarrassed.

The difference between rational and natural signification is that rational signification is *rationally necessary*, whereas natural signification is regular but not necessary. It is rationally necessary, for example, for every expression to have an utterer and for every contingent thing to be made by a necessary being, while it is regular but not necessary, for example, for the utterance "Aaah!" to be uttered by someone in pain, for paleness to follow from fear, and for redness to follow from embarrassment. This distinction between rational and natural significations is connected to the Ashʿarī theological position that the natural universe and all its properties are contingent.

Although all six of these are legitimate kinds of signification, logicians confine themselves to studying *conventional expressional signification*. This is because it (1) signifies the greatest number of meanings, (2) signifies with the most precision, and (3) is the easiest to learn and use. The rest of this chapter therefore focuses on conventional expressional signification.

2.1.1 *Conventional Expressional Signification*

A language is a collection of expressions that possess conventional signification among speakers of that language. Expressions that have been assigned meanings are *meaningful* (*mustaʿmal*), e.g., "man" and "horse"; those that have not been assigned meanings are *meaningless* (*muhmal*), e.g., "nam" (the reverse of "man") and "esroh" (the reverse of "horse"). Linguistic signification thus has three elements: (1) expressions, (2) meanings, and (3) the assignment

2. In many Arab societies, by contrast, moving the head down signifies assent and moving the head up signifies dissent, and this is the example that is traditionally mentioned in the manuals of the Muslim logicians.

of meanings to expressions. The speaker's *intended* meaning, however, is not an element of linguistic signification; expressions possess signification in virtue of their original linguistic assignment (*waḍʿ*) even if the speaker does not intend it.

Linguistic signification is divided into (1) *complete signification* (*dalālat al-muṭābaqa*), (2) *partial signification* (*dalālat al-taḍammun*), and (3) *entailed signification* (*dalālat al-iltizām*). The basis of this threefold division is that a meaningful expression may either (1) signify the exact meaning assigned to it, (2) signify part of that meaning, or (3) signify a meaning that is neither that exact meaning nor a part of it.

The first is the expression's complete signification. For example, the complete signification of the expression "human" is its relation to the meaning ‹rational animal› because this is the exact meaning that the expression has been linguistically assigned. The second is the expression's partial signification. For example, a partial signification of the expression "human" is its relation to the meaning ‹animal› because this is part of the meaning that the expression has been linguistically assigned, namely ‹rational animal›. The third is the expression's entailed signification. For example, an entailed signification of the expression "human" is its relation to the meaning ‹something capable of knowledge› because this meaning is entailed by the meaning that the expression has been linguistically assigned, namely ‹rational animal›.

These three kinds of significations often coincide, such as in the expression "human," which possesses all of them, but this is not strictly necessary. The table below displays which kinds of signification logically require or do not require the obtaining of others. The table reflects the fact that there are some basic meanings that cannot be divided into parts, such as the meaning of the geometric concept ‹point›. It also reflects the fact that, even though most meanings we express entail others, these entailments are *nonessential* properties of meanings.

	Requires	**Requires**	**Requires**
Complete	-	No	No
Partial	Yes	-	No
Entailed	Yes	No	-

The logicians endorse the use of complete and partial signification because these signify their meanings clearly. They only endorse the use of entailed signification, however, when the entailment meets several conditions, described below.

2.1.2 *Entailed Signification*

The *entailment* (*luzūm*) of meanings is divided into *direct entailment* (*luzūm bayyin*) and *indirect entailment* (*luzūm ghayr bayyin*). A meaning's entailment is indirect when understanding the *entailed meaning* (*lāzim*) from the *original meaning* (*malzūm*) requires an *intermediary premise* (*wasaṭ*). For example, understanding ‹necessary being› from ‹contingent being› requires the intermediary premise ‹Every contingent being requires a necessary being›.

A meaning's entailment is direct when understanding the entailed meaning from the original meaning does not require any intermediary premise. For example, understanding ‹something capable of knowledge› from ‹rational animal› does not require any intermediary premise, because rationality independently entails the capacity for knowledge.

Direct entailment is further divided into *independent direct entailment* (*luzūm bayyin bi-l-maʿnā al-akhaṣṣ*) and *collective direct entailment* (*luzūm bayyin bi-l-maʿnā al-aʿamm*). The difference between independent and collective entailment is that the meaning that is entailed independently requires conception of the original meaning alone, whereas the meaning that is entailed collectively requires conception of both the original and entailed meanings. For example, the entailment of ‹something capable of knowledge› by ‹rational animal› is an independent entailment because merely understanding ‹rational› in ‹rational animal› reveals a capacity for knowledge. On the other hand, the entailment of ‹something capable of writing› by ‹rational animal› is a collective entailment because merely understanding ‹rational animal› does not reveal a capacity for writing; rather, one needs to understand it while also understanding that writing is a kind of motion that relies on careful reflection. Another example of an independent direct entailment is the entailment of ‹evenness› by ‹two›.[3] Another example of a collective direct entailment is the entailment of ‹difference from ‹human› by the meaning ‹horse›.[4]

---

3. Some scholars argue that this is an indirect entailment because it requires an intermediate inference using the premise, ‹Two is divisible by two›. Others reply that this inference is *subconscious* (see 10.2.1.6), which renders the entailment direct.

4. Logicians stipulate that the use of entailed signification in expressions ought to involve independent rather than collective entailment because otherwise expressions alone would not indicate their intended meanings.

Direct entailment is also divided into *rational entailment* (*luzūm ʿaqlī*) and *conventional entailment* (*luzūm ʿurfī*). The difference between the two is that rational entailment is a priori and necessary, whereas conventional entailment is a posteriori and merely regular. For example, the entailment of ‹even number› by ‹two› is rational because ‹two› is necessarily even and its evenness is known a priori, whereas the entailment of ‹black› by ‹crow› is merely regular, because crows are only regularly black, not necessarily, and their blackness is only known a posteriori.

It is possible for one meaning to rationally entail another even in the case that their extramental coexistence is impossible. For example, the meaning ‹blindness› rationally entails the meaning ‹sight› because only something that can conceivably see—e.g., humans, horses, and lions—can be said to be blind, as opposed to that which cannot conceivably see—e.g., walls, doors, and tables—which cannot be said to be blind. The meaning ‹blindness› therefore rationally entails the meaning ‹sight› even though the two cannot coexist in the same object in the external world.

Many logicians stipulate that entailed signification must be rational rather than conventional. Conventional entailment, they argue, is inconclusive since it is hypothetically possible for an expression not to entail a meaning to which it relates merely regularly. For example, it is possible for "crow" not to entail ‹black›, because it is hypothetically possible to have a crow that is not black.

The scholars of Arabic eloquence (*balāgha*) disagree with the logicians, arguing that many figurative (*majāz*) and indirect (*kināya*) uses of expressions rely on their conventional entailments and their use is widespread in eloquent speech, particularly in the Qurʾān. This argument influenced a number of prominent logicians, most notably al-Taftāzānī himself, to accept both the rational and conventional entailments of expressions.

2.1.3 *Assignment of Expressions to Meanings*

The *linguistic assignment* (*waḍʿ*) is the conventional assignment of expressions to meanings by speakers of a particular language. It has three elements—(1) the expression, (2) the meaning, and (3) the assignment of the expression to the meaning—and can be divided into various categories from the perspective of each element.

From the perspective of the assigned expression, it is divided into (1) *assignment of an individual expression* (*waḍʿ shakhṣī*), e.g., the assignment of the individual expression "man" to the meaning ‹rational animal›, and (2) *assignment of a class of expressions* (*waḍʿ nawʿī*), e.g., the assignment of the class of nouns that end with "-s" (e.g., "tables," "chairs," and "books") to the pluralization of that noun.

From the perspective of the meaning, it is divided into (1) assignment to a *singular meaning* (*mawḍūʿ lahu khāṣṣ*), e.g., the assignment of the proper name "Omar" to the singular meaning of the particular man who is given that name, and (2) assignment to a *universal meaning* (*mawḍūʿ lahu ʿāmm*), e.g., the assignment of the common noun "man" to the universal meaning ‹rational animal›.

Finally, from the perspective of the assignment, it is divided into (1) *individual assignment* (*waḍʿ khāṣṣ*), i.e., an assignment that is intentionally directed to an individual meaning, e.g., the individual assignment of "Omar" to the individual meaning of the particular man who is given that name, and (2) *general assignment* (*waḍʿ ʿāmm*), i.e., an assignment that is intentionally directed to a general meaning. In consideration of the previous division, general assignment is divisible into (a) *general assignment to a universal meaning* (*waḍʿ ʿāmm li-mawḍūʿ lahu ʿāmm*), e.g., the general assignment of "man" to the universal meaning ‹rational animal› and (b) *general assignment to a class of singular meanings* (*waḍʿ ʿāmm li-mawḍūʿ lahu khāṣṣ*), e.g., the general assignment of the demonstrative pronoun "this" to any singular thing that the speaker physically points to.

These divisions lead to five combinations that are types of commonly used linguistic assignment:

1. *Individual assignment of an individual expression to a singular meaning*, e.g., the assignment of the expression "Omar" to the meaning of the man who is given that name.
2. *General assignment of an individual expression to a class of singulars*, e.g., the assignment of the demonstrative pronoun "this" to any singular meaning that the speaker physically points to.
3. *General assignment of an individual expression to a universal meaning*, e.g., the assignment of the expression "man" to the meaning ‹rational animal›.
4. *General assignment of a class of expressions to a class of singulars*, e.g., the assignment of the class of nouns that end with "-s" (e.g., "tables," "chairs," and "books") to the pluralization of every singular meaning.
5. *General assignment of a class of expressions to a universal meaning*, e.g., the assignment of the class of "*X* is *Y*" expressions (e.g., "Omar

is standing," and, "Fatima is sitting") to the universal meaning of the predication of *Y* to *X*.

Avicenna, al-Fārābī, and Quṭb al-Dīn al-Rāzī (d. 766/1365) held that expressions are linguistically assigned to the mental representations of extramental things, not to the actual extramental things, based on their philosophical position that the objects of our knowledge are mental representations rather than the extramental things they represent. Al-Ṭūsī (d. 672/1274), Quṭb al-Dīn al-Shīrāzī (d. 711/1311), al-Taftāzānī (d. 792/1389), al-Dawānī (d. 918/1512), and others held that they are assigned to extramental things themselves, arguing that expressions direct our attention to the extramental objects that mental representations represent, not to the mental representations themselves. The preferred position of the late scholarly tradition of logicians, however, is that expressions are assigned neither to extramental objects nor to their mental representations, but to meanings that possess reference. These meanings sometimes refer to extramental objects, in which case they are mental representations of extramental objects; sometimes they refer to meanings that refer to extramental objects in a general manner (such as with *indexicals*), and sometimes they refer to mental considerations that have no extramental existence.[5]

2.1.4 *Indexicals*

The logicians disagreed about the linguistic assignment of *indexicals*, namely personal pronouns (e.g., "I," "you," and "they"), demonstrative pronouns (e.g., "this," "that," and "those"), and relative pronouns (e.g., "which" and "that"). According to the late logicians, indexicals involve the general assignment of individual expressions to a class of singulars, as explained in the table below.

5. *Reference* is a frequently used technical term in the philosophy of language that is used variously by different philosophers. In the usage of the present book, expressions (or words) possess *signification*, not reference, while meanings (or thoughts) possess *reference*, not signification.

Indexical	Explanation of Linguistic Assignment
Personal Pronouns	The first-person pronoun "I" is generally assigned to every singular individual who is speaking. The first-person pronoun "we" is generally assigned to every group of singular individuals who are speaking. The second-person pronoun "you" is generally assigned to every singular individual (or individuals) who is (or are) addressed. The third-person pronoun "he" is generally assigned to every previously mentioned male singular individual who is spoken about. The third-person pronoun "she" is generally assigned to every previously mentioned female singular individual who is spoken about. The third-person pronoun "they" is generally assigned to every previously mentioned group of singular individuals who are spoken about.
Demon-strative Pronouns	The demonstrative pronoun "this" is generally assigned to every nearby singular individual that the speaker physically points to. The demonstrative pronoun "these" is generally assigned to every group of nearby singular individuals that the speaker physically points to. The demonstrative pronoun "that" is generally assigned to every faraway singular individual that the speaker physically points to. The demonstrative pronoun "those" is generally assigned to every group of faraway singular individuals that the speaker physically points to.
Relative Pronouns	The relative pronoun "which" is generally assigned to every singular individual that has been mentioned immediately before it. The relative pronoun "that" is generally assigned to every singular individual that has been mentioned immediately before it.

The early logicians did not recognize this kind of linguistic assignment. For the early logicians, indexicals instead involve the general assignment of an individual expression to a universal meaning. In other words, the linguistic assignment of indexicals is the same as the linguistic assignment of "man" or "horse." This position was taken by al-Taftāzānī but rejected by the overwhelming majority of other scholars of the late logical tradition.

The same disagreement extends to relational words, such as prepositions (e.g., "in" and "on"). In other words, according to the overwhelming majority of late logicians, these relational words are generally assigned to a class of singulars. For example, the expression "in" is generally assigned to the singular instances of containment by the word that is mentioned after it. The word "in" in the phrase "in this box" in other words, refers to the specific individual containment by the box that the speaker in pointing to, while in the phrase "in Arabia" it refers to the specific individual containment by the land of Arabia. Similarly, the expression "on" is generally assigned to the singular instances of above-ness with respect to the word that is mentioned after it. "On" in the phrase "on this table," in other words, refers to the above-ness with respect to the table that the speaker is pointing to, while in the phrase "on the tree" it refers to above-ness with respect to the individual tree that is referred to. According to the earlier logicians and al-Taftāzānī, on the other hand, the linguistic assignment of relational words is like the third type of assignment listed in the previous section. The arguments advanced respectively by the early and late logicians are discussed in manuals of the science of linguistic assignment (*ʿilm al-waḍʿ*).

2.2 Expressions

An expression is a sound that is composed of the letters of a particular language, e.g., "man" and its reverse, "nam." "Man" is an expression that possesses linguistic signification whereas "nam" is an expression that does not. Expressions that possess linguistic signification such as "man" are called *meaningful* (*mustaʿmal*) and those that do not are called *meaningless* (*muhmal*). Logicians are only concerned with meaningful expressions.

Meaningful expressions are divided into *basic expressions* (*lafẓ mufrad*), e.g., "man," and *composite expressions* (*lafẓ murakkab*), e.g., "The man is standing." The difference between basic and composite expressions is that composite expressions are composed of sub-expressions that possess linguistic signification whereas basic expressions are not. The linguistic signification of the sub-expressions must be intended by the speaker for the expression to be composite; otherwise, what appears to be a compound expression will actually be a basic expression. This occurs, for example, with compound expressions that are used as proper names, e.g., "Longfellow" (personal name), "Mount Everest" (place name), or "Eagle's Point" (place name). It is theoretically possible for any compound expression to turn into a basic expression in this manner—someone might, for example, name his son, "The man is standing," and what used to be a sentence will turn into a singular noun. This is more common in Arabic than in English.[6]

Composite expressions are divided into *sentences* (*murakkab tāmm*) and *phrases* (*murakkab nāqiṣ*). The difference between the two is that when someone is addressed by a sentence, e.g., "The man is in the house," he normally stops expecting more, whereas when he is addressed by a phrase, e.g., "The man is in...," he notices that the speech is incomplete and expects more.

2.2.1 *Sentences*

Sentences are either *propositional* (*khabarī*) or *non-propositional* (*inshā'ī*). The difference between the two is that propositions, e.g., "The man is in the house," can be true or false whereas non-propositional sentences, e.g., "Is the man in the house?" cannot. Non-propositional sentences include questions, commands, prohibitions, suggestions, expressions of praise, and expressions of blame. These are studied in the sciences of language. Logicians, on the other hand, only study propositional sentences.

It may appear at first glance that some kinds of propositions cannot be false, e.g., "Two is half of four" (noninferentially known), or, "God exists" (inferentially known), and that some kinds of propositions cannot be true, e.g., "Two is half of six" (noninferentially known to be false), or, "God does not exist" (inferentially known to be false). The logicians respond to this objection by explaining that what they mean by the possibility of truth and falsity is their possibility from the perspective of the expression's *structure*, without regard for its content or what is actually stated. Inasmuch as all these expressions are structured as propositional sentences, they can, indeed, be true or false. As for the fact that they are actually necessarily true or false, that is because of what they are saying, not because of their structures.

2.2.2 *Phrases*

Phrases are either *restrictive* (*taqyīdī*) or *non-restrictive* (*ghayr taqyīdī*). The difference between the two is that restrictive phrases restrict the referential

6. Famous examples include *'Abdallāh* ("God's slave"), *Ta'abbaṭa-sharran* ("he concealed evil"), and *Shāba-qarnāhā* ("her braids turned gray").

scope of an expression whereas non-restrictive phrases do not. For example, "tall man" and "your house" are both restrictive phrases because the adjective "tall" restricts the referential scope of "man" and the possessive pronoun "your" restricts the referential scope of "house." The phrases "in the house" and "certainly stood," on the other hand, are not restrictive phrases, because appending the preposition "in" does not restrict the referential scope of "the house," nor does appending the adverb "certainly" restrict the referential scope of "stood."

2.2.3 *Basic Expressions*

Basic expressions are the units that compose phrases and sentences. Note that although the goal of logicians when studying expressions is to study them in general, independently of any particular language, some linguistic particularities are unavoidable as every logician will explain how expressions signify meanings using the language that he speaks. Throughout this translation, examples from the Arabic language have been replaced with analogous examples from the English language. In this section, however, the differences between English and Arabic grow very wide, so original examples from the Arabic language have been retained.

2.2.3.1 Parts of Speech

The basic expressions that compose phrases and sentences in the Arabic language are of three types: (1) verbs (the Arab grammarians call a verb a *fiʿl*; the logicians call it a *kalima*), (2) nouns (*ism*), and (3) particles (the Arab grammarians call a particle a *ḥarf*; the logicians call it an *adāh*).[7]

Verbs and nouns are *notional expressions* that signify meanings independently. For example, the Arabic words *ḍaraba* ("he hit") and *yaktubu* ("he writes") are verbs that signify meanings independently rather than in relation to other expressions. Similarly, the Arabic words *Zayd* (proper name) and *insān* ("human") are nouns that signify meanings independently rather than in relation to other expressions.

Particles, on the other hand, are *relational expressions* that do not signify meanings independently, but only in relation to other expressions. For example, the Arabic word *fī* ("in") in the sentence *Zayd fī al-dār* ("Zayd is in

7. There is, strictly speaking, a difference between the *adāh* of the logicians and the *ḥarf* of the grammarians, the former being more inclusive. For example, conditional nouns and the auxiliary (*nāqiṣ*) verbs *kana* and its sisters are counted as logical *adawāt*. Since, however, these additional examples are rather specific grammatical categories, it is common to ignore these exceptional cases and simply treat the two as identical.

the house") signifies containment (*ẓarfiyya*), but not independently as signified by the noun "containment." Rather, it signifies the relational meaning of the containment that obtains between Zayd and the house. To take another example, the Arabic word *min* ("from") in the sentence *kharaja Zayd min al-masjid* ("Zayd exited from the mosque") signifies beginning (*ibtidāʾ*), but not independently as signified by the noun "beginning." Rather, it signifies the relational meaning of the beginning that obtains between Zayd's exiting and the mosque.

In consequence of this difference between verbs and nouns on one hand and particles on the other, the predicate of a propositional Arabic sentence may consist solely of a verb—e.g., *Zaydun kataba* ("Zayd wrote")—or solely of a noun—e.g., *Zaydun katibun* ("Zayd is someone who writes")[8]—but never solely of a particle. Because particles only signify meanings in relation to other expressions, they can only constitute the predicate along with their related expressions and are hence always a part of a phrasal predicate. In the two examples mentioned in the previous paragraph, these phrasal predicates are *ḥāṣil fī al-dār* ("exists in the house")[9] and *kharaja min al-masjid* ("exited from the mosque"), respectively.

The difference between a noun and a verb is that the *morphological structure* (*hayʾa*) of an Arabic verb signifies tense whereas the morphological structure of an Arabic noun does not. Nominal sentences default to the present tense and may also figuratively refer to the future tense, but this signification of tense is inferred from context rather than morphology.

2.2.3.2 Name-Meaning Relationships

Basic expressions are divided from the perspective of the meanings that they signify into expressions that have a single meaning and expressions that have multiple meanings.

Basic expressions that signify a single meaning are divided into two categories: (1) *proper names* (*ʿalam*) and (2) *common nouns* (*ism jins*).[10] A *prop-*

8. Arabic sentences do not use the copula "is," and Arabic nouns can hence function as predicates directly, unlike English nouns.

9. The word *ḥāṣil* ("exists") is an unstated but grammatically implied part of the sentence.

10. The glosses on the *Tahdhīb* point out that this division of basic expressions into proper names and common nouns is not entirely accurate because (1) these divisions technically do not apply to all kinds of basic expressions but only to nouns, unlike the other divisions, which apply to verbs and particles as well, and (2) these are actually divisions of the meanings that these expressions signify, not the expressions themselves. The division has nevertheless been

er name is an expression that is linguistically assigned to be predicated of only one thing, e.g., the personal name "Zayd" (can only be predicated of the particular man given that name) and the place-name "Mecca" (can only be predicated of the particular place given that name). *Indexicals* are not considered proper names because although they refer to singulars, they are not linguistically assigned to be predicated of only one thing. A *common noun* is an expression that is linguistically assigned to be predicated of many things, e.g., "man," which can be predicated of many different men (one can say, for example, that Zayd is a man and also that John is a man), and "red," which can be predicated of many different things (one can say, for example, that this book is red and also that this shirt is red).

Common nouns are further divided into: (a) *nouns that possess nonvarying reference* (*ism mutawāṭi'*), e.g., "man," since the universal meaning ‹man› applies equivalently to all its referents, and differences from one man to another are nonessential differences that return to something that is incidental to their humanness, such as knowledge, strength, or piety, and (b) *nouns that possess varying reference* (*ism mushakkik*), e.g., "red," since the universal meaning ‹red› applies to its referents in varying degrees. The mark that a universal has varying reference is that one can use it comparatively, e.g., "This book is *redder* than that shirt."

These varying degrees in the application of the latter type of universal meanings are either degrees of *precedence* (*awwaliyya*) or degrees of *strength* (*awlawiyya*). An example of a universal that has both kinds of variance is ‹existence›. It has varying degrees of precedence because its presence in God precedes its presence in the universe, and it has varying degrees of strength because its presence in God is stronger than its presence in the universe (God's existence is necessary whereas the universe's existence is contingent). The difference between the two kinds of degrees in this example is perspectival.

Some logicians, such Ibn al-Tilmisānī and al-Jurjānī, denied the existence of varying universals and held that names that appear to signify a varying universal meaning are actually *homonyms* (sg. *ism mushtarak*) signifying a number of distinct nonvarying universals. They argue that the purported variance arises either (a) from the linguistic assignments of such names, in which case they are homonyms, or (b) from a factor external to their linguistic assignments (i.e., nonessential variations in the instances that the expression refers to), in which case the expression is assigned to the essential commonality between

---

preserved for the sake of matching the presentation of the *Tahdhīb*.

the instances, which must be nonvarying. The majority of logicians did not accept the requirement that this latter commonality must be nonvarying.

Basic expressions that signify multiple meanings are divided into (1) expressions linguistically assigned to those multiple meanings, namely *homonyms* (sg. *ism mushtarak*)—e.g., "pupil," which is linguistically assigned to both ‹center of the eye› and ‹student in a class›—and (2) expressions that are not.

The second category is divided into two types. The first type is that of *expressions whose meaning has shifted* (*manqūl*) either by (a) being employed for a new meaning by revelation (e.g., the Arabic word *ṣalāh* originally meant ‹supplication› and its meaning shifted because of revelation to ‹ritual prayer›), or (b) being employed for a new technical meaning by the scholars of a science (e.g., the Arabic word *fāʿil* originally meant ‹agent› and Arabic grammarians shifted its meaning in their books to ‹grammatical subject›), or (c) taking on a new meaning due to changing linguistic conventions (e.g., the Arabic word *dābba* originally referred to all living things that walk on the earth, including humans, and then shifted because of linguistic conventions to refer exclusively to four-legged animals). The second type is that of *literal* (*ḥaqīqa*) and *figurative* (*majāz*) expressions (e.g., "lion," which can be used literally to refer to the predatory animal that lives in the jungle or figuratively to refer to a brave person).[11]

Sources

Section	Sources
2.1 Signification	*TB*, 83-84, 86-87; for further reading, see Street, *Najm al-Dīn*, 97-105; Ahmed, *Palimpsests*, 147-48; Riccardo Strobino, *Avicenna's Theory of Science: Logic, Metaphysics, Epistemology* (Oakland: University of California Press, 2021), 192-96
2.1.1 Conventional Expressional Signification	*TB*, 85, 88-89, 95, 99-103
2.1.2 Entailed Signification	*TB*, 88-98
2.1.3 Assignment of Expressions to Meanings	*TB*, 93-94, 104, 118; Yūsuf al-Dijwī, *Khulāṣat ʿilm al-waḍʿ* (Cairo: Maṭbaʿat al-Nahḍa, 1920), 1-12; ʿAbd al-Khāliq al-Shabrāwī, *al-Minḥa al-ilāhiyya fī al-qawāʿid al-waḍʿiyya* (Cairo: Maṭbaʿat al-Saʿāda, n.d.), 3-12

11. This second category of expressions is studied in the science of Arabic eloquence.

Section	Sources
2.1.4 Indexicals	*TB*, 117-18; al-Dijwī, Khulāṣa, 9-12; al-Shabrāwī, *al-Minḥa*, 21-22, 24-26
2.2 Expressions	*TB*, 103, 108-9; for further reading, see Street, Najm al-Dīn, 104-8; Ahmed, Palimpsests, 148-51
2.2.1 Sentences	*TB*, 106
2.2.2 Phrases	*TB*, 107-8
2.2.3 Basic Expressions	*TB*, 108, 112
2.2.3.1 Parts of Speech	TB, 110-16; Quṭb al-Dīn al-Rāzī, et al., *Shurūḥ al-Shamsiyya majmūʿat ḥawāshin wa-taʿlīqāt fī al-manṭiq* (repr., Cairo: al-Maktaba al-Azhariyya li-l-Turāth, 2011), 1: 200–208
2.2.3.2 Name-Meaning Relationships	*TB*, 116-25

II

CONCEPTUAL KNOWLEDGE

3

CONCEPTION

The previous chapters were not about logic *per se*. They were merely preparatory, preparing the way for the study of logic by addressing preliminary questions. Since logic studies how to arrive at new conception through definition and how to arrive at new judgment through argument, its investigations are divided into four categories, as we have seen: (1) concept-related investigations that are useful for definition, (2) definition, (3) judgment-related investigations that are useful for argument, and (4) argument. This chapter focuses on the first category.

It begins with a study of mental concepts. "Concept" (*mafhūm*), "meaning" (*maʿnā*), and "significate" (*madlūl*) are various names that refer to the same thing. The difference between them is perspectival: "concept" highlights the aspect of occurring in the mind (the Arabic word *mafhūm* literally means "that which is understood"); "meaning" highlights the aspect of being intended by expressions (the Arabic word *maʿnā* comes from the morphological root *ʿ-n-y*, which carries the meaning of intention); and "significate" highlights the aspect of being signified by expressions (the Arabic word *madlūl* literally means, "that which is signified").

Mental concepts have *referents* (sg. *mā-ṣadaq*) or *instances* (sg. *fard*) of which they are predicated. These referents and instances may either be mental or extramental. For example, the concept ‹human› has extramental referents, such as Zayd, John, and Mary, and the concept ‹universal› has mental referents, such as the universals ‹human›, ‹horse›, and ‹animal›.

3.1 Singular and Universal Concepts

Every concept is either *singular* (*juzʾī*) or *universal* (*kullī*). It is *singular* if, merely by virtue of the concept's occurrence in the mind, the mind judges without further reflection that it is *impossible* for the concept to be predicated of multiple instances. For example, the concept signified by the expression "Zayd" is a singular concept because it is impossible for it to be predicated of any instance other than the specific person that it refers to. The concept is *universal*, on the other hand, if, merely by virtue of its occurrence in the mind, the mind judges without further reflection that it is *possible* for the concept to be predicated of multiple instances. For example, the expression "human" signifies a universal concept because it is possible for ‹human› to be predicated of billions of instances of human beings.

Singularization (*tashakhkhuṣ* or *taʿayyun*) can refer to one of two things. It can refer to a mental concept being such that it is inconceivable that it be common to multiple instances, e.g., the singular concept ‹Zayd›. Or it can refer to a thing being extramentally distinct from all else by means of its various particular, nonessential, extramental properties. This latter meaning refers to the thing's *identity* (*huwiyya*), which is distinct from and superadded to its universal *essence* (*māhiyya*).

The division of concepts into singular and universal concepts is based on a consideration of concepts from the perspective of their mere occurrence in the mind without any further consideration. From this perspective, the concept ‹necessary existent› (*wājib al-wujūd*) is a universal concept because, when it is considered from the perspective of its mere occurrence in the mind, it can indeed be predicated of multiple instances. However, when one adds the consideration of the rational argument for the oneness of God, it is no longer a universal concept, because it can no longer be predicated of multiple instances.[1]

Singularity and *universality* are *second-order concepts* (*maʿqūlāt thāniya*) that are abstracted from other concepts in the mind. This is why the concept ‹singularity› is itself a universal; it can be predicated of many different concepts (e.g., ‹Zayd›, ‹Mecca›, ‹John›). It is the concepts that ‹singularity› is predicated of (e.g., ‹Zayd›, ‹Mecca›, ‹John›)—not the concept ‹singularity› itself—that cannot be predicated of many things.

---

1. In this case, it is neither singular nor universal because the distinction between singular and universal only applies when one considers a concept from the perspective of its mere occurrence in the mind. *TB*, 133.

Logicians are not concerned with singular concepts inasmuch as they are singular because singular concepts neither (1) help one acquire new knowledge through definition or argument nor (2) constitute the new knowledge that results from definition or argument. Both the acquisition of new knowledge and the new knowledge that is acquired depend on universal concepts. Although singular concepts might be present in the premises or conclusions of some arguments, their singularity is always incidental to the inference of the conclusion.

3.2 Extramental Existence of a Universal's Instances

The definition of *universal* as something that can be predicated of many instances might lead one to imagine that every universal must possess many instances. But that is not correct; all that is required for a concept to be a universal is for it to be *possible* for it to predicated of many instances, even if no such instances actually exist. In order to clarify this point, logicians divide universals into six categories from the perspective of the extramental existence of their instances.

1. The extramental existence of the universal's instances is impossible, e.g., ‹coexistence of opposites› and ‹second god›. These are called *hypothetical universals* (sg. *kullī farḍī*).
2. The extramental existence of the universal's instances is possible, but none actually exist, e.g., ‹hydra› and ‹unicorn›.
3. The extramental existence of the universal's instances is only possible for one existing instance, e.g., ‹necessary being›, whose only possible instance is God.
4. The extramental existence of the universal's instances is possible in any number, but only one actually exists, e.g., ‹sun›.[2]
5. The extramental existence of the universal's instances is possible in any number, and a finite number of them actually exist, e.g., ‹human› and ‹lion›.
6. The extramental existence of the universal's instances is possible in any number, and an infinite number of them actually exist. According to the *mutakallimūn*, it is impossible for an actual infinite number of things to exist in the universe, and hence no

2. Modern astronomy has revealed that millions of the stars in the heavens are suns in their own right, but this medieval example can still be construed correctly if "sun" is understood to mean ‹suns in our solar system›.

such universal concept exists with respect to the things in the universe, whether in this life or in the afterlife.[3] It is true that paradise is everlasting, yet the actual pleasures of paradise at any given moment will inevitably amount to a finite number. That is to say that the infinity of the pleasures of paradise is a potential infinity, not an actual one. It is, however, possible for there to be such universals with respect to God, such as the universal concepts ‹God's attributes of perfection›, ‹things that God knows›, and ‹things that God can do› because the arguments that *mutakallimūn* make for the impossibility of the existence of an actual infinite are all proofs by contradiction that take as their basis the things of the universe to prove the finitude of the universe. Hence, they do not apply to God.

The basis of this division is the extramental existence of the universal's instances; the representational existence of the instances in the mind, however, is always possible. After all, the mind posits and conceives the existence of impossible things in order to make the judgment that it is impossible for them to exist.[4]

3.3 Relationships Between Universals

The consideration of any two different universal concepts may lead one to ask how they are related in terms of their reference, that is, whether or not and to what extent the one concept refers to what the other concept refers to. There are four relationships between pairs of universal concepts in terms of their reference:

Disjointedness (*tabāyun*): The two universals have no mutually common referents, e.g., ‹human› and ‹horse›.

Equality (*tasāwī*): All referents of the two universals are mutually common, e.g., ‹human› and ‹laughing animal›.

Unconditional inclusiveness and inclusion (*ʿumūm wa-khuṣūṣ muṭlaq*): All referents of one universal are common to the other, though the reverse is not true, e.g., ‹human› and ‹animal›—‹animal› is unconditionally

3. For the *falāsifa* such as Avicenna who hold that the universe has no beginning and has existed for an infinite period of time, it is possible to have universal concepts with an actual infinite number of extramentally existing instances in the universe.

4. Some universals have neither mental nor extramental instances, such as the universal ‹nothing›.

more general than ‹human›, and ‹human› is unconditionally more specific than ‹animal›.

Perspectival inclusiveness and inclusion (*ʿumūm wa-khuṣūṣ min wajh*): Each universal has some referents in common with the other and some unique referents, e.g., ‹animal› and ‹upright thing›—‹animal› is more general than ‹upright thing› from the perspective of position, for there are animals without an upright position, and ‹upright thing› is more general than ‹animal› from the perspective of animate life, for there are upright things that are not animals.

3.3.1 *Propositional Mapping of Universal Relationships*

The four universal relationships described above can be mapped into groups of *actual* and *continuous* propositions (see 6.7.2) as shown below.

Relationship	Propositional Mapping	Example
Disjointedness (*tabāyun*)	It is always the case that every A is not B. It is always the case that every B is not A.	A: human B: horse
Equality (*tasāwī*)	It is actually the case that every A is B. It is actually the case that every B is A.	A: human B: laughing animal
Unconditional Inclusiveness (*ʿumūm wa-khuṣūṣ muṭlaq*)	It is always the case that some A is not B. It is actually the case that every A is B.	A: animal B: human
Perspectival Inclusiveness (*ʿumūm wa-khuṣūṣ min wajh*)	It is actually the case that some A is B. It is always the case that some A is not B. It is always the case that some B is not A.	A: animal B: upright thing

3.3.2 *Complementary Relationships*

After describing the four possible relationships between universal concepts, it is the custom of logicians to examine the relationship that results from considering the complement of each universal. The *complement* (*naqīḍ*) of a universal concept is its negation. For example, the complement of ‹human› is ‹non-human›.

The relationship between the complements of two disjoint universals is *partial disjointedness* (*tabāyun juz'ī*). *Partial disjointedness* is a combination of disjointedness and perspectival inclusion. For example, ‹human› and ‹horse› are disjoint (original relationship), and ‹non-human› and ‹non-horse› are partially disjoint (complementary relationship), i.e., disjoint with respect to referents that are horses or humans and perspectivally more and less inclusive with respect to all other referents.

The relationship between the complements of equal universals is equality. For example, ‹human› and ‹animal› are equal (original relationship) and ‹non-human› and ‹non-laughing-animal› are also equal (complementary relationship).

The relationship between the complements of universals that are unconditionally more and less inclusive is unconditional inclusiveness in the reverse direction. For example, ‹animal› is unconditionally more inclusive than ‹human› (original relationship), and ‹non-human› is unconditionally more inclusive than ‹non-animal› (complementary relationship).

The relationship between the complements of universals that are perspectivally more and less inclusive is partial disjointedness. For example, ‹animal› and ‹upright thing› are perspectivally more and less inclusive (original relationship), and ‹non-animal› and ‹non-upright-thing› are partially disjoint (complementary relationship), i.e., disjoint with respect to referents that are animals or upright and perspectivally more and less inclusive with respect to all other instances.

These relationships are summarized in the table below. The logicians present simple *proofs by contradiction* (sg. *dalīl al-khulf*) for each of these complementary relationships. These proofs have been omitted from this translation.

Original Relationship	**Relationship**
Disjointedness	Partial Disjointedness
Equality	Equality
Unconditional Inclusiveness	Unconditional Inclusiveness Reversed
Perspectival Inclusiveness	Partial Disjointedness

3.4 The Five Universals

Universal concepts are divided into two categories from the perspective of the instances that they are predicated of. If the universal concept is essential to the instance that it is predicated of (e.g., ‹Zayd is human›, where ‹human› is essential to Zayd), it is an *essential universal* (*kullī dhātī*); otherwise (e.g., ‹Zayd is someone tall›, where ‹someone tall› is not essential to Zayd), it is a *nonessential universal* (*kullī ʿāraḍī*).

There are three kinds of essential universals: (1) *genus* (*jins*), (2) *species* (*nawʿ*), and (3) *differentia* (*faṣl*). And, to complete the categorization of universals, there are two kinds of nonessential universals or *accidents* (sg. *ʿaraḍ*): (4) *special accident* (*khāṣṣa*) and (5) *general accident* (*ʿaraḍ ʿāmm*). These are collectively known as the *five universals* (*al-kulliyyāt al-khams*), and their study is an integral part of the science of logic because logicians use them to construct *definitions*. Understanding this fivefold division of universals requires us to first understand what it means to *predicate* these universals, which is the subject of the next subsection. The following subsection then builds on this to examine the three kinds of essential universals, and the subsection after that examines the two kinds of nonessential universals.

3.4.1 *Identity-Predication*

There are two kinds of predication: (1) identity-predications (*ḥaml muwāṭaʾa* or *ḥaml huwa huwa*) and (2) property-predications (*ḥaml ishtiqāqī or ḥaml dhū huwa*). An identity-predication is the assertion of a referential identity between two different concepts. For example, when one says, "Zayd is human," one asserts that the concepts ‹Zayd› and ‹human› are referentially identical (i.e., they have the same referent). This definition of identity-predication highlights the aspect of difference ("two different concepts") and the aspect of identity ("referential identity"). The reason for the stipulation of conceptual difference is that a predication between identical concepts (e.g., ‹Humans are human›) does not communicate anything useful. And the reason for the stipulation of referential identity is that a predication between concepts with different referents (e.g., ‹Humans are horses›) is a false predication. In other words, in order for an identity-predication to be meaningful, the concepts must be different, and in order for it to be true the reference must be identical.[5] The following sections use the concept of identity-predication to

5. Note that the reference here is not necessarily extramental. Though this is commonly the case, it is also possible that the reference be mental, as when the concepts involved in the predication (1) have no actual referents (e.g., ‹Unicorns have horns›), (2) are second-order

distinguish between the five kinds of universals. Property-predications are the assertion of the possession of a quality or action by the subject, such as "Zayd has the quality of strength" (or, simply, "Zayd is strong") or "Zayd is doing the action of laughing" (or, simply, "Zayd is laughing"). Property-predications are not used by logicians in this section. Related discussions on predication are found in 4.1 and 6.1.

3.4.1.1 Kinds of Identity-Predication

Identity-predication is divided into *conceptual predication* (*ḥaml awwalī*) and *ordinary predication* (*ḥaml shāʾiʿī*). If the predication equates one universal concept with another, it is a *conceptual predication*, e.g., ‹‹Human› is ‹rational animal››, i.e., the mental concept ‹human› is the same as the mental concept ‹rational animal›.[6] Definitions use conceptual predications.

If the predication conveys that the subject is an instance of the predicate or that the subject and predicate share an instance, it is an ordinary predication, e.g., ‹Zayd is human›, i.e., the person Zayd is an instance of the universal concept ‹human›. Most natural language identity-predications are ordinary predications, which is why the Arabic term for ordinary predication, *ḥaml shāʾiʿī*, literally means "prevalent predication."

3.4.1.2 Identity-Predication of Singulars

The logicians agree that it is not correct to predicate a singular to a universal, e.g., ‹‹Human› is Zayd›. They disagree, however, whether or not it is correct to predicate a singular to another singular. Many, such as al-Jurjānī, argue that it is not correct because the two singulars are either (a) identical, e.g., ‹Zayd is Zayd›, in which case the predication does not communicate anything of value, or (b) different, e.g., ‹Zayd is John›, in which case the predication is false. Problem cases, such as the sentence, "This is Zayd," where both subject and predicate appear to be singular, are interpreted by such logicians to mean ‹This is the-person-who-has-been-named-Zayd (*musammā Zayd*)›, which turns the apparently singular ‹Zayd› into the universal ‹person-who-has-been-named-Zayd›. Other logicians, such as al-Dawānī, have argued that it is possible to predicate a singular of another singular, as long as they

concepts whose actual referents are mental concepts (e.g., ‹‹Human› is a universal›), or (3) are hypothetical concepts (e.g., ‹The existence of another god is impossible›).

6. The description of this kind of predication as one that *equates* two concepts is for the sake of simplicity. Strictly speaking, the predication of a logical part, like ‹animal› of ‹human›, though it falls within the scope of conceptual predication (*ḥaml awwalī*), it is not a true equation and hence not a proper definition.

are perspectivally different. These logicians interpret sentences like, "This is Zayd," straightforwardly, saying that although both the subject and predicate are extramentally identical, their perspectival difference in the mind makes the predication useful.

3.4.2 *Essential Universals*

Essential universals (sg. *kullī dhātī*) are divided into three types: *genus* (*jins*), *species* (*nawʿ*), and *differentia* (*faṣl*). The following subsections will use the category-tree in the table below to illustrate these three types of essential universals. The tree represents a classical illustrative example that is used in virtually all classical books of logic. After assuming that we start generally with all things that exist in the physical world and classify them into the *ten categories* (*al-maqūlāt al-ʿashara*) that include properties (*aʿrāḍ*) and objects (*jawāhir*), the tree divides one of these categories, namely ‹object›, into ‹inanimate object› and ‹organism›. It then divides ‹organism› into ‹plant› and ‹animal›, then ‹animal› into its various species, focusing on a selection that includes ‹human›. Finally, it divides ‹human› into its specific instances, focusing on a selection of particular humans (in this example, Zayd, John, and Mary). At each stage of the division from the basic categories onwards, an additional element is added to the higher universal in order to constitute one of the lower universals, as illustrated in the table.

<table>
<tr><td colspan="7">Object</td></tr>
<tr><td rowspan="4">Non-living Thing
Object that does not grow</td><td colspan="6">Organism</td></tr>
<tr><td rowspan="3">Plant
Object that grows and does not move with volition</td><td colspan="5">Animal
Object that grows and moves with volition</td></tr>
<tr><td rowspan="2">Horse
...</td><td rowspan="2">Lion
...</td><td colspan="3">Human
Object that grows and moves with volition and is rational</td></tr>
<tr><td>Zayd</td><td>John</td><td>Mary</td></tr>
</table>

3.4.2.1 Genus

A *genus* (*jins*) is a universal that is predicated of multiple universal concepts that have different *essences* (sg. *ḥaqīqa* or *māhiyya*), in response to the question, "What is it?" For example, the genus of ‹human›, ‹horse›, and ‹lion› is ‹animal› because ‹human›, ‹horse›, and ‹lion› are all universals with difference essences, and the answer to the question, "What is ‹‹human›, ‹horse›, and ‹lion››?" is, "‹‹Human›, ‹horse›, and ‹lion›› is ‹animal›."

The question, "What is ‹‹A›, ‹B›, ‹C›, ...›?" uses the grammatically singular "is" rather than the plural "are" because it is assumed that the various universals (‹A›, ‹B›, ‹C›, ...) all share a common essential universal, and it is this common essential universal that is being asked about. The predication sought, in other words, is a *conceptual predication*, not an *ordinary predication*.

Another way of describing a genus is to say that it is a higher-level universal that is like a higher-level class for other universals that fall under it. This class, however, is an essential grouping that captures something that is common to the essences of the different universals that fall under it. To return to the example above, ‹animal› is an essential class that is a part of the essences of ‹human›, ‹horse›, and ‹lion›, all of which are its sub-categories. Each of these essences is constituted by the essence of ‹animal› plus some other element (in the case of ‹human›, this additional element is ‹rational›). The way that we know that ‹human›, ‹horse›, and ‹lion› all fall under ‹animal› is that ‹animal› can be predicated of each of them—one can say, "‹Human› is ‹animal›," and, "‹Horse› is ‹animal›," and, "‹Lion› is ‹animal›."

‹Animal› is everything that is intrinsically common to ‹human›, ‹horse›, ‹lion›, and all other species of ‹animal›. In other words, the most that ‹human›, ‹horse›, ‹lion›, and other species of ‹animal› have in common is that they are all ‹animal›. It is also possible to answer the question, "What is ‹‹human›, ‹horse›, and ‹lion››?" by saying, "‹‹Human›, ‹horse›, and ‹lion›› is ‹object›." ‹Object›, like ‹animal›, is common to all the different essences that are species of ‹animal›. Unlike ‹animal›, however, ‹object› is *not* the most that these species have in common; it is only *some* of what they have in common. ‹Object› is a part of the essence of ‹animal› (and thereby also of the species of ‹animal›, namely ‹human›, ‹horse›, and ‹lion›), making every animal an object, but not vice-versa. A genus that captures everything that all of its sub-universals have in common (like ‹animal› in our example above) is a *proximate genus* (*jins qarīb*); a genus that only captures some of what its sub-universals have in common (like ‹object› in our example above) is a *remote genus* (*jins baʿīd*). Remote genera vary in their remoteness. For example, ‹object› is a more remote genus of ‹human›, ‹horse›, and ‹lion› than is ‹organism›. The higher a genus lies on the category-tree, the more remote it is in relation to its lower species.

3.4.2.2 Species

A *species* (*nawʿ*) is a universal that is predicated of multiple singular concepts that have the same essence, in response to the question, "What is it?" For example, the species of the singular concepts ‹Zayd›, ‹John›, and ‹Mary› (each referring to a specific person with that name) is ‹human› because ‹Zayd›, ‹John›, and ‹Mary› are all singular concepts that have the same essence. Thus, the answer to the question, "What is ‹‹Zayd›, ‹John›, and ‹Mary››?" is "‹‹Zayd›, ‹John›, and ‹Mary›› is ‹human›."

As in the previous section, the question, "What is ‹‹A›, ‹B›, ‹C›, ...›?" uses the grammatically singular "is" rather than the plural "are" because it is assumed that the various universals (‹A›, ‹B›, ‹C›, ...) all share a common essential universal, and it is this common essential universal that is being asked about. The predication, in other words, is a *conceptual predication*, not an *ordinary predication.*

Two important differences feature in the respective definitions of *genus* and *species*. First, a genus is a universal that is common to *universal* concepts, whereas a species is a universal that is common to *singular* concepts. Second, a genus is a universal that is common to concepts with *different* essences, whereas a species is a universal that is common to concepts with the *same* essence.

This is how the term *species* is normally used, i.e., to refer to the essence that is common to multiple singular concepts. Sometimes, however, the term is used to refer to the universal concepts subordinate to a genus, lying below it on a category-tree. In this sense, ‹human›, ‹horse›, and ‹lion› are all different species of the overarching genus ‹animal›. When the term *species* is used in this way, the concept ‹species› is a *correlative* (*mutaḍāyif*) of the concept ‹genus›, meaning that it can only be conceived in correlation with ‹genus› and that ‹genus› can only be conceived in correlation with ‹species› because a species is only a species relative to some higher genus and a genus is only a genus relative to some lower species. This usage of the term *species* refers to the *relative species* (*nawʿ iḍāfī*), while the term's usage in the first sense discussed above refers to the *essential species* (*nawʿ ḥaqīqī*).

To further use logical terminology to understand these concepts, we can say that ‹essential species› and ‹relative species› are universals each of which is *perspectivally more general* than the other. They share, for example, the concept ‹human› as a referent; ‹human› is at once both an essential species (with respect to the singular concepts ‹Zayd›, ‹John›, and ‹Mary›) and a relative species (with respect to the genus ‹animal›). But while the proximate and remote genera of ‹human› (‹animal›, ‹organism›, ‹object›, etc.) are all referents for ‹relative species› (with respect to the genera above them), they are not referents for ‹essential species› (because they have no singular concepts directly below them). And, in the reverse, while basic, non-composite universal concepts such as the geometric concept ‹point› are referents for ‹essential species› (with respect to the singular points, for example, below them), they are not referents for ‹relative species› (because as basic concepts they do not belong to any higher genus).[7]

Given a category-tree, such as the one in Section 3.4.2, one can either proceed upward from the bottom or downward from the top. Proceeding upward from the bottom, one begins with singular concepts (e.g., ‹Zayd›, ‹John›, ‹Mary›), climbs up to their overarching essential species (e.g., ‹human›), then further to the species' proximate genus (e.g., ‹animal›), then to its remote genus (e.g., ‹organism›), until one final reaches the highest genus (e.g., ‹object›), above which there is no other genus. Proceeding downward from the top of the category-tree, one begins with one of the basic categories (e.g., ‹object›), descends into one of its relative species (e.g., ‹organism›), then further into its sub-species (e.g., ‹animal›), until one reaches the lowest species (e.g., ‹human›), beneath which there are no other species, only singular concepts (e.g., ‹Zayd›, ‹John›, ‹Mary›).

Following the Aristotelean tradition, Muslim logicians posit the existence of *ten basic categories* (*maqūlāt ʿashara*) that are the *highest genera* (*ajnās ʿāliya*) to which all contingent existent things belong.[8] Although we may loosely think of ‹existent thing› as a higher "category" under which the categories lie,

7. The medieval natural philosophies of the Sunni *kalām* tradition, the Muʿtazilī *kalām* tradition, and the *falsafa* tradition disagree over the precise definition of ‹point› (for the positions of each tradition, see *TB*, 164-68). This example is based on the Sunni *kalām* conception, according to which ‹point› is a *perspectival concept* (*amr iʿtibārī*) that the mind conceives when it considers objects from a particular perspective. Since perspectival concepts do not have any extramental reference, they are not existent things. And since the ten basic categories are categories of contingent existent things, perspectival concepts such as ‹point› do not have to fall under one of them. When such concepts are non-composite, as with our example here, they do not belong to any higher genus because universals that belong to a genus are always constituted by a composition of the genus's essence and the essence of their differentia.

8. According to the *mutakallimūn*, the ten categories are the highest genera of concepts that can be predicated of contingent things. This means that the sub-categories that fall under each category all share the essential attribute of their highest genus. For example, since ‹plant› and ‹animal› are sub-categories of ‹object›, they have in common the essential property of being objects. These ten basic categories are derived inductively based on observation (see 9.2.1), which means that it is possible for additional categories to be discovered. For a fuller description of the ten categories in the Muslim scholarly tradition, see Note 27.

logicians explain that ‹existent thing› is not really a genus for the categories because ‹existence› is not part of their essence—the ten categories can all be conceived without conceiving of ‹existent thing›. Strictly speaking, it is not a genus of the categories but rather a *general accident.*

3.4.2.3 Differentia

A *differentia* (*faṣl*) is that part of a species' essence that distinguishes it from the other species that share the same genus. For example, ‹rational› is the differentia of ‹human› because (a) it is part of the essence of ‹human› and (b) it distinguishes ‹human› from ‹horse›, ‹lion›, and all other species of ‹animal›.

More precisely, a *differentia* is a universal that is predicated of a species in response to the question, "What kind of ‹X› is ‹Y›, essentially?" where ‹X› is the genus and ‹Y› is the species. For example, the differentia of the species ‹human› is the concept ‹rational› because the answer to the question, "What kind of ‹animal› is ‹human›, essentially?" is "‹Human› is ‹rational animal›, essentially." The qualifying word "essentially" excludes *special accidents*, which are also universals that can be provided as answers to the question, "What kind of ‹X› is ‹Y›?" but are not *essential* to ‹Y›. For example, to the question, "What kind of ‹animal› is ‹human›?" one might correctly respond, "‹Human› is ‹animal capable of laughter›," yet ‹capable of laughter› is not a *differentia* because it is not part of the *essence* of ‹human›. As we will see, it is rather a *special accident* of ‹human›.

Like genera, differentiae are either *proximate differentiae* (sg. *faṣl qarīb*) or *remote differentiae* (sg. *faṣl baʿīd*). If a differentia differentiates a species from another species that shares the same *proximate genus*, it is a proximate differentia. If, on the other hand, it differentiates a species from another species that only shares a *remote genus*, it is a remote differentia. For example, ‹rational› is a proximate differentia of ‹human› because it differentiates it from other species of its proximate genus ‹animal› (e.g., from ‹horse› and ‹lion›). ‹Capable of voluntary motion›, on the other hand, is a remote differentia of ‹human› because it differentiates it from other species of its remote genus ‹organism› (e.g., from ‹plant›).

Differentiae are *divisive* (*muqassim*) with respect to the genera above and *constitutive* (*muqawwim*) with respect to the species below. For example, proceeding down the category-tree from ‹organism› to ‹animal› to ‹human›, the genus ‹animal› is ‹volitionally mobile organism› and its species ‹human› is ‹rational animal›. With respect to the higher genus ‹animal›, the differentia ‹rational› is divisive: it divides ‹animal› into ‹rational animal› and ‹non-rational animal›. With respect to the lower species ‹human›, on the other hand, it is constitutive: it constitutes the essence of ‹human› by adding the essential concept ‹rational› to the essence of the genus ‹animal›.

A differentia that divides a lower genus or species will also divide all higher genera. For example, ‹rational› divides ‹animal› into ‹rational animal› and ‹non-rational animal›. It will therefore similarly divide the higher genera ‹organism› and ‹object› into ‹rational organism› and ‹non-rational organism› or into ‹rational object› and ‹non-rational object›, respectively.[9] The reverse, however, is not true: a differentia that divides a higher genus will not divide its lower genera or species.

On the other hand, a differentia that constitutes a higher genus will also constitute all lower genera and species. For example, ‹organism› is ‹object that grows›. The differentia ‹growing› constitutes ‹organism› along with the latter's genus ‹object›. This differentia will also therefore constitute all genera and species that lie below ‹organism›; the essences of ‹animal›, ‹plant›, ‹human›, ‹horse›, and ‹lion› are all constituted by ‹growing› because they are all species of ‹organism› and must each therefore comprise its essence plus one or more differentiae. The reverse, however, is not true: a differentia that constitutes a lower genus or species will not necessarily constitute higher genera.

3.4.3 *Nonessential Universals*

Nonessential universals (sg. *kullī ʿaraḍī*) or *accidents* (sg. *ʿaraḍ*)[10] are divided into two categories: *special accidents* (sg. *khāṣṣa*) and *general accidents* (sg. *ʿaraḍ ʿāmm*). The category-tree described above illustrates a hierarchy of genera and species and is thus designed specifically to illustrate the three kinds of essential universals. The examples in the following subsections will make

9. In the above examples, ‹rational animal›, ‹rational organism›, and ‹rational object› are all equal to ‹human› because they feature its proximate differentia ‹rational›.

10. Nonessential universals, or accidents (*aʿrāḍ*) in the logical sense are not to be confused for properties (*aʿrāḍ*) in the metaphysical sense. While the Arabic term *ʿaraḍ* often indicates a property, i.e., that which subsists in a substrate when it exists extramentally, here it indicates a nonessential universal concept. The distinction has implications in predication: the predication of special and general accidents is always *identity-predication*, whereas the predication of properties is *property-predication*. *TB*, 185-186. Note that this ambiguity between the two senses of *ʿaraḍ* is sometimes replicated in English when translators render the term in both senses as "accident." In the interest of clarity, that is not the practice of the present work; the term *accident* is used only to refer to a nonessential universal, and the term *property* is used otherwise.

use of the same category-tree, but only indirectly, in order to illustrate that the universals described are nonessential.

The essentialness of the universals discussed above was brought out by means of certain kinds of questions, and the definitions of the essential universals were seen to involve predication in response to these questions. Since the universals discussed in this section are nonessential, their definitions do not involve predication in response to questions.

3.4.3.1 Special Accident

A *special accident* (*khāṣṣa*) is a universal that is exclusively predicated of instances that share an essence but without being part of that essence nor identical to it. For example, ‹thing that laughs› is a special accident of ‹human› because it is predicated of human instances (e.g., ‹Zayd, John, and Mary are things that laugh›) exclusively, as only humans are capable of laughter,[11] and because ‹thing that laughs› is neither part of ‹human› nor identical to it. The final qualification—"without being part of that essence nor identical to it"—excludes *species*, which, like a special accident, is exclusively predicated of instances that share a single essence, but, unlike a special accident, is itself identical to the essence of its instances. It also excludes *differentia*, which again is exclusively predicated of instances that share a single essence but is itself part of the essence of its instances. Another way of saying this is that the predication of special accidents is nonessential whereas the predication of species is essential.

This kind of special accident is also called an *absolutely special accident* (*khāṣṣa muṭlaqa*) to distinguish it from a *relatively special accident* (*khāṣṣa iḍāfiyya*), which is exclusive to instances of a particular essence *relative to instances of other particular essences*. For example, ‹thing that walks› is a relatively special accident of ‹human› with respect to ‹plant›, but it is not an absolutely special accident of ‹human› because it can also be predicated of other essences, such as ‹horse› and ‹lion›. A nonessential universal that is only relatively exclusive is in reality a *general accident*.

11. Laughter here does not mean the sound of laughter, which primates other than humans can also produce, but the laughter that results from actually finding something funny, which only humans can produce because the ability to find something funny presupposes rationality.

3.4.3.2 General Accident

A *general accident* (*ʿaraḍ ʿāmm*)[12] is a universal that is generally predicated of universal or singular concepts with different essences without being part of their essences nor identical to their essences. For example, ‹thing that walks› is a general accident that is predicated of ‹horse› (a universal), ‹human› (a universal with a different essence), Zayd (a singular), and this donkey (a singular with a different essence), without being part of or identical to their respective essences. The fact that a general accident is predicated of things with different essences distinguishes it from a special accident, and the fact that it is not part of nor identical to the essence of what it is predicated of distinguishes it from a genus, species, and differentia.

Like a differentia, a general accident can be used to divide genera into sub-categories. But whereas the categories that result from division through differentiae are species, the categories that result from division through general accidents are merely *types* (sg. *ṣinf*) because, unlike division through differentiae, division through general accidents is not exclusive to the essence of the genus in question. For example, ‹human› can be divided into ‹Turkic›, ‹Arab›, and other racial categories. These categories are types that are not exclusive to ‹human›; they may just as well result from the division of ‹horse› using the same general accidents.

3.4.3.3 Inseparable and Separable Nonessential Universals

Since, in predication, an essential universal is essential to its subject, essential universals are always *inseparable* from their subjects. Nonessential universals, however, whether special or general, may be either inseparable or separable. An *inseparable accident* (*ʿaraḍ lāzim*) is either *essentially inseparable* (*lāzim bi-l-naẓar ilā al-māhiyya*) or *coincidentally inseparable* (*lāzim bi-l-naẓar ilā al-wujūd*).

It is *essentially inseparable* when it is both mentally and extramentally inseparable, e.g., ‹even thing›[13] with respect to ‹thing that is four› since ‹even thing› is inseparable from the essence of ‹thing that is four› and is hence inseparable from it both with respect to its mental concept ‹thing that is four› and also with respect to its extramental instances, such as "those four books."

---

12. See Note 51.

13. Most logic manuals say "evenness" rather than "even thing" and "whiteness" rather than "white thing." The glosses on the *Tahdhīb*, however, point out that this is imprecise and that what is meant is ‹thing that is even› and ‹white thing› because the five universals all assume identity-predication. *TB*, 189.

(Note that ‹even thing› is a *general accident* of ‹four›, because it is predicated of other numbers as well, e.g., ‹thing that is six›, ‹thing that is eight›, ‹thing that is ten›, etc.)

An accident is *coincidentally inseparable* when it is only extramentally inseparable, e.g., ‹physically fit person› with respect to ‹Olympic champion› since ‹Olympic champion› always coincides extramentally with ‹physically fit person› even though ‹physically fit person› is not essential to ‹Olympic champion› and is hence mentally separable from it. (Note that ‹Olympic champion› is merely a nonessential *type* of ‹human›, not an essential species, and ‹physically fit person› is hence merely inseparable from this nonessential type of ‹human›, not from all humans. This shows that ‹physically fit person› is indeed not part of the *essence* of ‹Olympic champion› and is hence mentally separable from it.)

Both kinds of inseparability are either *directly entailed*, meaning that the inference of inseparability does not require an intermediary premise or *indirectly entailed*, meaning that it does. Direct entailment is either independent or collective. It is *independent* if the inference of inseparability only requires the conception of one of the two universals, and it is *collective* if the inference of inseparability requires the conception of both universals. An example of an independent direct entailment is the inseparability of ‹thing that is the double of one› from ‹thing that is two›; the inseparability of the two universals can be inferred merely from a conception of the latter. An example of a collective direct entailment is the inseparability of ‹thing that can be divided into two equal parts› from ‹thing that is four›; the inseparability of the two universals is only inferred from the collective conception of both universals. Finally, an example of an *indirect entailment* is the inseparability of ‹created thing› from ‹universe›; the inference of inseparability requires an intermediate premise. Inseparability that results in the mind from *intuition* or *empirical testing* is considered to be indirectly entailed.

A *separable accident* (*ʿaraḍ mufāriq*) is either *permanent* (*dāʾim*), *gradually disappearing* (*baṭīʾ al-zawāl*), or *quickly disappearing* (*sarīʿ al-zawāl*). An example of a permanent separable accident is ‹poor person› with respect to someone who is poor his entire life. An example of a gradually disappearing separable universal is ‹young person› with respect to all humans. An example of a quickly disappearing separable universal is ‹someone red with embarrassment› with respect to all humans.

3.4.4 *Relativity of the Five Universals*

The categorization of a universal into one of the five universals is a relative categorization that depends on the other universals or instances with respect to which the original universal is considered. The same universal concept, in other words, might fall into any one of the five categories when considered with respect to different things. For example, the universal ‹colored thing› is simultaneously:

1. *Genus* of ‹black thing›, ‹yellow thing›, ‹green thing›, etc.
2. *Species* of ‹thing that possesses sensible properties›, whose other species include ‹thing that has a taste›, ‹thing that has a smell›, etc.
3. *Differentia* of ‹opaque object›, differentiating it from its counterpart ‹transparent object›, both of which are species of the genus ‹object›.
4. *Special accident* of ‹composite object›, setting it apart from its counterpart ‹basic object›, both of which are species of the genus ‹object›.[14]
5. *General accident* of ‹animal›, because it is not exclusive to any of its species.

3.5 The Existence of Universals

The logical classification of mental concepts into universals and singulars has been historically associated with "the problem of universals," which is closely tied to the question of whether or not universals possess extramental existence.[15] This question is not, strictly speaking, a question of logic; logic studies concepts and propositions from the perspective of their leading to new mental concepts and propositions—whether or not universals possess extramental existence has no bearing on this study. Within the medieval Muslim scholarly tradition, the proper place for this question is the science of *falsafa*. But since the examples that logicians use naturally lead one to ask this question (and perhaps because of historical precedent), it is the custom of the logicians to treat it briefly at the end of the chapter on conception.

---

14. This is based on the natural philosophy of those *mutakallimūn* who held that the objects of the universe are all composed of basic indivisible particles that do not have any color and that color is a property that can only be possessed by objects that are composed of multiple basic indivisible particles.

15. See Gyula Klima, "Medieval Problem of Universals," *Stanford Encyclopedia of Philosophy* (Fall 2013), ed. Edward N. Zalta, http://plato.stanford.edu/archives/fall2013/entries/universals-medieval.

The examples that prompt this question are propositions like, "‹Animal› is a universal." The logicians explain that such propositions employ the universal in three different senses. Here, this proposition involves (1) the concept ‹universal› itself, (2) the concept ‹animal›, and (3) the combination of the two. A judgment concerning the extramental existence of universals requires that one first carefully define each sense. This then is the first step toward answering the question above.

The first sense, the concept ‹universal› itself, was previously defined as *a concept whose mere occurrence in the mind leads one to judge that it is possible to predicate it of multiple instances*. This kind of universal is called the *logicians' universal* (*kullī manṭiqī*) because this is the universal that logicians are most concerned with. It is a *second-order concept* that is *abstracted* (*muntazaʿ*) from mental concepts such as ‹animal›, ‹human›, ‹horse›, ‹lion›, and ‹plant›.

The second sense, represented in our example by ‹animal›, is the mental concept from which the logicians' universal is abstracted. This kind of universal is a *first-order concept* that is normally (but not always) abstracted from extramental instances and represents their *essences* or *natures* (sg. *ṭabīʿa*) and is hence called a *natural universal* (*kullī ṭabīʿī*). It is the subject of the judgment ‹‹X› is a universal›, where ‹X› is a concept such as ‹animal›, ‹human›, ‹horse›, ‹lion›, ‹plant›, etc. Each of these natures can be conceived without the concept of universality. ‹Animal›, for example, is ‹object that grows and moves with volition›, and ‹human› is ‹rational animal›. These nature-concepts are all mentally distinct from the concept of the logicians' universal which is *identity-predicated* of them (recall that identity-predication requires that the concept of the subject and the concept of the predicate be different; see 3.4.1). Though being a universal is not *part of the essence* of natural universals, they are universals because they meet the criterion of universality, i.e., they can have multiple instances.

The third sense, by contrast, does have the notion of *being a universal* in its essence. When we make the judgment ‹‹X› is a universal›, this results in a mental conception of this third kind of universal, which is a combination of the first two. In our example, the judgment ‹‹Animal› is a universal› results in the concept ‹the universal concept ‹animal››. In other words, it results in the conception of ‹animal› *as a universal concept*. This concept of the natural universal as a universal is a *mental universal* (*kullī ʿaqlī*).

The logicians use the expression "universal" equivocally, i.e., as a homonym, to refer to all three senses: the logicians' universal, the natural universal, and the mental universal. Since universals are divided into the five universals, the terms used to refer to the five universals are also equivocal in this way. For example, the statement, "Animal is a genus," refers to three different senses of genus: (1) the *logicians' genus* (*jins manṭiqī*), i.e., the second-order concept ‹genus› which is the predicate; (2) a *natural genus* (*jins ṭabīʿī*), i.e., the first-order concept ‹animal›, which is judged to be an instance of ‹genus›; and (3) a *mental genus* (*jins ʿaqlī*), i.e., the concept ‹the genus ‹animal››, which is a combination of the two.

In fact, the same is true even of the singular. The statement, "Zayd is a singular," for example, refers to three different senses of singular: (1) the *logicians' singular* (*juzʾī manṭiqī*), i.e., the second-order concept ‹singular› which is the predicate; (2) a *natural singular* (*juzʾī ṭabīʿī*), i.e., the first-order concept ‹Zayd›, which is judged to be an instance of ‹singular›; and (3) a *mental singular* (*juzʾī ʿaqlī*), i.e., the concept ‹the singular concept ‹Zayd›, which is a combination of the two.

The fact that this threefold division applies equally to singular and universal concepts illustrates that it is a division of mental concepts considered from the perspective of the predication of second-order concepts to first-order ones—it has nothing *per se* to do with *universality* or *singularity* at all. It follows from this that in none of the three senses does the universal—whether the logicians' universal, the natural universal, or the mental universal—have extramental existence. The same is true of the singular and of any concept associated with the predication of a second-order concept to a first-order one. All of these are merely mental concepts.

For a universal to exist extramentally would entail a contradiction: since a universal is one thing that is common to its instances, if it were to exist extramentally within all the singular instances to which it is common, it would have to simultaneously possess opposite properties. For example, if the universal ‹human› extramentally existed within every human being, it would simultaneously be tall and short, black and white, fat and thin, and so on because the various human beings that it would exist within possess these opposite properties. This is why extramental existence is limited to the extramental instances of singular concepts—Zayd, John, Mary, etc.—and the universal concepts that are predicated of them only exist mentally.

Within the Muslim *falsafa* tradition, the disagreement over the extramental existence of universals revolves around the extramental existence of something that is part of singular things that a natural universal might represent in the mind. The question, in other words, is whether or not there is an extramental humanness that is part of Zayd, another extramental humanness that is part of John, another extramental humanness that is part Mary, and so on, all of which are represented in the mind by the natural universal ‹human›. Avicenna argued that this extramental humanness did exist, and a number of later authorities, such as al-Siyālkūtī and al-ʿAṭṭār, concurred. Most later logicians, however, held that the extramental singular instances of Zayd, John, and Mary are non-composite in their singularity and uncomposed of parts such as humanness, and that the natural universal ‹human› is the mental representation of these non-composite singulars themselves rather than of a humanness within them.

Sources

Section	Sources
3 Conception	*TB*, 112-13, 149; for further reading, see Street, *Najm al-Dīn*, 108-26; Ahmed, *Palimpsests*, 147; Strobino, *Avicenna's Theory*, 13-40
3.1 Singular and Universal Concepts	*TB*, 112, 126-30, 133, 135, 160-61
3.2 Extramental Existence of a Universal's Instances	*TB*, 130-34
3.3 Relationships Between Universals	*TB*, 134-48
3.3.1 Propositional Mapping of Universal Relationships	TB, 134-48
3.3.2 Complementary Relationships	*TB*, 134-48
3.4 The Five Universals	*TB*, 149; for further reading, see Ahmed, *Palimpsests*, 153-58
3.4.1 Identity-Predication	*TB*, 151, 153-54; Muḥammad ʿAlī al-Tahānawī, *Kashhāf iṣṭilāḥāt al-funūn wa-l-ʿulūm al-islāmiyya* (repr., Beirut: Dār Ṣādir, n.d.), 1:353-54; for further reading, see Ahmed, *Palimpsests*, 167-70; Khaled El-Rouayheb, "Dawānī (d. 1502) and Dashtakī (d. 1498) on Primary (*awwalī*) and Familiar (*mutaʿāraf*) Predication," *Oriens* 51, no. 3-4 (2023): 367-92, https://doi.org/10.1163/18778372-12340031

Section	Sources
3.4.1.1 Kinds of Identity-Predications	al-Tahānawī, *Kashhāf*, 1:355
3.4.1.2 Identity-Predication of Singulars	*TB*, 154
3.4.2 Essential Universals	
3.4.2.1 Genus	*TB*, 150-58
3.4.2.2 Species	*TB*, 158-72
3.4.2.3 Differentia	*TB*, 172-83
3.4.2.3 Nonessential Universals	
3.4.3 Nonessential Universals	*TB*, 183
3.4.3.1 Special Accident	*TB*, 183-85
3.4.3.2 General Accident	*TB*, 163, 185-87
3.4.3.3 Inseparable and Separable Accidents	*TB*, 187-93
3.4.4 Relativity of the Five Universals	*TB*, 155
3.5 The Existence of Universals	*TB*, 193-204

4

DEFINITION

The goal of logic is to distinguish sound inference from flawed inference where *inference* is either the acquisition of knowledge of an unknown *concept* or the acquisition of knowledge of an unknown *judgment*. The first kind of inference is *definition*; the second is *argument*. This chapter focuses on *definition* (*taʿrīf*).

Definition is logically prior to argument because every argument consists of terms that signify concepts, and apprehending whether or not the argument's conclusion follows from its premises depends on first apprehending the meanings of those terms. The logicians frequently express this rule by saying, "Making a judgment about something depends on its conception" (*al-ḥukm ʿalā shayʾ farʿ ʿan taṣawwurihi*).

Consider, for example, the following argument taken from the science of *kalām*.

First Premise:	The universe exists contingently.
Second Premise:	Everything that exists contingently requires a determining agent.
Conclusion:	The universe requires a determining agent.

Evaluating the soundness of the conclusion presupposes an apprehension of the meaning of "universe" (*ʿālam*), the meaning of "contingent" (*mumkin*), the meaning of "existence" (*wujūd*), and the meaning of "determining agent" (*mukhaṣṣiṣ*). The method for precisely apprehending such meanings is definition.

This chapter explains the proper method of definition by first explaining the difference between predications in definitions and predication in propositions in Section 4.1, then the precise role of definitions in human knowledge in Section 4.2, then how to construct definitions using the *five universals* in Section 4.3, and then finally how to avoid common mistakes in definitions in Section 4.4.

4.1 Predication in Definition

The *definition* of a concept ‹X› is an *identity-predication* of something to ‹X› in order to bring about its conception. For example, the definition of ‹human› is, "‹Human› is ‹rational animal›." This definition comprises the predication of ‹rational animal› to ‹human› in order to bring about a conception of ‹human›. In other words, definition is a kind of inference that composes known concepts in order to bring about a new, previously unknown concept.

The predication in definitions is peculiar. Unlike most predications, its primary purpose is not judgment but rather conception. For example, the purpose of propositional predications such as "God exists," "Muḥammad is the messenger of God," or the mundane "It is raining outside" is to make judgments about God, the Prophet Muḥammad (God bless him and give him peace), or the weather outside. These judgments, inasmuch as they are judgments, can be true or false and are hence justified by *argument*. In contrast, the purpose of conceptual predications such as "‹Human› is ‹rational animal›" is to form a conception of the subject ‹human› using the predicate ‹rational animal›. The purpose of the predication in propositions is *judgment*, whereas the purpose of the predication in definitions is not judgment but *conception*. Since judgments can be true or false but conceptions cannot, predication in propositions can be true or false, and predication in definitions cannot.

Definitions, then, do not comprise judgments; they comprise merely a conception of the *defining expression* (*muʿarrif*) (for short, the *definition*) in a way that corresponds to the conception of the term defined, the *definiendum* (*muʿarraf*). The definition is merely a mirror that reflects the definiendum. This is why another name for definition in the vocabulary of the Muslim logicians is *qawl shāriḥ*, or "clarifying predication."[1]

Because of this distinction between definitions and propositions, some logicians (most notably al-Jurjānī) deny the existence of any predication in

1. Clarifying predications are *conceptual predications* whereas propositional predications are usually *ordinary predications*. *TB*, 206n.

definitions altogether. According to these logicians, neither is the definiendum (*mu'arraf*) a grammatical subject (*mubtada'*) nor is the definition (*mu'arrif*) a grammatical predicate (*khabar*). Definitions only have the appearance of predications. In reality, however, they are a different kind of grammatical construct that is peculiar to the conventions of the logicians.

This view is not accepted by most other logicians, who respond that no logician before al-Jurjānī ever claimed that definitions were a new kind of grammatical construct. Definitions are regular grammatical predications, but with the difference that their primary purpose is conception rather than judgment. The grammatical predication of definitions will unavoidably bring about a grammatical judgment (e.g., the identification of "human" with "rational animal"), but unlike propositional judgments, which are sought for their own sake, definitional judgments are sought for the sake of conception.

Sometimes, the same predication can serve both purposes. For example, when Gabriel (upon him be peace) asked the Prophet Muḥammad (God bless him and give him peace), "What is religious belief?" he responded, "That you believe in God, His angels, His books, His messengers, the Last Day, and in destiny—both the pleasant of it and the unpleasant," to which Gabriel replied, "You have said what is true."[2] In this example, Gabriel asked to what concept the scriptural term "religious belief" (*īmān*) corresponds. When the Prophet Muḥammad (God bless him and give him peace) replied that it corresponds to the six elements that he mentioned, his predication comprised an aspect of conception—it brought about a conception of ‹religious belief› in the minds of the listeners—and it also comprised an aspect of judgment—it asserted that the critically important scriptural expression "religious belief" means belief in the six elements—and it was from the perspective of this latter aspect that Gabriel confirmed the truth of the predication.

4.2 Names, Concepts, and Reality

Language as verbally uttered *signifies* (*dalāla*) concepts in the mind, and concepts in the mind *refer* (*ṣidq*) to real objects outside the mind. Definitions

2. This is part of a hadith that is famously known as the "Gabriel hadith" in which Gabriel comes in the form of a mysterious, handsome man to ask the Prophet (God bless him and give him peace) about the meaning of religious belief (*īmān*), submission (*islām*), spirituality (*iḥsān*), and the Last Day in order to teach the onlooking Companions about these things through the Prophet's responses (God bless him and give him peace). The hadith is part of the rigorously authenticated collection of Muslim and was selected by al-Nawawī as the second of the forty-odd hadiths in his famous hadith collection.

relate to all three—language, mind, and reality—for they involve expressions, mental concepts, and extramental objects. This section investigates definitions that relate to language, namely *lexical definitions* (sg. *taʿrīf lafẓī*); definitions that relate to concepts, namely *hypothetical definitions* (sg. *taʿrīf ismī*); and definitions that relate to real things, namely *real definitions* (sg. *taʿrīf ḥaqīqī*).

4.2.1 *What-Knowledge and Is-Knowledge*

The knowledge that humans seek is divided into (1) knowledge sought using the interrogative "what?"—we will call this *what-knowledge* (*maṭlab mā*)—and (2) knowledge sought using the interrogative "is?"—we will call this *is-knowledge* (*maṭlab hal*).

What-knowledge is then further divided into (1a) *hypothetical conception* (*taṣawwur bi-ḥasab al-ism*), i.e., knowledge of a thing purely with respect to its representational concept in the mind, regardless of whether that concept corresponds to something that actually exists extramentally; and (1b) *real conception* (*taṣawwur bi-ḥasab al-ḥaqīqa*), i.e., knowledge of a thing as it actually exists extramentally. Hypothetical conception is the answer to the question, "What is ‹X›, conceptually?" whereas real conception is the answer to the question, "What is X, really?" It is possible to have hypothetical conception of things that exist, as well as of things that do not, but it is only possible to have real conception of things that exist.

Is-knowledge is divided into (2a) *existential judgment* (*taṣdīq bi-wujūd al-shayʾ fī nafsihi*), i.e., knowledge of whether or not a thing exists extramentally; and (2b) *predicative judgment* (*taṣdīq bi-thubūt al-shayʾ li-ghayrihi*), i.e., knowledge of whether or not a predication is true of a thing or not (in other words, whether or not X is Y). Existential judgment is the answer to the question, "Is X something that exists?" whereas predicative judgment is the answer to the question, "Is X Y?"

Based on this fourfold division of knowledge, the proper order of seeking knowledge is to begin with hypothetical conception (1a), then move to existential judgment (2a), then to real conception (1b), and finally to predicative judgment (2b). For example, the proper order of seeking discursive knowledge of God[3] is to:

1. Begin by asking, "What is ‹God›, conceptually?" and acquiring

3. *Discursive knowledge* excludes *mystical knowledge*, which is an immediate and noninferential disclosure of God to the soul rather than a knowledge acquired through discursive inference. Mystical knowledge of God is the subject of the science of Sufism, or Islamic mysticism.

hypothetical conception of ‹God› as ‹the One who exists necessarily›[4] (1a).
2. Ask, "Does God exist?" and infer through *argument* the *existential judgment* ‹God exists› (2a).
3. Proceed by asking, "What is God, really?" and acquiring *real conception* of God as ‹the One who exists necessarily› (1b).
4. Follow with questions like, "Is God beginninglessly eternal?" and "Is God omnipotent?" and infer *predicative judgments* like ‹God is beginninglessly eternal›, ‹God is omnipotent›, etc.

Real conception logically presupposes *existential judgment,* which, in turn, logically presupposes *hypothetical conception*. It is, however, theoretically possible to move directly from *hypothetical conception* to *predicative judgment* (see 6.6) by investigating what might be predicated of something *were it to exist.* Yet it is preferable to move to predicative judgment only after real conception because predicative judgment of something that is real is better and more complete than predicative judgment of something that is only hypothetical.

The fourfold division above highlights that ‹existence› is a special predicate that is different from other predicates. The difference is that the predication of ‹existence› to a thing does not involve anything other than the thing itself because its existence is a concept that is abstracted from the extramental thing itself. This is why the *mutakallimūn* refer to existence as an *essential attribute* (*ṣifa nafsiyya*).[5] The predication of concepts other than existence, on the other hand, involves other things along with the thing itself.

4.2.2 *Hypothetical and Real Definitions*

Definition is divided into (1) *hypothetical definition* (*taʿrīf ismī*)[6] and (2) *real definition* (*taʿrīf ḥaqīqī*). *Hypothetical definitions* lead to conception of a thing without there being any judgment as to its existence, whereas *real definitions* lead to conception of a thing as it is known to exist. Through hypothetical definitions, we seek knowledge of mere mental concepts (e.g., ‹unicorn›); through real definitions, we seek knowledge of things as they actually exist extramentally (e.g., ‹human›).

4. Note that this is a *nonessential definition* since an *essential definition* of God is not possible.

5. This is also why, according to the *mutakallimūn*, the ontological argument for the existence of God begs the question. See Muṣṭafā Ṣabrī, *Mawqif al-ʿaql wa-l-ʿilm wa-l-ʿālam min rabb al-ʿālamīn wa-ʿibādihi al-mursalīn* (Beirut: Dār Iḥyāʾ al-Turāth al-ʿArabī, n.d.), 2: 224-8.

6. This is also called *nominal definition*.

Another way of saying this is that hypothetical definitions lead to *hypothetical conception,* whereas real definitions lead to *real conception.* Just as hypothetical conception is logically prior to real conception, hypothetical definitions are logically prior to real definitions. When something that has been conceptually defined is known to exist, i.e., when we have an affirmative *existential judgment* of it, the hypothetical definition becomes a real definition.

The definitions of the various religious and philosophical sciences that are conventionally mentioned by Muslim scholars in their prolegomena to each science (such as the prolegomenon to the science of logic described above in Chapter 1) are thus hypothetical definitions as a student begins his study of a given science, and they become real definitions when the student comprehends all of its questions by the end of his study.

4.2.3 *Proper and Lexical Definitions*

Hypothetical and real definitions are *proper definitions* (sg. *taʿrīf ḥaqīqī*)[7] and stand in contrast to *lexical definitions* (sg. *taʿrīf lafẓī*). Whereas a proper definition brings about a new conception in the mind, a lexical definition merely associates the unknown meaning of a relatively obscure expression with the already-known meaning of a relatively familiar one. For example, someone might come across the expression "melancholy," not know what it means, look it up in a dictionary, and find that it has the same meaning as the more common expression "sadness." The definition of "melancholy" as "sadness" is a lexical definition—it replaces a relatively obscure expression with a familiar one to bring the mind's attention to a concept that already exists within it. Lexical definitions merely specify concepts that already exist in the mind instead of leading to knowledge of new concepts.

Because lexical definitions do not bring about new conception, they differ from proper definitions in that their predicative purpose is *judgment,* not conception. To be more precise, the purpose of a lexical definition is to bring about the judgment that a particular expression (e.g., "melancholy") signifies a particular concept that already exists in the mind (e.g., the concept signified by the common expression "sadness"). As a result, unlike proper definitions, lexical definitions can be true or false.

Some logicians (most notably al-Taftāzānī himself and al-Dawānī) argue that lexical definition is a kind of *hypothetical definition.* This position,

7. The term *taʿrīf ḥaqīqī* is used for both real definition as described above and proper definition as described here.

however, is not accepted by most other logicians, who mention three important differences:

1. Hypothetical definitions bring about new conceptions in the mind, whereas lexical definitions merely direct the mind to concepts that already exist within it.
2. Hypothetical definitions comprise more basic concepts and cannot comprise mere synonyms, whereas lexical definitions can and frequently do.
3. Hypothetical definitions are used when defining the technical terms of a science, whereas lexical definitions are used in dictionaries to explain the linguistic significations of rare expressions.

Al-Dawānī countered these objections by arguing that the predicative purpose of lexical definitions is, indeed, conceptual—just like hypothetical definitions—with the sole difference that lexical definitions move a concept that has already existed in the mind from distant memory into the mental foreground, whereas hypothetical definitions bring concepts into the mental foreground by bringing about knowledge of a new concept that has never existed in the mind before. The difference is merely one of degree.

According to later authorities, lexical definitions are used for two main purposes. First, they are used by lexicographers to specify the concepts signified by expressions. Second, they are used by logicians to draw attention to *noninferential concepts*, which cannot be defined (and in this role are called *reminders*; see 1.1.4). The predicative purpose of the former is judgment, whereas the predicative purpose of the latter is conception.

4.3 Essential and Nonessential Definitions

Proper definition is a *clarifying predication* (*qawl shāriḥ*; def: 4.1) that leads to knowledge of a new conception. Before the knowledge of this new conception can be sought, there must already be some distant conception of the *definiendum* (*muʿarraf*) in the mind for it is not possible to direct oneself to seek knowledge of something absolutely unknown. The difference between this conception that is already present prior to definition and the conception that is brought about through definition is that the former is a vague, general, and remote conception, whereas the latter is a precise and detailed conception. In other words, the two concepts are referentially identical, but one is conceptually more precise and detailed than the other.

Proper definition is divided into *essential definition* (*ḥadd*) and (2) *nonessential definition* (*rasm*). *Essential definition* is predication that brings about the essential conception of the definiendum; *nonessential definition* is predication that merely distinguishes the definiendum from all other concepts. For example, the predication ‹‹Human› is ‹rational animal›› is an essential definition because it leads to knowledge of the essence of ‹human›, whereas on the other hand the predication ‹‹Human› is ‹laughing animal›› is a nonessential definition because it leads to a nonessential conception of ‹human› that merely distinguishes it from all other concepts.

4.3.1 *Complete and Incomplete Definitions*

Definitions are composed of three of the five universals: *genus*, *differentia*, and *special accident*. Whenever the definition comprises the differentia of the definiendum, it is an essential definition because the differentia distinguishes the definiendum through its essential characteristic. Whenever it comprises a special accident of the definiendum, it is a nonessential definition, because the special accident distinguishes the definiendum through a nonessential characteristic. The inclusion of the genus is optional for the validity of the definition; whenever it is included, the definition is said to be *complete* (*tāmm*), and whenever it is omitted, it is said to be *incomplete* (*nāqiṣ*) because some of the definiendum's essential elements are missing. This makes for four kinds of definition:

1. *Complete essential definition*, comprising the genus and differentia, e.g., ‹‹Human› is ‹rational animal››.
2. *Incomplete essential definition*, comprising the differentia only, e.g., ‹‹Human› is ‹rational thing››.
3. *Complete nonessential definition*, comprising the genus and a special accident, e.g., ‹‹Human› is ‹laughing animal››.
4. *Incomplete nonessential definition*, comprising a special accident only, e.g., ‹‹Human› is ‹laughing thing››.

This categorization assumes that the genus provided is *proximate*. When it is *remote*, the definition is also said to be incomplete because, once again, some of the definiendum's essential elements are missing from the definition. An example of an incomplete essential definition with a remote genus is ‹‹Human› is ‹rational organism››, and an example of an incomplete nonessential definition with a remote genus is ‹‹Human› is ‹laughing organism››. As the genus increases in remoteness, the definition becomes progressively more incomplete, culminating in the most incomplete definition when the genus is omitted altogether.

4.3.2 *Species and General Accidents*

According to the later logicians, as we have seen, only three of the five universals are used in definition: genus, differentia, and special accident. As for *species* and *general accident*, they are not used in definition and are only mentioned among the five universals for the sake of completion. The earlier logicians, however, allowed general accidents in definitions.

Some logicians argue that species can be used to define *nonessential types*. For example, the nonessential type ‹European› might be defined as ‹‹European› is ‹human born in Europe››. This definition uses ‹human›, which is a species, not a genus, because it is predicated of singular concepts (such as <Zayd>, <John>, or <Mary>). Other logicians respond that this argument assumes that such examples are *real definitions* of real concepts. In reality, however, they are *hypothetical definitions* of perspectival concepts—e.g., ‹human› is a conceptual genus divided from the *perspective* ‹place of birth› into various other universal concepts such as ‹European›, ‹Arab›, and ‹Turkic›. So <human> in this example is not a species, but a genus.

Since general accidents are nonessential to any given definiendum and since essential definitions are composed of the essential parts of the definiendum, general accidents cannot be used to compose essential definitions. Moreover, since they can be predicated generally of other concepts as of the definiendum, general accidents cannot distinguish the definiendum from other concepts and hence cannot be used in nonessential definitions either. For example, ‹breathing thing› is a general accident of ‹human›; thus, to say, "‹Human› is ‹breathing animal›," or "‹Human› is ‹breathing thing›," neither brings about an essential conception of ‹human› nor does it distinguish it from other kinds of ‹animal›.

4.3.3 *Definition by Extramental Parts*

Concepts whose referents are extramental and composed can be essentially conceived by the essential conception of all of their parts. For example, ‹house› can be essentially conceived by the essential conceptions of ‹wall› and ‹roof› as composed in a house-like form. Such cases led a number of logicians to conclude that whenever a concept refers to something extramentally composed, it is possible to form an essential definition of that thing by essentially conceiving its parts rather than by conceiving a genus and differentia. The difference between *essential definition by extramental parts* (*ḥadd bi-l-ajzāʾ al-khārijiyya*) and *essential definition by genus and differentia* is that the latter comprises both mental motions that constitute inference whereas the former only comprises one of the two. Essential definition by extramental parts does not involve the second mental motion, because the essential concepts of the extramental parts do not need to be logically arranged in order to bring about the essential conception of the definiendum—their mere conception in any order is sufficient to conceive the definiendum. Since most logicians stipulate that *inference* (*naẓar*) must comprise both mental motions, they do not consider this kind of definition to be inference, and hence do not conventionally list it as a kind of essential definition.

Other logicians argue that the mental composition of extramental parts is not a definition because it cannot be predicated of the definiendum. One cannot, for example, say, "‹House› is ‹wall and roof›." To make the predicate fit for a conceptual predication, this must be rendered, "‹House› is ‹thing that possesses a wall and a roof›," and on this rendering it becomes a nonessential definition.

4.4 Conditions of Definition

A definition is only sound on condition that the *defining expression* (*muʿarrif*) is (a) *referentially equal* to the definiendum and (b) *conceptually clearer* than the definiendum.

4.4.1 *Referential Equality*

The defining expression must be *referentially equal* to the definiendum, meaning that the concept that it signifies must exactly match the concept signified by the definiendum. The condition of *equality* (*tasāwī*) does not entail that the two given concepts are the same in terms of their precision—as explained previously, the concept of the defining expression must be more precise and detailed than the concept of the definiendum. Rather, what equality entails is that the concept signified by the defining expression be neither *more inclusive* or *general* (*aʿamm*) nor *more exclusive* or *specific* (*akhaṣṣ*) than the concept of the definiendum in terms of its *reference*.

The condition of referential equality can be analyzed into two propositions:

1. Everything that the defining expression refers to is also referred to by the definiendum.

2. Everything that the definiendum refers to is also referred to by the defining expression.

Whenever the defining expression is more general than the definiendum, it contradicts the first proposition, and the definition is unsound because it is too inclusive. For example, the definition ‹‹DNA› is ‹molecule›› is unsound because ‹molecule› includes referents that are not DNA, such as H_2O. A definition that is too inclusive is unsound because it neither meets the criteria of essential definition—it does not bring about an essential conception of the definiendum for it is not referentially equal—nor of nonessential definition—it does not distinguish the definiendum from all other concepts for it includes other concepts.

Whenever the defining expression is more specific than the definiendum, it contradicts the second proposition, and the definition is unsound because it is too exclusive. For example, the definition ‹‹Molecule› is ‹DNA›› is unsound because ‹DNA› is more specific in referential scope than ‹molecule›. A definition that is too exclusive is unsound because it neither meets the criteria of essential definition—for it is, again, not referentially equal—nor of nonessential definition—for it only distinguishes the part of the definiendum that it includes.

Referential equality is a condition of definition only according to the later logicians who stipulate that definition must either bring about an essential conception of the definiendum (as an essential definition) or distinguish it from *all* other concepts (as a nonessential definition). According to the early logicians, however, referential equality is only a condition for *complete definitions. Incomplete definitions*, on the other hand, do not need to distinguish the definiendum from *all* other concepts. For to simply distinguish it from *some* other concepts does bring about a remote conception of the definiendum, and this is sufficient for an incomplete definition. On this position, a defining expression that is more general or more specific than the definiendum does count as an incomplete definition.[8] This position was also adopted by some major authorities of the later logical tradition, such as al-Jurjānī and al-Dawānī.

According to this position, general accidents can form nonessential definitions on their own (as opposed to what was mentioned above in 4.3.2). And general accidents are useful in nonessential definitions because mentioning them alongside a given special accident brings about a more complete

8. To be more precise, incomplete *essential* definitions can be more general but not more specific, whereas incomplete *nonessential* definitions can be both more general or more specific.

conception of the definiendum than mentioning the special accident alone. For example, to say, "‹Human› is ‹animal that laughs and breathes›," is better than to simply say, "‹Human› is ‹animal that laughs›." Definitions that make use of general accidents are particularly common among lexicographers.

4.4.2 *Conceptual Clarity*

The defining expression must be conceptually *clearer* (*ajlā*) than the definiendum, meaning that its conception must precede the conception of the definiendum. If the defining expression is vaguer than the definiendum or even if it is of the same level of conceptual clarity, then the definition is unsound because in such a case knowledge of the defining expression is not obtained *before* knowledge of the definiendum, and hence the defining expression cannot be a means for acquiring knowledge of the definiendum. For example, the definition ‹‹Fire› is ‹object that resembles soul›› is unsound because ‹object that resembles soul› is vaguer than ‹fire›. And the definitions ‹‹Motion› is ‹non-stillness›› and ‹‹Human› is ‹human›› are both unsound because ‹non-stillness› is of the same level of clarity as ‹motion›[9] and ‹human› is of the same level of clarity as itself.

Sources

Section	Sources
4 Definition	For further reading, see Street, *Najm al-Dīn*, 135-40; Ahmed, *Palimpsests*, 159-62; Anil Gupta and Stephen Mackereth, "Definitions," *Stanford Encyclopedia of Philosophy* (Fall 2023), ed. Edward N. Zalta and Uri Nodelman, https://plato.stanford.edu/archives/fall2023/entries/definitions; Strobino, *Avicenna's Theory*, 283-304
4.1 Predication in Definition	*TB*, 205-7
4.2 Names, Concepts, and Reality	
4.2.1 What-Knowledge and Is-Knowledge	*TB*, 219-21

9. This assumes that motion and stillness are *contrary opposites*, i.e., positive concepts that are opposed yet conceived independently of each other. Others held that they are *privative opposites*, i.e., stillness is the absence of motion. On this latter position, ‹motion› (the positive concept) is clearer than ‹stillness› (the privative concept), which means that stillness can in fact be defined as the absence of motion, but not vice-versa. *TB*, 212.

Section	Sources
4.2.2 Hypothetical and Real Definitions	*TB*, 221
4.2.3 Proper and Lexical Definitions	*TB*, 219-22
4.3 Essential and Nonessential Definitions	*TB*, 209, 212-17
4.3.1 Complete and Incomplete Definitions	*TB*, 212-13
4.3.2 Species and General Accidents	*TB*, 212-14, 224
4.3.3 Definition by Extramental Parts	*TB*, 213-14
4.4 Conditions of Definition	*TB*, 209-12
4.4.1 Referential Equality	*TB*, 209-16
4.4.2 Conceptual Clarity	*TB*, 209-12

III

PROPOSITIONAL KNOWLEDGE

5

PROPOSITIONS IN GENERAL

The core topics of the science of logic are divided into two parts: one part on topics related to *conception* and another part on topics related to *judgment*. PART II of this book (Chapters 3 and 4) studied topics related to the first part; this chapter marks the beginning of PART III, which will study topics related to the second part. The primary purpose of studying topics related to judgment is to learn the rules of proper argument. Those rules will be studied in Chapters 9 and 10, the final chapters of PART III. This chapter, along with the next two chapters, studies topics related to propositions in order to prepare for the study of arguments in those final chapters.

There are two kinds of *sentences*: *propositional sentences* and *non-propositional sentences* (see 2.2.1). *Propositional* (*khabarī*) sentences or *propositions* (sg. *qaḍiyya*) are expressions that can be true or false, such as the affirmative statement, "Snow is white," or the negative statement, "It is not raining outside." *Non-propositional* (*inshāʾī*) sentences are expressions that cannot be true or false, such as the question, "Is it raining outside?"; the command, "Pick up the book"; and the exclamation, "What a beautiful day!" Since the goal of *argument* is the demonstration of truth or falsity, arguments are only composed of propositions.

A *proposition* (*qaḍiyya*) can be defined as a *sentential expression* (see 2.2) that can be true or false, e.g., "Snow is white." According to this definition, a proposition is a verbal *expression* (*lafẓ*) rather than a mental *concept* (*mafhūm*). Sometimes, however, logicians use the term *proposition* to refer not to the verbal expression (e.g., the expression, "Snow is white") but to the mental concept that it signifies (e.g., the concept ‹Snow is white› signified by the expression "Snow is white"). To distinguish between these two uses, the propositional expression is called an *expressional proposition* (*qaḍiyya lafẓiyya*) and the propositional concept is called a *mental proposition* (*qaḍiyya ʿaqliyya*). A *mental proposition* is a different kind of concept than the concepts studied in Chapters 3 and 4. Those concepts (e.g., ‹human›, ‹horse›, and ‹lion›) are *non-sentential*, and hence, unlike mental propositions, cannot be true or false.

Arguments are composed of two kinds of propositions: *simple propositions*, e.g., "It is raining outside," and *complex propositions*, e.g., "If it is raining outside, then the sidewalk is wet." Hence, following this chapter, which investigates propositions in general, Chapter 6 investigates *simple propositions* and Chapter 7 investigates *complex propositions*.

5.1 Correspondence to Reality

Mental propositions comprise the predication of a predicate to a subject. This predication *describes* (*ḥikāya*) an already-existing *extra-propositional reality* (*wāqiʿ*).[1] If the extra-propositional reality is as the predication describes it, we say that the proposition *corresponds* to that reality and is therefore true; if the extra-propositional reality is not as the predication describes it, then we say that the proposition *does not correspond* to that reality and is therefore false. The predication only exists in the mind (as part of the mental proposition); the reality exists extra-propositionally.

The relation between the mental predication and extra-propositional reality is a relation of *correspondence* (*muṭābaqa*), not a relation of *identity*. If the extra-propositional reality is as described by the predication, the predication corresponds to it; otherwise, it does not. The extra-propositional reality is the *referent* (*mā-ṣadaq*) of the predication, just as the particular human beings in the world are referents of the non-propositional concept ‹human›. But whereas the predication *describes* an extra-propositional reality, the non-propositional concept does not. That is why the predication can be described as being true or false, but the non-propositional concept cannot.

The difference between a *predication* and a *judgment* (or *propositional knowledge* [def: 1.1.3]) is that a predication is a concept that can be true or false, whereas a judgment is a kind of knowledge that relates to such a concept by actually perceiving whether or not it is true or false. The fact that

1. "Extra-propositional" is broader than "extramental." As explained below in Section 5.1.2, the concepts and predications of valid propositions must refer to something beyond themselves. The referent, however, can be either mental or extramental, and either actual or hypothetical.

both *predication* and *judgment* can be signified by the Arabic term *ḥukm* sometimes results in confusion.[2]

Unlike propositional statements, non-propositional statements do not describe an already-existing extra-propositional reality; instead, they bring about new states of affairs through their expression. For example, interrogative expressions solicit responses that do not yet exist, and exclamatory statements bring about amazement through their very expression. It is because they do not describe an already-existing extra-propositional reality that non-propositional statements cannot be described as being true or false.

Definitions, too, do not describe an extra-propositional reality; they merely clarify the concept of the subject by means of the concept of the predicate. The correspondence of a definition is thus not its correspondence to an extra-propositional reality but the correspondence of the concept of the definiendum to the concept of the defining expression, and it hence cannot be described as being true or false.

5.1.1 *The Meaning of "Reality"*

The *extra-propositional reality* (*wāqiʿ*) against which the truth of a proposition is measured is the extra-propositional state of its subject's referents. If that state is such that it is correct to assert that the referents extra-propositionally *are* the predicate, then the proposition is true; otherwise, it is false. The nature of this subject-state varies from predication to predication.[3]

In propositions that make an essential predication, the subject-state or reality that determines whether the proposition is true or false is the subject's essence, that is, *what the subject is*. For example, the proposition ‹Zayd is human› essentially predicates ‹human› of Zayd. Whether or not this proposition is true depends on the essence of the subject Zayd. If Zayd's extramental essence is humanness, the predication is true; otherwise, it is false.

In propositions that predicate existence (*wujūd*) to contingent things, the subject-state or reality that determines whether the proposition is true or false is the subject's having been made to exist by God. For example, the proposition ‹Zayd exists› predicates existence to Zayd. Whether or not this

2. This confusion leads to disagreement over whether or not a *hesitative proposition* (*qaḍiyya mashkūka*) should be considered a proposition. *TB*, 228. Since the disagreement is based entirely on a semantic confusion that is clarified and corrected in the glosses, the discussion has been omitted in this book.

3. Though the following examples are all of simple propositions, similar examples can also be constructed for complex propositions.

proposition is true depends on God's having made him exist. If God has made him exist, the predication is true; otherwise, it is false.

In propositions that predicate *particular descriptions* (sg. *waṣf ʿaynī*), the subject-state or reality that determines whether the proposition is true or false is the subject's possession of the extramentally real basis for that description. For example, the proposition ‹Zayd is knowledgeable› predicates of Zayd the description of being someone knowledgeable. Whether or not this proposition is true depends on Zayd's possession of the property of knowledge. If Zayd possesses the property of knowledge, the predication is true; otherwise, it is false.

In propositions that predicate privative concepts (*ʿadamiyyāt*), the subject-state or reality that determines whether the proposition is true or false is the mental relation of the subject's non-possession of the concept that is denied. For example, the proposition ‹Zayd is something that is not hungry› predicates the privative concept ‹thing that is not hungry› of Zayd. Whether or not the proposition is true depends on Zayd's extramental non-possession of hunger. If Zayd does not possess hunger, the predication is true; otherwise, it is false.

In propositions that predicate relative concepts (*iḍāfiyyāt*), the subject-state or reality that determines whether the proposition is true or false is the subject's relation to another thing. For example, the proposition ‹Zayd is John's son› affirms the correlation of father-ness and son-ness between Zayd and John. Whether or not the proposition is true depends on Zayd's relation to John by a father-son relationship. If this relationship exists, the predication is true; otherwise, it is false.

5.1.2 *The Liar Paradox*

The *liar paradox* (*mughālaṭat al-jadhr al-aṣamm*) is the statement, "Everything that I say today is false," when it is made by someone who says nothing else on that day. The paradox in this statement is that it appears to be both true and false at the same time—the statement's truth entails its falsity, and its falsity entails its truth. Its truth entails that the following two premises are simultaneously true: (1) the statement is the only thing that the one who stated it said that day, and (2) everything he said that day is false, thereby entailing the conclusion that the statement is false. But the statement's falsity entails that the following two premises are simultaneously true: (1) the statement is the only thing that he said that day, and (2) it is false that everything he said that day is false, thereby entailing the conclusion that the statement is true.

The logicians historically responded to this paradox in several ways. One of the most famous responses was offered by al-Dawānī, who said that *propositional sentences* (sg. *khabar*) must describe an *extra-propositional reality* that the sentential predications either correspond to (in which case they are true) or not (in which case they are false). They cannot, however, describe the sentential predications that they themselves comprise. The reason for this is that the possibility of a sentential predication's being true or false requires the possibility of that mental predication coexisting with a corresponding reality (in which case it would be true) and with a non-corresponding reality (in which case it would be false). If, however, the propositional sentence is merely describing itself—as in this case, where the proposition, "Everything that I said today is false," is only describing itself because it was the only thing that was said that day—then it is not possible for its predication to coexist with and without its corresponding reality because it is its own reality and it must always exist. The solution to the paradox, then, is that the paradoxical statement is not a proposition at all and hence can neither be true nor false. It is not a proposition because a statement can only be a proposition if it is possible for its predication to coexist both with a corresponding reality and a non-corresponding one, and that is not the case with this statement.[4]

This is why the statement, "This statement is true," is only a proposition if it refers to a statement other than itself. If it refers to itself, it is not a proposition because the predication that it comprises is self-referential and does not describe an extra-propositional reality. This line of reasoning follows from the logicians' representational account of knowledge, according to which a judgment is the perception of an extra-propositional reality through its representation in the mind. According to this account, a self-referential predication is not knowledge because it does not represent anything outside of itself.

Other logicians explained this further by saying that the function of propositional sentences is to describe a reality that is prior to themselves to which they can correspond or not correspond. The description of this prior reality is what sets them apart from non-propositional sentences, such as interrogatives, exclamations, commands, and prohibitions. When they describe themselves, they are no longer describing a prior reality and cease to be propositional.

4. This solution is analogous to how someone like al-Dawānī would analyze Russell's paradox and its solution—just as a proposition must only describe an extra-propositional reality in order to be coherent, a set must only comprise members other than itself to be coherent.

5.2 The Ontology of Predication

The referent of a predication can be said to *exist* in one three ways: (1) *extramentally*, (2) *mentally*, and (3) *in-itself*. The *extramental existence* (*wujūd khārijī*) of a thing means that it exists in the real world, independently of being perceived by minds. Everything in the universe, for example—the earth, the sun, the sky, and so on—exists extramentally regardless of whether we know about it or not.

When we come to know of something that exists extramentally, such as, for example, when we observe an extramentally existing tree, it comes to exist in our minds. Its existence in our minds does not mean that the tree itself comes to inhere in our minds. Rather, it means that a representational concept of the tree (created by God) comes to exist in our minds when we observe it. The logicians call this representational existence of something in our minds its *mental existence* (*wujūd dhihnī*). Since a thing's mental existence normally derives from its extramental existence, the extramental existence of things is also called their *primary existence* (*wujūd aṣlī* or *wujūd muta'aṣṣil*) and their mental existence is also called their *secondary existence* (*wujūd ẓillī*). It is only by their original, or extramental, existence that things have effects. For example, it is only by its extramental existence that fire burns. In terms of its secondary, mental existence, the concept ‹fire› does not burn the mind.

The kind of mental existence that has been described above is *abstracted existence* (*wujūd intizāʿī*). There is another kind of mental existence, *imagined existence* (*wujūd ikhtirāʿī*), which is not derived from anything's extramental existence but simply imagined in the mind. For example, the concept ‹sea of mercury› is a concept that we can imagine in the mind even though it does not exist extramentally. Whereas the abstracted mental existence of a thing derives from its extramental existence, a thing's imagined mental existence does not. A sea of mercury, then, exists mentally (if we bring it to mind) but not extramentally.

Finally, a thing's *existence-in-itself* (*wujūd fī nafs al-amr*) means simply that it is the case. For something to be the case, it does not have to exist extramentally. For example, the contingency of the universe is the case, meaning that the universe is, in fact, contingent, even though the concept ‹contingency› is a mental concept without any extramental existence. In fact, for the contingency of the universe to actually exist (or, in other words, for it to be the case), it does not even have to exist in the mind—the universe actually is contingent, regardless of whether or not anyone conceives its contingency in his mind. A thing's existence-in-itself refers to its being the case independently of its being thought about in the mind and regardless of whether or not it exists extramentally.

The conceptual relationships between these three modes of existence are as follows:

1. ‹Existence in-itself› is *unconditionally more inclusive* than ‹extramental existence›, meaning that everything that exists extramentally also exists in-itself but not vice-versa. An example of something that both exists extramentally and in-itself is God. An example of something that exists in-itself but not extramentally is the contingency of the universe.
2. ‹Existence in-itself› is *perspectivally more and less inclusive* than ‹mental existence›, meaning that there are some things that exist in-themselves but not mentally (e.g., the unknown depths of the universe), others that exist mentally but not in-themselves (e.g., a sea of mercury), and others that both exist mentally and in-themselves (e.g., a person who is observed to exist).
3. ‹Mental existence› is *perspectivally more and less inclusive* than ‹extramental existence›, meaning that there are some things that exist mentally but not extramentally (e.g., a sea of mercury), others that exist extramentally but not mentally (e.g., the unknown depths of the universe), and others that both exist mentally and extramentally (e.g., a person who is observed to exist).

5.3 Distinct Types of Judgments in *Kalām* Epistemology

Propositional knowledge or *judgment* (def: 1.1.3) is a perception of reality. The Muslim logicians' analysis of this propositional knowledge, particularly their analysis of *propositional modality*, is based on an epistemology that they share with the *kalām* theologians. This epistemology distinguishes judgments of three categories: (1) *metaphysical judgments* (sg. *ḥukm ʿaqlī*), (2) *regularity judgments* (sg. *ḥukm ʿādī*), and (3) *revelatory judgments* (sg. *ḥukm sharʿī*). These three distinct categories of judgments are intertwined in cosmological arguments for the existence of God from contingency and creation.

5.3.1 *Metaphysical Judgments*

A *metaphysical judgment* (*ḥukm ʿaqlī*)[5] is the mind's perception that a predication is *rationally necessary* (*wājib ʿaqlī*), *rationally impossible* (*mustaḥīl ʿaqlī*), or *rationally possible* (*jāʾiz ʿaqlī*). Each one of these perceptions is either *noninferential* or *inferential*. A predication is *rationally necessary* when the mind perceives that it cannot *not* be the case. An example of a noninferential judgment of rational necessity is ‹‹One› is ‹half of two››. An example of an inferential judgment of rational necessity is ‹God exists›. A predication is *rationally impossible* when the mind perceives that it cannot be the case. An example of a noninferential judgment of rational impossibility is ‹‹Two› is ‹half of one››. An example of an inferential judgment of rational impossibility is ‹More than one god exists›. A predication is *rationally possible* when the mind perceives that it can either be or not be the case. An example of a noninferential judgment of rational possibility is ‹This book is red›. An example of an inferential judgment of rational possibility is ‹Believers will dwell forever in paradise›.

Each of these judgments is a mental perception of reality. The mind perceives, in other words, that it is metaphysically necessary for God to exist, metaphysically impossible for more than one god to exist, and metaphysically possible for believers to dwell in paradise. The mind's ability to perceive these metaphysical qualities is so fundamental to human rationality that some theologians, most notably al-Juwaynī (d. 478/1085), defined the human mind as knowledge of these three judgments.[6]

5.3.2 *Regularity Judgments*

A *regularity judgment* (*ḥukm ʿādī*) is the mind's perception of a *regular association* (*rabṭ ʿādī*) between two *rationally possible* matters, whether *existential* (*amr wujūdī*) or *privative* (*amr ʿadamī*). For example, the mind perceives a regular association between ‹eating›, an existential rationally possible matter,

5. The term *ḥukm ʿaqlī* is often used to refer to any judgment that is made by the mind without recourse to any perception of a regular association or to revelation. In this sense, *ḥukm ʿaqlī* could be translated as "purely mental judgment." However, the primary purpose of this category in the context of the three-part *kalām* classification is to characterize the kind of judgment we make when we judge a thing in the universe to be contingent, which is the mental perception of a metaphysical modality (see 6.7.1). The translation of this term as "metaphysical judgment" emphasizes this primary purpose and corrects the tendency among many contemporary students of *kalām* to translate and explain this term in a way that separates it from the real world and confines it to mathematical tautologies that only exist in the mind.

6. Al-Dasūqī, *Ḥāshiyat Umm al-barāhīn*, 51.

and ‹satiation›, an existential rationally possible matter; ‹non-eating›, a privative rationally possible matter, and ‹hunger›, an existential rationally possible matter; ‹eating›, an existential rationally possible matter, and ‹non-hunger›, a privative rationally possible matter; and ‹non-eating›, a privative rationally possible matter, and ‹non-satiation›, a privative rationally possible matter.

This perception arises upon repeatedly observing the conjunction of two matters (whether existential or privative) in the universe. When we observe more than once, for example, that fire and burning are conjoined, we perceive a regular association between the two, on the basis of which we perceive the truth of the proposition ‹Fire burns›. This perception is called a *regularity judgment.*

The association that the mind perceives here is a *regular association* (*rabṭ ʿādī*), not a *rational association* (*rabṭ ʿaqlī*) as with *metaphysical judgments* described above. *Continual association,* in other words, does not entail *necessary association.* This means that for a regular association to be interrupted would not entail any rational contradiction. The interruption of regular associations, in fact, forms the basis of the third kind of judgments, namely revelatory judgments, which are described below in the next section.

5.3.3 *Revelatory Judgments*

Whereas metaphysical judgments are mental perceptions of propositional knowledge unaided by either regular association or revelation, a *revelatory judgment* (*ḥukm sharʿī*) is the mind's perception that a predication is true by virtue of God informing us that it is the case, i.e., through genuine revelation from God. This perception relies first on an *inference* that a given claimant to messengerhood is a genuine messenger from God. This inference takes as its starting points: (1) a given regularity judgment (e.g., that fire burns), (2) the inferential judgment that every event in the universe is directly created by God,[7] (3) the context of a prophetic miracle (*muʿjiza*) at the hands of someone claiming that his proof that he is genuinely conveying something from God is that God will now interrupt some regularity (e.g., that a particular fire will cease to burn), and (4) the fact that the regularity is interrupted at that time

7. This is inferred through the *argument for divine oneness by mutual prevention,* (*dalīl al-tamānuʿ*). The argument gains its inspiration from the verse, "Were there any gods therein [i.e., in the heavens and the earth] apart from God, neither would have existed" (Qur'ān 21:22). The argument builds on the *argument from createdness* (*dalīl al-ḥudūth*), which demonstrates the existence of a necessary, omnipotent, omniscient, volitional being, and goes on to argue that this being cannot be more than one because for more than one omnipotent being to exist would entail a logical contradiction.

(e.g., something is thrown into the fire and it does not burn it). Whenever the mind perceives these four things, God creates within it the knowledge that our witnessing the prophetic miracle in that context is equivalent to God's saying to us, "This servant of mine is truthful in everything that he conveys from Me."

The prophetic miracles of the Prophet Muḥammad (God bless him and give him peace) were numerous. Among them was the eloquence of the Qur'ān, which interrupted the regularity within the norms of human eloquence in the Arabic language on the Arabian Peninsula. Through these prophetic miracles, we infer that the Qur'ān and the Sunna, the two categories of revelation that the Prophet Muḥammad (God bless him and give him peace) conveyed to us from God, are genuinely from God.

From these two sources, we can infer two kinds of *revelatory judgments*: *moral revelatory judgments* and *informative revelatory judgments*. A *moral revelatory judgment* is the mind's perception that God has declared an action of a morally responsible agent to be obligatory, recommended, permissible, offensive, or unlawful. The mind infers this declaration through divine commands and prohibitions in the Qur'ān and Sunna. The moral revelatory judgments transmitted to us by the Prophet Muḥammad (God bless him and give him peace) from God are recorded in the science of sacred law (see 11.5.3).[8] An *informative revelatory judgment* is the mind's perception that God has, in the present, or will, in the future, realize some rationally possible proposition. An example of a rationally possible proposition that the mind knows to be true *in the present* by virtue of revelation is ‹Unseen beings exist called jinn, whom God has made from fire just as has He has made us from clay›. An example of a rationally possible proposition that the mind knows to be true *in the future* by virtue of revelation is ‹Believers will dwell eternally in paradise›.

Thus, a proposition that the mind, without the aid of revelation, judges to be *intrinsically possible* can become *extrinsically necessary* by virtue of God informing us that He has actualized or will actualize it through His will and

8. For the Sunni *mutakallimūn*, moral responsibility is defined by God's commands and prohibitions, which are unrestricted by any contingent criterion. God is, in other words, free to command or prohibit whatever He wills and when we perceive His commands and prohibitions, we perceive the moral revelatory judgments described here. These moral revelatory judgments are thus defined by the divine command alone, not by any objective quality or thing in nature. However, God has created a moral sense within us through which can know, for example, that it is good to give charity and that it is bad to steal. As a mercy from God, His moral revelatory judgments *actually* correspond to this contingent moral sense that God has created within us. But the contingency of that moral sense entails that His moral revelatory judgments do not *necessarily* correspond to it. (This is a modal difference. See: 6.7.1.)

power. The metaphysical judgments of necessity, impossibility and possibility described above are thus judgments of *intrinsic necessity* (*wujūb dhātī*), *intrinsic impossibility* (*istiḥāla dhātiyya*), and *intrinsic possibility* (*jawāz dhātī*). For example, the mind perceives that for God to exist is *intrinsically* (or *in-itself*; see 5.2) necessary, for more than one God to exist is *intrinsically* (or *in-itself*) impossible, and for believers to dwell in paradise is *intrinsically* (or *in-itself*) possible. Something that is intrinsically possible becomes *extrinsically necessary* (*wājib li-ghayrihi*) or *extrinsically impossible* (*mustaḥīl li-ghayrihi*) when considered from the perspective of what revelation tells us about it. For example, we perceive that for believers to dwell forever in paradise is *intrinsically possible* (this is a perception of how it is *in-itself*, namely a contingent event whose realization or non-realization is utterly subject to God's will and power), but *extrinsically necessary* because true revelation from God informs us that God will, in fact, make believers dwell in paradise (this is a perception of how the contingent event will, in fact, turn out to be). Similarly, we perceive that for believers to dwell forever in hellfire is also intrinsically possible (this is a perception of how it is *in-itself*, namely a contingent event whose realization or non-realization is utterly subject to God's will and power), but extrinsically impossible because true revelation from God informs us that God will, in fact, make believers dwell in paradise and not in hellfire (this is a perception of how the contingent event will, in fact, turn out to be). This intrinsic-extrinsic distinction only applies to matters that are *intrinsically possible*. Matters that are *intrinsically necessary* or *intrinsically impossible* cannot be extrinsically otherwise. For them to be extrinsically otherwise would be a contradiction because something that is intrinsically necessary cannot *not* be the case and something that is intrinsically impossible cannot *be* the case. It is only *intrinsically possible* things that can be the case or not be the case and hence become necessary or impossible from the perspective of what revelation tells us about them.

Sources

Section	Sources
5 Propositions in General	TB, 227; for further reading, see Street, *Najm al-Dīn*, 140-45; Ahmed, *Palimpsests*, 162; Khaled El-Rouayheb, "Does a Proposition Have Three Parts or Four? A Debate in Later Arabic Logic," *Oriens* 44, no. 3-4 (2016): 301-31, https://doi.org/10.1163/18778372-04403001

III.5: PROPOSITIONAL KNOWLEDGE

Section	Sources
5.1 Correspondence to Reality	TB, 225
5.1.1 The Meaning of "Reality"	TB, 225-26
5.1.2 The Liar Paradox	TB, 226; for further reading, see Ahmed, Palimpsests, 150; Khaled El-Rouayheb, "The Liar Paradox in Fifteenth-Century Shiraz: The Exchange between Ṣadr al-Dīn al-Dashtakī and Jalāl al-Dīn al-Dawānī," *British Journal for the History of Philosophy* 28, no 2. (2020): 251-75, https://doi.org/10.1080/09608788.2019.1616156; Hassan John Rezakhany, "Jalāl ad-Dīn ad-Dawānī's Solution to the Liar Paradox and Its Reception in Qāḍī Mubārak and Mullā Mubīn," *Journal of South Asian Intellectual History* 1, no. 2 (2018): 183-220, https://doi.org/10.1163/25425552-12340007
5.2 The Ontology of Predication	TB, 249-50
5.3 Epistemological Division of Judgments	
5.3.1 Metaphysical Judgments	al-Sharqāwī, *Ḥāshiya*, 26-28
5.3.2 Regularity Judgments	al-Sharqāwī, *Ḥāshiya*, 23-25
5.3.3 Revelatory Judgments	al-Sharqāwī, *Ḥāshiya*, 17-19, 21-23

6

SIMPLE PROPOSITIONS

There are two kinds of propositions: the *simple proposition* (*qaḍiyya ḥamliyya*) and the *complex proposition* (*qaḍiyya sharṭiyya*). The *simple proposition* is the kind of proposition that has been used in almost all propositional examples cited thus far. It is a simple propositional statement that affirms or negates the *predication* (*nisba* or *ḥukm*) of a *predicate* (*maḥmūl*) to a *subject* (*mawḍūʿ*). Simple propositions in English typically consist of three terms: (1) the *subject*, which is usually mentioned first; (2) the *predicate*, which is usually mentioned afterward; and (3) the *copula* (*rābiṭ*), which is usually mentioned between the subject and predicate. For example, in the proposition, "Snow is white," the subject is "snow," the predicate is "white," and the copula is "is."

The copula signifies the predicative relationship between the subject and the predicate. This relationship is called the *predication* (*nisba* or *ḥukm*). A simple proposition either affirms this predication (e.g., ‹Snow is white›), in which case it is called an *affirmative proposition* (*qaḍiyya mūjaba*), or it negates this predication (e.g., ‹Snow is not black›), in which case it is called a *negative proposition* (*qaḍiyya sāliba*). The propositional property of being an affirmative or negative proposition is called the proposition's *quality* (*kayf*). If the affirmation or negation of the predication corresponds to reality, the proposition is *true* (*ṣādiq*); if it does not, it is *false* (*kādhib*).

Arabic propositional statements do not have copulas. The predicative relationship between the subject and predicate is signified instead by the grammatical inflective signs of words in the sentence (see 11.5.1). For example, the English propositional statement, "Zayd is standing," consists of three words—the subject "Zayd," the predicate "standing," and the copula "is." Its

Arabic equivalent is, *Zayd*^{un} *qā'im*^{un}, which only consists of two words—the subject *Zayd* and the predicate *qā'im*. The predicative relationship between the Arabic subject and predicate is signified by the vowels at the ends of the words (transliterated into English in this example by the superscript *-un*). That being said, Greek propositional statements, like English, do have copulas. When Islamic civilization translated the texts of Greek logic into Arabic, the copula was translated using the third-person pronoun *huwa* (e.g., *Zayd*^{un} *huwa qā'im*^{un}) or the verb *kāna* (e.g., *Zayd*^{un} *kāna qā'im*^{an}). The logicians of the later logical tradition point out, however, that such translations reflected the influence of Greek and were not native to the Arabic language. The inclusion of the third-person pronoun *huwa* or the verb *kāna* does not change the fact that the predicative relationship is signified in Arabic by inflective signs.

When only the subject and predicate of a proposition are stated, the Arabic-speaking logicians call it a *two-part proposition* (*qaḍiyya thunā'iyya*). When the copula is stated (albeit unnecessarily), it is called a *three-part proposition* (*qaḍiyya thulāthiyya*). Simple propositions also have a fourth integral part called the *stated modality* (*jiha*). When this part is explicitly added, the proposition is called a *four-part proposition* (*qaḍiyya rubā'iyya*). Other propositional elements, such as negations and *quantifiers*, are not required to constitute the proposition, although they may be useful.

6.1 Predication in Simple Propositions

The predication of simple propositions is an *ordinary predication*, meaning that it signifies that the subject is an instance of the predicate (see 3.4.1.1). For example, the predication of the simple proposition ‹Zayd is human› conveys that the person Zayd is an instance of the universal concept ‹human›. A more precise analysis of this predication is as follows. The person or *instance* Zayd has been *referred to* (or, in modern terminology, *denoted*) by the *concept* ‹Zayd› in the mind of the speaker, which is *signified* by the expression "Zayd" on the tongue of the speaker. This same instance, Zayd, has been *co-referred-to* by the *universal concept* ‹human› in the mind of the speaker, which is signified by the expression "human" on the tongue of the speaker. The predication uses the singular concept ‹Zayd› to specify the instance Zayd and then conveys that Zayd is an instance of the universal concept ‹human›.

This analysis reveals that the predication of a simple proposition has three elements: (1) the propositional *subject-concept* (*'unwān al-mawḍū'*), (2) the propositional *predicate-concept* (*'unwān al-maḥmūl*), and (3) an extra-propositional *referent*.[1] The predication affirms a referential identity between the subject-concept and the predicate-concept. *Referential identity* is not the same as *conceptual identity*—conceptually, the subject-concept and predicate-concept are different; it is only referentially that they are the same. If they were conceptually identical, the predication would not be an *ordinary predication* but a *conceptual predication*. The predication has, in other words, an aspect of identity—the extra-propositional referent—and an aspect of difference—the conceptual difference between the subject-concept and the predicate-concept.[2]

With respect to the predication, what is sought by the subject-expression is the *referent* of its concept (not its concept *per se*) and what is sought by the predicate-expression is its concept *per se* (not its referent). The purpose of the subject-concept, in other words, is to refer to its referents, whereas the purpose of the predicate-concept is to be predicated to those referents. The value of the subject-concept is *reference*; the value of the predicate-concept is *predication*.

The subject-concept refers to the extra-propositional referent—termed the *subject-referent* (*dhāt al-mawḍūʿ*)—through *conventional expressional signification* (def: 2.1.1). This reference between the subject-concept and the subject-referent is called the *reference of signification* (*ʿaqd al-waḍʿ*). The predicate-concept, by contrast, refers to the extra-propositional referent through the propositional predication itself. This reference of the predicate-concept to the referent is called the *reference of predication* (*ʿaqd al-ḥaml*). These two types of reference, the reference of signification and the reference of predication, are what constitute the *mental simple proposition*.

1. That is, the *extension* (*mā-ṣadaq*). The qualification "extra-propositional" here means that the referent is outside the mental conception of the proposition and outside the verbal expression of the proposition. It is not enough to say that the referent is *extramental*, for the referent may indeed be a mental concept, e.g., in the proposition, ‹The simultaneous existence and nonexistence of a thing is impossible›, where the subject, ‹the simultaneous existence and nonexistence of a thing›, is not an extramental entity but rather a merely mental one. Importantly, this referent is not the referent of the proposition insofar as it is the subject of the proposition; rather, it is the referent insofar as it is a mental concept that is conceived independently, before, and "outside" of the conceiving of the proposition.

2. In modern logical terminology, the subject-concept is the *intension* of the subject-term and the subject-referent is its *extension*. The predicate-concept is the intension of the predicate-term. To reiterate the analysis in this terminology, the predication of a simple proposition affirms an *extensional identity* between the subject-term and the predicate-term *by means of their intensions*. The Muslim logicians were aware that the intension of the subject-term can affect the truth of modal propositions, and their precise analysis of predication eliminates problems like the morning-star paradox (see Note 100).

6.2 Subject-Concepts

The *subject-concept* of a simple proposition is either a *singular concept* or a *universal concept*. If it is a universal concept, then then its *referent* (*mā-ṣadaq*) is either the concept itself or the instances of the concept. Simple propositions are thus divided from the perspective of their subjects into three kinds.

1. *Singular propositions* (sg. *qaḍiyya shakhṣiyya*), e.g., ‹Zayd is wise›. This proposition conveys that the singular instance Zayd referred to by the singular concept ‹Zayd› is characterized by wisdom.
2. *Concept-propositions* (sg. *qaḍiyya ṭabīʿiyya*), e.g., ‹‹Animal› is a genus›. The purpose of the subject-concept ‹animal› is to refer not to the instances of ‹animal› but rather to the concept ‹animal› itself. The proposition says, in other words, "The concept ‹animal› is a genus-concept." Contrast this with the proposition ‹Every animal is either an herbivore or a carnivore›, where the purpose of ‹animal› is to refer to its instances.[3]
3. *Instance-propositions*, e.g., ‹Every human is wise›.[4] The purpose of the subject-concept ‹human› is to refer to its instances. Thus, the proposition conveys that all the singular instances referred to by the concept ‹human› are characterized by wisdom.

The logicians do not use *concept-propositions* because they are not useful for propositional inferences.[5] This is illustrated in the following example, where

3. Since the predication of this proposition is an *ordinary predication*, ‹animal› is in different ways both the subject-concept and the subject-referent. The predication involves two concepts that are both signified by "animal"—a concept that is the subject-concept of the proposition and hence refers to something else (call it the "referring-concept") and a concept that is the subject-referent of the proposition and hence referred to by the former concept (call it the "referent-concept"). This proposition conveys that the mentally existing referent-concept ‹animal› (the subject-referent) that is referred to by the referring-concept ‹animal› (the subject-concept) is a genus-kind-of-concept (the characterization conveyed by the predicate-concept). *TB*, 238.

4. Al-Taftāzānī does not give this category a name, but an appropriate name is given here for clarity. It is hence not a translation of any Arabic term.

5. Al-Khabīṣī in his commentary on the *Tahdhīb*, like most commentators and glossers of the *Shamsiyya*, says that the reason why logicians do not examine concept-propositions is that logic serves the *philosophical sciences* (i.e., the Aristotelian corpus of sciences that the Muslims inherited through Avicenna whose goal is to study all things without reference to revelation; see Karamali, *Madrasa Curriculum*, 6), which only study extramentally existing things. Since concepts are not extramentally existing things, concept-propositions are not about extramentally existing things, and hence not useful to the philosophical sciences, and hence not useful to logicians. *TB*, 237-38. This, as Ibn Saʿīd notes in his gloss on al-Khabīṣī's commentary, is not an entirely accurate explanation because the philosophical sciences do,

using concept-propositions in the argument leads to an incorrect conclusion.

Minor Premise:	Zayd is a human. (Instance-proposition)
Major Premise:	‹Human› is a species. (Concept-proposition)
Conclusion:	Zayd is a species. (Incorrect)

Logical inference depends instead on *instance-propositions*, and they are the propositions that logicians are primarily concerned with. The use of instance-propositions in a valid logical argument is illustrated in the following example, which has the same form as the previous example, with the exception that the premises are all instance-propositions. When the concept-proposition is replaced with an instance-proposition, the argument leads to a correct conclusion:

Minor Premise:	Every human is an animal. (Instance-proposition)
Major Premise:	Every animal is an organism. (Instance-proposition)
Conclusion:	Every human is an organism. (Correct)

In addition to this, another reason why it is instance-propositions that are the primary concern of logicians is that the structure of logical arguments is based on the *quantification* of simple propositions, and quantification only applies to instance-propositions—neither singular propositions nor concept-propositions can be quantified.

Thus, as with concept-propositions, *singular propositions* are not useful for logical inference because the *usefulness* of a proposition in logical inference is determined by whether or not it can play the role of the major premise and, like concept-propositions, singular propositions cannot play that role (see 9.1.1). They are, however, still studied by logicians because singular propositions are parts of instance-propositions: instance-propositions make judgments on groups of instances, while singular propositions make judgments on single instances. Additionally, unlike concept-propositions, singular propositions can at least *appear* to play the role of a major premise. For example:

in fact, study non-extramentally existing things as well. Ḥasan b. Muḥammad al-ʿAṭṭār and Muḥammad b. ʿAlī b. Saʿīd, *Ḥāshiyat al-ʿAṭṭār ʿalā sharḥ al-Khabīṣī wa-bi-hāmishihā ḥāshiyat al-ʿallāma Ibn Saʿīd* (Cairo: ʿĪsā al-Bābī al-Ḥalabī, 1960), 151-52. The reason for the logicians' disinterest in concept-propositions that is mentioned above, namely that they are not useful for logical inference, which is also mentioned in the glosses on the *Tahdhīb*, is hence the more pertinent reason.

Minor Premise:	This is Zayd. (Singular proposition)
Major Premise:	Zayd is a human. (Instance-proposition)
Conclusion:	This is a human. (Correct)

Here, it appears that the major premise is a singular proposition. However, since the identity-predication of singulars is impossible, the predicate of the minor premise is not the singular concept ‹Zayd›, but rather the implicitly universal concept ‹person named "Zayd"› (see 3.4.1.2). Since the predicate of the minor premise must be the same as the subject of the major premise, the subject of the major premise, too, is the same implicitly universal concept. The major premise is hence an instance-proposition even though it appears to be a singular proposition.[6]

6.3 Characterization of Subject-Referents

Al-Fārābī and Avicenna[7] disagreed on whether an ordinary predication signifies that the subject-referent is *broadly possibly* or *broadly actually* characterized by the subject-concept. *Possibility* and *actuality* here are not opposites; rather, broad possibility is the opposite of *rational impossibility*, whereas actuality is the opposite of *potentiality*.[8] Al-Fārābī held that the subject-referent of

6. According to those who hold that the identity-predication of singulars is possible, such as al-Dawānī, a singular proposition can indeed serve as the major premise of a simple proposition, and hence the reason singular propositions are mentioned by the logicians is simply that they are directly useful to their purposes.

7. In the terminology of the Muslim logicians, al-Fārābī and Avicenna are collectively referred to as *al-Shaykhān* ("the Two Shaykhs"), and Avicenna is referred to as *al-Shaykh al-Ra'īs* ("the Leading Shaykh") or simply as *al-Shaykh*. This is how they are referred to in this passage. *TB*, 260.

8. *Broad possibility* is for it not to be metaphysically impossible for a thing to be a particular way. *Impossibility* is for it to be metaphysically impossible to be that way. *Potentiality* is for it to be natural for a thing be a particular way but to not yet be that way. *Actuality* is for it to be natural for a thing to be a particular way and to be that way. The word "possibility" (as with the Arabic word *imkān*) equivocates between the meaning of broad possibility just described and between the meaning of potentiality. This often leads to confusion between the two terms. There are three ways in which one can distinguish between potentiality and possibility. First, something that is potentially X is not actually X whereas something that is broadly possibly X can be (and more often than not is) actually X. Second, potentiality does not apply equally to a thing during its nonexistence and existence, whereas possibility does. We can say, "Broadly possibly, fire is hot," intending both before and after it exists, whereas with potentiality we only say, "Potentially, this wood is hot" (i.e., if it is lit into a fire) or, "Actually, this fire is hot." Third, when something that is potential becomes actual, the thing itself changes—e.g., "Wood is potentially fire"—or its attributes change—e.g., "Someone who is unlettered potentially writes." Possibility is therefore *perspectivally more and less inclusive* than potentiality: the first example can be correctly stated with potentiality but not possibility (it is incorrect to say,

instance predications is *broadly possibly* characterized by the subject-concept. According to him, a proposition such as ‹Every sweet thing is X› would, by default, refer not only to things like sugar but also to things like salt because it is *rationally possible* for salt to be characterized by sweetness. A proposition stated in the form, "Every A is B," is thus really the statement, "Everything that is possibly A is B." In contrast, Avicenna held that the subject-referent of instance-propositions is *broadly actually* characterized by the subject-concept. According to him, the proposition ‹Every sweet thing is X› refers only to things that are actually sweet. Salt would hence not normally be included in the statement because even though it is *possibly* sweet, it is not *actually* sweet.

Avicenna's position does not require that the subject-referent be characterized by the subject-concept in reality; rather, the subject-referent might also be hypothesized to be characterized by the subject-concept in order to test whether or not that is actually the case.[9] To return to the example just cited, if salt were hypothesized to be sweet in order to make a statement about it as a sweet thing and then test whether or not that is the case, then salt could be included in the statement, "Every sweet thing is X." This is still an actual characterization (albeit hypothetical) of the subject-referent by the subject-concept, not merely a possible one. The proposition, "Every A is B," according to Avicenna, hence means, "Everything that actually (whether hypothetically or non-hypothetically) is A is B."

Avicenna's position is the preferred one. Although it is possible for instance-propositions to be intended to function as al-Fārābī held they did, the way that they function in ordinary language corresponds to Avicenna's position because people normally make statements about things that have happened or will actually happen. For instance-propositions to be understood as al-Fārābī understood them, they would have to be explicitly stated as, "Everything *that is possibly* A is B." Of note, a third position was held by Averroes, namely, that when the *intended modality* of the predication is *possibility*, then the subject-referent is understood to be *possibly* characterized by the subject-concept, whereas, when the intended modality of the predication

"Wood is possibly fire," because it is impossible for wood to be fire); the second example can be correctly stated with both potentiality and possibility; and statements of actuality can be stated with possibility but not potentiality. *TB*, 272-73.

9. This is an interpretation of Avicenna's position by later logicians. Others insist that his position does indeed require that the subject-referent be characterized by the subject-concept in reality. *TB*, 342.

is *actuality*, *continuity*, or *necessity*, then the subject-referent is understood to be *actually* characterized by the subject-concept.[10]

6.4 Quantification in Simple Propositions

Instance-propositions use a universal subject-concept to predicate the predicate-concept to the universal's singular instances. For example, in the proposition ‹Humans are rational›, the concept ‹human› is used to refer to instances of humans, so that the concept ‹rational› may be predicated to them. In this example, the subject-instances are unquantified. It has not been specified, in other words, whether the predication applies to all instances of the subject-concept or merely to some of its instances. This proposition is hence called an *unquantified proposition* (*qaḍiyya muhmala*).

If the proposition specifies that the predication applies to all of the instances of the subject-concept, such as in the affirmative propositions ‹Every human is rational› and ‹Every human is rational› and in the negative proposition ‹Every human is not non-rational›, it is called a *universally quantified proposition* (*qaḍiyya kulliyya*).[11] If the proposition specifies that the predication applies to some instance of the subject-concept, i.e., one or more, such as in the affirmative proposition ‹Some human is rational› or in the negative proposition ‹Some human is not rational›, it is called a *particularly quantified proposition* (*qaḍiyya juz'iyya*). Universally and particularly quantified propositions are both *quantified propositions* (sg. *qaḍiyya maḥṣūra* or *qaḍiyya musawwara*). The expression that is used to quantify the subject-instances[12] of a proposition, such as "all" or "some," is a *quantifier* (*sūr*).

From the perspective of logical inference, an *unquantified proposition* can be treated as a particularly quantified proposition, meaning that whenever

10. This was Averroes' interpretation of Aristotle on the matter. The Muslim logicians transmitted that Alexander of Aphrodisias held the same position as Avicenna. Ibrāhīm al-Bājūrī, *Ḥāshiyat Ibrāhīm al-Bājūrī 'alā mukhtaṣar al-Sanūsī fī fann al-manṭiq* (Cairo: Maṭba'at al-Taqaddum al-'Ilmiyya, 1321H), 84.

11. The most common universal quantifier in the Arabic language is the word *kull*, which can be synonymously used in the meaning of "all" or "every," as in the propositions cited above, or in the meaning of a collective group, such as *ḥamala kull al-rijāl al-ṣakhra*, which means, "All of the men together lifted the boulder." This latter kind of *kull* is called *al-kull al-majmū'ī* ("the collective *kull*") and is not a universal quantifier. Propositions that begin with this kind of *kull* are singular propositions because the word *kull* refers to a specific collection of parts. *TB*, 242.

12. It is the subject's instances that are quantified, not the predicate, because the ordinary predication of simple propositions affirms the predicate-concept of the subject-instances, not the other way around. In other words, whereas the subject-concept is used to refer to its instances, the predicate-concept is not used to refer to any instances; it is merely applied to

one is true, the other is also true. The reason for this is that an unquantified proposition is either actually a particularly quantified proposition, or else it is a universally quantified proposition, which includes the particularly quantified proposition. Therefore, it may be treated at minimum as a particularly quantified proposition.

6.5 Complemented Simple Propositions

The element within a negative proposition (*qaḍiyya sāliba*) to which the negation applies is the proposition's predication. For example, the negation within the proposition ‹Every human does not live forever› applies to the predication of ‹living forever› to humans. If a negation within a proposition is applied instead to one of its two terms, thereby changing the term into its *complement* (def: 3.3.2), the proposition is called a *complemented proposition* (*qaḍiyya maʿdūla*). If the negation is applied to the subject, the proposition is called a *subject-complemented proposition* (*qaḍiyya maʿdūlat al-mawḍūʿ*); if it is applied to the predicate, it is called a *predicate-complemented proposition* (*qaḍiyya maʿdūlat al-maḥmūl*). In each case the proposition as a whole can be either affirmative (if the predication is not negated) or negative (if the predication is negated). The various possibilities are summarized in the table below.

	Example	Kind of Proposition
1	Every human is rational.	Affirmative uncomplemented proposition
2	Every human does not live forever.	Negative uncomplemented proposition
3	Some non-human is alive	Affirmative subject-complemented proposition
4	Some non-human is not alive.	Negative subject-complemented proposition
5	Every horse is non-rational.	Affirmative predicate-complemented proposition
6	Every human is not non-rational.	Negative predicate-complemented proposition
7	Every non-human is non-rational.	Affirmative subject-and-predicate-complemented proposition
8	Some non-horse is not non-rational.	Negative subject-and-predicate-complemented proposition

the instances that the subject-concept refers to. *TB*, 241-42.

A proposition whose terms have not been complemented is either an *uncomplemented affirmative proposition* (*qaḍiyya muḥaṣṣila*),[13] such as Example 1 in the table above, or an *uncomplemented negative proposition* (*qaḍiyya sāliba basīṭa*), such as Example 2 in the table above. The difference between an *uncomplemented negative proposition* (*qaḍiyya sāliba basīṭa*), e.g., ‹Every human does not live forever›, and a *predicate-complemented affirmative proposition* (*qaḍiyya mūjaba maʿdūlat al-maḥmūl*), e.g., ‹Every human is a non-living-forever-thing›, is that the existence of the subject is not a condition for the truth of the former whereas it is for the truth of the latter (see *existential import*; 6.6). The former is hence true in a greater number of cases than the latter.

6.6 Existential Import in Simple Propositions

Affirmative simple propositions have *existential import*, meaning that their truth requires the existence of their subject-referents. For example, the proposition ‹Every logician is tall› can only be true if some logician exists—if no logicians exist, they cannot be tall. In other words, if the referent of a concept does not exist, nothing can be affirmed of it. The truth of negative simple propositions, on the other hand, does not require the existence of its subject-referents. For example, the proposition ‹Every unicorn is not brown› can be true if unicorns exist and none of them are brown, or it can be true if no unicorns exist—if there are no unicorns, in other words, it is true that it is not the case that unicorns are brown.

The existential import of an affirmative simple proposition is of three kinds, depending on the kind of existence that it implicitly affirms for its subject-referents: (1) the existential import of *extramental propositions* (which may be called *real-world propositions*), (2) the existential import of *common propositions* (which may be called *possible-world propositions*), and (3) the existential import of *mental propositions* (which may, in some cases, be called *impossible-world propositions*). These are described in turn in the following subsections.

6.6.1 *Extramental Propositions*

An *extramental proposition* (*qaḍiyya khārijiyya*) makes a predicative judgment on subject-referents that *exist extramentally* in the real world. With

13. The term *qaḍiyya muḥaṣṣila* is often used to refer to any uncomplemented proposition, regardless of whether it is affirmative or negative. *TB*, 252.

extramental propositions, when we say, "Every S is P," we mean, "Every extramental referent of ‹S› is extramentally P." For example, if the proposition, "Every human is rational," is taken as an extramental proposition, it means that all humans who exist extramentally in the real world are rational in the real world. Since humans do exist in the real world, and since all of them are rational, this proposition is true. On the other hand, if the proposition, "Every unicorn has a horn," is taken as an extramental proposition, it means that all unicorns that exist extramentally in the real world have a horn in the real world. Since unicorns do not exist in the real world, this proposition is false.

Because extramental propositions make a predicate judgment about things in the real world, they can also be called *real-world propositions*. The existential import of extramental or real-world propositions pertains to the real world, meaning that their subjects must exist in the real world in order for the propositions to be true. The truth of extramental or real-world predicative judgments hence depends on what is the case in the extramental world. In this respect, they are distinguished from *common propositions* and *mental propositions* whose truth does not depend on what is the case in the extramental world because their subjects either do not exist in the extramental world (if they are mental propositions) or need not exist in the extramental world (if they are common propositions).

6.6.2 *Common Propositions*

A *common proposition* (*qaḍiyya ḥaqīqiyya*) makes a predicative judgment on subject-referents that could, hypothetically, exist in the real world (they are called *common propositions* because most propositions that we use fall into this category). With common propositions, when we say, "Every S is P," we mean, "Everything[14] which, if it existed extramentally, would be S, is such that, if it existed, it would extramentally be P."[15] For example, if the proposition

---

14. The existence of these things must be possible. Otherwise, the proposition would be a mental proposition. Whereas common or possible-world propositions suppose the existence of things whose existence is possible, mental or impossible-world propositions posit the existence of things whose existence is impossible in order to say that their existence is impossible. *TB*, 247.

15. This is not the same as, "If S existed, then it would be P," because it would then be a complex proposition. Since common propositions are simple propositions, they do not comprise any condition. What is intended by the apparent conditional in the explanation of the meaning of common propositions (i.e., "... if it existed, it would be S,...if it existed, it would be P") is the expansion of the subject's referential scope. The goal of the conditional, in other words, is simply to expand the scope of the reference of the subject-concept to include nonexistent-but-possible things. *TB*, 247.

‹Every unicorn has a horn› is taken as a common proposition, it means that everything which, if it existed, would be a unicorn, is such that, if it existed, it would have one horn." Since it is possible for unicorns to exist, and since, if they existed, they would have one horn, this proposition is true as a common proposition, even though it is false as an extramental proposition.

The predicative judgment of common propositions is not restricted to extramentally nonexistent things like unicorns—it applies just as well to extramentally existent things. The predication of the proposition ‹Every human is rational›, when considered as a common proposition, applies both to those humans who exist as well as those who do not exist but could possibly exist. Common propositions are therefore of two kinds: (1) those whose subject-referents do not exist but hypothetically could exist (e.g., unicorns) and (2) those whose subject-referents encompass a group of referents that do exist and another group that do not exist but hypothetically could exist (e.g., humans).

Whereas the predicative judgment of *extramental propositions* applies to subject-referents that actually exist extramentally in the real world, the predicative judgment of *common propositions* applies to subject-referents that could, possibly, exist in the real world. From this perspective, common propositions can also be called *possible-world propositions*.[16] We may say that the existential import of common or possible-world propositions pertains to "possible worlds," meaning that their subjects must exist in some possible world—i.e., in the hypothesis of the mind—in order for the propositions to be true.[17]

6.6.3 *Mental Propositions*

A *mental proposition* (*qaḍiyya dhihniyya*) makes a predicative judgment about subject-referents that only exist in the mind. Since the subject-referents only

16. The distinction between extramental and common propositions cannot be applied to complex propositions because the conjunction between their sub-propositions encompasses all theoretically possible realities and is not restricted to the reality that actually and extramentally is. *TB*, 252. (Note: al-ʿAṭṭār's gloss seems to extend this to both conditional and disjunctive propositions, but it seems that it only applies to conditional propositions.)

17. One of the key differences between classical and modern logic in the Western tradition is the existential import of universally quantified propositions. Since Frege, modern logic denies the existential import of universally quantified propositions, interpreting, "Every S is P," as, "For all x, if x is S, then x is P." From the perspective of the Muslim logicians, the universally quantified proposition, too, must have existential import, but not necessarily real-world existential import. The confusion over existential import, in other words, arises from not making a distinction between the various kinds of existence. See especially 6.6.5 below.

exist in the mind, the existential import of mental propositions pertains to *mental existence*. There are three kinds of mental propositions: (1) those whose subject-referents are mental concepts, (2) those whose predicates are related to existence, and (3) those whose subject-referents are posited instances of impossible concepts.

6.6.3.1 Mental Propositions Whose Subject-Referents Are Mental Concepts

The first category of mental propositions is that of those whose subject-referents are mental concepts. The clearest example of these kinds of mental propositions are questions of logic, which predicate *second-order concepts* (sg. *maʿqūl thānawī*) to mental concepts. For example, the proposition ‹‹Human› is a universal› predicates the second-order concept ‹universal› to the mental concept ‹human›.

The predication within these propositions is, like the predication within all simple propositions, an identity-predication. In other words, the predication affirms that the instances referred to by the subject-concept are characterized by the predicate-concept. But the fact that the subject-referents of mental propositions only exist in the mind complicates their analysis as identity-predications because the subject-concept appears to be referring to itself, which is inadmissible.

For example, the subject-concept in the proposition ‹‹Human› is a universal› is the mental concept ‹human›, and this subject-concept itself refers to the mental concept ‹human›. The logicians resolved this problem by saying that there are two mental concepts involved in the subject: there is on the one hand a mental concept, ‹human›, that *exists in-itself* as a concept in the mind, and there is on the other hand another mental concept of ‹human› that the mind abstracts from this original concept. The existence of the first is *primary*—we can call this the *primary concept*; the existence of the second is *secondary* and depends on the first—we can call this the *secondary concept* (see 5.2).

Using this distinction to analyze the identity-predication of the mental proposition ‹‹Human› is a universal›, we say that the primary concept ‹human› that the secondary concept ‹human› refers to is a universal. The subject-concept, in other words, is the secondary concept ‹human›; the subject-referent is the primary concept ‹human›; and the predicate concept is the second-order concept ‹universal›.

6.6.3.2 Mental Propositions Whose Predicates Are Related to Existence

As discussed previously, the knowledge of *what something is* is logically prior to the knowledge *that it is* (see 4.2.1). Another way of saying this is that existence is predicated of essences.[18] We first conceive of an essence and only afterward investigate whether or not it exists. If we discover that it exists, we predicate existence of it. In the proposition ‹Lions exist›, the concept ‹things-that-possesses-the-essence-of-lions› is mentally characterized as possessing extramental existence. The subject of the predication is not extramentally existing things, but a mental concept.

By the same reasoning, those concepts *of which existence is a corollary*, such as ‹contingency› and ‹extrinsic necessity›, are also only predicated of the concept of something that possesses some essence. For example, in the proposition ‹Zayd is contingent›, the concept ‹Zayd› is mentally characterized as possibly possessing extramental existence. As another example, in the proposition ‹Zayd is extrinsically necessary›, the concept ‹Zayd› is mentally characterized as necessarily possessing extramental existence.

As with the previous category of mental propositions, the fact that the subject-referents exist only in the mind complicates the analysis of these propositions as identity-predications. The resolution of this complication is similar to the resolution of the complication involved in the previous category: the mental concepts ‹lions› and ‹Zayd› have a primary existence that is the subject-referent and a secondary existence that is the subject-concept. The predicate-concepts ‹existence›, ‹contingency›, and ‹extrinsic necessity› are predicated to the primary concept via its reference by the secondary concept.

6.6.3.3 Mental Propositions Whose Subject-Referents Are Posited Instances of Impossible Concepts

The last category is that of mental propositions whose predicates are related to *necessary nonexistence*. The subject-concept of a mental proposition of this category is an impossible concept, i.e., something whose instances cannot exist in the real world, such as a partner in God's divinity. The logicians mention, however, that instances of impossible concepts can be posited in the mind for the sake of predication even if they cannot exist extramentally. These instances exist mentally, but not extramentally nor in-themselves.

18. Essence here refers generally to the result of essential definitions as well as nonessential definitions.

With this category of mental propositions, when we say, "S is P," we use the subject-concept to refer to these mentally posited instances and then predicate ‹necessary nonexistence› to them. For example, when we say, "Partners in God's divinity are necessarily nonexistent," we use the subject-concept ‹partners in God's divinity› to refer to the mentally posited instances of partners in God's divinity, which exist neither extramentally nor in-themselves, and then predicate ‹necessary nonexistence› to these posited instances. The table below gives four examples.

Example Proposition	Analysis
Partners in God's divinity are necessarily nonexistent.	Mentally posited instances of partners in God's divinity are mentally characterized as being necessarily nonexistent extramentally.
The coexistence of opposites is impossible.	Mentally posited instances of the coexistence of opposites are mentally characterized as being impossible.
The absolute unknown is unreceptive to predication.	A mentally posited instance of the absolute unknown is mentally characterized as being unreceptive to predication.

Since the subject-referents of these propositions cannot exist in any possible world, these propositions can also be called *impossible-world propositions*.

6.6.4 *Mental Existential Import*

Instance-propositions have, strictly speaking, two kinds of existential import. The first is the kind that has been described in the sections above. This kind of existential import relates to the truth of propositions or, in other words, to the subject-referent *extra-propositionally* and *in-itself* being characterized by the predicate-concept. This kind of existential import belongs to affirmative instance-propositions, as described above. The second kind of existential import belongs to *negative propositions*. Since negative propositions, too, are instance-propositions, they, too, require an extra-propositional subject-referent that is first *referenced by signification* by the subject-concept and then *referenced by predication* by the predicate-concept. This extra-propositional subject-reference must possess *mental existence* in order for the predicative judgment of the proposition to take place.

The question that this second kind of existential import raises, however, is this: Is there a difference between the mental existential import of affirmative *mental propositions* and the mental existential import of negative propositions? If there is no difference, this would imply that existential import is not limited to affirmative instance-propositions but encompasses all instance-propositions, regardless of whether they are affirmative or negative.

There is, in fact, a difference between the two kinds of existential import.[19] Whereas the first kind refers to the kind of existence that the subject-referent must have in order to *in-itself* or *extra-propositionally* be characterized by the predicate-concept, the second kind refers to the kind of existence that the subject-referent must have in order for that characterization to happen during the mental act of predication, independently of *existence in-itself* or *extra-propositional reality*. Because it is a requirement of the mental act of predication, this second kind of existential import, in fact, encompasses all kinds of propositions, whether negative or even affirmative. This, then, is the difference between the two kinds of existential import: the first is with respect to the truth of the proposition and with respect to the *extra-propositional reality* of the predication; the second is with respect to the *mental act of predication* regardless of whether the predication is true or false.

As a result of this difference, the latter kind of existential import only requires the mental existence of the subject-referent at the moment of predication. The former, however, requires the in-itself existence (whether extramental, mental, or possible-world-related) of the subject-referent in accordance with the requirements of extra-propositional reality. For example, the negative proposition ‹Every unicorn is not brown› only requires the mental existence of unicorns at the moment of predication. The affirmative proposition ‹‹Human› is a universal›, too, requires this mental existence (by virtue of its being a predication) but in addition to that, it requires that ‹human› always be a universal (since that is always true), and this always-in-itself-being-a-universal requires an always-in-itself-existence of ‹human›, since ‹human› can only be a universal if ‹human› exists.

6.6.5 *Existential Import in Affirmative Predicate-Complemented Propositions*

Fakhr al-Dīn al-Rāzī argues that *affirmative predicate-complemented propositions*, such as ‹Lions are non-rational›, do not have existential import,

19. This is the majority position of the logicians. Later logicians note that al-Taftāzānī, however, in his commentary on the *Shamsiyya*, mistakenly holds that there is no difference between *mental propositions* and *negative propositions*, and that only *extramental propositions* and *common propositions* have existential import, to the exclusion of mental propositions. *TB*, 250-51.

effectively making them identical to their corresponding negative propositions—in this case, ‹Every lion is not rational›. His argument is as follows.

1. Take a hypothetical nonexistent thing, A, and an existential predicate, e.g. ‹rational›.
2. The predicate's complement (‹non-rational›) is either (*a*) predicated to A or (*b*) not predicated to A.
3. If (*a*) it is predicated to A, then the proposition does not have existential import.
4. If (*b*) it is not predicated to A, then the uncomplemented predicate (‹rational›) is predicated to it because the subject cannot be uncharacterized by one of a pair of contradictory opposites.
5. But then something existential (i.e., rationality) would be predicated to a nonexistent subject, which is impossible.
6. Therefore, the complement of the existential predicate must be predicated to any nonexistent subject, meaning the proposition does not have existential import.

The response of later logicians is that al-Rāzī's argument is flawed at Premise 4. The consequent of the conditional clause, "if the complement of the existential predicate is not predicated to A," should not be, "then the uncomplemented predicate is predicated to it," but rather, "then the negation of the existential predicate is predicated to it." To illustrate, if it is false that ‹Lions are non-rational›, then this does not imply ‹Lions are rational› but rather ‹Lions are not non-rational›. Moreover, Premise 4 is flawed also because it is only impossible for a subject that exists to be uncharacterized by either member of a pair of contradictory opposites. As for a subject that does not exist, it is indeed possible for it to be uncharacterized by either member of a pair of contradictory opposites.

Despite the flaw in al-Rāzī's argument, many logicians agree with him that affirmative predicate-complemented propositions do not have existential import. Others, like al-Dawānī, argue that they do for the same reason that all other affirmative propositions have existential import. Their existential import, however, is only mental because a complemented predicate exists neither extramentally nor in-itself and therefore can only be predicated to the subject mentally.

6.7 Modality in Simple Propositions

Simple propositions are typically conceived as consisting of three parts—subject, predicate, and copula—but this is not accurate. There is a fourth integral part of every simple proposition: its *modality*. For when we perceive the occurrence or non-occurrence of a predication, we additionally perceive a *quality* (*kayfiyya*) pertaining to that occurrence or non-occurrence. This is the proposition's *modality* or "predication-occurrence-quality" (*kayfiyyat al-nisba*). For example, when we perceive the truth of the proposition ‹Humans are rational›, we also perceive in the occurrence of its predication the quality of *necessity* (*ḍarūra*)—we perceive that it is *metaphysically impossible* (def: 5.3.1) for the proposition to not be true. And when we perceive the truth of the proposition ‹Crows are black›, we perceive that this truth has the predication-occurrence-quality of *possibility* (*imkān*)—we perceive that it is *metaphysically possible* (def: 5.3.1) for the proposition to not be true because, the existence of a white crow would entail no metaphysical impossibility.

A proposition's modality is an integral part of the proposition. Without it, the proposition is not complete, and any reasoning based on the proposition is susceptible to error. This is because in order for a proposition to correspond to reality, not only must its mere *predication* correspond to reality, but so must its *modality*. For example, the truth or falsity of the proposition ‹God exists› is not dependent merely on God's actual existence or nonexistence, but also on what kind of predication-occurrence-quality the proposition is taken to have, and whether that quality corresponds to reality. Until that quality, that modality, is stated as part of the proposition, the proposition is incomplete, and its truth cannot be precisely evaluated.[20] The modality might, for example, be taken as *necessity*, in which case the complete proposition is ‹God *necessarily* exists›.[21] It might also, on the other hand, be taken as *possibility*,

20. In modern logic, modality is not an integral constitutive part of a proposition, which is why it is possible to form logical statements like $P \rightarrow \Diamond P$, i.e., "If P is actually the case (i.e., without any modality), then it is broadly possibly the case (i.e., with the modality of broad possibility)." In the terminology of the Muslim logicians, this would be expressed instead as, "If P is *broadly actually* true, then P is *broadly possibly* true," where both *broad actuality* and *broad possibility* are predication-occurrence-qualities or modalities. Modern logic does not define modality as a predication-occurrence-quality and distinguishes modal from non-modal propositions by examining whether the proposition is a statement about an actual fact (which is a non-modal proposition) or about "how things could, must, or could not have been" (which is also a non-modal proposition). See the introductory paragraphs in Anand Vaidya, "Epistemology of Modality," *Stanford Encyclopedia of Philosophy* (Summer 2015), ed. Edward N. Zalta, http://plato.stanford.edu/archives/sum2015/entries/modality-epistemology.

21. Words expressing propositional modality are italicized to distinguish them from other

in which case the complete proposition is ‹God *strictly possibly* exists›. Now, if the intended modality is necessity, then the proposition is true; but if the intended modality is *strict possibility*, then the proposition is false. This is because, in reality, the predication of existence to God is necessarily true, not merely possibly true.[22]

To take another example, an evaluation of the truth of the proposition ‹Believers will dwell eternally in paradise› requires first that it be completed with a stated modality. According to the Muʿtazilīs, for example, this proposition is true *necessarily*—they formulate the proposition as, "Believers will *necessarily* dwell eternally in paradise." The Sunnis, however, hold the proposition in this formulation to be false because the residence of believers in paradise is a contingent occurrence that can only be realized through God's will and power, which bear equal potential relations to the residence of believers in paradise and to the negation thereof. The correct formulation of the proposition according to the Sunnis is thus, "Believers will *actually* dwell eternally in paradise." *Actuality* here is the proposition's modality.

As an element in the formulation of a proposition, a modifier indicating the modality (e.g., "necessarily" or "possibly") is termed the *stated modality* (*jiha*) of the proposition whether it is expressed in an *expressional proposition* or mentally noted in a *mental proposition*. This *stated modality* either corresponds or does not correspond to the proposition's *real* or *metaphysical modality* (*māddat al-qaḍiyya* or *kayfiyya fī nafs al-amr*). The mind's perception of a proposition's real modality, in other words, reflects extra-propositional reality. The mind is able to perceive through inference, for example, that it is really the case that, necessarily, God exists, and that, actually, believers will dwell in paradise. The logicians express this by saying that God's existence is *necessary in-itself* and that the believers' dwelling in paradise is *actual in-itself*. Another way of saying this is that predication-occurrences possess *existence in-themselves* (see 5.2), not merely *imaginary mental existence*.

The reason that the logicians distinguished *real* or *metaphysical modality* from *stated modality* is that, when determining the conclusion of a pair of

propositional elements.

22. The necessity of God's existing is only known through inference. Inference similarly demonstrates the necessity of God's possession of twenty attributes (or thirteen, depending on how the attributes are didactically counted), including beginningless eternality, power, knowledge, and others. It is the first obligation of human beings to make these inferences, whether informally and semi-intuitively by observing the universe, as with most Muslims, or formally by a careful study of the precise logical arguments, as with students of the science of *kalām*. Al-Bājūrī, *Tuḥfat al-murīd*, 66-83.

propositions that are brought together into a syllogism, what is important to consider is what the propositions *state* and not what quality is possessed by the predication-occurrences that actually exist in-themselves. Only after one determines what the propositions state can one determine whether the propositions are true, i.e., whether they correspond to reality. And only after one determines what the propositions state can one determine whether a given conclusion can be validly derived from those propositions or not (see Chapter 9).

6.7.1 *Real Modality*

A real modality is either one of *necessity* or *non-necessity*, and it is also either one of *continuity* or *non-continuity*. Modalities related to necessity are corollaries of *metaphysical judgments* (def: 5.3.1), and modalities related to continuity are corollaries of *regularity judgments* (def: 5.3.29). These modalities all derive from various kinds of metaphysical necessity and various kinds of metaphysical continuity.[23]

6.7.1.1 Kinds of Real Necessity

A predication is *necessary* if its non-occurrence is *rationally impossible* for its subject-referent.[24] Real necessity is of five kinds.

1. *Eternal necessity* (*ḍarūra azalīyya*) is for a predication to be necessary in both *beginningless eternity* (*azal*) into the "past" and *everlasting eternity* (*abad*) into the "future." This kind of necessity applies to predications of God, Who exists eternally without beginning or end; thus, ‹God *eternally necessarily* exists›, and ‹God *eternally necessarily* possesses knowledge›. The words "past" and "future" in this context are figurative because they are temporal concepts, whereas this kind of eternity is non-temporal; God is not subject to time, which applies only to the created universe. To say that God

23. In modern logic, there are three notions of modal necessity: (1) *logical necessity*, (2) *metaphysical necessity*, and (3) *natural* (or *nomic*) *necessity*. (See Vaidya, "Epistemology of Modality") For the Muslim logicians, *logical necessity* is not a propositional modality, as it is merely the validity of formal logical entailments and tautologies, whereas *propositional modality* is defined as a quality of useful and meaningful predication-occurrences of instance-propositions with different subject-concepts and predicate-concepts. *Metaphysical necessity*, on the other hand, is the same as the modality of necessity described in this subsection. As for *natural necessity*, it is not a necessity at all; instead, it is equivalent to the modality of *continuity*.

24. *Extrinsic necessity* (def: 5.3.3) is not considered here because everything that is extrinsically necessary is intrinsically possible (or contingent). What is pertinent to the logicians is not this extrinsic necessity but rather necessity as an intrinsic, real modality discerned by the mind. *TB*, 269.

is *beginninglessly eternal* is to say that His existence is *logically* unpreceded by nonexistence, and to say that He is *everlastingly eternal* is to say that His existence is *logically* unfollowed by nonexistence.[25]

2. *Extensional necessity* (*ḍarūra dhātiyya*) is for a predication to be necessary through the duration of the existence of the subject-referents—thus it is a necessity in virtue of the *extension* of the subject-concept, namely, the referents to which the subject-concept applies. The characteristic mark of extensional necessity is that the predication's necessity accompanies the existence of the subject-referent; whenever the subject-referent exists, the necessity does, too, and whenever the subject-referent ceases to exist, the necessity ceases with it. An example is the proposition ‹Every human *extensionally necessarily* is rational›. It is necessary for humans to be rational because rationality is essential to humans; thus, this necessity applies even though the subject-referent does not exist in eternity as in the category above. Whenever something does exist as a human, it is necessary for it to be rational. According to the logicians, *eternal necessity* is a special case of *extensional necessity*, such that the latter can be divided into *eternal extensional necessity* and *non-eternal extensional necessity*. Eternal necessity is hence not typically treated as a proper kind of modality in its own right.[26]

3. *Intensional necessity* (*ḍarūra waṣfiyya*) is the necessity of a predication by virtue of the subject-referents being characterized by the subject-concept—that is, the necessity of a predication as a result of the *intension* of the subject-concept. The standard example in traditional manuals of logic is ‹Every writer, *as long as he is a writer, necessarily* moves his fingers›. The concept <writer> refers to human beings, and it is not necessary for human beings to be moving their fingers. But if they are referenced by the concept <writer>, then that means that they are writing, which means that they must be moving their fingers. From this perspective, i.e., as a result of their being

25. Note that eternal necessity cannot be expressed using Kripke's possible-world semantics, which express the necessary truth of a proposition with its being true in all possible worlds. But since God is the creator of all possible things, what it means for something to be necessarily true of Him is not that it is true in all the worlds that He has created but simply that they cannot not be the case in a way that it is unrelated to time.

26. Al-Dawānī objects that non-eternal extensional necessity is not really a necessity because as long as the existence of the subject-referent is merely *metaphysically possible*, any predication to it will also be merely metaphysically possible and hence not necessary. Al-Siyālkūtī responds that al-Dawānī's objection would hold only if the logicians had defined extensional necessity as a necessity that *requires* the existence of its subject-referent. However, they define it instead as a necessity that *accompanies* the existence of the subject-referent. According to this definition, the objection does not hold. *TB*, 258.

characterized by the subject-concept <writer>, it is, in fact, necessary for them to be moving their fingers.[27] This is how most Muslim logicians read intensionally necessary propositions. We will call this the first reading of intensional necessity.

Some logicians understood intensional necessity temporally rather than as a result of being characterized by the subject-concept: they said that ‹Every writer, *as long as he is a writer, necessarily* moves his fingers› means that it is necessary for the writer to be moving his fingers during the times that he is writing, not by virtue of his being a writer. On this reading of intensional necessity, this proposition would be false because it is never necessary for a writer to be writing, and therefore it is never necessary for him to be moving his fingers while he is writing; it is true that he is *actually* moving his fingers while he is writing, but not that he is *necessarily* moving his fingers while he is writing. We will call this the second reading of intensional necessity.

These two readings of intensional necessity are *perspectivally more and less inclusive* than each other.[28] When the predication is necessary as a result of characterization by the subject-concept, but not intrinsically necessary during that time, then it is intensionally necessary on the first reading but not on the second. When it is intrinsically necessary during the time of its characterization by the subject-concept, but not necessary as a result of it, then it is intensionally necessary on the first reading but not on the second. And when it is both necessary as a result of characterization by the subject-concept and intrinsically necessary during that time, then it is intensionally necessary on both readings. The table below summarizes the three possibilities.

27. The "morning-star paradox" is resolved in virtue of, first, the definition of simple propositions as the characterization of the subject-referent (or *extension* of the subject expression) by the predicate-concept (or *intension* of the predicate expression), by means of the latter's reference through the subject-concept, and, second, the subsequent definition of *conceptual* (or *intensional*) *necessity* based on this understanding of propositional predication. The reason why the proposition, "The morning star rises in the morning," which may also be expressed, "The morning star *necessarily* rises in the morning," appears to result in a paradox is that the integral elements of the proposition have not been explicitly stated. When formulated in terms of *intensional necessity*, the proposition appears as follows: "The morning star, *as long as it is characterized as a morning star, necessarily* rises in the morning." The paradox has disappeared. See Melvin Fitting, "Intensional Logic," *Stanford Encyclopedia of Philosophy* (Summer 2015), ed. Edward N. Zalta, http://plato.stanford.edu/archives/sum2015/entries/logic-intensional.

28. Someone might imagine that the second reading is simply more inclusive that the first reading, but this is not the case. *TB*, 265.

	Example Proposition	True in First Reading	True in Second Reading
1	Every writer, *as long as he is a writer, necessarily* moves his fingers.	Yes	No
2	Every writer, *as long as he is a writer, necessarily* is human.	No	Yes
3	Every eclipsed thing, *as long as it is an eclipsed thing, necessarily* darkens.	Yes	Yes

4. *Temporal necessity* (*ḍarūra bi-ḥasab al-waqt*) is the necessity of a predication at some specified or unspecified[29] time, regardless of whether the predication is necessary as long as the subject-referent exists, and regardless of whether the necessity depends on the characterization of the subject-referent by the subject-concept. The abovementioned temporal reading of intensional necessity (the second reading) can be understood as a kind of temporal necessity, since it means that the intrinsic necessity of the predication merely coincides with the time during which the subject-referent is characterized by the subject-referent (rather than meaning that the characterization actually brings about the necessity). For example, in Proposition 2 in the table above, the necessity of writers being human does not arise as a result of the characterization of the subject-referents by ‹writer›; rather, the necessity simply coincides with that characterization. The example can be stated as a proposition that is temporally necessary at a specified time, as in, "Every writer, *when he is a writer, necessarily* is human." This proposition is true because the referents identified by ‹writer› always happen to be human, and the characterization of humans by ‹human› is obviously necessary.

In the above example, the proposition is in fact true regardless of the temporal delimitation; the necessity has nothing to do with the time specified. The Muslim logicians, however, were more concerned with examples in which the necessity really is restricted to some time. The standard examples were variations of Proposition 3 in the table above, e.g., ‹The moon, *when the earth obstructs it, necessarily* is eclipsed›, which exemplifies temporal necessity at a specified time, and ‹The moon, *at some time, necessarily* is eclipsed›, which exemplifies temporal necessity at an unspecified time. These examples were

29. Necessity at an unspecified time is not, strictly speaking, a *real modality* but rather a *stated modality* because, in reality, every temporal event must occur at some specific time; for it to occur at an unspecific time is impossible. *TB*, 267.

based on the natural philosophy of the Avicennan *falāsifa*, who held that natural effects are necessarily caused by the essences of things. For the Sunni *mutakallimūn*, however, the only effective causal necessity is that whatever God wills and creates must come to be. This is an extrinsic necessity, a necessity that is not intrinsic to the essences of created things but rather results from an external agent, namely God. The universe is entirely contingent and created, and all regular occurrences in creation are not effects of natural necessity but are merely *regular associations* (see 5.3.2).

For the Sunni *mutakallimūn*, the closest examples of non-continuous temporal necessity are thus propositions that are extrinsically necessary, like those about events that God has informed us will occur. One might say, for example, "The dead, *at the time when the Archangel Isrāfīl blows the trumpet, necessarily* will be resurrected" (example of temporal necessity at a specified time), and, "The dead, *at some time, necessarily* will be resurrected" (example of temporal necessity at an unspecified time).[30] Strictly speaking, however, these are not examples of temporal necessity because *extrinsically necessary* propositions are, in fact, *intrinsically possible,* and their real modality is thus *possibility*, not *necessity*.

5. *Predicate necessity* (*ḍarūra bi-sharṭ al-maḥmūl*) is the necessity of a predicate's being predicated (or denied) of a subject-referent on condition of the predicate's being predicated (or denied) of the subject-referent, such as the proposition ‹The universe, *as long as it exists, necessarily* exists›. The logicians normally mention this kind of necessity to explain that it is not a propositional modality, or, more precisely, that it does not affect the necessity or non-necessity of a predication. Whereas the necessity of a predication might be affected by the extension (*1* and *2* above), the intension (*3* above), or (according to some) the temporal delimitation (*4* above), it is not affected by the predicate-concept. In other words, qualifying or not qualifying the subject-referent by the predicate-concept does not affect the necessity of a predication. To say that a proposition is necessarily true as long as its subject-referent is characterized by the predicate-concept is not to state the proposition's modality but to state the law of non-contradiction. For example, the proposition just cited, "The universe, *as long as it exists, necessarily* exists," means, "The universe, *as long as it exists, necessarily* cannot not exist." This is simply to say that it is impossible for a thing to exist and not exist at

30. An example of a scriptural basis for these extrinsic necessities is, "The trumpet shall be sounded and then, all of a sudden, they will rush forth to their Lord from their graves" (Qur'ān 36:83).

the same time, which is a statement of the law of non-contradiction, not a propositional modality.

Since the statement, "S, *as long as it is P, necessarily* is P," is a statement of the law of non-contradiction, the only one who would deem it a significant statement is a skeptic who does not hold the law of non-contradiction to be necessary or who wants to create confusion about rational truths through sophistry. In this particular case—the case of the proposition, "The universe, *as long as it exists, necessarily* exists"—the goal of the skeptic might be to give the false impression that it is intrinsically necessary for the universe to exist in order to escape arguments for the existence of God that are based on its contingency. His goal, in other words, is to escape the proposition ‹The universe *strictly possibly* exists› since it entails that the universe needs a necessary being to make it exist.[31]

6.7.1.2 Kinds of Real Continuity

A predication is *continuous* if its non-occurrence is never *actual* for its subject-referent. For a predication to *actually* never be separated from its subject-referent is weaker than for it to *necessarily* never be separated from its

31. *Necessary existence* is for a thing's nonexistence to entail a contradiction, *impossible existence* is for its existence to entail a contradiction, and *contingent existence* and *contingent nonexistence* are for neither its supposed existence nor nonexistence to entail any contradiction. Based on this division, the universe's existence is contingent and hence needs a being that is external to it to make it exist, because all things that exist contingently need something to make them exist and cannot be the cause of their own existence. In order to avoid infinite regress and circular causation (both of which are impossible), this external being must exist necessarily.

The skeptics described above use predicate necessity to escape this argument. If predicate necessity is a real modality (as they claim), then *necessary existence* is for it to be impossible for it to not exist while it exists (therefore everything that does exist does so necessarily), *impossible existence* is for it to be impossible for it to exist while it does not exist (therefore everything that does not exist does so necessarily), *contingent existence* is for it to be possible for it to superadd existence to its nonexistence, and *contingent nonexistence* is for it to be possible for it to superadd nonexistence to its existence.

Apart from the fact that predicate necessity is not a real modality, the skeptical position is not a response to the argument for God's existence from contingency, because the necessity, impossibility, and contingency that the argument refers to are all intrinsic to their subject-referents regardless of their being characterized by any predicate-concept. The necessity, impossibility, and contingency that skeptics refer to, on the other hand, are all extrinsic to the subject-referent and only arise by virtue of the referent being characterized by the predicate-concept. This characterization remains contingent, as a result of which the argument for God's existence still stands. Al-Bājūrī, *Ḥāshiya fī fann al-manṭiq*, 96. The appeal to predicate-necessity continues to be a feature of atheistic arguments even today, such as when they say that the universe's existence is inevitable because it exists.

subject-referent—necessary occurrence implies continuous occurrence but continuous occurrence does not imply necessary occurrence. The fact that a predication's occurrence is continuous merely indicates a *regular association* between the subject and predicate, not a *metaphysically necessary association.* This distinction between necessity and continuity lies at the heart of the study of modality in the tradition of the Muslim logicians. There are three kinds of continuity.

1. *Eternal continuity* (*dawām azalī*) is a predication's continuity in both *beginningless eternity* (*azal*) into the "past" and *everlasting eternity* (*abad*) into the "future." This kind of continuity applies to predications of God, Who exists eternally without beginning or end—e.g., ‹God *always* exists› and ‹God *always* possesses knowledge›. Note that these examples are the same as those cited above in the previous section for *eternal necessity.* The same propositions have been examined from different perspectives, previously as eternally necessary and here as eternally continuous. Although the former perspective implies the latter, they are conceptually distinct. But the distinction is merely conceptual. In terms of real modality, there are no actual instances of eternally continuous predication that are not also eternally necessary, for eternally continuous predications are only true of God.[32] For this reason, as with eternal necessity, the words "past" and "future" have been placed in quotation marks, accounting for the fact that God is not subject to time.

2. *Extensional continuity* (*dawām dhātī*) is the continuity of a predication throughout the existence of its subject-referents. The characteristic mark of this kind of continuity is that it accompanies the existence of the subject-referent; whenever the subject-referent exists, the predication is continuous, and whenever the subject-referent disappears, the continuous predication disappears with it. An example is the proposition ‹Every technician *always* is at least one foot tall›. Technicians are continuously at least one foot tall throughout their existence.

This example illustrates that, whereas an eternally continuous predication must also be eternally necessary, an extensionally continuous predication does not have to be extensionally necessary. Technicians are extensionally continuously at least one foot tall, but it is not necessary that they be so—for them to be less than one foot tall does not entail any *metaphysical impossibility.* In this manner, all propositions about laws of nature are extensionally continuous but not extensionally necessary, e.g., ‹Fire *always* burns› or ‹Two

32. This is proven in the science of *kalām* through arguments for the beginning of the universe and for the impossibility of an infinite regress of created events.

bodies *always* attract each other with a force that is proportional to their masses and inversely proportional to the square of the distance between them›.[33] But although an extensionally continuous proposition does not have to be extensionally necessary, all extensionally necessary propositions are, in fact, also extensionally continuous and can be considered from their modal aspect of continuity just as they are considered from their modal aspect of necessity. The example cited above in the previous section for extensional necessity can thus be recast as an example of extensional continuity: ‹Every human *always* is rational›. Finally, just as *eternal necessity* is a special case of *extensional necessity*, *eternal continuity* is also a special case of *extensional continuity*, which the logicians traditionally divide into *eternal extensional continuity* and *non-eternal extensional continuity*. Eternal continuity is hence not typically treated as a proper kind of modality in its own right.

3. *Intensional continuity* (*dawām waṣfī*) is the continuity of a predication on condition of the subject-referent being characterized by the subject-concept. An example is the proposition ‹Every believer, *as long as he is a believer*, *always* is better in the sight of God than a disbeliever›.[34] This predicational continuity is dependent on the characterization of the human beings by the subject-concept ‹believer›; thus, the intension of ‹believer› brings about the continuity. If the same referents were referred to by a different concept, like ‹human being›, the predication would not be continuous. Intensionally continuous propositions do not have to be intensionally necessary—it is not *necessary* for believers to be better in the sight of God than disbelievers, as this superiority is a divine favor rather than a human right.[35] But although an intensionally continuous proposition does not have to be intensionally necessary, all intensionally necessary propositions are, in fact, also intensionally continuous and can be considered from their modal aspect of continuity. The standard example of intensional necessity cited above in the previous section

33. The authors of glosses on the *Tahdhīb* provide examples of physical laws from medieval Aristotelian natural philosophy, e.g., ‹Every celestial body *extensionally continuously* moves›. *TB*, 269. The fact that they categorize such laws as continuous reflects an adjustment on the part of the Muslim logicians that is based on their position that there is a distinction between regular and metaphysically necessary association. According to this distinction, the modality of propositions expressing physical laws is demoted from one of necessity to one of continuity.

34. Logicians derive this proposition from the verse, "A male slave is better than a male polytheist, even if you find him attractive [i.e., for marrying your womenfolk to]" (Qur'ān 2:221). *TB*, 271.

35. This is the position of the Sunni *mutakallimūn*. The Mu'tazilīs, on the other hand, generally held that this predication is in fact necessary, and that the superiority is indeed a right that human beings have over God.

can thus be recast as an example of intensional continuity: ‹Every writer, *as long as he is a writer*, *always* moves his fingers›.

The three kinds of continuity parallel the first three kinds of necessity: eternal continuity parallels eternal necessity, extensional continuity parallels extensional necessity, and intensional continuity parallels intensional necessity. *Temporal necessity*, however, has no parallel in continuity, because for a proposition to be continuous at a particular time (whether a specified time or an unspecified time) makes no sense—if it is continuous, it must be continuous at all times. *Predicate necessity* also has no parallel, because, as explained above, it is not really a necessity at all, and is only examined by the logicians in response to skeptical sophistry.

6.7.2 *Stated Modality*

In the tradition of the Muslim logicians, there are four kinds of stated modalities which may be verbally expressed or mentally noted in a proposition:

1. *Necessity* (*ḍarūra*), in which a predication-occurrence is stated to be metaphysically necessarily, e.g., ‹Humans *necessarily* are rational›.
2. *Continuity* (*dawām*), in which a predication-occurrence is stated to be always the case whether necessarily or non-necessarily, e.g., ‹Fire *always* is hot›.
3. *Actuality* (*iṭlāq*), in which a predication-occurrence is stated to be actually the case whether continuously or non-continuously, and whether necessarily or non-necessarily, e.g., ‹Humans *actually* die›.
4. *Possibility* (*imkān*), in which a predication-occurrence is stated to be possibly the case whether actually or potentially, whether continuously or non-continuously, and whether necessarily or non-necessarily.

These four stated modalities have been listed in increasing order of inclusiveness—the stated modality of necessity is *unconditionally less inclusive* than the stated modality of continuity, which is *unconditionally less inclusive* than the stated modality of actuality, which is in turn *unconditionally less inclusive* than the stated modality of possibility. In other words, a predication-occurrence that is stated to be *possible* might in reality be actual, continuous, necessary, or merely possible; one that is stated to be *actual* might in reality be continuous, necessary, or merely actual (but not merely possible); one that is stated to be *continuous* might in reality be necessary or merely continuous (but not merely possible or merely actual); and one that is stated to be *necessary* can in reality be neither merely continuous, merely actual, nor merely possible. To put it another way, a predication-occurrence that is in reality *necessary* is also continuous, actual, and possible; one that is in reality *continuous* is also actual and possible but may or may not be necessary; one that is in reality *actual* is also possible but may or may not be continuous or necessary; and one that is in reality *possible* may or may not be actual, continuous, or necessary. From this perspective, necessity is the strongest modality and possibility is the weakest.

Each of these four kinds of modalities has several sub-kinds. Together, these are all termed the *basic modalities* (*kayfiyyāt basīṭa* or *basāʾiṭ*). These basic modalities can be combined to form various kinds of *composite modalities* (*kayfiyyāt murakkaba* or *murakkabāt*). Basic and composite modalities are described below in turn.

6.7.2.1 Basic Stated Modalities

There are eight kinds of basic stated modalities: four modalities of *necessity*, two modalities of *continuity*, one modality of *actuality*, and one modality of *possibility*. Examples of propositions that possess these modalities are summarized in the following table and described below in turn.

	Kind of Modal Proposition	**Affirmative Example**	**Negative Example**
1	Extensionally Necessary Proposition *ḍarūriyya muṭlaqa*	Every human *necessarily* is an animal.	Every human *necessarily* is not a rock.
2	Broadly Intensionally Necessary Proposition *mashrūṭa ʿāmma*	Every writer, *as long as he is a writer, necessarily* moves his fingers.	Every writer, *as long as he is a writer, necessarily* does not keep his fingers still.
3	Broadly Specific-Time Necessary Proposition *waqtiyya muṭlaqa*	Every moon, *when obstructed by the earth, necessarily* is eclipsed.	Every moon, *when illumined by the sun, necessarily* is not eclipsed.

	Kind of Modal Proposition	Affirmative Example	Negative Example
4	Broadly Sometime Necessary Proposition *muntashira muṭlaqa*	Every human *sometime necessarily* breathes.	Every human *sometime necessarily* does not breathe.
5	Extensionally Continuous Proposition *dā'ima muṭlaqa*	Every human *always* is an animal.	Every human *always* is not a rock.
6	Broadly Intensionally Continuous Proposition *'urfiyya 'āmma*	Every writer, *as long as he is a writer, always* moves his fingers.	Every writer, *as long as he is a writer, always* does not keep his fingers still.
7	Broadly Actual Proposition *muṭlaqa 'āmma*	Every human *broadly actually* breathes.	Every human *broadly actually* does not breathe.
8	Broadly Possible Proposition *mumkina 'āmma*	Every fire *broadly possibly* is hot.	Every hot thing *broadly possibly* is not cold.

Let us now discuss each of these modalities in turn.

Four Modalities of Necessity

1. An *extensionally necessary proposition* (*ḍarūriyya muṭlaqa*)[36] possesses either *eternal necessity* or *extensional necessity*. This is the strongest type of necessary modality and is indicated simply by the expression "necessarily." Two examples of propositions with this modality are ‹God *necessarily* exists› (that is, *eternally extensionally necessarily*) and ‹Every human *necessarily* is an animal› (that is, *non-eternally extensionally necessarily*). This is the most important kind of modality for Muslim theologians because it is the modality possessed by most tenets of religious belief—namely, those propositions

36. Literally, an "unconditionally necessary" proposition. It is called "unconditionally" necessary because it is the only kind of necessary proposition whose necessity is unconditioned. *TB*, 258. For example, the necessity of intensionally necessary propositions is conditioned by the characterization of the subject-referent by the subject-concept, and the necessity of specific-time necessary propositions is conditioned by a specified time.

affirming God's perfections—and the first obligation of human beings is to perceive the truth of these tenets with this modality.[37]

2. A *broadly intensionally necessary proposition* (*mashrūṭa ʿāmma*)[38] broadly possesses *intensional necessity*. This is a weaker modality than extensional necessity because extensional necessity unconditionally accompanies the existence of the subject-referent, whereas this necessity only accompanies its existence on condition of its characterization by the subject-concept. An example of a proposition with this modality is ‹Every writer, *as long as he is a writer, necessarily* moves his fingers›. Whereas extensional necessity is indicated simply by the word "necessarily," this kind of necessity is indicated by "necessarily" qualified with a clause of the form, "as long as X is characterized by the subject-concept."

3. A *broadly specific-time necessary proposition* (*waqtiyya muṭlaqa*)[39] broadly possesses *temporal necessity at a specific time*. An example is the proposition ‹Every writer, *when he is a writer, necessarily* is a human›. The difference between this and the previous kind of necessity is that, with the previous kind, the subject-referent's characterization by the subject-concept is the *cause* of the necessity, whereas here it merely delimits the *time* of the necessity.

4. A *broadly sometime necessary proposition* (*muntashira muṭlaqa*)[40] broadly possesses *temporal necessity at an unspecified time*. An example is the proposition ‹Every human *sometime necessarily* breathes›.

Extensional necessity (*1* above) is *unconditionally less inclusive* than *specific-time necessity* and *sometime necessity* (*3* and *4* above), meaning that every extensionally necessary proposition is also specific-time and sometime necessary, but not vice-versa. For example, the extensionally necessary proposition ‹Every human *necessarily* is an animal›, is also true as a specific-time

37. See Note 95 above.

38. Literally, a "general conditioned" proposition. It is called "conditioned" because its necessity is conditioned by the subject-referent's characterization by the subject-concept, and it is called "general" to distinguish it from *strictly intensionally necessary* propositions, which are conditioned by an additional modality and are hence more exclusive. *TB*, 262.

39. Literally, an "unconditioned temporal" proposition. It is called "temporal" because it includes a reference to a specified time, and it is called "unconditioned" to distinguish it from *strictly specific-time necessary* propositions, which are conditioned by an additional modality. *TB*, 267.

40. Literally, an "unconditioned distributed" proposition. It is called "distributed" because the time that it references could be any time and is hence "distributed" across all times, and it is called "unconditioned" to distinguish it from *strictly sometime necessary* propositions, which are conditioned by an additional modality. *TB*, 267.

necessary proposition for any given time and as a sometime necessary proposition. Meanwhile, the proposition ‹Every writer *necessarily* moves his fingers›, where the necessity is qualified by either a specified time or an unspecified time, is not true as an extensionally necessary proposition.

Intensional necessity (*2* above) is *perspectivally more and less inclusive* than specific-time necessity and sometime necessity (*3* and *4* above), meaning that, although the two kinds of modality overlap in some propositions, there are also some propositions that possess only one and not the other. An example of an intensionally necessary proposition that is also specific-time and sometime necessary is ‹Every writer *necessarily* moves his fingers›. An example of a specific-time and sometime necessary proposition that is not intensionally necessary is ‹Every writer *necessarily* is human›. And an example of an intensionally necessary proposition that is not specific-time nor sometime necessary is ‹Every eclipsed thing *necessarily* is dark›.

These relationships between intensional necessity and specific-time and sometime necessity were discussed above in 6.7.1.1. As explained previously, there is no real temporal necessity. This section, however, is about *stated modalities*, not *real modalities*, and the fact that there is no real temporal necessity does not make it invalid to state a predication to be temporally necessary. Temporal necessity is thus a valid stated modality.

Two Modalities of Continuity

5. An *extensionally continuous proposition* (*dāʾima muṭlaqa*)[41] possesses either *eternal continuity* or *extensional continuity*. This is the strongest type of continuous modality and is indicated simply by the expression "always." Two examples of propositions with this modality are ‹God *always* exists› (that is, *eternally extensionally continuously*) and ‹Every human *always* is an animal› (that is, *non-eternally extensionally continuously*). The non-modal parts of these example propositions are the same as the non-modal parts of the examples cited above for extensionally necessary propositions. In fact, every extensionally necessary predication is also extensionally continuous because the rational impossibility of a predication not occurring for its subject-referent (i.e., its *extensional necessity*) entails the continuous occurrence of that predication for its subject-referent (i.e., its *extensional continuity*).

41. Literally, an "unconditionally continuous" proposition. It is called "unconditionally" continuous because it is the only kind of continuous proposition whose continuity is unconditioned. *TB*, 268. By contrast, for example, the necessity of intensionally continuous propositions is conditioned by the subject-referent's characterization by the subject-concept.

6. A *broadly intensionally continuous proposition* (*ʿurfiyya ʿāmma*)[42] broadly possesses *intensional continuity*. This kind of continuity is weaker than extensional continuity because extensional continuity unconditionally accompanies the existence of the subject-referent, whereas this continuity only accompanies its existence on condition of its characterization by the subject-concept. An example of a proposition with this modality is ‹Every writer, *as long as he is a writer, always* moves his fingers›. Whereas extensional continuity is indicated simply by the word "always," this kind of necessity is indicated by the word "always" qualified by a clause of the form "as long as X is characterized by the subject-concept." Once again, the non-modal parts of these example propositions are the same as the non-modal parts of the examples cited above for *intensionally necessary propositions*. In fact, every intensionally necessary proposition is also intensionally continuous, because the rational impossibility of a predication not occurring for its subject-referent, when it is characterized by the subject-concept (i.e., the predication's *intensional necessity*), entails the continuous occurrence of that predication for its subject-referent when it is characterized by the subject-concept (i.e., the predication's *intensional continuity*).

One Modality of Actuality

Actuality is the modal counterpart of *continuity*; whereas a predication's *continuity* is for it to *always* occur for its subject-referent, its *actuality* is merely for it to occur at some time.

42. Literally, a "general conventionally understood" proposition. It is called "conventionally understood" because intensional continuity is conventionally understood in such propositions when it is not explicitly stated. This is reflected in an interpretive principle of legal theory (*uṣūl al-fiqh*) according to which the predication of the predicate-concept to the subject-referent via the subject-concept conventionally indicates that the subject-concept is the underlying reason (*ʿilla*) for the predication, which in turn indicates that as long as the subject-referent is characterized by the subject-concept, it will also be characterized by the predicate-concept—in other words, that it is intensionally continuous (the rule as stated in Arabic is: *taʿlīq al-ḥukm bi-l-mushtaqq yushʿiru bi-ʿilliyyat mā minhu al-ishtiqāq*). *TB*, 271. For example, the proposition, "Everyone who is sleeping will not hear you when you speak," conventionally indicates that the reason why the subject-referent will not hear you when you speak is that he is sleeping (the subject-concept), which in turn indicates that as long as he is characterized by being asleep, he will not hear you when you speak. The proposition has been understood, in other words, as an *intensionally continuous proposition*, namely, ‹Every sleeping person, *as a sleeping person, always* will not hear you when you speak›. This kind of modal proposition is called "general" to distinguish it from *strictly intensionally continuous* propositions, which are conditioned by an additional modality and are hence more exclusive.

7. A *broadly actual proposition* (*muṭlaqa ʿāmma*)[43] broadly possesses non-continuity, meaning that the predication occurs for the subject-referent regardless of whether it is continuous (or non-continuous) or necessary (or non-necessary). An example of a proposition with this modality is ‹Every human *broadly actually* breathes›. Here, the predication of breathing to humans is neither necessary nor continuous but merely actual. This is an example of a proposition whose real modality is actuality. But to state that a predication is *broadly actual* is not to state that it is *strictly actual*. Broad actuality includes strict actuality as well as continuity and necessity. As a result, all of the examples cited thus far in this section could be stated to possess this modality—e.g., ‹Every human *broadly actually* is rational› or ‹Every writer *broadly actually* moves his fingers›.

Quṭb al-Dīn al-Rāzī (d. 766/1365) objects that actuality is not a propositional modality because a modality is an attribute or quality of a predication-occurrence whereas actuality is the predication-occurrence itself, not its quality. To state that a predication-occurrence is *necessary* or *continuous* is indeed to state a modality because one thereby describes a quality of the predication-occurrence, whereas to state that it is *actual* is merely to assert that a predication obtains, not to describe a quality it possesses. Later logicians, however, respond that actuality is indeed a quality of a predication-occurrence. To state that a predication-occurrence is actual is to state that it possesses the quality of *broadly* occurring, which is more general than occurring necessarily or continuously; this is a description of a quality of a predication-occurrence, not merely a statement that the predication has occurred.

One Modality of Possibility

Just as *actuality* is the modal counterpart of *continuity*, *possibility* is the modal counterpart of *necessity*.

8. A *broadly possible proposition* (*mumkina ʿāmma*)[44] broadly possesses non-necessity, meaning that its negation is not necessary. An example of a

43. Literally, an "general unconditioned" proposition. It is called "unconditioned" not because it is unconditioned, but because when a proposition is stated without being conditioned by any modality, this is the default modality that is understood from it (at the very least, in other words, a proposition's predication must have occurred in order to be true). It is called "general" to distinguish it from *non-necessary actual* and *non-continuous actual* propositions, which are conditioned by an additional modality and are hence more exclusive. *TB*, 272-74.

44. Literally, a "general possible" proposition. It is called "possible" because it comprises the modality of possibility, and it is called "general" to distinguish it from *strictly possible* propositions, which are conditioned by an additional modality and are hence more exclusive. *TB*, 275.

proposition with this modality is ‹Every fire *broadly possibly* is cold›. This is a true statement because for fire to not be cold is not necessary. That fire be hot and that fire be cold are both *metaphysically possible*. Note that the example proposition is true even though the predication is not *actual*. To state that a proposition is *broadly possible*, in other words, is to state that it could possibly be the case (or that it is not *rationally impossible* for it to be the case), even if it is not actually the case. It is thus a more general modality than actuality, continuity, or necessity, and all of the examples cited thus far in this section could be stated to possess this modality—e.g., ‹Every human *broadly possibly* is rational› and ‹Every human *broadly possibly* breathes›.

Quṭb al-Dīn al-Rāzī objects that possibility is not a propositional modality because a proposition that merely states what is possibly the case does not state that something is the case (a predication); it merely supposes that something might be the case. But in order for a statement to be a proposition, it must comprise a predication. Because *broadly possible propositions* do not necessarily state what is the case, they do not comprise any predication at all and are hence not propositions.

Some later logicians respond that for something to *be possibly the case* is in fact a kind of predication, while others agree with al-Rāzī that the existence of a predication requires actuality. At the crux of the dispute is a more fundamental disagreement about whether there is a difference between something *being the case possibly* and something *possibly being the case*. Logicians who hold that there is no difference consequently hold that a broadly possible proposition states what is merely *possibly the case* and hence does not comprise a predication; because nothing is the case, the proposition is not a proposition at all. Those who hold that there is a difference, on the other hand, hold that a broadly possible proposition is the case (but only possibly), which is a kind of predication; because something is the case, the proposition is indeed a proposition. According to the former position, possibility is only mentioned as a modality because it is the negation of necessity, which for its part is a proper propositional modality; according to the latter position, possibility is a proper propositional modality in its own right.

6.7.2.2 Composite Stated Modalities

We have seen that *basic stated modalities* (*basāʾiṭ*) merely affirm or negate one of the four basic predication-occurrence qualities—necessity, continuity, actuality, or possibility. *Composite stated modalities* (*murakkabāt*), on the other hand, condition this basic affirmation or negation with one of two additional modal negations—either the *negation of extensional necessity* (*lā-ḍarūra*) or the *negation of extensional continuity* (*lā-dawām*). Thus, new kinds of propositions may be derived from the eight basic modal propositions, as illustrated in the table below.

	Original Basic Modal Proposition	**Modal Addition**	**New Composite Modal Proposition**
1	Extensionally Necessary Proposition *ḍarūriyya muṭlaqa*		
2	Broadly Intensionally Necessary Proposition *mashrūṭa ʿāmma*	Not Extensionally Continuous	Strictly Intensionally Necessary Proposition *mashrūṭa khāṣṣa*
3	Broadly Specific-Time Necessary Proposition *waqtiyya muṭlaqa*	Not Extensionally Continuous	Strictly Specific-Time Necessary Proposition *waqtiyya*
4	Broadly Sometime Necessary Proposition *muntashira muṭlaqa*	Not Extensionally Continuous	Strictly Sometime Necessary Proposition *muntashira*
5	Extensionally Continuous Proposition *dāʾima muṭlaqa*		
6	Broadly Intensionally Continuous Proposition *ʿurfiyya ʿāmma*	Not Extensionally Continuous	Strictly Intensionally Continuous Proposition *ʿurfiyya khāṣṣa*
7	Broadly Actual Proposition *muṭlaqa ʿāmma*	Not Extensionally Necessary	Non-Necessary Actual Proposition *wujūdiyya lā-ḍarūriyya*
		Not Extensionally Continuous	Non-Continuous Actual Proposition *wujūdiyya lā-dāʾima*
8	Broadly Possible Proposition *mumkina ʿāmma*	Not Extensionally Necessary	Strictly Possible Proposition *mumkina khāṣṣa*

The value of this modal composition is to reduce the scope of any of the six *broad* basic modalities. For example, *broad actuality* includes those predication-occurrences that are *strictly actual* as well as those that are necessary or continuous. This broad or inclusive scope of *broadly actual propositions* can be reduced by either excluding (i.e., negating) *necessity* (resulting in a *non-necessary actual proposition*) or by excluding (i.e., negating) *continuity* (resulting in a *non-continuous actual proposition*). As illustrated in the table above, this kind of modal composition is conventionally applied to all of the basic modal propositions described in the previous section except for *extensionally necessary propositions* and *extensionally continuous propositions*. To apply it to extensionally necessary propositions is not possible because that would be a logical contradiction. The negation of necessity could, however, be applied to extensionally continuous propositions, but it is not the convention of the logicians to study non-necessary continuous propositions.

The composition of *non-necessity* or *non-continuity* with the remaining basic modal propositions leads to the seven composite modal propositions listed in the table above. This is not an exhaustive list of all possible composite modal propositions but merely a list of those composite modal propositions that are conventionally studied by the Muslim logicians. These seven composite modal propositions are summarized in the following table and then explained in further detail below. Other possible composite modal propositions are described in the footnotes of these descriptions below.

	Kind of Modal Proposition	**Example of Affirmative Proposition**	**Example of Negative Proposition**
1	Strictly Intensionally Necessary Proposition *mashrūṭa khāṣṣa*	Every writer, *strictly as long as he is a writer, necessarily* moves his fingers.	Every writer, *strictly as long as he is a writer, necessarily* does not keep his fingers still.
2	Strictly Specific-Time Necessary Proposition *waqtiyya*	Every moon, *strictly when obstructed by the earth, necessarily* is eclipsed.[45]	Every moon, *strictly when illumined by the sun, necessarily* is not eclipsed.
3	Strictly Sometime Necessary Proposition *muntashira*	Every human, *strictly sometime, necessarily* draws in a breath.	Every human, *strictly sometime, necessarily* does not draw in a breath.

45. As discussed previously, examples like the ones for this row and the next are not true according to the Sunni theologians

	Kind of Modal Proposition	Example of Affirmative Proposition	Example of Negative Proposition
4	Strictly Intensionally Continuous Proposition *ʿurfiyya khāṣṣa*	Every writer, *strictly as long as he is a writer, always* moves his fingers.	Every writer, strictly as long as he is a *writer, always* does not keep his fingers still.
5	Non-Necessary Actual Proposition *wujūdiyya lā-ḍarūriyya*	Every human *actually but not necessarily* draws in a breath.	Every human *actually but not necessarily* does not draw in a breath.
6	Non-Continuous Actual Proposition *wujūdiyya lā-dāʾima*	Every human *actually but not always* draws in a breath.	Every human *actually but not always* does not draw in a breath.
7	Strictly Possible Proposition *mumkina khāṣṣa*	Every fire *strictly possibly* is hot.	Every fire *strictly possibly* is not hot.

Every composite modal proposition can be broken down into two basic modal propositions: (1) the original basic modal proposition and (2) either a *broadly possible proposition*, if the additional modality is the negation of *extensional necessity*,[46] or a *broadly actual proposition*, if the additional modality is the negation of *extensional continuity*.[47] The latter proposition will have the same subject, predication, and quantification as the original proposition but will differ in affirmation or negation. Each type of composite modal proposition is analyzed below with examples.

---

46. If the *affirmation* of a predication is not necessary, then it means that there is at least one predication-instance whose negation is possible regardless of whether it is possible continuously or non-continuously, and this is the meaning of a *negative broadly possible proposition*. On the other hand, if the *negation* of a predication is not necessary, then it means that there is at least one predication-instance whose affirmation is possible regardless of whether it is possible continuously or non-continuously, and this is the meaning of an *affirmative broadly possible proposition*. *TB*, 281.

47. If the *affirmation* of a predication is not continuous, then it means that there is at least one predication-instance that does not occur regardless of whether it does not occur necessarily or non-necessarily, and this is the meaning of a *negative broadly actual proposition*. On the other hand, if the *negation* of a predication is not continuous, then it means that there is at least one predication-instance that does occur regardless of whether it occurs necessarily or non-necessarily, and this is the meaning of an *affirmative broadly actual proposition*. *TB*, 278.

Composite Modalities of Necessity

1. A *strictly intensionally necessary proposition* (*mashrūṭa khāṣṣa*) is a broadly intensionally necessary proposition with the additional stated modality of non-extensional-continuity. If it is *affirmative*, it is composed of (*i*) an affirmative *broadly intensionally necessary proposition*, which represents the original basic modal proposition, and (*ii*) a negative *broadly actual proposition*, which represents the additional stated modality. If it is *negative*, it is composed of (*i*) the original negative *broadly intensionally necessary proposition* and (*ii*) an additional affirmative *broadly actual proposition.*

<table>
<tr><td colspan="2">COMPOSITE AFFIRMATIVE
Every writer, strictly as long as he is a writer, always moves his fingers.</td></tr>
<tr><td>ORIGINAL AFFIRMATIVE
Every writer, as long as he is a writer, always moves his fingers.</td><td>ADDITIONAL NEGATIVE
Every writer broadly actually does not move his fingers.[48]</td></tr>
<tr><td colspan="2">COMPOSITE NEGATIVE
Every writer, strictly as long as he is a writer, always does not keep his fingers still.</td></tr>
<tr><td>ORIGINAL NEGATIVE
Every writer, as long as he is a writer, always does not keep his fingers still.</td><td>ADDITIONAL AFFIRMATIVE
Every writer broadly actually keeps his fingers still.</td></tr>
</table>

2. A *strictly specific-time necessary proposition* (*waqtiyya*) is a broadly specific-time necessary proposition with the additional stated modality of non-extensional-continuity. If *affirmative*, it is composed of (*i*) the original affirmative *broadly specific-time necessary proposition* and (*ii*) an additional negative *broadly actual proposition.* If *negative*, it is composed of (*i*) the original negative *broadly specific-time necessary proposition* and (*ii*) an additional affirmative *broadly actual proposition.*

48. This proposition asserts that, for every referent of subject-concept ‹writer›, it is broadly actually true that that referent at some time does not move his fingers. The proposition does not assert that there is never at any time a writer that moves his fingers.

<table>
<tr><td colspan="2">COMPOSITE AFFIRMATIVE
Every moon, strictly when obstructed by the earth, necessarily is eclipsed</td></tr>
<tr><td>ORIGINAL AFFIRMATIVE
Every moon, when obstructed by the earth, necessarily is eclipsed.</td><td>ADDITIONAL NEGATIVE
Every moon broadly actually is not eclipsed.</td></tr>
<tr><td colspan="2">COMPOSITE NEGATIVE
Every moon, strictly when illumined by the sun, necessarily is not eclipsed.</td></tr>
<tr><td>ORIGINAL NEGATIVE
Every moon, when illumined by the sun, necessarily is not eclipsed.</td><td>ADDITIONAL AFFIRMATIVE
Every moon broadly actually is eclipsed.</td></tr>
</table>

3. A *strictly sometime necessary proposition* (*muntashira*) is a broadly sometime necessary proposition with the additional stated modality of non-extensional continuity. If *affirmative*, it is composed of (*i*) the original affirmative *broadly sometime necessary proposition* and (*ii*) an additional negative *broadly actual proposition*. If *negative*, it is composed of (*i*) the original negative *broadly sometime necessary proposition* and (*ii*) an additional affirmative *broadly actual proposition*.

<table>
<tr><td colspan="2">COMPOSITE AFFIRMATIVE
Every human, strictly sometime, necessarily breathes.</td></tr>
<tr><td>ORIGINAL AFFIRMATIVE
Every human sometime necessarily breathes.</td><td>ADDITIONAL NEGATIVE
Every human broadly actually does not breathe.</td></tr>
<tr><td colspan="2">COMPOSITE NEGATIVE
Every human, strictly sometime, necessarily does not breathe.</td></tr>
<tr><td>ORIGINAL NEGATIVE
Every human sometime necessarily does not breathe.</td><td>ADDITIONAL AFFIRMATIVE
Every human broadly actually breathes.</td></tr>
</table>

Composite Modalities of Actuality

4. A *strictly intensionally continuous proposition* (*ʿurfiyya khāṣṣa*) is a broadly intensionally continuous proposition with the additional stated modality of non-extensional-continuity. If *affirmative*, it is composed of (*i*) the original affirmative *broadly intensionally continuous proposition* and (*ii*) an additional negative *broadly actual proposition*. If *negative*, it is composed of (*i*) the

original negative *broadly intensionally continuous proposition* and (*ii*) an additional affirmative *broadly actual proposition.*

<table>
<tr><td colspan="2">COMPOSITE AFFIRMATIVE
Every writer, strictly as long as he is a writer, always moves his fingers.</td></tr>
<tr><td>ORIGINAL AFFIRMATIVE
Every writer, as long as he is a writer, always moves his fingers.</td><td>ADDITIONAL NEGATIVE
Every writer broadly actually does not move his fingers.</td></tr>
<tr><td colspan="2">COMPOSITE NEGATIVE
Every writer, strictly as long as he is a writer, always does not keep his fingers still.</td></tr>
<tr><td>ORIGINAL NEGATIVE
Every writer, as long as he is a writer, always does not keep his fingers still.</td><td>ADDITIONAL AFFIRMATIVE
Every writer broadly actually keeps his fingers still.</td></tr>
</table>

Composite Modalities of Actuality

5. A *non-necessary actual proposition* (*wujūdiyya lā-ḍarūriyya*) is a broadly actual proposition with the additional stated modality of non-extensional-necessity. If *affirmative,* it is composed of (*i*) the original affirmative *broadly actual proposition* and (*ii*) an additional negative *broadly possible proposition.* If *negative,* it is composed of (*i*) the original negative *broadly actual proposition* and (*ii*) an additional affirmative *broadly possible proposition.*

<table>
<tr><td colspan="2">COMPOSITE AFFIRMATIVE
Every human, strictly sometime, necessarily breathes.</td></tr>
<tr><td>ORIGINAL AFFIRMATIVE
Every human broadly actually breathes.</td><td>ADDITIONAL NEGATIVE
Every human broadly possibly does not breathe.</td></tr>
<tr><td colspan="2">COMPOSITE NEGATIVE
Every human, actually but not necessarily does not breathe.</td></tr>
<tr><td>ORIGINAL NEGATIVE
Every human broadly actually does not breathe.</td><td>ADDITIONAL AFFIRMATIVE
Every human broadly possibly breathes.</td></tr>
</table>

6. A *non-continuous actual proposition* (*wujūdiyya lā-dā'ima*) is a broadly actual proposition with the additional stated modality of non-extensional-continuity. If *affirmative,* it is composed of (*i*) the original affirmative *broadly*

actual proposition and (*ii*) an additional negative *broadly actual proposition*. If *negative*, it is composed of (*i*) the original negative *broadly actual proposition* and (*ii*) an additional affirmative *broadly actual proposition*.

COMPOSITE AFFIRMATIVE Every human, *actually but not always* breathes.	
ORIGINAL AFFIRMATIVE Every human *broadly actually* breathes.	ADDITIONAL NEGATIVE Every human *broadly actually* does not breathe.
COMPOSITE NEGATIVE Every human, *actually but not always* does not breathe.	
ORIGINAL NEGATIVE Every human *broadly actually* does not breathe.	ADDITIONAL AFFIRMATIVE Every human *broadly actually* breathes.

Composite Modality of Possiblity

7. A *strictly possible proposition* (*mumkina khāṣṣa*) is a broadly possible proposition with the additional stated modality of non-extensional-necessity. If *affirmative*, it is composed of (*i*) the original affirmative *broadly possible proposition* and (*ii*) an additional negative *broadly possible proposition*. If *negative*, it is composed of (*i*) the original negative *broadly possible proposition* and (*ii*) an additional affirmative *broadly possible proposition*.

COMPOSITE AFFIRMATIVE Every fire *strictly possibly* is hot.	
ORIGINAL AFFIRMATIVE Every fire *broadly possibly* is hot.	ADDITIONAL NEGATIVE Every fire *broadly possibly* is not hot.
COMPOSITE NEGATIVE Every hot thing *strictly possibly* is not cold.	
ORIGINAL NEGATIVE Every hot thing *broadly possibly* is not cold.	ADDITIONAL AFFIRMATIVE Every hot thing *broadly possibly* is cold.

6.7.2.3 Summary of Stated Modalities

The Muslim logicians thus conventionally mention a total of fifteen modalities, i.e., the eight *basic modalities* and the seven *composite modalities* described above. These are summarized in the table below.

		Kind of Modal Proposition	**Basic or Comp**	**Example**
Necessity	1	Extensionally Necessary Proposition *ḍarūriyya muṭlaqa*	B	Every human *necessarily is* an animal.
	2	Broadly Intensionally Necessary Proposition *mashrūṭa ʿāmma*	B	Every writer, *as long as he is a writer, necessarily* moves his fingers.
	3	Strictly Intensionally Necessary Proposition *mashrūṭa khāṣṣa*	C	Every writer, *strictly as long as he is a writer, necessarily* moves his fingers.
	4	Broadly Specific-Time Necessary Proposition *waqtiyya muṭlaqa*	B	Every pair of like electrical charges, *broadly when brought together, necessarily* repels.[49]
	5	Strictly Specific-Time Necessary Proposition *waqtiyya*	C	Every pair of like electrical charges, *strictly when brought together, necessarily* repels.
	6	Broadly Sometime Necessary Proposition *muntashira muṭlaqa*	B	Every chicken *sometime necessarily* hatches from an egg.
	7	Strictly Sometime Necessary Proposition *muntashira*	C	Every chicken *strictly sometime necessarily* hatches from an egg.

49. This is based on the false but prevalent assumption of materialism, which holds that the contingent causes in the universe independently and necessarily bring about their effects.

		Kind of Modal Proposition	Basic or Comp	Example
Continuity	1	Extensionally Continuous Proposition *dā'ima muṭlaqa*	B	Every piece of wood *always* is carbon-based.
	2	Broadly Intensionally Continuous Proposition *'urfiyya 'āmma*	B	Every scholar, *as long as he is a scholar, always* possesses scholarly knowledge.
	3	Strictly Intensionally Continuous Proposition *'urfiyya khāṣṣa*	C	Every scholar, *strictly as long as he is a scholar, always* possesses scholarly knowledge.
Actuality	1	Broadly Actual Proposition *muṭlaqa 'āmma*	B	Every wolf *broadly actually* howls.
	2	Non-Necessary Actual Proposition *wujūdiyya lā-ḍarūriyya*	C	Every wolf *actually but not necessarily* howls.
	3	Non-Continuous Actual Proposition *wujūdiyya lā-dā'ima*	C	Every wolf *actually but not always* howls.
Possibility	1	Broadly Possible Proposition *mumkina 'āmma*	B	Every light *broadly possibly* illuminates.
	2	Strictly Possible Proposition *mumkina khāṣṣa*	C	Every light *strictly possibly* illuminates.

These fifteen modalities may be considered in relation to each other as universals. Their relations, whether relations of *absolute generality and specificity* (a), of *perspectival generality and specificity* (p), or of *disjointedness* (d), are illustrated below.

	Non-Cnt. Act.	Non-Nec. Act.	S. Smt. Nec.	S. Sp. Tm. Nec.	S. In. Cnt.	S. In. Nec.	B. Pos.	B. Act.	B. In. Cnt.	Ex. Cnt.	B. Smt. Nec.	B. Sp. Tm Nec.	B. In. Nec	Ex. Nec.
Ex. Nec.														
B. In. Nec														p
B. Sp. Tm Nec.													p	a
B. Smt. Nec.												a	p	a
Ex. Cnt.											p	p	p	a
B. In. Cnt.										a	p	p	a	a
B. Act.									a	a	a	a	a	a
B. Pos.								a	a	a	a	a	a	a
S. In. Nec.							a	a	a	d	p	p	a	d
S. In. Cnt.						p	a	a	a	d	p		p	d
S. Sp. Tm. Nec.					p	p	a	a	p	d	a	a	p	d
S. Smt. Nec.				a	p	p	a	a	p	d	a	a	p	d
Non-Nec. Act.			a	a	a	a	a	a	p	p	p	p	p	d
Non-Cnt. Act.		a	a	a	a	a	a	a	p	d	p	p	p	d
S. Pos.	a	a	a	a	a	a	a					p	p	d

Studying the contradictions and converses of these fifteen kinds of modal propositions (see 8.1 and 8.2) reveals six additional kinds of modal propositions, which are described later. These are the (1) *broadly intensionally possible proposition* (*ḥīniyya mumkina*), the (2) *broadly specific-time possible proposition* (*mumkina waqtiyya*), the (3) *continuously possible proposition* (*mumkina dā'ima*), the (4) *broadly intensionally actual proposition* (*ḥīniyya muṭlaqa*), the (5) *intensionally non-continuously actual proposition* (*ḥīniyya muṭlaqa lā-dā'ima*), and the (6) ***broadly intensionally continuous proposition that is non-continuous in some cases*** (*'urfiyya lā-dā'ima fī al-ba'ḍ*). This amounts to a total of 21 kinds of stated modalities considered by the Muslim logicians.[50]

Sources

Section	Sources
6 Simple Propositions	*TB*, 229-36; al-Bājūrī, *Ḥāshiya fī fann al-manṭiq*, 82-83; for further reading, see Street, *Najm al-Dīn*, 145-52; Ahmed, *Palimpsests*, 162-64; 165-70
6.1 Predication in Simple Propositions	*TB*, 231-32, 245-59; for further reading, see Ahmed, *Palimpsests*, 167-70
6.2 Subject-Concepts	*TB*, 224, 237-38
6.3 Characterization of Subject-Referents	*TB*, 260; al-Bājūrī, *Ḥāshiya fī fann al-manṭiq*, 83-84
6.4 Quantification in Simple Propositions	*TB*, 239-43
6.5 Complemented Simple Propositions	*TB*, 251-53
6.6 Existential Import in Simple Propositions	*TB*, 243-45
6.6.1 Extramental Propositions	*TB*, 245-46, 248
6.6.2 Common Propositions	*TB*, 247-48
6.6.3 Mental Propositions	*TB*, 247-48; Muḥammad Ḥasanayn Makhlūf, *al-Ḥāshiya al-thāniya 'alā al-Jawāhir al-muntaẓamāt fī 'uqūd al-maqūlāt* (Cairo: Maṭba'at Muṣṭafā al-Bābī al-Ḥalabī, 1971), 6-7
6.6.3.1 Mental Propositions Whose Subject-Referents are Mental Concepts	
6.6.3.2 Mental Propositions Whose Predicates are Related to Existence	

50. Some logicians add a twenty-second kind, namely the *sometime actual proposition* (*muṭlaqa muntashira*). See Note 141.

6.6.3.3 Mental Propositions Whose Subject-Referents are Posited Instances of Impossible Concepts	
6.6.4 Mental Existential Import	*TB*, 250-51
6.6.5 Existential Import in Affirmative Predicate-Complemented Propositions	*TB*, 244-45
6.7 Modality in Simple Propositions	*TB*, 253-56; al-Bājūrī, *Ḥāshiya fī fann al-manṭiq*, 83-85; for further reading, see Street, *Najm al-Dīn*, 166-79; Ahmed, *Palimpsests*, 170-74; Asad Ahmed, "The *Jiha/Tropos-Mādda/Hūlē* Distinction in Arabic Logic and its Significance for Avicenna's Modals," in *The Unity of Science in the Arabic Tradition: Science, Logic, Epistemology and their Interactions*, eds. Shahid Rahman, et al. (Dordrecht: Springer, 2008), 229-53; Strobino, Avicenna's Theory, 138-50
6.7.1 Real Modality	
6.7.1.1 Kinds of Real Necessity	*TB*, 262-66, 276; al-Bājūrī, *Ḥāshiya fī fann al-manṭiq*, 94-96
6.7.1.2 Kinds of Real Continuity	*TB*, 268-71, 276
6.7.2 Stated Modality	
6.7.2.1 Basic Stated Modalities	*TB*, 256-76
6.7.2.2 Composite Stated Modalities	*TB*, 276-86
6.7.2.3 Summary of Stated Modalities	*TB*, 345

7

COMPLEX PROPOSITIONS

Whereas a *simple proposition* affirms or negates a predicative relationship between a non-propositional subject and a non-propositional predicate, a *complex proposition* (*qaḍiyya sharṭiyya*) affirms or negates a predicative relationship between two (or sometimes more) propositions. For example, ‹Zayd is human› is an affirmative simple proposition that affirms a predicative relationship between ‹Zayd› and ‹human›, neither of which are propositions; likewise, ‹Zayd is not a horse› is a negative simple proposition that negates a predicative relationship between ‹Zayd› and ‹horse›, neither of which are propositions. On the other hand, the proposition ‹If the sun has risen, then daytime exists› is a *complex proposition* because it affirms a predicative relationship between the two *sub-propositions* ‹The sun has risen› and ‹Daytime exists›. Specifically, it affirms that when the first sub-proposition is true then the second one is also true, and when the second one is false, then the first one is also false. This predicative relationship can also be negated. For example, the complex proposition ‹It is not the case that if the sun has not risen, then daytime exists› negates the predicative relationship just described between the two sub-propositions ‹The sun has not risen› and ‹Daytime exists›. This kind of complex proposition is called a *conditional complex proposition* (*qaḍiyya sharṭiyya muttaṣila*).

There is another kind of complex proposition, called a *disjunctive complex proposition* (*qaḍiyya sharṭiyya munfaṣila*), that affirms or negates a different kind of predicative relationship between its sub-propositions. The affirmative disjunctive complex proposition ‹Number X is exclusively either even or odd›, for example, affirms a *strong exclusivity* between the two sub-propositions

‹Number X is even› and ‹Number X is odd›, meaning that if one of the two is true, then the other one is false, and vice versa. And the negative disjunctive complex proposition ‹It is not the case that Horse X is exclusively black or white› negates a strong exclusivity between the two sub-propositions ‹Horse X is black› and ‹Horse X is white›. These two kinds of complex propositions are described in turn below.

7.1 Conditional Complex Propositions

A *conditional complex proposition* (*qaḍiyya sharṭiyya muttaṣila*)[1] comprises a *judgment* of the dependence of the hypothetical truth of one simple proposition, called the *consequent* (*tālī*), on the hypothetical truth of another simple proposition, called the *antecedent* (*muqaddam*). That is, it is a judgment that, if, hypothetically, the antecedent were true, then on that hypothesis the consequent would be true. For example, the proposition ‹If the sun has risen, then daytime exists› comprises a judgment that the consequent proposition, ‹Daytime exists›, would be true given the truth of the antecedent proposition, ‹The sun has risen›, meaning that if, hypothetically, it is true that the sun has risen, then on that hypothesis it will be true that daytime exists.

This dependence of the truth of the consequent on the truth of the antecedent is called *truth-dependence* (*ittiṣāl*). The example conditional proposition just cited affirms such a truth-dependence and is hence called an *affirmative conditional proposition* (*qaḍiyya muttaṣila mūjaba*). The truth-dependence could also, however, be negated, such as in the proposition ‹It is not the case that if the sun has risen, then nighttime exists›, which negates any truth-dependence between the consequent, ‹Nighttime exists›, and the antecedent, ‹The sun has risen›. This kind of conditional proposition is called a *negative conditional proposition* (*qaḍiyya muttaṣila sāliba*).

There is a difference between *negating truth-dependence* (*salb al-ittiṣāl*) and the *truth-dependence of negative sub-propositions* (*ittiṣāl al-salb*). The proposition ‹It is not the case that if the sun has risen, then nighttime exists› negates the truth-dependence of the affirmative consequent, ‹Nighttime exists›, on the affirmative antecedent, ‹The sun has risen›. This is an example of *negating truth-dependence*, and the conditional proposition is hence a negative conditional proposition. On the other hand, the proposition ‹If the sun has not risen, then daytime does not exist› is an example of the *truth-dependence of negative sub-propositions*. It in fact *affirms* the truth-dependence of the negative

1. Henceforth, *conditional complex proposition* will be abbreviated *conditional proposition*.

consequent, ‹Daytime does not exist›, on the negative antecedent, ‹The sun has not risen›. Because it affirms this truth-dependence, it is an example of an affirmative conditional proposition. Even though its *sub-propositions* are negative, the complex proposition is affirmative. Ultimately, then, whether a conditional proposition is affirmative or negative depends on whether it affirms or negates the truth-dependence of its consequent on its antecedent. This is unaffected by whether the consequent and antecedent are themselves affirmative or negative sub-propositions. Thus, in terms of affirmation and negation, conditional propositions possess a total of eight possible configurations: the conditional proposition as a whole is either affirmative or negative (two possibilities); the consequent is either affirmative or negative (two possibilities, yielding four configurations when factored with the previous two); and the antecedent is either affirmative or negative (two possibilities, yielding eight total configurations).

If the judgment of truth-dependence in a conditional proposition is based on a discernable *real connection* (*ʿalāqa*) between the antecedent and the consequent, the proposition is called a *real conditional proposition* (*qaḍiyya muttaṣila luzūmiyya*); otherwise, it is called a *coincidental conditional proposition* (*qaḍiyya muttaṣila ittifāqiyya*). This real connection between the antecedent and the consequent is a causal connection[2] in which either the antecedent may be the cause, e.g., ‹If the sun has risen, then daytime exists›, or the consequent may be the cause, e.g., ‹If daytime exists, then the sun has risen›. Both example propositions affirm a *real truth-dependence* (*luzūm*) between the antecedent and the consequent based on the perceived real connection between the rising of the sun and the existence of daytime. The

2. Some logicians argued for the possibility of two kinds of non-causal connections, namely (1) the connection between two effects by means of an underlying cause of both and (2) the connection between two *correlatives* (*mutaḍāyifān*)—two concepts each of which is only conceivable through the conception of the other, e.g., ‹father› and ‹child›. The first kind was critiqued by al-Ṭūsī, who argued that it would entail that everything in the universe is causally connected since everything in the universe is made to exist by God. The correct position, he argued, is that connection through a common cause is insufficient to render the conditional proposition real; rather, the common cause must bring about a causal connection between the two in order for the conditional proposition to be real. As a result, this putative kind of non-causal connection is ultimately in fact a kind of causal connection. The second kind was critiqued by ʿAbd al-Ḥakīm al-Siyālkūtī, who argued that the conceptual dependence of correlatives on each other is distinct from their metaphysical dependence on a cause. For example, although ‹father› and ‹child› are correlatives in the sense that neither can be conceived without the other, they are, in reality, each caused by the event of childbirth. All correlatives thus have a common cause, which, as al-Ṭūsī argued, is insufficient to render a conditional proposition real. *TB*, 289-90.

one who formulates the proposition does so on the basis of a perception that the rising of the sun regularly causes the existence of daytime. The connection between the rising of the sun and the existence of daytime is hence a *real connection* (*luzūm*) and the proposition is a *real conditional proposition.* On the other hand, the proposition ‹If humans are rational, then donkeys bray› affirms a *coincidental truth-dependence* (*ittifāq*) between the antecedent and the consequent.[3] There is no perceived real connection, in other words, between humans being rational and donkeys braying. The connection between the truth of the antecedent and the truth of the consequent is merely a *coincidental connection* (*ittifāq*).[4]

With *negative* propositions, the connection whose perception makes the proposition a real conditional proposition is the *absence* of any real connection that results in the truth-dependence of the consequent on the antecedent. For example, the proposition ‹It is not the case that if the sun has risen, then nighttime exists› is a real conditional proposition because it negates the truth-dependence of the consequent on the antecedent based on the perceived fact that the two sub-propositions do not bear a connection of truth-dependence.

7.2 Disjunctive Complex Propositions

A *disjunctive complex proposition* (*qaḍiyya sharṭiyya munfaṣila*)[5] comprises a *judgment* that two[6] simple propositions are *exclusive* (*mutanāfī*). For example,

3. In modern logic, there is no distinction between real and coincidental connection in conditional propositions. A proposition of the form, ‹If P, then Q›, follows the rules of *material implication*, which means that it is *always* a true proposition *unless* the antecedent is true while the consequent is false. This is irrespective of whether there is or is not a real connection between P and Q, and thus includes both those propositions that the Islamic logicians would call *real* and also those they would call *coincidental.*

4. Many logicians hold that every connection, including coincidental connections, is the result of some underlying causal relation between the antecedent and the consequent. According to these logicians, the difference between real and coincidental connections is then merely that with real connections the underlying cause is discernable, whereas with coincidental connections the underlying cause is not discernable. But ʿAbd al-Ḥakīm al-Siyālkūtī, an important late authority, explains that a connection is *not* always the result of an underlying causal relation between the antecedent and the consequent: it is possible that they *both be effects* of the same cause from different perspectives, and hence it is possible that they be dissociated. *TB*, 289. This in some ways parallels contemporary discussions in the metaphysics of causation that critique the explanation of causation as connection, based on the existence of epiphenomena.

5. Henceforth abbreviated as *disjunctive proposition.*

6. Although according to some logicians, disjunctive propositions can be composed of more

the proposition ‹This number is either even or odd› comprises a judgment that the simple sub-propositions ‹This number is even› and ‹This number is odd› are exclusive, meaning that if one of them is true, this excludes the truth of its counterpart, and if one of them is false, this excludes the falsity of its counterpart.[7] There are three kinds of disjunctive propositions:

1. Strongly exclusive (*ḥaqīqiyya* or *māniʿat al-jamʿ wa-l-khulū*) disjunctive propositions.
2. Truth-exclusive (*māniʿat al-jamʿ*) disjunctive propositions.
3. Falsity-exclusive (*māniʿat al-khulū*) disjunctive propositions.

Strongly exclusive disjunctive propositions are those whose sub-propositions can neither simultaneously be true nor simultaneously be false, e.g., ‹This number is either even or odd›. Strongly exclusive disjunction requires that the predicate-concepts of the sub-propositions be either *actual complements* (sg. *naqīḍ*) or *effective complements* (sg. *musāwī li-l-naqīḍ*). The actual complement of a predicate-concept is its *negation*, e.g., ‹non-even› with respect to ‹even›, whereas the effective complement is an independent concept that does not necessarily comprise a negation but is nevertheless *referentially equal* to the predicate-concept's actual complement, e.g., ‹odd› with respect to ‹even›.

Truth-exclusive disjunctive propositions are those whose sub-propositions cannot simultaneously be true but can simultaneously be false, e.g., ‹This thing is either a tree or a boulder›. The sub-propositions ‹This thing is a tree› and ‹This thing is a boulder› cannot simultaneously be true because a thing cannot both be a tree and a boulder, but they can however be simultaneously false because a thing can be neither a tree nor a boulder (by being a human, for instance). Truth-exclusive disjunction requires that the predicate-concept of one sub-proposition be *unconditionally less inclusive* than the *complement* of the other. To take the example just cited, the predicate-concept ‹boulder› is

than two sub-propositions, e.g., ‹This screen is either black or white or neither black nor white›, this section focuses on disjunctive propositions with only two sub-propositions. Nevertheless, the features of disjunctive propositions discussed here can be analogously applied to disjunctive propositions with more than two sub-propositions. Note that other logicians hold that disjunctive propositions can only be composed of two sub-propositions and that those that are composed of more are actually *nested complex propositions*. *TB*, 301.

7. The proposition ‹This number is either even or odd› could also be understood as a simple proposition whose subject is ‹this number› and whose predicate is ‹either even or odd›. What the logicians intend by this syntactic structure, however, is a disjunctive proposition as described above. An unambiguous formulation of a disjunctive proposition would explicitly state both sub-propositions and place the disjunction-word, in this case the word "or," between them, e.g., "Either this number is even, or this number is odd." *TB*, 292.

unconditionally more specific than the concept ‹non-tree›; every boulder is a non-tree but not every non-tree is a boulder (some, for instance, are humans).

Falsity-exclusive disjunctive propositions are those whose sub-propositions cannot simultaneously be false but can simultaneously be true, e.g., ‹Zayd is either in a body of water or he is not drowning›. The sub-propositions ‹Zayd is in a body of water› and ‹Zayd is not drowning› cannot be simultaneously false but they can simultaneously be true. To illustrate why they cannot both be false, we can take the *contradictory opposite* of each sub-proposition (see 8.1) and show that the two contradictory opposites cannot both be true. The contradictory opposite of the first is ‹Zayd is not in a body of water›, and the contradictory opposite of the second is ‹Zayd is drowning›. These two propositions cannot both be true because Zayd cannot be drowning unless he is in a body of water. The two sub-propositions can, however, simultaneously be true—Zayd can be in a body of water without drowning if he is swimming safely from one end to the other. Falsity-exclusive disjunction requires that the predicate-concept of one sub-proposition be *unconditionally more inclusive* than the *complement* of the other. To take the example just cited, the predicate-concept ‹someone in a body of water› is unconditionally more general than the concept ‹non-someone-not-drowning› (i.e., ‹someone drowning›). In other words, everyone drowning is in a body of water, but not everyone in a body of water is drowning.

The examples cited above are all *affirmative disjunctive propositions* (sg. *qaḍiyya munfaṣila mūjaba*). Whereas an affirmative disjunctive proposition comprises a judgment that two sub-propositions are exclusive, a *negative disjunctive proposition* (*qaḍiyya munfaṣila sāliba*) comprises a judgment that two sub-propositions are *not exclusive*—either *not strongly exclusive, not truth-exclusive*, or *not falsity-exclusive*. An example of a negative *strongly exclusive disjunctive proposition* is ‹It is not the case that this person either has a sister or knows how to write›. In other words, it is not the case that the sub-propositions ‹This person has a sister› and ‹This person knows how to write› cannot simultaneously be true or false; that is, they can indeed simultaneously be true or false. The only requirement for the truth of a negative strongly disjunctive proposition is that either the two sub-propositions can simultaneously be true or that they can simultaneously be false. For a negative *truth-exclusive proposition*, on the other hand, it is specifically required that the two sub-propositions can simultaneously be true, and for a negative *falsity-exclusive proposition* it is specifically required that the two can simultaneously be false. Since, in the example above, the two sub-propositions both can simultaneously be true and can simultaneously be false, the same example can be used to illustrate negative truth-exclusive propositions and negative falsity-exclusive propositions. Note from this explanation that *negative* disjunctive propositions are not, strictly speaking, disjunctions. That is why logicians remark that to call them "disjunctive propositions" is merely a terminological convention.

Just as we saw above with the connections in conditional propositions, the disjunctions in disjunctive propositions may be either real or coincidental. If the sub-propositions of a disjunctive proposition are *intrinsically* mutually exclusive, it is called a *real disjunctive proposition* (*qaḍiyya munfaṣila ʿinādiyya*); otherwise, it is called a *coincidental disjunctive proposition* (*qaḍiyya munfaṣila ittifāqiyya*). For example, the proposition ‹This number is either even or odd› affirms a *strong exclusion* between the sub-propositions ‹This number is even› and ‹This number is odd›. This strong exclusion is *intrinsically* entailed by the sub-propositions; since ‹odd› is the *effective complement* of ‹even›, the simultaneous truth or falsity of the sub-propositions would result in a logical contradiction of the form ‹‹A is B› and ‹A is non-B››. The disjunctive proposition as a whole is hence a *real disjunctive proposition.* The other two examples cited previously—the truth-exclusive disjunction ‹This thing is either a tree or a boulder› and the falsity-exclusive disjunction ‹Zayd is either in a body of water or he is not drowning›—similarly *intrinsically* entail their respective exclusivity. In contrast, if we suppose the existence of a girl who has a sister and does not know how to write and formulate the proposition ‹This girl either has a sister or knows how to write›, then it is coincidentally the case that the two sub-propositions ‹This girl has a sister› and ‹This girl knows how to write› are neither simultaneously true nor are they simultaneously false; the first just happens to be true and the second just happens to be false. The strong exclusivity between the two sub-propositions does not arise intrinsically, but merely because the girl happens to be such that she does not simultaneously have a sister and the ability to write, nor does she simultaneously lack a sister and the ability to write. This is hence a coincidental disjunctive proposition. Similar examples can be devised for coincidental truth-exclusivity and coincidental falsity-exclusivity.

7.3 Quantification in Complex Propositions

Just as simple propositions can be *quantified*, complex propositions too can be quantified. But whereas the quantification of simple propositions pertains to the instances of their subject-concepts, the quantification of complex propositions pertains to the *states-of-affairs* (*awḍāʿ*) that can accompany their antecedents. An example of a quantified complex proposition is ‹Whenever Zayd is human, then he is an animal›. Here, the antecedent, ‹Zayd is human›, is quantified with respect to the *times* with which this proposition can possibly coexist. This example hence illustrates the quantification of complex propositions with the most general state-of-affairs, namely, time. Since the quantifier "whenever" encompasses all times, this is a *universally quantified conditional proposition*. The table below gives examples of *universally quantified*, *particularly quantified*, *singular*, and *unquantified* complex propositions, both conditional and disjunctive.

Quantification	Conditional Proposition	Disjunctive Proposition
Universally Quantified	Whenever Zayd is human, then he is an animal.	At all times, numbers are either even or odd.
Particularly Quantified	Sometimes, when a thing is an animal, then it is human.	Sometimes, either the sun has risen, or nighttime exists.
Singular	If you visit me today, then I will honor you.	Today, either the sun has risen, or nighttime exists.
Unquantified	If you visit me, then I will honor you.	Zayd is either in a body of water, or he is not drowning.

The general state-of-affairs of *time* can be detailed further by the specification of particular states-of-affairs during the times that accompany the antecedent, e.g., ‹Whenever he is lying down, if Zayd closes his eyes, then he falls asleep›. Here, the state-of-affairs of *Zayd lying down* specifies the general state-of-affairs of time; it is at the times that Zayd is lying down that the truth-dependence between the antecedent and the consequent is affirmed. Note that impossible states-of-affairs are not considered, e.g., ‹Whenever they are horses, humans are animals›—since it is not possible for humans to be horses, quantification with this state-of-affairs is invalid.

It is also valid to quantify complex propositions with non-temporal states-of-affairs, e.g., ‹Assuming that this thing is a number, it is either even or odd›. Here, the state-of-affairs is *this thing being a number*. And it is valid to use temporal states-of-affairs to quantify propositions with non-temporal antecedents. For example, the proposition ‹Whenever God exists, then He possesses knowledge› is a validly quantified proposition and is not invalidated by the fact that God does not exist in time because what it states is that, at every time (as we experience it), it is the case that if God exists then He possesses knowledge. Finally, it is also valid to temporally quantify complex propositions whose antecedent's subject is *time* itself, e.g., ‹Whenever time exists, the celestial spheres are moving›.[8] Even though time itself cannot be said to be in time, this is a validly quantified proposition because what it states is that, at every time (as we experience it), it is the case that if time exists then the celestial spheres are moving.

7.4 Nested Complex Propositions

Conditional propositions are always formed from the composition of two sub-propositions.[9] These two sub-propositions are normally *simple propositions*, such as all the examples cited above. But they can also be *complex propositions*, in which case the overarching complex proposition is a *nested complex proposition*. For example, the following nested conditional proposition is composed of two sub-propositions, each of which are in turn conditional propositions: ‹Whenever ‹If this thing is human, then it is an animal›, then ‹If this thing is not an animal, then it is not human››. This nested conditional proposition affirms the truth-dependence of the truth-dependence of the consequent on the truth-dependence of the antecedent. To take another example, the following nested conditional proposition is composed of two sub-propositions, one of which is a conditional proposition and the other a disjunctive proposition: ‹If ‹Whenever the sun has set, then nighttime exists›, then ‹Either the sun has set, or nighttime does not exist››. Other possibilities of propositional nesting can be devised based on these two examples.

7.5 Complemented Complex Propositions

Traditionally, the logicians do not discuss how complex propositions can be complemented, leaving it to students to analogically infer the complements of complex propositions from the complements of simple propositions. Recall that in a simple proposition, the relationship affirmed or negated in the proposition *as a whole* is a relationship between non-propositional terms, e.g., the

8. This example is based on the position of the *falāsifa* that time arises as a result of the motion of the celestial spheres that Avicenna's premodern natural philosophy posited to explain the structure and working of the universe.

9. There is disagreement on whether this also applies to disjunctive propositions. See Note 130.

terms ‹snowflake› and ‹cold thing› in the proposition ‹Every snowflake is cold›. But we saw that it is also possible to consider and classify simple propositions with respect to the affirmation and negation of their terms, i.e., the subject and predicate. ‹Every burning coal is non-cold› is a *complemented* proposition because its predicate, ‹non-cold›, is complemented—it is the complement or negation of ‹cold›. Because this negation pertains to an individual term and not to the predication of the proposition *as a whole*, we do not say that the proposition ‹Every burning coal is non-cold› is negative; we say that it is affirmative but that it is *predicate-complemented*.

Now let us turn to complex propositions. Unlike in simple propositions where the relationship affirmed or negated in the proposition is a relationship between non-propositional terms, the relationship affirmed or negated in complex propositions is between sub-propositions. The quality of a complex proposition as a whole, i.e., whether it is affirmative or negative, pertains to this relationship *between* its two sub-propositions. Now, complex propositions can also be considered and classified with respect to the predicative relationships *within* their sub-propositions. For example, the conditional proposition ‹If what is inside my hand is a hot coal then I am in pain› is affirmative and uncomplemented: it affirms a conditional relationship between the sub-propositions ‹What is inside my hand is a hot coal› and ‹I am in pain›, and each of these sub-propositions in turn affirms a predicative relationship. When we make the consequent negative, e.g., ‹If what is inside my hand is a hot coal, then I am not comfortable›, the complex proposition remains affirmative, but it is now a *consequent-complemented* proposition. Note the difference between this example and the uncomplemented negative proposition ‹It is not the case that if what is inside my hand is a hot coal, then I am in comfort›. The table below classifies the various possibilities, with the examples illustrating different quantifications and alternating between conditional and disjunctive propositions.

	Example	**Kind of Proposition**
1	Right now, either what is inside your hand is a hot coal, or you are comfortable.	Affirmative uncomplemented proposition
2	At any given time, it is not the case that if what is inside your hand is a hot coal, then you are comfortable.	Negative uncomplemented proposition

	Example	Kind of Proposition
3	This next moment, if your immediate reaction is not to drop the hot coals, then you are in a medical emergency.	Affirmative antecedent-complemented proposition
4	It is not the case that either the donuts are not made yet, or Zayd is bringing them now.	Negative antecedent-complemented proposition
5	Either he has five donuts, or his willpower is not normal.	Affirmative consequent-complemented proposition
6	It is not the case that if Zayd eats some donuts, then there will not be any donuts left.	Negative consequent-complemented proposition
7	If we are not on a safari, then we are not enjoying ourselves.	Affirmative antecedent-and-consequent-complemented proposition
8	After they opened the local zoo, it is not the case that either we are not in town, or we are not seeing exotic animals.	Negative antecedent-and-consequent-complemented proposition

7.6 Existential Import in Complex Propositions

Unlike simple propositions, complex propositions do not have existential import. This is because the truth of a complex proposition depends on the hypothetical relationship between two predications. Unlike affirmative simple propositions where the subject needs to exist so that one may make a judgment about its characterization by the predicate, in complex propositions the antecedent need only be *hypothesized* to allow a judgment about its relationship with the consequent. This applies to both conditional and disjunctive propositions. For example, in ‹If Zayd is righteous, then he is sincere before God›, the relationship of truth-dependence between the predication in ‹Zayd is righteous› and the predication in ‹Zayd is sincere before God› does not require that we suppose either that Zayd is righteous or that he is sincere before God. We assess the truth-dependence of these two sub-propositions, i.e., the truth of the complex proposition as a whole, independently of whether or not the respective predications in the sub-propositions actually occur. The same applies to the disjunctive proposition ‹Either Zayd is sincere before God, or he is not righteous› and to the relationship between its sub-propositions. The proposition as a whole does not carry existential import.

Sources

Section	Sources
7 Complex Propositions	*TB*, 235-37; for further reading, see Street, *Najm al-Dīn*, 179-89; Ahmed, *Palimpsests*, 164-65; 174-79
7.1 Conditional Complex Propositions	*TB*, 286-91
7.2 Disjunctive Complex Propositions	*TB*, 292-96
7.3 Quantification in Complex Propositions	*TB*, 296-301
7.4 Nested Complex Propositions	*TB*, 301-3
7.5 Complemented Complex Propositions	*TB*, 286
7.6 Existential Import in Complex Propositions	*TB*, 244

8

PROPOSITIONAL REASONING

This chapter concerns the various formal relationships between propositions that allow us to make inferences about the truth or falsity of one proposition on the basis of the truth or falsity of another proposition. These kinds of inferences are not the kinds of inferences that we make when we draw conclusions from arguments composed of multiple premises—those are the subject of the next chapter. Rather, they are *immediate inferences*, inferences from the truth or falsity of a single proposition to the truth or falsity of another proposition. The kinds of immediate inference are *contradiction*, *conversion*, *contraposition*, and *negated contraposition*, each of which is defined and proven in this chapter. Ultimately, as we will see, all proofs for the validity of any kind of immediate inference reduce to the law of identity and the law of non-contradiction.

8.1 Contradiction

Contradictory opposition (*tanāquḍ*)[1] is for two propositions[2] to formally differ in a manner that leads the truth of one of them to entail the falsity of the other and vice-versa. For example, the two propositions ‹Zayd is standing› and ‹Zayd is not standing› *contradict* each other because the difference in their forms—‹A is B› and ‹A is not B›—entails that if the former proposition is true, then the latter proposition is false, and if the latter is true, then the former is false. The formal difference between contradictory propositions

1. In modern mathematical logic, contradictory opposition is studied as a kind of logical operation, namely, the logical operation of *negation*. The contradictory opposite propositions that are described in this section are in these terms the "negations" of the original propositions.

2. Contradiction in this sense is not a relationship between concepts.

entails, in other words, that it is impossible for both of them to simultaneously be true or for both of them to simultaneously be false.

By contrast, the difference between the two propositions ‹Zayd is moving› and ‹Zayd is not still› is not a contradictory opposition, because although they are different, these propositions do not oppose each other and can be (and in fact always are) simultaneously true or simultaneously false. It is also not the case that the difference between the two propositions ‹Zayd is human› and ‹Zayd is not rational› is a contradictory opposition. Unlike the previous pair of propositions, each proposition in this pair does, in fact, oppose its counterpart, because of which the two propositions cannot simultaneously be true nor can they simultaneously be false. If it is true that Zayd is human, then it must be false that he is not rational, and if it is true that he is not rational, then it must be false that he is human. But these propositions still do not oppose each other in the manner of *contradiction* because the impossibility of their being simultaneously true and simultaneously false is not an entailment of their difference in *form*; rather, it is an entailment of their difference in the *matter* of their predicates. To state this more clearly, the general forms of the two propositions are ‹A is B› and ‹A is not C›. This difference in *form* does *not* entail that the two propositions cannot be simultaneously true or simultaneously false. To illustrate, the two propositions ‹Zayd is human› and ‹Zayd is not a doctor› display this same difference in form, yet they can be simultaneously true (assuming for example that Zayd does not successfully graduate from medical school) or simultaneously false (assuming that Zayd does successfully graduate from medical school). But the reason why it is impossible for the propositions ‹Zayd is human› and ‹Zayd is not rational› to be simultaneously true or false is not because of the form of their difference but because of the material relationship between the specific predicates that materially constitute each proposition. That is, since ‹rational› is a *differentia* of ‹human›, anything that is human must also be rational and anything that is not rational cannot be human.

The difference between the two propositions ‹Every human is an animal› and ‹Every human is not an animal› is also not a contradictory difference because, again, the fact that the pair of propositions cannot simultaneously be true or false is an entailment of the material relationship between the specific subjects and predicates that materially constitute the propositions. This is not as obvious as in the previous example, and is best illustrated by another pair of propositions that have the same respective forms yet can be simultaneously false. The general forms of these two propositions are ‹Every A is B› and ‹Every A is not B›. The following pair of propositions exhibits these forms: ‹Every student passed the exam› and ‹Every student did not pass the exam›. Suppose now that some students passed the exam while some did not. Both of these propositions will now simultaneously be false, even though they are of the same form as the former pair of propositions. The reason why the former pair, like this latter pair, cannot simultaneously be false is because the subjects of the former pair, i.e., ‹human›, are *unconditionally less inclusive* than their predicates, i.e., ‹animal›, and it is hence necessary for every subject-referent, i.e., every human, to be characterized by the predicate-concept, i.e., ‹animal›.

These examples illustrate that in order for two propositions to contradict each other, they must have certain precise aspects of formal difference—they must differ in affirmation and negation, for example, and the quantification of their subjects must differ in a well-defined way—and they must also have certain precise aspects of formal identity—their subjects and predicates, for example, must be identical. The goal of this section is to comprehensively study the aspects of formal difference and the aspects of formal identity that lead a pair of propositions to contradict each other.

8.1.1 *Quality and Quantification in Contradiction*

The true contradictory opposite of a proposition is simply the *negative complement* (*rafʿ*) of the original proposition. For example, the contradictory opposite of the proposition ‹Every A is B› is ‹It is not the case that all A is B›. What logicians are interested in, however, is the *simplified logical equivalent* of this true contradictory opposite (*al-musāwī li-l-naqīḍ*). In the example just cited, this simplified logical equivalent is the proposition ‹Some A is not B›.

Forming the simplified logical equivalent of the negative complement of a proposition involves changing the proposition's *quality* (*kayf*), *quantification* (*kamm*), and *stated modality* (*jiha*). In order for two propositions to contradict each other in their simplified logical form, they must appropriately differ in each of these three aspects of their form.

The required formal difference in the proposition's *quality* is straightforward: in order for two propositions to contradict each other, the affirmation of the original proposition must be changed to a negation or its negation to an affirmation. In non-modal singular propositions, which cannot be quantified, this is all that is required to form the logical equivalent of the true contradictory opposite. For example, the proposition ‹Zayd is standing› simply needs to be changed to ‹Zayd is not standing›.

The required formal difference in the proposition's *quantification* is summarized in the following table.

Kind of Proposition	Original	Contradictory
Singular	A is B	A is not B.
Quantified Universal	Every A is B.	Some A is not B.
	Some A is B.	Every A is not B.
	Some A is not B.	Every A is B.
	Every A is not B.	Some A is B.
Unquantified Universal	A is B (Some A is B)	Every A is not B.
	A is not B (Some A is not B)	Every A is B.

As the table shows, if the proposition is a singular proposition, it cannot be quantified and its contradiction is formed by simply changing its quality. If, on the other hand, the proposition is a universal proposition, then it is either quantified or unquantified. If the proposition is a quantified universal proposition, then in addition to its quality, its quantification too must be changed, that is, from universal quantification to particular quantification or vice-versa. This means that if a proposition is affirmative and universally quantified (i.e., ‹Every A is B›), its contradictory opposite will be negative and particularly quantified (i.e., ‹Some A is not B›) and vice-versa; and if a proposition is negative and universally quantified (i.e., ‹Every A is not B›), its contradictory opposite will be affirmative and particularly quantified (i.e., ‹Some A is B›) and vice-versa. If the proposition is an unquantified universal proposition, then, for the purposes of logical inference, it can be treated as a particularly quantified proposition and its contradictory opposite will be an affirmative or negative universally quantified proposition.

8.1.2 *Modality in Contradiction*

The required formal difference in the stated modality (*jiha*) of contradictory propositions is more complex than that of their quality or quantification. Recall that propositional modality is one of the four integral parts of a proposition; in the absence of its modality, a proposition has not been completely formulated. Formal difference in the modality of two propositions is a requirement for two propositions to contradictorily oppose each other. To illustrate why this is the case, consider two propositions whose *real modality* is *strict possibility* and which formally differ in a contradictory manner with respect to their quality and their quantification, e.g., ‹Every human writes› and ‹Some human does not write›. If these two propositions are both stated as *extensionally necessary propositions*—i.e., ‹Every human *necessarily* writes› and ‹Some humans *necessarily* do not write›—then they are both false. And if they are both stated as *strictly possible propositions*—i.e., ‹Every human *strictly possibly* writes› and ‹Some humans *strictly possibly* do not write›—then they are both true. This is because in order for the two propositions to contradict each other, they must also differ appropriately in their stated modalities.

As explained above, the true contradictory opposite of a proposition is its negative complement. The true contradictory opposite of the modal proposition ‹Every human *necessarily* writes› is thus simply ‹It is not the case that every human *necessarily* writes›. But, again, as explained above, what interests the logicians is not this negative complement, but rather its simplified logical equivalent (*al-musāwī li-l-naqīḍ*). In the example just cited, this simplified logical equivalent is the proposition ‹Some human *broadly possibly* does not write›. Logicians study the *logical equivalents of the negative complements of modal propositions* (simplified henceforth to *contradictory opposites of modal propositions*) in two parts: (1) the contradictory opposites of *basic modal propositions* and (2) the contradictory opposites of *composite modal propositions*. These are discussed in turn below.

8.1.2.1 Contradiction of Basic Modal Propositions

The logicians traditionally study eight kinds of *basic stated modalities* (see 6.7.2.1). But the contradictory opposites of modal propositions that are formulated with these eight basic modalities cannot all be expressed with these eight modalities. In order to express the contradictory opposites of all of these eight kinds of basic modal propositions, the logicians had to define four additional kinds of basic modal propositions: (*i*) the *broadly intensionally possible proposition* (*mumkina ḥīniyya*), (*ii*) the *broadly specific-time possible proposition* (*mumkina waqtiyya*), (*iii*) the *continuously possible proposition* (*mumkina dā'ima*), and (*iv*) the *broadly intensionally actual proposition* (*ḥīniyya muṭlaqa*). These are all highlighted in the section summary table below.[3]

3. Some logicians add a fifth new kind of modal proposition, namely the *sometime actual proposition* (*muṭlaqa muntashira*). See Note 7.

	Original Modal Proposition	Contradictory Modal Proposition
1	Extensionally Necessary Proposition *ḍarūriyya muṭlaqa*	Broadly Possible Proposition *mumkina ʿāmma*
2	Broadly Intensionally Necessary Proposition *mashrūṭa ʿāmma*	(i) Broadly Intensional Broadly Possible Proposition *mumkina ḥīniyya*
3	Broadly Specific-Time Necessary Proposition *waqtiyya muṭlaqa*	(ii) Broadly Specific-Time Broadly Possible Proposition *mumkina waqtiyya*
4	Broadly Sometime Necessary Proposition *muntashira muṭlaqa*	(iii) Broadly Continuous Broadly Possible Proposition *mumkina dāʾima*
5	Extensionally Continuous Proposition *dāʾima muṭlaqa*	Broadly Actual Proposition[4] *muṭlaqa ʿāmma*
6	Broadly Intensionally Continuous Proposition *ʿurfiyya ʿāmma*	(iv) Broadly Intensional Broadly Actual Proposition *ḥīniyya muṭlaqa*
7	Broadly Actual Proposition *muṭlaqa ʿāmma*	Extensionally Continuous Proposition[5] *dāʾima muṭlaqa*
8	Broadly Possible Proposition *mumkina ʿāmma*	Extensionally Necessary Proposition *ḍarūriyya muṭlaqa*

The general principle behind the contradictory opposition of basic modal propositions is that the contradictory opposite of *extensional necessity* is *broad possibility*, and the contradictory opposite of *extensional continuity* is *broad actuality*. Just as the remaining basic modalities are modal modifications of these four kinds of modalities, the remaining contradictory opposites are also modal modifications of these four kinds of modalities. The remainder of this section begins with a demonstration of the fact that extensional necessity and broad possibility are contradictory opposites and then uses that demonstration to derive the contradictory opposites of the remaining kinds of necessary propositions. It then demonstrates that extensional continuity and broad actuality are contradictory opposites and finally uses that

4. See Note 7.

5. See Note 7.

demonstration to derive the contradictory opposites of the remaining kinds of continuous and actual propositions.

Contradictory Opposition of Necessary and Possible Basic Modal Propositions

First, the fact that the contradictory opposite of *extensional necessity* is *broad possibility* can be derived by: (1) forming the negative complement of the definition of the affirmation of extensional necessity and showing that it is semantically equivalent to the definition of negation with broad possibility; and (2) forming the negative complement of the definition of the negation of extensional necessity and showing that it is semantically equivalent to the definition of affirmation with broad possibility. This is done below.

1. By definition, the affirmation of extensional necessity is for the predication to necessarily occur. The negative complement of this affirmation is for it not to necessarily occur. This is semantically equivalent to saying that its occurrence is not necessary. That, by definition, is negation with broad possibility. For example, the contradictory opposite of the proposition ‹God *necessarily* exists› is the proposition ‹God *broadly possibly* does not exist›.
2. By definition, the negation of extensional necessity is for the predication to necessarily not occur. The negative complement of this negation is for it not to necessarily not occur. This is semantically equivalent to saying that its non-occurrence is not necessary. That, by definition, is affirmation with broad possibility. For example, the contradictory opposite of the proposition ‹More than one god *necessarily* does not exist› is the proposition ‹More than one god *broadly possibly* exists›.

Therefore, the contradictory opposite of an extensionally necessary proposition is a broadly possible proposition, and vice-versa. This is illustrated in Rows 1 and 8 of the summary table above.

Broad intensional necessity is necessity that obtains while the subject-referent is characterized by the subject-concept,[6] which is a kind of necessity that is *unconditionally less inclusive* than extensional necessity. It therefore follows that if the contradictory opposite of necessity is possibility, then the contradictory opposite of necessity that pertains while the subject-referent is characterized by the subject-concept is possibility that pertains while the

6. Note that the temporal reading of intensional necessity is used here for simplicity.

subject-referent is characterized by the subject-concept. A proposition with this kind of stated modality is a *broadly intensionally possible proposition* (*ḥīniyya mumkina*). This is illustrated in Row 2 of the summary table above. An example of an affirmative broadly intensionally necessary proposition and its contradictory opposite is ‹Every writer, *broadly while a writer, necessarily* moves his fingers› and ‹Some writer, *broadly while a writer, broadly possibly* does not move his fingers›. An example of a negative broadly intensionally necessary proposition and its contradictory opposite is ‹Every writer, *broadly while a writer, necessarily* does not keep his fingers still› and ‹Some writer, *broadly while a writer, broadly possibly* keeps his fingers still›.[7]

Broad specific-time necessity is necessity at a specified time, which is also *unconditionally less inclusive* than extensional necessity. It therefore follows that if the contradictory opposite of necessity is possibility, then the contradictory opposite of necessity at a specified time is possibility at a specified time. A proposition with this kind of stated modality is a *broadly specific-time possible proposition* (*mumkina waqtiyya*). This is illustrated in Row 3 of the summary table above. An example of an affirmative broadly specific-time necessary proposition and its negative broadly specific-time possible contradictory proposition is ‹Every writer, *broadly when he is a writer, necessarily* moves his fingers› and ‹Some writer, *broadly when he is a writer, broadly possibly* does not move his fingers›. An example of a negative broadly specific-time necessary proposition and its affirmative broadly specific-time possible contradiction proposition is ‹Every writer, *broadly when he is a writer, necessarily* does not keep his fingers still› and ‹Some writer, *broadly when he is a writer, broadly possibly* keeps his fingers still›.

Broad sometime necessity is necessity at an unspecified time. The negation of necessity at an unspecified time is semantically equivalent to possibility at all times. A proposition with this kind of modality is a *continuously possible proposition* (*mumkina dā'ima*). This is illustrated in Row 4 of the summary table above. An example of an affirmative broadly sometime necessary proposition and its negative continuously possible contradictory proposition is ‹Every human *broadly sometime necessarily* breathes› and ‹Some human *broadly always broadly possibly* does not breathe›. An example of a negative

7. This analysis is according to the less prevalent definition of intensional necessity as necessity *during the times when* the subject-referent is characterized by the subject-concept, as described above in 6.7.1.1. According to the more prevalent definition of intensional necessity as predicative necessity *as a result of* the subject-referent being characterized by the subject-concept, broad intensional possibility would not contradict intensional necessity. *TB*, 317.

broadly sometime necessary proposition and its affirmative continuously possible contradictory proposition is ‹Every human *broadly sometime necessarily* does not breathe› and ‹Some human *broadly always broadly possibly* breathes›.

Contradictory Opposition of Continuous and Actual Basic Modal Propositions

Now let us turn to the contradictory opposition between continuous and actual basic propositions. The fact that the contradictory opposite of *extensional continuity* is *broad actuality* can be derived by (1) forming the negative complement of the definition of the affirmation of extensional continuity and showing that it is semantically equivalent to the definition of negation with broad actuality; and (2) forming the negative complement of the definition of the negation of extensional continuity and showing that it is semantically equivalent to the definition of affirmation with broad actuality. This is done below.

1. By definition, the affirmation of extensional continuity is for a predication to occur always. The negative complement of this affirmation is for it not to occur always. This is semantically equivalent to saying that at some time it does not occur. That, by definition, is negation with broad actuality. For example, the contradictory opposite of the proposition ‹Fire *always* burns› is the proposition ‹Fire *broadly actually* does not burn›.
2. By definition, the negation of extensional continuity is for a predication to not occur always. This is semantically equivalent to saying that at some time, it does not occur. The negative complement of this negation is for it not to not occur at some time. This is semantically equivalent to saying that at some time it does occur. That, by definition, is affirmation with broad actuality. For example, the contradictory opposite of the proposition ‹Fire *always* is not cold› is the proposition ‹Fire *broadly actually* is cold›.

Therefore, the contradictory opposite of an extensionally continuous proposition is a broadly actual proposition, and vice-versa.[8] This is illustrated in Rows 5 and 7 of the summary table above.

8. This is not entirely accurate, because a broadly actual proposition does not affirm that the predication occurs at some time; rather, it negates that a predication is continuous. The latter is *unconditionally more inclusive* than the former because it includes non-temporal predications (i.e., predications about God or predications about time) whereas the former only applies to temporal predications. According to al-Taftāzānī in another work, the contradiction of an

Broad intensional continuity is continuity that pertains while the subject-referent is characterized by the subject-concept, which is a kind of continuity *unconditionally less inclusive* than extensional continuity. It therefore follows that if the contradictory opposite of continuity is actuality, then the contradictory opposite of continuity that obtains while the subject-referent is characterized by the subject-concept is actuality that obtains while the subject-referent is characterized by the subject-concept. A proposition with this kind of stated modality is a *broadly intensionally actual proposition* (*ḥīniyya muṭlaqa*). This is illustrated in Row 6 of the summary table above. An example of an affirmative broadly intensionally continuous proposition and its contradictorily opposite proposition is ‹Every writer, *broadly while a writer, always* moves his fingers› and ‹Some writer, *broadly while a writer, broadly actually* does not move his fingers›. An example of a negative broadly intensionally necessary proposition and its contradictorily opposite proposition is ‹Every writer, *broadly while a writer, always* does not keep his fingers still› and ‹Some writer, *broadly while a writer, broadly actually* keeps his fingers still›.[9]

8.1.2.2 Contradiction of Composite Modal Propositions

The contradictory opposites of basic modal propositions described above can be used to derive the contradictory opposites of *composite modal propositions* as follows. Every composite modal proposition can be expressed as the combination of two basic modal sub-propositions (see 6.7.2.2). The complement of the composite modal proposition is therefore the complement of one or both of the two sub-propositions. The logicians conventionally formulate this proposition as a *falsity-exclusive disjunctive complex proposition* that is composed of the contradictory opposites of the two basically modal sub-propositions. For example, an affirmative *strictly intensionally necessary proposition* is composed of an affirmative *broadly intensionally necessary proposition* and a negative *broadly actual proposition*. The contradictory opposite of the first sub-proposition is a negative *broadly intensionally possible proposition*, and the contradictory opposite of the second sub-proposition is

extensionally continuous proposition is not a broadly actual proposition as is prevalently stated by most logicians, but a *sometime actual proposition* (*muṭlaqa muntashira*), which affirms the occurrence of a predication at some time as described above (this is a fifth kind of basic modal proposition that is sometimes introduced in this chapter in addition to the four kinds listed in the table above). The contradiction of a broadly actual proposition, then, is not an extensionally continuous proposition, but some other kind of modal proposition that is not conventionally investigated by the logicians. Other logicians disagreed with al-Taftāzānī. *TB*, 316.

9. This is according to the less prevalent definition of intensional continuity.

an affirmative *extensionally continuous proposition*. The contradictory opposite of the composite strictly intensionally necessary proposition as a whole can hence be approximated with a falsity-exclusive disjunctive proposition composed of these two contradictory opposites: ‹It is always the case[10] that either the contradictory opposite of the first sub-proposition is true or that the contradictory opposite of the second sub-proposition is true.› The "or" in this disjunctive proposition is *falsity-exclusive*, meaning that the disjunctive proposition is only false when both sub-propositions are false, and that it is true when either one or both of the sub-propositions are true. For the "or" to be *strongly exclusive* or *truth-exclusive* would be insufficient because the disjunctive proposition would then be false when both sub-propositions are true, whereas what is required in that case is for the disjunctive proposition to be false because the original composite modal proposition is true.

Let us illustrate this by applying it to a specific example of an affirmative strictly intensionally necessary proposition: ‹Every writer, *strictly as long as he is a writer, necessarily* moves his fingers›. The contradictory opposite of this proposition is: ‹It is always the case that either some writer, *as long as he is a writer, broadly possibly* does not move his fingers, or some writer *always* moves his fingers›, where the disjunctive "or" is falsity-exclusive, meaning that both sub-propositions cannot be false, but one or both of them can be true.

The contradictory opposites of the remaining composite modal propositions listed in 6.7.2.2 are summarized in the table below with illustrative examples.

	Original Modal Proposition	Contradictory Modal Proposition
1	Strictly Intensionally Necessary Proposition *mashrūṭa khāṣṣa*	Either (a) opposite-quality *intensionally broadly possible proposition* or (b) same-quality *extensionally continuous proposition*.
	Every writer, *strictly as long as he is a writer, necessarily* moves his fingers.	It is always the case that either (a) some writer, *as long as he is a writer, broadly possibly* does not move his fingers, or (b) some writer *always* moves his fingers.

10. This is a universal quantifier on the disjunctive proposition. See 7.3.

	Original Modal Proposition	Contradictory Modal Proposition
2	Strictly Specific-Time Necessary Proposition *waqtiyya* Every moon, *strictly when obstructed by the earth, necessarily* is eclipsed.	Either (a) opposite-quality *specific-time broadly possible proposition* or (b) same-quality *extensionally continuous proposition.* It is always the case that either (a) some moon, *when the earth obstructs it, broadly possibly* is not eclipsed, or (b) some moon *always* is eclipsed.
3	Strictly Sometime Necessary Proposition *muntashira* Every human, *strictly sometime*, necessarily breathes.	Either (a) opposite-quality *continuously broadly possible proposition* or (b) same-quality *extensionally continuous proposition.* It is always the case that either (a) some human a*lways broadly possibly* does not breathe, or (b) some human *always* breathes.
4	Strictly Intensionally Continuous Proposition *ʿurfiyya khāṣṣa* Every writer, *strictly as long as he is a writer, always* moves his fingers.	Either (a) opposite-quality *intensionally actual proposition* or (b) same-quality *extensionally continuous proposition.* It is always the case that either (a) some writer, *as long as he is a writer, actually* does not move his fingers, or (b) some writer *always* moves his fingers.
5	Non-Necessary Actual Proposition wujūdiyya lā-ḍarūriyya Every human *actually but not necessarily* breathes.	Either (a) opposite-quality *extensionally continuous proposition* or (b) same-quality extensionally necessary proposition. It is always the case that either (a) some human *always* does not breathe, or (b) some human *necessarily* breathes.

	Original Modal Proposition	Contradictory Modal Proposition
6	Non-Continuous Actual Proposition *wujūdiyya lā-dā'ima* Every human *actually but not always* breathes.	Either (a) opposite-quality *extensionally continuous proposition* or (b) same-quality *extensionally continuous proposition.* It is always the case that either (a) some human *always* does not breathe, or (b) some human *always* breathes.
7	Strictly Possible Proposition mumkina khāṣṣa Every fire *strictly possibly* is hot.	Either (a) opposite-quality *extensionally necessary proposition* or (b) same-quality *extensionally necessary proposition.* It is always the case that either (a) some fire *necessarily* is not hot, or (b) some fire *necessarily* is hot.

The formulation of the contradictory opposite of composite modal propositions with disjunctive propositions in this manner is, however, merely an approximation. This is because, strictly speaking, complex propositions describe a relationship between two sub-propositions, whereas what is ideally sought here is a simple proposition that affirms or negates a predication-occurrence to a non-propositional subject. In reality, the contradictory opposite of an affirmative[11] composite modal proposition is not the disjunctive approximation described above, but the predication to the appropriately quantified subject of the complex predicate-concept ‹one or both of (*a*) the negation of the first predicate qualified with its contradictory modality and (*b*) the affirmation of the second predicate qualified with its contradictory modality›. Let us illustrate this by applying this to the example ‹Every writer, *strictly as long as he is a writer, necessarily* moves his fingers›. The disjunctive approximation of its contradictory opposite was ‹It is always the case that either (*a*) some writer, *as long as he is a writer, broadly possibly* does not move his fingers, or (*b*) some writer *always* moves his fingers›. The simple proposition that this disjunctive proposition approximates is ‹Some writer either (*a*) *broadly possibly* does not move his fingers *as long as he is a writer*, or (*b*) *always* moves his fingers›, where the "or" is falsity-exclusive, meaning that both predications cannot not be the case but one or both of them can.

11. The contradictory opposite of a negative proposition would be the same except that the affirmations and negations of the two predicates would be reversed.

The reason why a disjunctive complex proposition is a good approximation of this simple proposition is because the disjunctive complex proposition is true whenever this simple proposition is true and false whenever it is false. This disjunctive approximation only works, however, when the original proposition is *universally quantified* (as has been the case with all examples so far), not when it is particularly quantified. To see why this is the case, consider the following table.

Particularly Quantified Subject	Quasi-Disjunctive Simple Proposition	Some A is either B or C
	Corresponding Truly Disjunctive Proposition	It is always the case that either some A is B or that some A is C
Universally Quantified Subject	Quasi-Disjunctive Simple Proposition	Every A is either B or C
	Corresponding Truly Disjunctive Proposition	It is always the case that either every A is B or that every A is C

This table places a *quasi-disjunctive simple proposition* (*ḥamliyya shabīha bi-l-munfaṣila*) beside its corresponding *truly disjunctive proposition* (*munfaṣila ḥaqīqiyya*).[12] The proposition "Some A is either B or C" is a quasi-disjunctive simple proposition. It is properly interpreted as a simple proposition because the disjunctive term "either" is placed after the subject term, but it resembles a disjunctive proposition because the presence of the disjunctive term allows it also to be interpreted as a disjunctive proposition. As a simple proposition, it signifies the predication of the concept ‹either B or C› (a predicate-concept that means ‹one or both of B and C›) to some referent of A. The corresponding *truly disjunctive proposition* ‹It is always the case that either some A is B or that some A is C› is how the simple proposition might

12. A *quasi-disjunctive simple proposition* is an equivocally simple proposition because it can also be interpreted as a disjunctive proposition. A *truly disjunctive proposition* is an unequivocally disjunctive proposition because it can only be interpreted as a disjunctive proposition, never as a simple proposition. Depending on (*a*) whether the disjunctive term "either" is placed before or after the subject term and (*b*) whether or not the two sub-propositions of the disjunctive complex proposition are stated in their complete form, simple and disjunctive propositions fall into one of four categories: (1) *unequivocally simple propositions*, i.e., simple propositions without any disjunctive term whatsoever, e.g., "Every A is B"; (2) *equivocally simple propositions*, i.e., simple propositions that might be mistaken for disjunctive propositions because they comprise a disjunctive term in their predicates, e.g., "Every A is either B or C"; (3) *unequivocally disjunctive propositions*, i.e., disjunctive propositions whose sub-propositions are completely stated with their subjects as well as their predicates, e.g., "Either A is B, or A is C"; and (4) *equivocally disjunctive propositions*, i.e., disjunctive propositions whose sub-propositions are incompletely stated, e.g., "Either A is B or C." *TB*, 320.

also have been interpreted. This proposition is a complex proposition that signifies the affirmation of a falsity-exclusive disjunctive relationship between the proposition ‹Some A is B› and the proposition ‹Some A is C›. Although the simple and disjunctive propositions state different things, they are logically equivalent in terms of when they are true or false.

This logical equivalence does not, however, hold with the second pair of propositions where the subject-term of the simple proposition is universally quantified. As a simple proposition, "Every A is either B or C," is not logically equivalent to the disjunctive proposition, "It is always the case that either every A is B or that every A is C." For example, when some A is B, some A is not B, some A is C, and some A is not C, the simple proposition is true, but the disjunctive proposition is false. What this means is that the contradictory opposites of *universally quantified* composite modal propositions can be approximated with disjunctive propositions (because the simple proposition that is approximated by the disjunctive proposition is particularly quantified), but the contradictory opposites of *particularly quantified* composite modal propositions cannot (because the simple proposition that would be approximated by the disjunctive proposition is universally quantified and hence not logically equivalent to it). The contradictory opposites of particularly quantified composite modal propositions can hence only be expressed with the simple proposition, not with the disjunctive proposition that approximates it.[13]

Let us illustrate this by applying it to the particularly quantified non-continuous actual proposition, "Some object *actually but not always* is an animal." This original proposition is false because it states that there is some object that is sometimes an animal and sometimes not an animal, whereas, in reality, every object is either continuously an animal or continuously not an animal. Because this proposition is particularly quantified, the disjunctive approximation of its contradictory opposite will fail[14]—applying the method

13. It would have been better for the logicians to have used the simple proposition to represent the contradictory opposite of both universally and particularly quantified composite modal propositions. This would have been clearer because using the disjunctive approximation in one case and the original simple proposition in the other complicates the presentation. It would also have been simpler because the disjunctive proposition consists of two sub-propositions and is hence more unwieldy than the original simple proposition, which only consists of one. *TB*, 326.

14. The logicians carefully chose this case because the disjunctive approximation fails for it. But, in fact, the disjunctive approximation will succeed in some specific cases and fail in others. The reason why the disjunctive approximation is not valid for the contradictory opposites of particularly quantified propositions is not because it fails in *all* cases, but because it fails in *some* cases. What is valid should never fail.

of forming the disjunctive approximation described above, we obtain the proposition ‹It is always the case that either (1) every object *always* is not an animal, or (2) every object *always* is an animal›. Both sub-propositions are false. The first is false because there are, indeed, some objects that are continuously animals. The second is false because there are other objects that are continuously not animals. Since the original proposition is false and this disjunctive proposition, too, is false, the disjunctive proposition has not approximated the original proposition's *contradictory opposite*. The simple proposition that this disjunctive proposition failed to approximate correctly is ‹Every object is either *always* an animal or *always* not an animal›. Unlike the disjunctive approximation, this simple proposition is true and properly contradicts the original proposition.[15]

8.1.3 *The Eight Aspects of Formal Identity*

In order for two propositions to *contradict* each other, they must formally differ in the three aspects discussed above—*quality*, *quantification*, and *stated modality*—and they must be formally identical in all other aspects, which the early Muslim logicians summarized as the *eight aspects of formal identity* (*al-waḥadāt al-thamāniya*): (1) identity of subjects, (2) identify of predicates, (3) identity of time, (4) identity of place, (5) identity of correlation, (6) identity of conditions, (7) identity of potentiality and actuality, and (8) identity of parts and wholes. These eight aspects of identity are illustrated in the table below.

	Aspect of Identity	Example of Non-Contradiction	
1	Subject *mawḍūʿ*	Zayd is standing.	ʿAmr is not standing.
2	Predicate *maḥmūl*	Zayd is standing.	Zayd is not sitting.
3	Time[16] *zamān*	Zayd is standing (i.e., at nighttime).	Zayd is not standing (i.e., at daytime).

15. This was one of several methods that the Muslim logicians used to remedy the inconsistency of the disjunctive approximation for particularly quantified composite modal propositions. Among their other methods was to maintain the disjunctive approximation but to modify with a third sub-proposition as follows, ‹It is always the case that either (1) every object *always* is not an animal, (2) every object *always* is an animal, or (3) some object *always* is an animal and some object *always* is not an animal›. *TB*, 325.

16. Some logicians object that identity of time is not always a requirement for the realization of a contradiction, such as, for example, in the two propositions (1) ‹Zayd is ʿAmr's father yesterday› and (2) ‹Zayd is not ʿAmr's father today›, where the difference in time does not

Aspect of Identity		Example of Non-Contradiction	
4	Place[17] *makān*	Zayd is standing (i.e., in the mosque).	Zayd is not standing (i.e., in the marketplace).
5	Correlation *iḍāfa*	Zayd is a father (i.e., to Bakr).	Zayd is not a father (i.e., to ʿAmr).
6	Condition *sharṭ*	Radiation is harmful (i.e., on condition of its having a high frequency).	Radiation is not harmful (i.e., on condition of its having a low frequency).
7	Potentiality and Actuality *al-quwwa wa-l-fiʿl*	The fermenting grape-juice is intoxicating (i.e., potentially).	The fermenting grape-juice is not intoxicating (i.e., actually).
8	Part and Whole *al-kull wa-l-juzʾ*	Zebras are black (i.e., partially).	Zebras are not black (i.e., wholly).

The examples in the table first illustrate that if the subjects or predicates are not identical, then formally changing the proposition from affirmative to negative or vice-versa does not result in a logical contradiction (Rows 1 and 2). The remaining examples are more subtle, illustrating that one must also take care to ensure that the times when the two predications occur are identical (Row 3); that the places where the predicates exist are identical (Row 4); that when the predicates are *correlatives*, their corresponding correlatives are identical (Row 5); that any unstated conditions or qualifications on the subjects are identical (Row 6); that the if one predication is intended potentially, then the other one must be, too, and if it is intended actually, then the other one must be, too (Row 7); and, finally, that if one predication is intended to apply to part of the subject, then the other one must be, too, and if it is intended to apply to all of the subject, then the other one must be, too (Row 8).

affect the fact that the two propositions are contradictory. This objection was not, however, accepted as correct by the logical scholarly tradition, which held that these two propositions are not, in fact, contradictory, because of the difference in time. The reason why it is not possible for them to be simultaneously true or false is not because of the *form* of the difference but because the specific predicate that materially constitutes the propositions (i.e., ‹father›) happens not to change with time. *TB*, 309.

17. Some logicians objected that time and place are the same aspect because they always metaphysically accompany each other as entailments of an object's existence. This objection was not, however, accepted as correct by the normative logical scholarly tradition, which held that place normally qualifies the *predicate*, whereas time qualifies the *predication*. *TB*, 309.

The early Muslim logicians did not intend these eight aspects of identity as an exhaustive list; they merely intended to train students to examine propositions carefully and not hastily assume that every pair of propositions that appears to be contradictory is, in fact, contradictory. In order for a pair of propositions to really be contradictory, the propositions must be identical in every single aspect except for the three aspects of difference described above in the previous section, and these aspects of identity are often left unstated. Discerning whether two propositions do, indeed, contradict each other thus requires careful reflection on all possible aspects of identity. These aspects of identity are, in fact, innumerable and often specific to the particular situation at hand, but studying eight common examples is normally sufficient to train students of logic to be alert to other aspects that might prevent two apparently contradictory propositions from, in fact, contradicting each other. Examples of other aspects of identity include identity of *instrument* (*āla*) in the two propositions ‹Zayd is writing (i.e., with a Japanese pen)› and ‹Zayd is not writing (i.e., with a German pen)› and the identity of *circumstantial qualifier* (*ḥāl*) in the two propositions ‹Zayd is singing (i.e., while riding)› and ‹Zayd is not singing (i.e., while standing)›.

Later Muslim logicians reduced all aspects of identity to two aspects, namely, *identity of subject* and *identity of predicate*. Identity of condition (Row 6) and identity of part and whole (Row 8) can both be restated as identities of the subject, and the rest of the identities can all be restated as identities of the predicate. This is illustrated in the table below.

Aspect of Identity		Example of Non-Contradiction	
3	Difference in time (*zamān*) as a difference in predicate	Zayd is standing (i.e., at nighttime).	Zayd is not standing (i.e., at daytime).
		Zayd is *standing at nighttime.*	Zayd is not *standing at daytime.*
4	Difference in place (*makān*) as a difference in predicate	Zayd is standing (i.e., in the mosque).	Zayd is not standing (i.e., in the marketplace).
		Zayd is *standing in the mosque.*	Zayd is *standing in the marketplace.*
5	Difference in correlation (*iḍāfa*) is a difference is predicate	Zayd is a father (i.e., to Bakr).	Zayd is not a father (i.e., to ʿAmr).
		Zayd is *Bakr's father.*	Zayd is not *ʿAmr's father.*

	Aspect of Identity	Example of Non-Contradiction	
6	Difference in condition (*sharṭ*) is a difference in subject	Radiation is harmful (i.e., on condition of its having a high frequency).	Radiation is not harmful (i.e., on condition of its having a low frequency).
		High-frequency radiation is harmful.	*Low-frequency radiation* is not harmful.
7	Difference in potentiality and actuality (*al-quwwa wa-l-fiʿl*) is a difference in predicate	The fermenting grape-juice is intoxicating (i.e., potentially).	The fermenting grape-juice is not intoxicating (i.e., actually).
		The fermenting grape-juice is *potentially intoxicating.*	The fermenting grape-juice is not *actually intoxicating.*
8	Difference in part and whole (*al-kull wa-l-juzʾ*) is a difference in subject	Zebras are black (i.e., partially).	Zebras are not black (i.e., wholly).
		Parts of zebras are black.	*The entirety of zebras* is not black.

Other later logicians noted that it is best to say that it is *possible* to reduce differences in time, place, correlation, condition, potentiality and actuality, and whole and part to differences in subject or predicate, without specifying which differences reduce to a difference in the subject and which ones reduce to a difference in the predicate, because each difference can be reduced to either a difference in the subject or a difference in the predicate depending on how the proposition is stated. For example, a difference in time can be reduced to a difference in predicate as illustrated in the table, or it can be reduced to a difference in subject by re-stating the propositions as, "The one who is standing at nighttime is Zayd," and, "The one who is standing at daytime is not Zayd." Similar modifications can be devised for the other differences.

For this reason, and also because the possible aspects of identity are innumerable, late Muslim logicians reduced all aspects of identity to a single aspect, namely, *identity of predication* (*waḥdat al-nisba*). Since every predication includes within it the subject and the predicate,[18] differences in either entail a difference in the predication.

18. The wording of this statement reflects the position that the concepts of the subject and predicate are *parts* (*arkān*) of the predication (see 1.1.3). The conclusion, however, would be

8.2 Conversion

Conversion (*ʿaks*) is the switching of the two parts of a proposition in a way that preserves its *truth* and *quality*. When a proposition is *converted* to another proposition, the resultant proposition is called the *converse* (*ʿaks*)[19] of the original proposition. Conversion applies to both *simple propositions*, in which case the two parts that are switched are the proposition's subject and predicate,[20] and to *conditional complex propositions*, in which case the two parts that are switched are the proposition's antecedent and consequent. For example, the converse of the universally quantified simple proposition ‹Every human is rational› is the particularly quantified simple proposition ‹Some rational thing is human›, and the converse of the universally quantified conditional complex proposition ‹It is always the case that when fire exists, heat exists› is the particularly quantified conditional complex proposition ‹It is sometimes the case that when heat exists, fire exists›. In each of these examples, the converse proposition switches the two parts of the original proposition in a way that preserves its truth (meaning that whenever the original proposition is true, the converse is also true) as well as its quality (meaning whenever the original proposition is affirmative the converse is also affirmative, and whenever the original proposition is negative, the converse is also negative).

Conversion does not, however, apply to *disjunctive complex propositions*, because, unlike simple and conditional complex propositions, which are *naturally ordered* (*murattab bi-l-ṭabʿ*), disjunctive complex propositions are merely *semantically ordered* (*murattab bi-l-waḍʿ*). A *naturally ordered proposition* is a proposition whose parts' order affects the proposition's meaning. Simple propositions are naturally ordered because switching their subjects and the predicates changes their meaning. The original proposition ‹Every human is rational› has a different meaning than its converse, ‹Some rational things are human›. Conditional complex propositions are also naturally ordered because switching their antecedents and consequents changes their meaning. The original proposition ‹It is always the case that when fire exists, heat exists› has a

true if the concepts of the subject and predicate were *conditions* (*shurūṭ*) rather than parts of the predication.

19. The Arabic expression *ʿaks* is thus equivocal. Used literally, it refers to the conversion process; used figuratively, it refers to the resultant proposition. *TB*, 329-30.

20. Strictly speaking, it is not the subjects and predicates themselves that are switched, but only the expressions that signify them. Switching the subjects and predicates themselves is not possible, because what is sought from the subject is its referent and what is sought from the predicate is its concept (see 6.1), and when the subject-expression is switched for the predicate-expression, these things are not switched with them. *TB*, 330.

different meaning than its converse, ‹It is sometimes the case that when heat exists, fire exists›. A merely *semantically ordered proposition*, on the other hand, is a proposition whose parts' order does *not* affect the proposition's meaning. Disjunctive complex propositions are merely semantically ordered, because switching their sub-propositions does not change their meaning. For example, the disjunctive complex proposition, "Either this number is even, or this number is odd," has the same meaning as, "Either this number is odd, or this number is even." Although the order of the two parts has been changed, the meaning of the proposition—i.e., the affirmation of a disjunctive relationship between the two sub-propositions—remains the same. Even though switching the order of the two parts in such propositions preserves their truth, the logicians do not consider this to be *conversion* because their study focuses on mental meanings rather than verbal expressions.

The process of propositional conversion only preserves *truth*, not *falsity*. This means that if the original proposition is true, then the converse will also be true, but if the original proposition is false, then the converse may or may not be false. The relationship between the original proposition and its converse can thus be represented by the following conditional complex proposition: ‹If the original proposition is true, then its converse is true›. In other words, the truth of the original proposition entails the truth of its converse, and the falsity of the converse entails the falsity of the original proposition.

Although conversion *preserves* truth, it does not *require* truth. In other words, if a proposition happens to actually be false, the conversion process is still valid. For example, even though the proposition ‹Every human is non-rational› is actually false, it is still correct to say that its converse is ‹Some non-rational things are human›. This is because conversion relates to the *form* of propositions, not to their *matter*. If a proposition on the form of the original proposition is true, then the proposition on the form of the converse will also be true. The fact that conversion is a transformation that retains truth by virtue of propositional *form* excludes examples where switching the two parts of a proposition retains truth by virtue of the specific subjects and predicates that materially constitute the proposition. For example, changing the proposition ‹Every human is rational› to the proposition ‹Every rational thing is human› preserves truth, but only because of the specific subjects and predicates of these propositions, not because of their form. That is why transforming other propositions that have the same form, e.g., ‹Every crow is black›, does not preserve their truth—it is true that all crows are black, but it is not true that all black things are crows.

8.2.1 *Quantification in Conversion*

As described above, propositional conversion requires preservation of a proposition's quality. It does not, however, require preservation of the proposition's *quantification*, which is sometimes kept the same and at other times changed. That is, the converse proposition's quantification is negotiated in order to preserve the proposition's truth when its two parts are switched while it retains its original quality. The results of this negotiation are summarized in the table below for both simple and conditional complex propositions.

	Original Proposition	**Converse Proposition**
Affirmative Universally Quantified	Every A is B.	Some B is A
	It is always the case that if A then B.,	It is sometimes the case that if B, then A.
Affirmative Particularly Quantified	Some A is B	Some B is A
	It is sometimes the case that if A, then B.	It is sometimes the case that if A, then B.
Negative Universally Quantified	Every A is not B.	Every B is not A.
	It is never the case that if A, then B.	It is never the case that if B, then A.
Negative Particularly Quantified	Some A is not B.	No valid converse
	It is sometimes not the case that if A, then B.	No valid converse

The first thing to note from this table is that conversion only applies to those propositions that can be quantified, namely *universal propositions*. *Singular propositions*, which cannot be quantified, cannot be converted, because predicates of their converse propositions would then be singular, and the predication of a singular is impossible (see 3.4.1.2). Now, the quantified universal propositions in the table are divided into two categories, namely, affirmative propositions and negative propositions. Let us examine these in turn.

8.2.1.1 Conversion of Affirmative Propositions

The converse of an affirmative proposition—whether simple or complex and whether universally quantified or particularly quantified—is always particularly quantified. The fact that the converse of a *particularly quantified* proposition is a particularly quantified is obvious. It is obvious with simple propositions because if it is the case that some A is B, then in those cases when A is B, B is A, and therefore it is true that some B is A. It is obvious as well with conditional complex propositions because if it is the case that A sometimes entails B, then in those cases where A entails B, B also entails A, and therefore it is true that B sometimes entails A.

However, the fact that the converse of a *universally quantified* proposition is a particularly quantified proposition is not as obvious and requires a two-part inferential sequence as follows. The first part is to show that an affirmative universally quantified proposition does not validly convert to a universally quantified proposition:

1. The original proposition is an affirmative universally quantified proposition, either simple or conditional complex.
2. It is possible for the predicate (of the original simple proposition) or the consequent (of the original conditional complex proposition) to be *unconditionally more inclusive* than the subject or antecedent, respectively, such as in the propositions ‹Every human is an animal› and ‹It is always the case that if fire exists, then heat exists›.
3. If the original proposition were to validly convert to a universally quantified proposition, then in this case, for simple propositions, it would entail the predication of a concept that is *unconditionally more inclusive* to the instances of a concept that is *unconditionally less inclusive*; similarly, for conditional complex propositions, it would entail that something that is *unconditionally more inclusive* implies something that is *unconditionally less inclusive*. Both of these outcomes are impossible.

To illustrate (3), the hypothetical converses of the example propositions above are ‹Every animal is human› and ‹It is always the case that when heat exists, then fire exists›. The first is false because the fact that the predicate-concept ‹human› is unconditionally less inclusive than the subject-concept ‹animal› entails that there are some animals that are not humans. The second is false because the fact that the consequent proposition ‹Fire exists› is unconditionally less inclusive than the antecedent proposition ‹Heat exists› (i.e., the cases when the consequent is true are a strict subset of the cases when the antecedent is true) means that there are some cases when it is true that heat exists but false that fire exists, such as when the heat is a result of sunlight.

The second part of the inference is to show that every affirmative universally quantified proposition validly converts to a particularly quantified proposition:[21]

4. Assume that affirmative universally quantified propositions do not validly convert to particularly quantified propositions. In other words, the truth of ‹Every A is B› does not entail the truth of ‹Some B is A›, and the truth of ‹It is always the case that if A is true, then B is true› does not entail the truth of ‹It is sometimes the case that if B is true, then A is true›.
5. Therefore, affirmative universally quantified propositions entail the truth of the *contradictory opposites* of their particularly quantified converses. In other words, the truth of ‹Every A is not B› entails the truth of ‹Some B is A›, and the truth of ‹It is never that case that if A is true, then B is true› entails the truth of ‹It is sometimes the case that if B is true, then A is true›.
6. Construct a *simple syllogism* with the contradictory opposite as the *minor premise* and the original proposition as the *major premise*. This syllogism entails that some A is not A, which is false because it is impossible to deny something of itself.[22]
7. Therefore, affirmative universally quantified propositions do not entail the truth of the contradictory opposite of the particularly quantified converses.

21. The first step proves that affirmative universally quantified propositions do not validly convert to universally quantified propositions. This alone does not entail that they convert to particularly quantified propositions; rather, it entails that *if* universally quantified propositions do validly convert, then they can only validly convert to particularly quantified propositions. The fact that they do validly convert (and to particularly quantified propositions) is proven in this second step. *TB*, 333-34.

22. This is how the Muslim logicians stated what is now known as the law of identity. The entailment is illustrated in the table below.

	Simple Proposition	Conditional Proposition
Minor Premise	Every A is B.	It is always the case that if A is true, then B is true.
Major Premise	Some B is not A.	It is sometimes not the case that if B is true, then A is true.
Conclusion	Some A is not A.	It is sometimes the case that if A is true, then A is not true.

8. Therefore, the assumption in (*4*) is false, and affirmative universally quantified propositions do indeed validly convert to particularly quantified propositions.

This is a proof by contradiction (*dalīl al-khulf*) that creates a contradiction by placing the contradictory opposite of the converse in a simple syllogism with the original proposition. This is the standard method of proof that is used throughout the rest of this section on conversion.

8.2.1.2 Conversion of Negative Propositions

Negative *universally quantified* propositions convert to universally quantified propositions by the same argument just described above, namely, a proof by contradiction that proceeds by placing the contradictory opposite of the converse in a simple syllogism with the original proposition. The logical proof is as follows:

1. Assume that negative universally quantified propositions do not validly convert to universally quantified propositions. In other words, the truth of ‹Every A is not B› does not entail the truth of ‹Every B is not A›, and the truth of ‹It is never the case that if A is true, then B is true› does not entail the truth of ‹It is never the case that if B is true, then A is true›.
2. Therefore, negative universally quantified propositions entail the truth of the contradictory opposites of their universally quantified converses. In other words, the truth of ‹Every A is B› does entails the truth of ‹Some B is not A›, and the truth of ‹It is always that case that if A is true, then B is true› does entails the truth of ‹It is sometimes not the case that if B is true, then A is true›.
3. Construct a *simple syllogism* with the contradictory opposite as the *minor premise* and the original proposition as the *major premise*. This syllogism entails that some A is not A, which is false because it is impossible to deny something of itself.[23]
4. Therefore, negative universally quantified propositions do not entail

23. The entailment of this violation of the law of identity is illustrated in the table below.

	Simple Proposition	Conditional Proposition
Minor Premise	Every A is not B.	It is never the case that if A is true, then B is true.
Major Premise	Some B is A.	It is sometimes the case that if B is true, then A is true.

the truth of the contradictory opposite of their universally quantified converses.

5. Therefore, the assumption in (*1*) is false and negative universally quantified propositions do indeed validly convert to universally quantified propositions.

As for negative *particularly quantified* propositions, they do not validly convert, neither to universally quantified propositions nor to particularly quantified propositions. The logical proof is as follows:

1. The original proposition is a negative particularly quantified proposition, either simple or conditional complex.
2. It is possible for the subject (of the original simple proposition) or the antecedent (of the original conditional complex proposition) to be *unconditionally more general* than the predicate or the consequent, respectively, such as in the propositions ‹Some animal is not human› and ‹It is sometimes not the case that if heat exists, then fire exists›.
3. If the original proposition were to validly convert (whether to a universally quantified or a particularly quantified proposition), then in this case, for simple propositions, it would entail that a predicate unconditionally more general than its subject is not predicated to it, and, for conditional complex propositions, it would entail that a consequent unconditionally more general than its antecedent is not entailed by it. Both of these outcomes are impossible.

To illustrate (*3*), the hypothetical converse of the example simple proposition above would either be ‹Every human is not an animal› (universally quantified) or ‹Some humans are not animals› (particularly quantified). But each of these is false because it entails that some human is not an animal, which is impossible, because the concept ‹human› is unconditionally more specific than the concept ‹animal›. Similarly, the hypothetical converse of the example conditional complex proposition above would either be ‹It is

	Simple Proposition	**Conditional Proposition**
Conclusion	Some A is not A.	It is sometimes the case that if A is true, then A is not true.

If it be objected that the proposition, ‹Some A is not A›, can be true when A does not exist because negative propositions have no existential import (see 6.6), then the response would be that A does, indeed, exist, because this is the conclusion of a syllogism whose minor premise (an affirmative proposition) requires the existence of A. *TB*, 335.

never the case that if fire exists, then heat exists› (universally quantified) or ‹It is sometimes not the case that if fire exists, then heat exists› (particularly quantified). But each of these is false because it entails that sometimes the existence of fire does not entail the existence of heat, which is impossible, because the existence of fire is unconditionally more specific than the existence of heat, meaning that the cases where the proposition ‹Fire exists› is true are a strict subset of the cases where the proposition ‹Heat exists› is true.

8.2.2 *Modality in Conversion*

As was the case with contradiction, conversion requires that the modality of a proposition be considered. Let us examine the conversions of affirmative and negative modal propositions in turn.

8.2.2.1 Conversion of Affirmative Modal Propositions

The table below lists the conversions of affirmative modal propositions of various basic and composite stated modalities. Every affirmative modal proposition that validly converts results in an affirmative particularly quantified modal proposition. The validity of the conversion can be proven for each kind of modal proposition.

	Original Affirmative Modal Proposition	**Converse**
N1 Basic	Extensionally Necessary Proposition *ḍarūriyya muṭlaqa* E.g., Every A *necessarily* is B.	Broadly Intensionally Actual Proposition *ḥīniyya muṭlaqa* E.g., Some B, *broadly as* B, *broadly actually* is A.
N2 Basic	Broadly Intensionally Necessary Proposition *mashrūṭa ʿāmma* E.g., Every A, *broadly as* A, *necessarily* is B.	Broadly Intensionally Actual Proposition *ḥīniyya muṭlaqa* E.g., Some B, *broadly as* B, *broadly actually* is A.

	Original Affirmative Modal Proposition	**Converse**
N3 Comp.	Strictly Intensionally Necessary Proposition *mashrūṭa khāṣṣa* E.g., Every A, *strictly as* A, *necessarily* is B.	Intensionally Non-Continuously Actual Proposition *ḥīniyya muṭlaqa lā-dā'ima* E.g., Some B, as B, *actually but not always* is A.
N4 Basic	Broadly Specific-Time Necessary Proposition *waqtiyya muṭlaqa* E.g., Every A, *broadly at a specified time, necessarily* is B.	Broadly Actual Proposition *muṭlaqa ʿāmma* E.g., Some B *broadly actually* is A.
N5 Comp.	Strictly Specific-Time Necessary Proposition *waqtiyya* E.g., Every A, *strictly at* a specified time, *necessarily* is B.	Broadly Actual Proposition *muṭlaqa ʿāmma* E.g., Some B *broadly actually* is A.
N6 Basic	Broadly Sometime Necessary Proposition *muntashira muṭlaqa* E.g., Every A *broadly sometime necessarily* is B.	Broadly Actual Proposition *muṭlaqa ʿāmma* E.g., Some B *broadly actually* is A.
N7 Comp.	Strictly Sometime Necessary Proposition *muntashira* E.g., Every A, *strictly sometime, necessarily* is B.	Broadly Actual Proposition *muṭlaqa ʿāmma* E.g., Some B *broadly actually* is A.
C1 Basic	Extensionally Continuous Proposition *dā'ima muṭlaqa* E.g., Every A *always* is B.	Broadly Intensionally Actual Proposition *ḥīniyya muṭlaqa* E.g., Some B, *broadly as* B, *broadly actually* is A.

	Original Affirmative Modal Proposition	Converse
C2 Basic	Broadly Intensionally Continuous Proposition *ʿurfiyya ʿāmma* E.g., Every A, *broadly as* A, *always* is B.	Broadly Intensionally Actual Proposition *ḥīniyya muṭlaqa* E.g., Some B, *broadly as* B, *broadly actually* is A.
C3 Comp.	Strictly Intensionally Continuous Proposition *ʿurfiyya khāṣṣa* E.g., Every A, *strictly as* A, *always* is B.	Intensionally Non-Continuously Actual Proposition *ḥīniyya muṭlaqa lā-dāʾima* E.g., Some B, as B, *actually but not always* is A.
A1 Basic	Broadly Actual Proposition *muṭlaqa ʿāmma* E.g., Every A *broadly actually* is B.	Broadly Actual Proposition *muṭlaqa ʿāmma* E.g., Some B *broadly actually* is A.
A2 Comp.	Non-Necessary Actual Proposition *wujūdiyya lā-ḍarūriyya* E.g., Every A *actually but not necessarily* is B.	Broadly Actual Proposition *muṭlaqa ʿāmma* E.g., Some B *broadly actually* is A.
A3 Comp.	Non-Continuous Actual Proposition *wujūdiyya lā-dāʾima* E.g., Every A *actually but not always* is B.	Broadly Actual Proposition *muṭlaqa ʿāmma* E.g., Some B *broadly actually* is A.
P1 Basic	Broadly Possible Proposition *mumkina ʿāmma* E.g., Every A *broadly possibly* is B.	*No valid converse*
P2 Comp.	Strictly Possible Proposition *mumkina khāṣṣa* E.g., Every A *strictly possibly* is B.	*No valid converse*

As the table above shows, the conversions of affirmative propositions that are

(N1) Extensionally necessary

(C1) Extensionally continuous

(N2) Broadly intensionally necessary

(C2) Broadly intensionally continuous

all result in *broadly intensionally actual propositions* (sg. *ḥīniyya muṭlaqa*). To see why this is the case, recall first that the predication in ‹Every A is B› uses the subject-concept ‹A› to refer to all the concept's referents and then affirms that these referents are all characterized by the predicate-concept ‹B›. To say that this predication is extensionally necessary or extensionally continuous is to say that the *referents* of ‹A› are such that their characterization by ‹B› is necessary or continuous, respectively, independently of their characterization by the concept ‹A›. The role of the concept ‹A›, in other words, is simply to pick out its referents in order to affirm that their characterization by ‹B› is necessary or continuous. As for their characterization by ‹A›, it neither has to be necessary nor continuous. All that is required is that it picks out its referents, which merely requires that their characterization by it be *actual*. For example, in the propositions ‹Every writer *extensionally necessarily* is human› or ‹Every writer *extensionally continuously* is human›, the characterization of the referents of the subject-concept ‹writer› by the predicate-concept ‹human› is both necessary and continuous, but their characterization by the subject-concept ‹writer› itself is neither necessary (it is possible for a human to not be a writer) nor continuous (a human may only sometimes be a writer). All that is required for the proposition to be true is that *some referent* be characterized by the concept ‹writer› (otherwise there would be no writers, which would violate the affirmative proposition's requirement of existential import; see 6.6). That is to say, all that is required for the proposition to be true is for the referents of the subject-concept ‹writer› to be *actually* characterized by ‹writer›.

This example was chosen to illustrate that it is possible for the subject-referents of extensionally necessary or continuous propositions to be *strictly actually* characterized by the subject-concept. It is also possible, however, for them to be necessarily characterized by their subject-concept (e.g., ‹Every rational thing is human›) or to be continuously characterized by their subject-concept (e.g., ‹Every potentially laughing thing is human›). Putting all these cases together, we can say that the subject-referents of extensionally necessary or continuous propositions must be *broadly actually* characterized by their subject-concepts, where *broad actuality* includes actuality, continuity, and necessity.

Note that each of these three examples—‹Every writer is human›, ‹Every rational thing is human›, and ‹Every potentially laughing thing is human›—can also be rendered as broadly intensionally necessary and broadly intensionally continuous. By the same line of reasoning applied in the case of extensionally necessary and extensionally continuous propositions, the subject-referents of broadly intensionally necessary and broadly intensionally continuous propositions too must be *broadly actually* characterized by their subject-concepts.

We are now ready to see why these four kinds of modal propositions—extensionally necessary propositions, extensionally continuous propositions, broadly intensionally necessary propositions, and broadly intensionally continuous propositions—all convert to *broadly intensionally actual propositions.* When each of these propositions is converted, the subject-concept and predicate-concept are switched; ‹Every A is B› becomes ‹Some B is A›. Whereas the original subject-concept ‹A› was sought merely for the sake of picking out its subject referents, it is now sought for the sake of the subject-referents being characterized by it. The modality of the proposition thus changes from being a description of the subject-referents' being characterized by the old predicate-concept ‹B› (in the converse proposition this is now the subject-concept) to a description of their being characterized by the old subject-concept ‹A› (in the converse proposition this is now the predicate-concept). And, as we have just shown above, the subject-referents are broadly actually characterized by the old subject-concept, which is the new predicate-concept. Thus, the modality of the new predication, that of the converse proposition, is *broad actuality.*

There are two kinds of actuality. First, there is *extensional* actuality, an actuality that exists as a result of the subject-referent's existence; second, there is *broadly intensional* actuality, an actuality that exists as a result of the subject-referent's characterization by the subject-concept. The latter is "broad" because it is *unconditionally more general* than the former. That is, if an actuality exists given the existence of the subject-referent, it also exists given the subject-referent's characterization by the subject-concept. The question thus becomes whether, in the converse proposition, the broad actuality of the subject-referent's characterization by the old subject-concept is *extensional* or *broadly intensional.* The original proposition ‹Every writer is a human› illustrates that it is possible for the original subject-concept to be such that it does not characterize the subject-referent as long as it exists. Therefore the broad actuality of the subject-concept's being characterized by the original subject-concept is *broad intensional* actuality.

Let us now formalize this explanation of the conversion of these four kinds of affirmative modal propositions into a proof with two parts. The first part is a proof that the truth of each of the four kinds entails the truth of its *broadly intensionally actual* converse:

1. Assume that each of these four kinds of affirmative modal propositions does not entail the truth of its broadly intensionally actual converse.
2. Therefore, each of these propositions entails the truth of the contradictory opposite of its broadly intensionally actual converse, which is a *broadly intensionally continuous proposition.*
3. Construct a *simple syllogism* with the contradictory opposite as the *minor premise* and the original modal proposition as the *major premise.* This syllogism entails that some A is not A, which is false because it is impossible to deny something from itself. This is illustrated in the table below.
4. Therefore, these affirmative modal propositions do not entail the truth of the contradictory opposite of their broadly intensionally actual converses.
5. Therefore, the assumption in (*1*) is false and these affirmative modal propositions do indeed entail the truth of their broadly intensionally actual converse propositions.

Original	Converse	Contradictory	Conclusions
N1. Every A *nec.* is B. N2. Every A, as A, *nec.* is B. C1. Every A *alw.* is B. C2. Every A, *as* A, *alw.* is B.	Some B, *broadly as* B, *broadly act.* is A.	Every B, *as* B, *alw.* is not A.	1. Every B *nec.* is not B. 2. Every B, *as* B, *nec.* is not B. 3. Every B *alw.* is not B. 4. Every B, *as* B, *alw.* is not B.

Original	Converse	Contradictory	Conclusions
N1. Some A *nec.* is B.	Some B, *broadly as* B, *broadly act.* is A.	Every B, *as* B, *alw.* is not A.	1. Some B *nec.* is not B.
N2. Some A, *as* A, *nec.* is B.			2. Some B, as B, *nec.* is not B.
C1. Some A alw. is B.			3. Some B *alw.* is not B.
C2. Some A, *as* A, *alw.* is B.			4. Some B, *as* B, *alw.* is not B.

The second part of the proof for the conversion of these four kinds of affirmative modal propositions is a proof that the truth of none of the four kinds entails the truth of any converse proposition that has wider modal truth-scope[24] than the broadly intensionally actual converse proposition:

6. The extensionally necessary proposition is the *unconditionally most specific* of the four modal propositions, meaning that whenever it is true, every other one of the four propositions is true, but not vice-versa.
7. The subject-concept and predicate-concept of an extensionally necessary proposition need not be *extensionally equal.* For example, in the proposition ‹Every laughing thing *necessarily* is human›, it is possible for the concepts ‹laughing thing› and ‹human› to not refer to all the same referents—a human who is not laughing is a referent of the latter but not the former.
8. Therefore, the characterization of the subject-referent by the subject-concept in the converse proposition does not entail its characterization by the predicate-concept but merely its characterization by the predicate-concept at some times when it is characterized by the subject-concept. For example, in the converse proposition ‹Some human is a laughing thing›, the fact that the subject-referent is human does not entail that it is a laughing thing. Rather, the referent of ‹human› is only a laughing thing at some times when it is characterized by the concept ‹human›.
9. The notion of being characterized by the predicate-concept at some times when characterized by the subject-concept is equivalent to the notion of *broad intensional actuality*. Therefore, the converse of an extensionally necessary proposition has no wider modal truth-scope than broad intensional actuality. For example, the converse of ‹Every laughing thing *necessarily* is human› is not with wider modal truth-scope than ‹Some human, *broadly while human, actually* is

24. By the term *modal truth-scope*, what is meant is the set of cases where propositions with a particular modality are true.

a laughing thing›.

10. Therefore (from *6* and *9*), the converse of none of the four kinds of modal propositions has wider modal truth-scope than broadly intensionally actual propositions.

Let us now turn to the conversions of affirmative modal propositions that are

(N3) Strictly Intensionally Necessary

(C3) Strictly Intensionally Continuous.

Each of these two kinds of propositions converts to an *intensionally non-continuously actual proposition* (*ḥīniyya muṭlaqa lā-dā'ima*). This is a new kind of composite modal proposition that is conventionally mentioned by logicians in this section on conversion rather than in the early section on composite stated modalities. *Intensionally non-continuously actual* propositions are broadly intensionally actual propositions conditioned by non-continuity. They are thus equivalent to a same-quality broadly intensionally actual proposition composed with an opposite-quality broadly actual proposition.

The logical proof that strictly intensionally necessary and strictly intensionally continuous propositions convert to intensionally non-continuously actual propositions can thus be broken into two parts. First, it must be proven that the truth of strictly intensionally necessary and strictly intensionally continuous propositions entails the truth of their converse broadly intensionally actual propositions. Second, it must be proven that the truth of strictly intensionally necessary and strictly intensionally continuous propositions entails the truth of the proposition that is the same as the converse broadly actual propositions except that it has the opposite propositional quality. The proof proceeds as follows:

1. The truth of broadly intensionally necessary propositions and broadly intensionally continuous propositions entails the truth of their converse broadly intensionally actual propositions.
2. Strictly intensionally necessary propositions and strictly intensionally continuous propositions are *unconditionally more specific* in their truth-scope than broadly intensionally necessary propositions and broadly intensionally continuous propositions, respectively.
3. Any proposition that is entailed by a proposition is also entailed by

those propositions that are unconditionally more specific than it.[25]

4. Therefore, the truth of strictly intensionally necessary propositions and strictly intensionally continuous propositions entails the truth of their converse broadly intensionally actual propositions.

With the entailment demonstrated, we move to the second part of the proof, which is that either kind of affirmative proposition entails a proposition that differs only in *quality* with the converse broadly actual proposition:

5. Assume that these two kinds of affirmative modal propositions do not entail the truth of the negative converse broadly actual proposition.
6. Therefore, these propositions entail the truth of the contradictory opposites of the negative converse broadly actual proposition, which is an *extensionally continuous proposition*.
7. Construct two *simple syllogisms*: one with the contradictory opposite as the *minor premise* and the first part of the original modal proposition as the *major premise* and another with the contradictory opposite as the minor premise and the second part of the original modal proposition as the major premise. The conclusion of one of these two syllogisms entails that some A is not A, which is false because it is impossible to deny something of itself.[26] This is illustrated in the table below.
8. Therefore, these affirmative modal propositions do not entail the truth of the contradictory opposite of the negative converse broadly actual proposition.
9. Therefore, the assumption in (5) is false, and these affirmative modal propositions do indeed entail the truth of the negative converse broadly actual proposition.

---

25. This is true because more specific propositions are included within those propositions that are more general than them. In order for the more general propositions to entail something, the propositions that they include must also entail that thing.

26. The original text of the *Tahdhīb* indicates that the reason why the simple syllogisms entail something false is because their conclusions contradict each other. Al-ʿAṭṭār explains in his gloss that the affirmation of something to itself is a meaningless tautology, and the real reason why the assumption is false is that one of the two simple propositions entails the negation of something from itself. *TB*, 339.

Original Composite (Major)	Negative Partial Converse	Contradictory (Minor)	Conclusions with First Original Part	Conclusions with Second Original Part
N3. Every A, *as* A, *nec.* is B; & Every A broad-*ly act.* is not B. C3. Every A, *as* A, *alw.* is B; & Every A *broad-ly act.* is not B.	Some B *broadly act.* is not A.	Every B *alw.* is A.	1. Every B *alw.* is B. 2. Every B *alw.* is B.	1. Every B *broadly act.* is not B. 2. Every B *broadly act.* is not B.
N3. Some A, *as* A, *nec.* is B; & Some A *broadly act.* is not B. C3. Some A, *as* A, *alw.* is B; & Some A *broad-ly act.* is not B.	Some B *broadly act.* is not A.	Every B *alw.* is A.	1. Some B *alw.* is B. 2. Some B *alw.* is B.	1. Some B *broadly act.* is not B. 2. Some B *broadly act.* is not B.

Let us proceed to the conversions of affirmative modal propositions that are

(N4) Broadly Specific-Time Necessary

(N5) Strictly Specific-Time Necessary

(N6) Broadly Sometime Necessary

(N7) Strictly Sometime Necessary

(A1) Broadly Actual

(A2) Non-Necessary Actual

(A3) Non-Continuous Actual.

These seven kinds all convert to *broadly actual propositions*. The proof is as follows:

1. Assume that these seven kinds of affirmative modal propositions do not entail the truth of their broadly actual converse.
2. Therefore, these propositions all entail the truth of the contradictory opposites of their broadly actual hypothetical converse, which is also an extensionally continuous proposition.
3. Construct a simple syllogism with the contradictory opposite as the minor premise and the original modal proposition as the major premise. This syllogism entails that some B is not B, which is false because it is impossible to deny something from itself. This is illustrated in the table below.
4. Therefore, these affirmative modal propositions do not entail the truth of the contradictory opposite of their broadly actual hypothetical converses.
5. Therefore, the assumption in (*1*) is false and these affirmative modal propositions do indeed entail the truth of their broadly actual converse propositions.

Original (Major)	**Converse**	**Contradictory (Minor)**	**Conclusion**
Every A [*modality*] is B.	Some B *broadly* act. is A.	Every B *alw.* is not A.	Every B [*modality*] is not B.
Some A [*modality*] is B.	Some B *broadly* act. is A.	Every B *alw.* is not A.	Some B [*modality*] is not B.

Finally, let us move to the conversions of affirmative modal propositions that are

(P1) BROADLY POSSIBLE

(P2) STRICTLY POSSIBLE.

Recall that, according to Avicenna and the logical tradition after him, the meaning of the proposition ‹Every A *possibly* is B› is that everything that is *actually* characterized by the subject-concept ‹A› is *possibly* characterized by the predicate-concept ‹B› (see 6.3). The fact that the propositional referents are only possibly characterized by the predicate-concept ‹B› means that they may in fact never *actually* be characterized by it. Thus, when this original proposition is converted to ‹Some B is A›, the subject-concept and predicate-concept are switched, and the propositional referents must now be *actually* characterized by the original predicate-concept ‹B›. In the case when the propositional referents are never actually characterized by ‹B›, the original proposition is true but its converse is false. For this reason, both *broadly possible* and *strictly possible* propositions do not convert.

To illustrate, suppose that Zayd only actually rides horses and never actually rides donkeys. In this case, the broadly or strictly possible proposition ‹Every donkey *possibly* is something that Zayd rides› means that everything that is actually characterized as being a donkey is possibly characterized as being something that Zayd rides. The converse of the proposition is ‹Some of what Zayd rides *possibly* is a donkey›, which means that some of what is actually characterized as being something that Zayd rides is possibly characterized as being a donkey. Since everything that is actually characterized as being something that Zayd rides is a horse, and since it is impossible for something that is actually a horse to be a donkey, this converse proposition is false.

Note that on al-Fārābī's position on predication, the converse proposition takes a different meaning, that is, that some of what is *possibly* characterized as being something that Zayd rides is possibly characterized as being a donkey. The subject-referent here is not what Zayd actually rides but what he possibly rides. Since Zayd can indeed possibly ride a donkey, the converse proposition is true. Thus, on al-Fārābī's position, broadly and strictly possible propositions do in fact convert, respectively, to broadly and strictly possible propositions.

8.2.2.2 Conversion of Negative Modal Propositions

The table below lists the conversions of the negative counterparts for the kinds of affirmative modal propositions examined above. These conversions can be proven as well.

	Original Negative Modal Proposition	**Converse**
N1 Basic	Extensionally Necessary Proposition *ḍarūriyya muṭlaqa* E.g., Every A *necessarily* is not B.	Extensionally Continuous Proposition *dā'ima muṭlaqa* E.g., Some B *always* is not A.

	Original Negative Modal Proposition	**Converse**
N2 Basic	Broadly Intensionally Necessary Proposition *mashrūṭa ʿāmma* E.g., Every A, *broadly as* A, *necessarily* is not B.	Broadly Intensionally Continuous Proposition *ʿurfiyya muṭlaqa* E.g., Some B, *broadly as* B, *always* is not A.
N3 Comp	Strictly Intensionally Necessary Proposition *mashrūṭa khāṣṣa* E.g., Every A, *strictly as* A, *necessarily* is not B.	Broadly Intensionally Continuous Proposition, Non-Continuous in Some Cases *ʿurfiyya lā-dāʾima fī al-baʿḍ* E.g., Some B, *broadly as* B, *always* is not A; & Some B *broadly actually* is A.
N4 Basic	Broadly Specific-Time Necessary Proposition *waqtiyya muṭlaqa* E.g., Every A, *broadly at a specified time, necessarily* is not B.	*No valid converse*
N5 Comp.	Strictly Specific-Time Necessary Proposition *waqtiyya* E.g., Every A, *strictly at a specified time, necessarily* is not B.	*No valid converse*
N6 Basic	Broadly Sometime Necessary Proposition *muntashira muṭlaqa* E.g., Every A *broadly sometime necessarily* is not B.	*No valid converse*
N7 Comp.	Strictly Sometime Necessary Proposition *muntashira* E.g., Every A, *strictly sometime, necessarily* is not B.	*No valid converse*

	Original Negative Modal Proposition	Converse
C1 Basic	Extensionally Continuous Proposition *dā'ima muṭlaqa* E.g., Every A *always* is not B.	Extensionally Continuous Proposition *dā'ima muṭlaqa* E.g., Some B *always* is not A.
C2 Basic	Broadly Intensionally Continuous Proposition *'urfiyya 'āmma* E.g., Every A, *broadly as* A, *always* is not B.	Broadly Intensionally Continuous Proposition *'urfiyya muṭlaqa* E.g., Some B, *broadly as* B, *always* is not A.
C3 Comp.	Strictly Intensionally Continuous Proposition *'urfiyya khāṣṣa* E.g., Every A, *strictly as* A, *always* is not B.	Broadly Intensionally Continuous Proposition, Non-Continuous in Some Cases *'urfiyya lā-dā'ima fī al-ba'ḍ* E.g., Some B, *broadly as* B, *always* is not A; & *Some* B *broadly actually* is A.
A1 Basic	Broadly Actual Proposition *muṭlaqa 'āmma* E.g., Every A *broadly actually* is not B.	*No valid converse*
A2 Comp.	Non-Necessary Actual Proposition *wujūdiyya lā-ḍarūriyya* E.g., Every A *actually but not necessarily* is not B.	*No valid converse*
A3 Comp.	Non-Continuous Actual Proposition *wujūdiyya lā-dā'ima* E.g., Every A *actually but not always* is not B.	*No valid converse*

	Original Negative Modal Proposition	Converse
P1 Basic	Broadly Possible Proposition *mumkina ʿāmma* E.g., Every A *broadly possibly* is not B.	*No valid converse*
P2 Comp.	Strictly Possible Proposition *mumkina khāṣṣa* E.g., Every A *strictly possibly* is not B.	*No valid converse*

Of the six types of negative modal propositions that validly convert, only two of them validly convert when particularly quantified: *strictly intensionally necessary* and *strictly intensionally continuous* propositions.[27] These two convert to *strictly intensionally continuous* propositions. The remaining four must be universally quantified to validly convert.

As the table above shows, the conversions of negative modal propositions that are

(N1) EXTENSIONALLY NECESSARY

(C1) EXTENSIONALLY CONTINUOUS

result in *extensionally continuous propositions*. Below is the proof that each of these negative propositions entails its extensionally continuous converse:

Assume that these two kinds of negative modal propositions do not entail their extensionally continuous converses.

Therefore, each entails the truth of the contradictory opposite of its extensionally continuous converse, which is a *broadly actual proposition.*

Construct a *simple syllogism* with the contradictory opposite as the *minor premise* and the original modal proposition as the *major premise*. This syllogism entails that some A is not A, which is false because it is impossible to deny something from itself. This is illustrated in the table below.

Therefore, these negative modal propositions do not entail the contradictory opposites of their extensionally continuous converses.

27. Even though, as mentioned previously, negative particularly quantified propositions do not, as a general rule, validly convert, these two kinds of modal propositions do validly convert on condition of their respective stated modalities.

Therefore, the assumption in (*1*) is false, and these negative modal propositions do indeed entail the extensionally continuous converse proposition.

Original (Major)	**Converse**	**Contra-dictory (Minor)**	**Conclusion**
N1. Every A *nec.* is not B. C1. Every A *alw.* is not B.	Every B *alw.* is not A.	Some B *broadly act.* is A.	1. Some B *nec.* is not B. 2. Some B *alw.* is not B.

Note that extensionally continuous propositions convert to propositions with the same modality, but extensionally necessary propositions do not. This is based on Avicenna's position on the characterization of the subject-referent, as discussed previously (see 6.3). The following counterexample proves that negative extensionally necessary propositions do not convert to propositions with the same modality. Suppose that Zayd only actually rides horses and never actually rides donkeys. In this case, on Avicenna's position, the extensionally necessary proposition ‹Everything that Zayd rides *necessarily* is not a donkey› is true. The reason why it is true is that the proposition means that, necessarily, nothing that is *actually* characterized as being something that Zayd rides is characterized as being a donkey. But we know that everything Zayd *actually* rides is a horse, and of course it is necessarily the case that no horse is a donkey. Now, the extensionally necessary converse of the proposition is ‹Everything that is a donkey *necessarily* is not something that Zayd rides›. Whereas the original proposition was true, this proposition is false, because it means that, necessarily, nothing that is *actually* characterized as being a donkey is characterized as being something that Zayd rides—yet of course it is possible for things that are characterized as being donkeys to be something that Zayd rides. Since, in this counterexample, the original extensionally necessary proposition is true and the converse extensionally necessary proposition is false, extensionally necessary propositions do not convert to propositions of the same modality. Note that changing the modality of the converse proposition to *broad intensional continuity* successfully produces the true proposition: ‹Everything that is a donkey *always* is not something that Zayd rides›.

Let us now turn to the conversions of negative modal propositions that are

(N2) Broadly Intensionally Necessary

(C2) BROADLY INTENSIONALLY CONTINUOUS.

These convert to *broadly intensionally continuous propositions*. The logical proof that the truth of each of these negative propositions entails the truth of their broadly intensionally continuous converse is given below.

Assume that these two kinds of negative modal propositions do not entail their broadly intensionally continuous converses.

Therefore, each proposition entails the contradictory opposite of its broadly intensionally continuous converse, which is a *broadly intensionally actual proposition*.

Construct a *simple syllogism* with the contradictory opposite as the *minor premise* and the original modal proposition as the *major premise*. This syllogism entails that some A is not A, which is false because it is impossible to deny something from itself. This is illustrated in the table below.

Therefore, these negative modal propositions do not entail the contradictory opposites of their broadly intensionally continuous converses.

Therefore, the assumption in (*1*) is false, and these propositions do indeed entail the broadly intensionally continuous converse proposition.

Original (Major)	Converse	Contradictory (Minor)	Conclusion
N1. Every A, *as* A, *nec.* is not B. C1. Every A, *as* A, *alw.* is not B.	Every B, *as* B, *alw.* is not A.	Some B, while B, *broadly act.* is A.	1. Some B *nec.* is not B. 2. Some B *alw.* is not B.

Note, again, that broadly intensionally *continuous* propositions convert to propositions with the same modality, but broadly intensionally *necessary* propositions do not. This is analogous to the case discussed above with respect to the respective conversions of negative extensionally necessary and extensionally continuous propositions. Since, as a consequence of Avicenna's reading of predication, there can be cases where the original broadly intensionally necessary proposition is true while the converse broadly intensionally necessary proposition is false, it is not valid to convert the former to another broadly intensionally necessary proposition; it is converted instead to a broadly intensionally continuous proposition.

As for negative propositions that are

(N3) STRICTLY INTENSIONALLY NECESSARY

(C3) Strictly Intensionally Continuous

these convert to *broadly intensionally continuous propositions that are non-continuous in some cases* (sg. *ʿurfiyya lā-dāʾima fī al-baʿḍ*). This is a new kind of composite modal proposition that is conventionally mentioned by logicians in this section on conversion rather than in the earlier section on composite stated modalities. This kind of proposition is a broadly intensionally continuous proposition conditioned by *non-extensional-continuity* in *some* of its referents. It is thus equivalent to a same-quality (in this case, negative) broadly intensionally continuous proposition composed with an opposite-quality (i.e., affirmative) particularly quantified broadly actual proposition. This is illustrated in the table below.

Original Composite	Original Decomposed	Converse Composite	Converse Decomposed
Every A, *strictly as* A, *nec.* is not B.	1. Every A, as A, *nec.* is not B. 2. Every A *broadly act.* is B	Every B, not *extensionally cnt. in some cases*, as B, *alw.* is not A.	1. Every B, *broadly as* B, *alw.* is not A. 2. Some B *broadly act.* is A.
Every A, *strictly as* A, *alw.* is not B.	1. Every A, as A, *alw.* is not B. 2. Every A *broadly act.* is B.	Every B, not *extensionally cnt. in some cases*, *broadly as* B, *alw.* is not A.	1. Every B, *broadly as* B, *alw.* is not A. 2. Some B *broadly act.* is A.

The logical proof that negative strictly intensionally necessary and strictly intensionally continuous propositions convert to *broadly intensionally continuous propositions that are non-continuous in some cases* can be broken into two parts: first, a proof that the truth of strictly intensionally necessary and strictly intensionally continuous propositions entails the truth of their converse broadly intensionally continuous propositions, and, second, a proof that the truth of strictly intensionally necessary and strictly intensionally continuous propositions entails the truth of the proposition that is the same as the particularly quantified converse broadly actual proposition except that it has the opposite propositional quality. We begin with the first:

1. The truth of *broadly* intensionally necessary propositions and *broadly* intensionally continuous propositions entails the truth of their converse broadly intensionally continuous propositions.
2. Strictly intensionally necessary propositions and strictly

intensionally continuous propositions are *unconditionally more specific* in their truth-scope than broadly intensionally necessary propositions and broadly intensionally continuous propositions respectively.

3. Any proposition that is entailed by a proposition is also entailed by those propositions that are unconditionally more specific than it.[28]
4. Therefore, the truth of strictly intensionally necessary propositions and strictly intensionally continuous propositions entails the truth of their converse broadly intensionally continuous propositions.

To proceed to the second part, that is, the proof that both of these kinds of negative modal propositions entails the proposition that is identical to the particularly quantified converse *broadly actual proposition* except that it has the opposite *quality*:

5. Assume that the two negative propositions under consideration, namely, ‹Every A, *strictly as A, necessarily* is not B› and ‹Every A, *strictly as A, always* is not B›, do not entail the truth of the proposition ‹Some B *broadly actually* is A›.
6. Therefore, each of the two propositions must entail this latter proposition's contradictory opposite, namely, ‹Every B *always* is not A›.
7. This contradictory opposite entails its converse proposition, namely, ‹Every A *always* is not B›.
8. This converse proposition and the original two composite propositions cannot simultaneously be true because this converse is contradictorily opposed to the second part of each, namely, ‹Some A *broadly actually* is B›.
9. Therefore, the assumption in (5) is false and the two negative modal propositions under consideration do indeed entail the proposition ‹Some B *broadly actually* is A›.

Strictly intensionally necessary and continuous propositions are broadly intensionally necessary and continuous propositions with the additional modal qualification of non-extensional-continuity. Some logicians objected that since this additional modal qualification is the negation of extensional continuity, and since negative extensionally continuous propositions convert to the same modality as themselves, the modal qualification should carry

28. As mentioned previously, more specific propositions are included within those propositions that are more general than them. In order for the more general propositions to entail something, the propositions that they include must also entail that thing.

over into the converse propositions of strictly intensionally necessary and continuous propositions. The converse would thus be a broadly intensionally continuous proposition that is non-continuous in *all* cases—i.e., a strictly intensionally continuous proposition (*ʿurfiyya khāṣṣa*)—rather than a broadly intensionally continuous proposition that is non-continuous in *some* cases.

Other logicians responded to this objection by saying that negative strictly intensionally necessary and continuous propositions are composite modal propositions that can be broken down into two parts: (*a*) a universally quantified *negative* broadly intensionally necessary or continuous proposition and (*b*) a universally quantified *affirmative* broadly actual proposition. The modal qualification that negates extensional continuity is thus equivalent to a universally quantified *affirmative* proposition, not a universally quantified *negative* proposition. Whereas a universally quantified *negative* extensionally continuous proposition converts to the same quantification and modality as itself, a universally quantified *affirmative* broadly actual proposition converts to the same modality but not to the same quantification; that is, affirmative *universally quantified* propositions convert to affirmative *particularly quantified* propositions. Because of this change in quantification, the negation of extensional continuity converts to only a partial negation of extensional continuity rather than a universal one. This is al-Taftāzānī's position, as well as the position of prominent late logicians, such as al-ʿAṭṭār.

Other prominent late logicians, such as Yāsīn and al-Shirbīnī, argued that this response is flawed because it assumes that the converse of the whole composite proposition is the same as the composition of the converses of the two sub-propositions that can represent it. This assumption, they argued, is incorrect. Even though the whole negative composite proposition can be represented by a negative original proposition and an affirmative additional proposition, the propositional quality of the whole proposition remains negative. It is a well-known principle among all logicians that whether a proposition is negative or affirmative is determined by the quality of its first sub-proposition, i.e., the original proposition, not the second sub-proposition that represents the additional modal quantification.

Some of these late logicians then presented the following logical argument to prove that strictly intensionally necessary and continuous propositions convert to strictly intensionally continuous propositions, not to broadly intensionally continuous propositions that are non-continuous in some cases:

1. Assume that the two negative propositions under consideration, namely, ‹Every A, *strictly as A*, *necessarily* is not B› and ‹Every A, *strictly as A*, *always* is not B›, do not entail the proposition ‹Every B *broadly actually* is A›.
2. Therefore, each of the two propositions also does not entail this proposition's converse, namely, ‹Some A *broadly actually* is B›.
3. Therefore, the two propositions entail the truth of the contradictory opposite of this converse, namely, ‹Every A *always* is not B›.
4. This contradicts the original propositions' sub-proposition ‹Some A *broadly actually* is B›.
5. Therefore, the assumption in (*1*) is false, and the two negative modal propositions under consideration do indeed entail the truth of the proposition ‹Every B *broadly actually* is A›.

The remaining kinds of negative modal propositions do not validly convert, whether universally or particularly quantified. This can be demonstrated by considering that the *strictly specific-time necessary* proposition is the strongest and most specific of the remaining kinds of modal propositions. As a general rule, if a relatively more specific kind of proposition does not convert, then a relatively more general kind does not convert either.[29] The fact that strictly specific-time necessary propositions do not convert can be shown by considering the proposition ‹Every moon, *strictly when exposed to the sun*, *necessarily* does not undergo a lunar eclipse›, which, if supposed true (in accordance with the natural philosophy of the *falāsifa*), does not entail the truth of the converse with the most general conceivable modality, namely that of broad possibility, as in ‹Something that undergoes a lunar eclipse *broadly possibly* is not a moon›. If the latter proposition is false, then in virtue of the fact that it has the most general kind of stated modality, it is false with any modality. Thus, the strictly specific-time necessary proposition above does not validly convert. Thus because it is the most specific of the remaining kinds of negative modal propositions, none of the remaining kinds of negative modal propositions convert.

29. The ability to convert is the inseparable property (*lāzim*) of any proposition that validly converts. If any given inseparable property is present in a more general (*aʿamm*) thing, then it is also present in every more specific (*akhaṣṣ*) thing that falls under the category of that general thing. Thus, if a property is not present in the most specific kind of a group of modal propositions, then that property is not present in any of the other kinds in that group, since all those kinds are more general. *TB*, 349.

8.3 Complemented Conversion

The logicians discuss two types of *complemented conversion* (*ʿaks al-naqīḍ*). These conversions are termed *complemented* since either the subject and predicate of the proposition are complemented or only the subject is complemented. Like (uncomplemented) conversion (*al-ʿaks al-mustawī*), discussed above, these are methods of immediate inference from a given proposition. The method of the early logicians to form the complemented conversion is to take the complement of the subject and predicate and then switch each for the other while preserving the truth, quantity, and quality of the proposition. This is *contraposition*. The method of the later logicians is to take the complement of the predicate, switch the subject and predicate, and change the quality, while preserving the truth and quantity of the proposition. This is *negated contraposition*. Each type is discussed in more detail below.

Some logicians held that, unlike conversion, *contraposition* and *negated contraposition* are not useful for arguments in the sciences. Specifically, they reasoned that, in the sciences, the standard practice is to construct arguments in the first figure, using propositional reasoning to change the positions of the terms in one's premises until the premises take the form of the first figure. This is often done by means of conversion, and the validity of the argument is retained in the process. However, attempting to draw a conclusion from an argument in which one premise is changed into its complemented converse, be it the contrapositive or the negated contrapositive, invalidates the argument. This is because, whereas in conversion the subject and predicate of the proposition are used as they are in the original statement without modification, in complemented conversion these terms are complemented, which changes them. Thus, according to the logicians, only conversion is suitable for arguments used in the sciences. Other logicians held that contraposition does not invalidate the argument, and that negated contraposition is the only type of conversion that is not useful.[30]

8.3.1 *Contraposition*

Contraposition (*ʿaks al-naqīḍ al-muwāfiq*), the early logicians' method of complemented conversion, involves the replacement of the subject and predicate terms with their respective complements and the switching of the positions of the subject and predicate with each other. Thus, the subject complement

30. *TB*, 355. Al-Khabīṣī notes that al-Taftāzānī mentioned the rules of conversion only for the contrapositive, disregarding negated contraposition, either because the latter is considered not to be useful in arguments or for the sake of brevity.

becomes the predicate, and the predicate complement becomes the subject. For the contraposition to be sound, the truth and quality of the original proposition must be maintained. Since the contrapositive proposition agrees with the original proposition in quality and quantification, this type of conversion is termed "agreeing" (*muwāfiq*). Take the following example of the contraposition of a universal affirmative proposition. The original proposition is ‹Every tree is a plant›. After contraposition, the proposition becomes ‹Every non-plant is a non-tree›.

The various valid inferences that can be made through contraposition are similar to those that can be made through conversion. The validity of *affirmative contrapositions* follows the validity of *negative conversions* and the validity of *negative contrapositions* follows the validity of *positive conversions*. The valid results of contraposition are as follows. A universal affirmative proposition contraposes validly to a universal affirmative. A particular affirmative is not contraposed validly in any case. A universal or particular negative proposition is contraposed validly to a negative particular proposition. The contraposition of universal negative propositions requires limitation, by which they are contraposed to particular negative propositions as opposed to universal negative ones. These cases are illustrated below.

Type	Original	Contrapositive	Original Example	Contrapositive Example
Universal Affirmative	Every A is B.	Every non-B is non-A.	Every tree is a plant.	Every non-plant is a non-tree.
Universal Negative	Every A is not B.	Some non-B is not non-A.	Every seal is not a fish.	Some non-fish is not a non-seal.
Particular Affirmative	Some A is B.	N/A	Some bird is a penguin.	N/A
Particular Negative	Some A is not B.	Some non-B is not non-A.	Some reptile is not an iguana.	Some non-iguana is not a reptile.

The manner of proof for valid contrapositions is the same as that given for conversions with the general principle previously mentioned that the validity of affirmative propositions in contraposition follows the validity of negative propositions in conversion and vice-versa. However, there are two kinds of modal propositions for which logicians use a different proof than those above.

The contraposition of particular affirmative *strictly intensionally necessary* and *strictly intensionally continuous* propositions to *strictly intensionally continuous* propositions is demonstrated with a proof by *hypothetical assertion* (*dalīl al-iftirāḍ*) as opposed to a proof by non-contradiction. This method is also used to demonstrate the validity of the *conversion* of particular negative strictly intensionally continuous propositions and strictly intensionally continuous propositions to strictly intensionally continuous propositions.

Let us begin with the proof by hypothetical assertion for the conversion of these latter kinds of propositions, and then turn to the contraposition of the corresponding kinds.

1. When, whether conceptually necessary or conceptually continuous, the following is true: ‹Some A, *strictly as A*, is not B›, meaning ‹Some B *actually* is A›, then the following is true: ‹Some B, *strictly as B*, is not A›, meaning ‹Some A *actually* is B›.
2. Assume there is some C. ‹Some A is C›, so ‹Some C is A› and ‹Some C is B›, due to the non-continuity of the original proposition, since the meaning of non-continuity is ‹Some A *actually* is B›, while we assumed that the "some" is C, so ‹Some C is B›, due to the non-continuity.
3. Moreover, ‹C, *strictly as B*, is not A›. Otherwise, ‹C, *as B*, is A› and ‹C, *as A*, is B›. But ‹B, *strictly as B*, is not A›. This is a contradiction.
4. When B and A both extend to C and do not extend to it, meaning when it is A, it would not be B, and when it is B, it would not be A, then it would be true that ‹Some B, *strictly as B*, is not A›. This is the first part of the conversion.
5. When it is true that ‹C *actually* is A›, then ‹Some B *actually* is A› is true. This is the meaning of non-continuity. Thus, the conversion of both parts is valid.

This is the conversion of the two particular negative strictly intensional propositions.

Here is the formal explanation of the contraposition of a particular affirmative *strictly intensionally continuous* proposition to a strictly intensionally continuous proposition.

1. When, whether intensionally necessary or intensionally continuous, the following is true: ‹Some A, *strictly as A*, is B›, meaning ‹Some A *actually* is non-B›, then ‹Some non-B, *strictly as non-B*, is non-A›,

meaning ‹Some non-B *actually* is not A›.

2. Assume there is some C. ‹Some C *actually* is non-B›, due to the non-continuity of the original proposition, since the meaning of non-continuity is ‹Some A *actually* is not B›, while we assumed that that the "some" is C, so ‹C is non-B›, due to the non-continuity.
3. Moreover, ‹C, *strictly as non-B*, is non-A›. Otherwise, ‹C, *as non-B*, is A›, so ‹C, *strictly as A*, is non-B›; however, ‹C, *as A*, is B›, from the original proposition. As well, ‹C *actually* is A›. This is a contradiction.
4. When ‹C is non-B› and ‹C, *strictly as non-B*, is not A› is true, then ‹Non-B, *strictly as non-B*, is non-A›. This is the first part of the conversion.
5. When ‹C *actually* is A› is true, then ‹Some non-B *actually* is A›, in actuality, is true, which is the meaning of non-continuity. Thus, the conversion of both parts is valid.

8.3.2 *Negated Contraposition*

Negated contraposition, the later logicians' method of complemented conversion, involves the replacement of the predicate with its complement and the switching of the positions of the subject and predicate with each other. Thus, the subject becomes the predicate, and the complement of the predicate becomes the subject, while maintaining the truth of the original proposition despite differing from it in quality. If the original proposition was affirmative, then the negated contrapositive proposition will be negative, and vice-versa. Since the negated contrapositive proposition differs from the original proposition in quality, it is termed "differing" (*mukhālif*). The following example shows the procedure: ‹Every tree is a plant› becomes ‹Every non-plant is not a tree›.

The method of negated contraposition is different from the method of *obversion* in the western logical tradition, where the subject and predicate are not switched. In obversion, all four types of propositions obvert validly and without limitation.[31]

There are valid negated contrapositions for universal affirmative propositions and universal and particular negative propositions. The following is a simplified presentation of the possibilities for negated contraposition, ignoring the complexities of modality and the ontological status of the subject, as described, for instance, in the *Shamsiyya* of Shams al-Dīn al-Kātibī. A

31. Recall 6.6.5 and the discussion of existential import. Perhaps the reason why the later Muslim logicians did not consider the method of obversion was based on the issue of existential import.

universal affirmative proposition becomes a universal negative proposition. A universal negative proposition becomes a particular affirmative proposition. A particular negative proposition becomes a particular affirmative proposition. A particular affirmative proposition does not validly undergo negated contraposition in any case.

Type	Original	Negated Contrapositive	Original Example	Neg. Cpv. Example
Universal Affirmative	Every A is B.	Every non-B is not A.	Every tree is a plant.	Every non-plant is not a tree.
Universal Negative	Every A is not B.	Some non-B is A.	Every seal is not a fish.	Some non-fish is a seal.
Particular Affirmative	Some A is B.	N/A	Some bird is a penguin.	N/A
Particular Negative	Some A is not B.	Some non-B is A.	Some reptile is not an iguana.	Some non-iguana is a reptile.

Sources

Section	Sources
8 Propositional Reasoning	For further reading, see Street, *Najm al-Dīn*, 189-224; Ahmed, *Palimpsests*, 179-84
8.1 Contradiction	TB, 304-7; for further reading, see Laurence R. Horn, "Contradiction," *Stanford Encyclopedia of Philosophy* (Summer 2024), ed. Edward N. Zalta and Uri Nodelman, https://plato.stanford.edu/archives/sum2024/entries/contradiction
8.1.1 Quality and Quantification in Contradiction	TB, 307-9
8.1.2 Modality in Contradiction	TB, 308
8.1.2.1 Contradiction of Basic Modal Propositions	TB, 313-25
8.1.2.2 Contradiction of Composite Modal Propositions	TB, 320, 325-28
8.1.3 Eight Aspects of Formal Identity	TB, 309-13
8.2 Conversion	TB, 329
8.2.1 Quantification in Conversion	TB, 330-31

Section	Sources
8.2.1.1 Conversion of Affirmative Propositions	TB, 332-34
8.2.1.2 Conversion of Negative Propositions	TB, 334-35
8.2.2 Modality in Conversion	TB, 335-52; Tony Street, "Afḍal al-Dīn al-Khūnajī (d. 1248) on the Conversion of Modal Propositions," *Oriens* 24, no. 3-4 (2014): 454-513
8.2.2.1 Conversion of Affirmative Modal Propositions	TB, 335-43
8.2.2.2 Conversion of Negative Modal Propositions	TB, 343-52
8.3 Complemented Conversion	TB, 352-63
8.3.1 Contraposition	TB, 354-63
8.3.2 Negated Contraposition	TB, 354-55; Muḥammad Riḍā al-Muẓaffar, *al-Manṭiq*, ed. Ghulām Riḍā al-Fayyāḍī (Qom: Mu'assasat al-Nashr al-Islāmī, 1393H), 227; al-Rāzī, et al., *Shurūḥ al-Shamsiyya*, 2:169-82

9

ARGUMENTS

The ultimate goal of logic is to distinguish sound propositional inferences from flawed propositional inferences, which is the direct goal of this chapter. Chapters 3 and 4 (PART II) investigated how to precisely define the terms of propositions, and Chapters 5, 6, 7, and 8 (PART III) investigated how to precisely form propositions using those terms and how to precisely understand the meanings and entailments of single propositions. This chapter uses those investigations to study how to precisely arrange multiple propositions into an argument from which one can infer new propositions.

There are two ways to acquire knowledge that an inferential proposition is true: through *deductive argument* (*qiyās*) or through *non-deductive argument*. Since deductive arguments afford *conclusive knowledge* whereas non-deductive arguments normally only afford *probabilistic knowledge*, the logicians are primarily concerned with deductive arguments, or syllogisms, which they study in great detail, and non-deductive forms of argument are typically only studied as a supplement (*mulḥaq*) to the study of syllogisms.

Note that this chapter studies each of these kinds of arguments from the perspective of their *form*, not from the perspective of their *matter*. The form of an argument, in contradistinction to its matter, is its abstract structure without regard for the specific terms that compose its premises. For example, the form of the argument,

Minor Premise: The universe is contingent.
Major Premise: Everything that is contingent depends on a necessary being.

is,

Minor Premise: A is B.
Major Premise: Every B is C.

When we study this argument in terms of its form, we abstract away the specific terms, "universe," "something that is contingent," and "something that depends on a necessary being," and study whether or not the two premises *formally* entail their conclusion. To put this another way, we study whether or not the truth of the premises entails the truth of the conclusion regardless of whether these specific premises composed of these specific terms are true or false. That is, we study whether or not an argument is *valid*, not whether it is *sound* and produces a true conclusion.

9.1 Deductive Arguments

A *deductive argument* or *syllogism* (*qiyās*) is a composition of propositions whose truth conclusively and formally entails the truth of a different proposition. The propositions that compose the argument are called its *premises* (*muqaddimāt*). The proposition that is entailed by the premises is called the *conclusion* (*natīja*). For example, the composition of the premises ‹The universe is contingent› and ‹Everything that is contingent depends on a necessary being› formally entails the conclusion ‹The universe depends on a necessary being›. According to this definition, a deductive argument has three requirements:

1. The composition of propositions, or premises.
2. The conclusive entailment of a different proposition, a conclusion.
3. That this entailment arises as a result of the *compositional form* (*hay'a*).

The example above is a deductive argument because it comprises each of these things. First, it features the composition of the two premises ‹The universe is contingent› and ‹Everything that is contingent depends on a necessary being›. Second, this composition conclusively entails[1] a conclusion that is different from the premises, namely, ‹The universe depends on a necessary being›. Third, this entailment arises as a result of the compositional form, i.e.,

1. This entailment might be a *direct entailment*, as with the first figure of the simple syllogism, or an *indirect entailment*, as with its remaining figures. *TB*, 364.

the composition of a proposition possessing the form ‹A is B› with another proposition possessing the form ‹Every B is C›.

The first requirement excludes the various kinds of propositional reasoning described in Chapter 8. Contradictory, converse, contrapositive, and negated contrapositive propositions are all inferred from a single original proposition, not from a *composition* of multiple propositions. Propositional reasoning is therefore not deductive argument, nor any argument at all, as all arguments require the composition of multiple propositions.[2] The second requirement excludes non-deductive arguments, namely, *inductive generalizations* and *causal analogies*, which only entail their conclusions *probabilistically*, not conclusively.[3]

The second requirement excludes *pointless argument* (*hadhayān*) and argument that *begs the question* (*muṣādara ʿalā al-maṭlūb*).[4] An argument is pointless when it does not lead to the discovery of something that is not already known. An argument begs the question when it assumes the conclusion as part of its premises.

The third requirement excludes *relational syllogisms* (sg. *qiyās musāwāh*), such as the entailment from the premises ‹Zayd is the brother of ʿAmr› and ‹ʿAmr is the brother of Ḥasan› of the conclusion ‹Zayd is the brother of Ḥasan›,

2. Some logicians objected that the definition does not exclude the inference of the contradictory premise of *composite modal propositions*. Since composite modal propositions are represented as a composition of *two basic modal propositions*, the inference of their contradictory premise involves an inference that comprises the composition of two propositions, even though that inference is an example of propositional reasoning rather than an example of deductive argument. The logicians gave two responses to this objection. The first response is that a composite modal proposition is, in fact, a single proposition that is qualified by an additional modal qualifier (such as non-continuity) and is not, in fact, two propositions. Thus, the first requirement excludes the inference of the contradictory of composite modal propositions from the definition of deductive argument. The second response is that, even if one were to admit that composite modal propositions are composed of two propositions, the composition that is sought in deductive arguments is a special kind of generalized and abstract composition that entails a conclusion (e.g., the composition of ‹A is B› and ‹Every B is C›, which entail ‹Every A is C›), whereas the supposed composition of composite modal propositions is not general and does not formally entail the contradictory. Thus, the second requirement excludes the inference of the contradictory of composite modal propositions from the definition of deductive argument. *TB*, 365.

3. In modern logic, the conclusive entailment of deductive arguments is associated with the modal notion of *logical necessity*. In the terminology of the Muslim logicians, however, "necessity" and "possibility" are used to describe not entailments but predications (see 6.7), and it would hence not be correct to describe the entailment of deductive arguments as *necessary*.

4. The Arabic term *muṣādara ʿalā al-maṭlūb* literally means "rushing to the conclusion," which is another name in English for the logical fallacy of *begging the question*.

which is not a *formal* entailment. The general form of a relational syllogism is ‹A is X of B› and ‹B is X of C›. In order for an argument of this form to entail ‹A is X of C›, as in the example just cited, the relation ‹X› must be such that the X of the X of A is the X of A. This is not always the case. Consider the relation of friendship: ‹Zayd is the friend of ʿAmr› and ‹ʿAmr is the friend of Ḥasan›: this does not entail ‹Zayd is the friend of Ḥasan›. The conclusion of relational syllogisms therefore does not arise as a result of the *compositional form* of the two premises alone; it arises with the help of an implicit premise of the form ‹The X of the X of A is the X of A›.

There are two kinds of deductive argument: the *simple syllogism* (*qiyās iqtirānī*) and the *complex syllogism* (*qiyās istithnāʾī*). A *simple syllogism* is a deductive argument in which the parts of the conclusion are dispersed between the two premises and the *composite form* (*hayʾa*) of the conclusion is not included in any one of the two premises. A *complex syllogism*, in contrast, is a deductive argument in which the composite form of the conclusion is mentioned in one of the two premises.[5] This difference is illustrated in the table below.

	Simple	**Complex**
Example	(Minor) Everything in the physical universe is contingent. (Major) Every contingent thing depends on a necessary being. (Conclusion) Everything in the physical universe depends on a necessary being.	(Major) Whenever the sun has risen, then daytime exists. (Minor) The sun has risen. (Conclusion) Daytime exists.

5. Some logicians argued that a more precise description of a complex syllogism is that it either mentions the composite form of the conclusion *or* the *composite form of the contradiction of the conclusion* in one of its premises. An example of where the contradiction of the conclusion is mentioned is: ‹Whenever the sun has risen, then daytime exists›; but, ‹Daytime does not exist›; therefore, ‹The sun has not risen›. Here, the conclusion is ‹The sun as not risen›, whereas what is mentioned in the major premise is its contradiction, namely, ‹The sun has risen›. Other logicians disagreed, arguing that what is meant by the *composite form* of the conclusion is the order of the subject and predicate, regardless of whether the predicate is affirmed or denied of the subject. On this understanding, the composite form of a premise is identical to that of its contradictory opposite, and the description of the complex syllogism mentioned above needs no modification. *TB*, 374-75.

	Simple	Complex
Relation Between Conclusion and Premises	The parts of the conclusion are dispersed between the two premises. The subject of the conclusion (‹physical universe›) is mentioned in the minor premise, and the predicate of the conclusion (‹began to exist›) is mentioned in the major premise.	The conclusion (‹Daytime exists›) is mentioned in its complete composite form in one of the premises, namely, the major premise.

9.1.1 *Simple Syllogisms*

Simple syllogisms are a pair of premises that collectively consist of three *terms* (sg. *ḥadd*): the *minor term* (*ḥadd aṣghar*), the *major term* (*ḥadd akbar*), and the *middle term* (*ḥadd awsaṭ*). The minor term is the subject of the conclusion, and the premise that contains the minor term is called the *minor premise* (*muqaddima ṣughrā* or simply *ṣughrā*). The major term is the predicate of the conclusion, and the premise that contains the major term is called the *major premise* (*muqaddima kubrā* or simply *kubrā*). The middle term is repeated in each of the minor and major premises and its role is to connect the two premises in such a way that they collectively constitute a compositional form that entails the conclusion. Through its relation to both the subject of the conclusion in the minor premise and the predicate of the conclusion in the major premise, the middle term establishes a relationship between the two that is expressed in the conclusion. Without the connective role of the middle term, the only way for the subject and predicate of the conclusion to be related is for the mere conception of one to entail the conception of the other, in which case the conclusion would be a noninferential *self-evident judgment*, obviating the need for any deductive argument.[6]

The middle term can occupy either the subject or the predicate position in the minor and major premises. As a result, simple syllogisms can have one of four abstract compositional forms, conventionally termed the first, second, third, and fourth *figures* (sg. *shakl*) of the simple syllogism: in the *first figure* (*shakl awwal*), the middle term is the predicate of the minor premise

6. According to most of the logicians, it is this connective role of the middle term and the intermediate premise that gives this kind of syllogism its Arabic name as the "*connective*" (*iqtirānī*) *syllogism*. Others hold that the reason why this kind of deductive argument is called a connective syllogism is that the conclusion arises as a result of connecting the two premises with the conjunction "and," in contrast with the complex syllogism, where the two premises are separated with the disjunction "but." *TB*, 375.

and the subject of the major premise; in the *second figure* (*shakl thānī*), it is the predicate of both premises; in the *third figure* (*shakl thālith*), it is the subject of both premises; and, in the *fourth figure* (*shakl rābiʿ*), it is the subject of the minor premise and the predicate of the major premise. The compositional forms of each of these four figures are illustrated in the table below. In this table and throughout the following sections, "A" formally represents the minor term, "B" formally represents the middle term, and "C" formally represents the major term. The figure of a syllogism is entirely determined by the positions of these three terms; the quality and quantification of the premises is irrelevant.

	First Fig.	**Second Fig.**	**Third Fig.**	**Fourth Fig.**
Compositional Form	A B B C	A B C B	B A B C	B A C B
Example	Everything in the physical universe is contingent. Every contingent thing depends on a necessary being.	Every human is an animal. Every inanimate thing is not an animal.	Every human is an animal. Every human is rational.	Every human is an animal. Every rational thing is a human.
Example	Everything in the physical universe depends on a necessary being.	Every human is not an inanimate thing.	Some animal is rational.	Some animal is rational.

The four figures are ordered from the best to the worst form of argument. The first figure is the best because it is the closest of the four figures to the way that we naturally reason—whereas the first figure entails its conclusion *directly*, the remaining figures only entail it indirectly through deductive inference.[7] The second figure comes next because it shares the best premise of the first figure, namely, the minor premise (the minor premise contains the subject of the conclusion, and the subject is the primary part of a proposition). The third figure comes next because it shares the major premise of

7. This is because, in the first figure, the mind naturally moves from the minor term to the middle term to the major term, in that order, to naturally form the conclusion without any further inference, whereas the other figures need to be converted to this order in order to discover their conclusions. *TB*, 378.

the first figure. The fourth figure is the last because it does not share any of the premises of the first figure.[8] It is extremely unnatural to reason using the fourth figure. For this reason, al-Fārābī, Avicenna, and al-Ghazālī all omitted its mention. The logicians also point out that, whereas deductive arguments of the first three figures are found in the Qur'ān, there is no argument to be found on the fourth figure.[9]

Simple syllogisms are most frequently composed of *simple propositions*, but they may also be composed of *complex propositions*, either partially or completely, as illustrated in the table below.[10] A simple syllogism that is entirely composed of simple propositions is a *pure simple syllogism* (*qiyās iqtirānī ḥamlī*), while one that is partially or completely composed of complex propositions is an *impure simple syllogism* (*qiyās iqtirānī sharṭī*).

8. Another reason that the logicians give for the evaluative ranking of the figures is that the first figure produces the greatest variety of conclusions: both affirmative and negative, and both universally and particularly quantified. The second figure comes next: although it only produces negative conclusions, it produces universally quantified conclusions, which are more useful than particularly quantified conclusions. The third and fourth figures only produce particularly quantified conclusions. Of these two, the third figure is better because it produces affirmative particularly quantified conclusions, whereas the fourth figure only produces negative ones. Logicians mention other reasons as well. Ultimately, however, the ranking is a matter of convention. *TB*, 379.

9. An example of a Qur'ānic argument on the first figure is the prophet Abraham's challenge (upon him be peace), "God causes the sun to rise from the east: so cause it to rise from the west" (Qur'ān 2:258), which can be logically represented: (Minor Premise) ‹You cannot make the sun rise from the west›; (Major Premise) ‹Everyone who cannot make the sun rise from the west is not my Lord›; (Conclusion) ‹You are not my Lord›. An example of an argument on the second figure is Abraham's reasoning in a different setting: "When it set, he said: 'I love not those that set'" (Qur'ān 6:76), which can be logically represented: (Minor Premise) ‹This thing sets›; (Major Premise) ‹Every true god does not set›; (Conclusion) ‹This is not a true god›. An example of an argument on the third figure is God's Most High rebuttal of the Jews' claim, "God has never revealed anything to a human" (Qur'ān 6:91) with the argument, "Say: 'Who revealed the book that Moses brought?'" (Qur'ān 6:91), which can be logically represented: (Minor Premise) ‹Moses is a human›; (Major Premise) ‹Moses has been given a book revealed by God›; (Conclusion) ‹Some human has been given a book revealed by God›. Al-Akhḍarī et al., *Ḥāshiya ʿalā Sharḥ al-Sullam li-l-Mallawī*, 128.

10. The table only illustrates impure simple syllogisms composed of conditional complex propositions, but disjunctive complex propositions, too, can compose simple syllogisms, either completely, partially alongside a simple proposition, or partially alongside a conditional proposition.

Pure Simple Syllogism	**Impure Simple Syllogism**	
	Partially Composed of Complex Propositions	Completely Composed of Complex Propositions
(Minor) Everything in the physical universe is composed.	(Minor) Whenever something is a human, it is an animal.	(Minor) Whenever the sun has risen, daytime exists.
(Major) Every composed thing began to exist.	(Major) Every animal is an object.	(Major) Whenever daytime exists, people are awake.
(Conclusion) Everything in the physical universe began to exist.	(Conclusion) Whenever something is a human, it is an object.	(Conclusion) Whenever the sun has risen, people are awake.

The discussion in the following subsections focuses on pure simple syllogisms, but many of the conclusions apply equally to impure simple syllogisms.

The way that the premises in a simple syllogism entail their conclusion is as follows. By predicating the middle term to the minor term, the minor premise places the instances of the minor term within the scope of the middle term. The major premise then places those instances within the scope of the major term by predicating the major term to the middle term. The role of the middle term is thus to carry the instances of the minor term into the scope of the major term. The conclusion reflects this outcome by predicating the major term to the minor term.

There is a well-known objection to this deductive process that the logicians cite and refute for the purpose of instruction. According to the objection, since the minor term is an instance or instances of the middle term, then to say (as one says in the major premise) that all instances of the middle term are characterized by the major term ‹P› requires that one already know that the instances of the minor term are characterized by ‹P›. But this is precisely what is supposedly learned as a *conclusion* of the argument. Therefore, one must know the conclusion in order to produce the conclusion, and therefore, deductive argumentation is circular and provides no new knowledge.

This objection can be refuted in more than one way. One way is to point out that the conclusion is an *explicit* or *precise* judgment about the minor term, while the major premise merely *implicitly* or *summarily* makes that judgment. The summary knowledge expressed in the major premise does not depend on having the precise knowledge that the conclusion provides. Thus one does gain new knowledge by means of the syllogism: one's summary knowledge becomes detailed, precise knowledge. Another way of responding to the objection is to point out that two different judgments obtain when one knows a predication to be true of a given subject-referent with one subject-concept and with another subject-concept. When one makes a deduction, one begins with the knowledge that a given predication applies to the referents of the middle term with the subject-concept of the middle term, and one gains the new knowledge that the predication also applies to the referents of the minor term with the subject-concept of the minor term. Thus, deduction can afford new knowledge, and the deductive process is not circular.

Deduction affords new knowledge whenever the quality, quantification, and modality of the premises are such that the middle term carries the instances of the minor term into the scope of the major term. Such a syllogism is a *valid argument* (*qiyās muntij*), and its conclusion validly predicates the major term to the minor term. Whenever the quality, quantification, or modality of the premises prevent the middle term from carrying the instances of the minor term into the scope of the major term, the syllogism is an *invalid argument* (*qiyās ʿaqīm*) and does not have a valid conclusion. The following four sections analyze the four figures in order to discern which qualities, quantifications, and modalities of their premises result in a valid argument. The qualities, quantifications, and modalities that are required for each figure are called its *conditions of validity* (*shurūṭ al-intāj*).

9.1.1.1 The First Figure

The conditions for the validity of the first figure are that the minor premise be affirmative and *actual* (i.e., of any modality except for *broad possibility* or *strict possibility*), and that the major premise be universally quantified. These conditions are summarized in the table below.

Quality	Minor premise must be affirmative
Quantification	Major premise must be universally quantified
Modality	Minor premise must be actual

A consequence of the requirement that the minor premise be affirmative is that it is invalid for it to comprise the word "only," which implies a negation. For example, the proposition ‹Only humans laugh› is equivalent to the combination of the affirmative proposition ‹Humans laugh› with the negative proposition ‹Everything other than humans does not laugh›. This is why the following syllogism is invalid and its conclusion false:

Minor Premise: Only humans laugh.
Major Premise: Everything that laughs is an animal.
Conclusion: Only humans are animals.

The reason why the minor premise must be affirmative is that if it were negative, then no instances of the minor term would be placed into the scope of the middle term, which would in turn be unable to perform its function of placing them within the scope of the major term. In other words, if ‹B› (the middle term) is affirmed of ‹A› (the minor term), then when ‹C› (the major term) is predicated to ‹B›—whether affirmatively or negatively—then the predication to ‹B› is also a predication to ‹A›. But if ‹B› is denied of ‹A›, then the predication of ‹C› to ‹B› is no longer a predication to ‹A›.[11]

The reason why the major premise must be universally quantified is that if it were particularly quantified, then there would be no guarantee that the instances of the minor term that the minor premise places into the scope of the intermediary term are the same instances that the major premise places into the scope of the major term. To illustrate, if all A is B but only some B is C, then there is no guarantee that the B that is C is the same B that is A.

---

11. The logicians considered and responded to two objections against the stipulation that the minor premise be affirmative. The first objection is that it is not a requirement for the minor premise to be affirmative, because in some cases it is possible to infer a true conclusion from a first-figure syllogism that has a negative minor premise. In particular, this is possible when the middle term is *referentially equal* to the major term, in which case everything of which the middle term is denied will be such that the major term, too, will be denied of it. For example, the terms "horse" and "something that neighs" are conceptually equal, as a result of which the following syllogism concludes truthfully: (Minor Premise) ‹Every human is not a horse›; (Major Premise) ‹Every horse neighs›; (Conclusion) ‹Every human does not neigh›. The logicians responded to this objection by saying that denying the major term of the minor term in such cases is an entailment of the *matter* of the argument. In other words, the entailment relies on the additional premise that everything of which one of two referentially equal predicates is denied is such that the other predicate, too, will be denied of it. The second objection is that negative *composite modal propositions* are composed of an original negative basic modal proposition and an additional affirmative modal proposition. Unlike the higher-level composite modal proposition, which is negative and hence cannot validly be the minor premise of a first-figure syllogism, this lower-level proposition is affirmative and hence can validly be a minor premise. With respect to this lower-level affirmative proposition, then, the higher-level composite modal proposition does, indeed, validly conclude, even though it is negative. The logicians responded to this second objection by drawing a distinction between the negative *composite* modal proposition being the minor premise of a valid first-figure syllogism and merely its affirmative *sub-proposition* being the minor premise of a valid first-figure syllogism; what the logicians deny is valid is the former, not the latter, and the stipulation that the minor premise be affirmative thus still holds. *TB*, 379-80.

The reason why the minor premise needs to be actual is that the major premise only predicates the major term to those referents that are actually characterized by the concept of the middle term. When the stated modality of the minor premise is mere *possibility* (whether broad or strict), there is no guarantee that there are any referents of the middle term that are actually characterized by its concept such that it can perform its function of placing the instances of the minor term into the scope of the major term. (Note that, according al-Fārābī's position on predication (see 6.3), the major premise predicates the major term of any referent that is *possibly* characterized by the concept of the middle term, and so the entailment would in fact be valid even when the minor premise is merely possible.)

Given these requirements, the first figure has four valid *moods* (sg. *ḍarb*), that is, four configurations of the premises in terms of quality and quantification that create a valid argument. These four moods, along with the remaining twelve invalid moods, are illustrated in the table below. Unlike the valid moods of the other three figures, the conclusions of the four valid moods of the first figure are noninferentially known to be entailed by the premises and do not require any logical proof.

	Minor Premise	Major Premise	Conclusion	Mood
1	Every A is B.	Every B is C.	Every A is C.	1
2		Every B is not C.	Every A is not C.	2
3		Some B is C.	-	
4		Some B is not C.	-	
5	Every A is not B.	Every B is C.	-	
6		Every B is not C.	-	
7		Some B is C.	-	
8		Some B is not C.	-	
9	Some A is B	Every B is C.	Some A is C.	3
10		Every B is not C.	Some A is not C.	4
11		Some B is C.	-	
12		Some B is not C.	-	

	Minor Premise	Major Premise	Conclusion	Mood
13	Some B is not C	Every B is C.	-	
14		Every B is not C.	-	
15		Some B is C.	-	
16		Some B is not C.	-	

9.1.1.2 The Second Figure

The conditions for the validity of the second figure are that the minor premise and the major premise differ in their quality, that the major premise be universally quantified, and that one of two alternative conditions be met with regard to the modality of the premises. The first of the alternative conditions is that neither premise possess the modality of *possibility*, and also either that (*i*) the minor premise be *broadly continuous* or else that (*ii*) the major premise have a modality that validly converts with negative propositions. The second of the alternative conditions is that *one* of the two premises possess the modality of *possibility* and that, if it be the minor premise, the major premise be extensionally or intensionally necessary, and, if it be the major premise, the minor premise be extensionally necessary. These conditions are summarized in the table below.

Quality	Minor and major premises must differ	
Quantification	Major premise must be universally quantified	
Modality	If neither premise is *possible,* then it must be that either (i) minor premise is *broadly continuous*, or (ii) major premise has a modality that validly converts with negative propositions	If one premise is *possible,* then it must be that either (i) minor premise is *possible* and major premise is *extensionally* or *continuously necessary,* or (ii) major premise is *possible* and minor premise is *extensionally necessary*

Given these requirements, there are four valid moods in the second figure. These four moods, along with the remaining twelve invalid moods, are illustrated in the table below.

	Minor Premise	Major Premise	Conclusion	Mood
1	Every A is B.	Every C is B.	-	
2		Every C is not B.	Every A is not C.	1
3		Some C is B.	-	
4		Some C is not B.	-	
5	Every A is not B.	Every C is B.	Every A is not C.	2
6		Every C is not B.	-	
7		Some C is B.	-	
8		Some C is not B.	-	
9	Some A is B	Every C is B.	-	
10		Every C is not B.	Some A is not C.	3
11		Some C is B.	-	
12		Some C is not B.	-	
13	Some B is not C	Every C is B.	Some A is not C.	4
14		Every C is not B.	-	
15		Some C is B.	-	
16		Some C is not B.	-	

Unlike the conclusions of the valid moods of the first figure, which are noninferentially known to be entailed by their premises, the conclusions of the four valid moods of the second figure are *inferentially* known to be so. There are three kinds of logical proofs that can be used to make the inference. Each proof uses some kind of *propositional reasoning* to transform either the conclusion or the major premise or the minor premise, and then uses that transformed proposition to construct a simple syllogism of the *first figure* to prove that the conclusion follows from the premises. However, some of these proofs are valid for some moods and not others.

Let us examine the first of the three proofs, which is a *proof by contradiction*, and which is valid for all four moods:

1. Assume that the minor and major premises are true and that the conclusion is false.
2. Therefore, the contradiction of the conclusion is true.
3. Make the contradiction of the conclusion the minor premise of the original syllogism.
4. This will result in a simple syllogism of the first figure whose

conclusion is the contradiction of the original minor premise.

5. This is an impossible outcome because of the assumption in (*1*) is that the original minor premise is true.
6. Therefore, the contradiction of the conclusion is false.
7. Therefore, the conclusion is true.

Let us illustrate these steps using Mood 2 in the table above, that is, the syllogism of the form,

Minor Premise: Every A is B.
Major Premise: Every C is not B.
Conclusion: Every A is not C.

The proof can be applied to this syllogism as follows:

1. Assume that ‹Every A is B› and ‹Every C is not B› are true and that ‹Every A is not C› is false.
2. Therefore, ‹Some A is C›, the contradiction of the conclusion, is true.
3. Form a first-figure simple syllogism with this contradiction and the original major premise, as follows:

Minor Premise: Some A is C.
Major Premise: Every C is not B.

4. Therefore, ‹Some A is not B›, the conclusion of this valid first-figure syllogism, is true.
5. But ‹Every A is B›, the contradiction of this conclusion, was assumed true.
6. Therefore, ‹Some A is C›, the contradiction of the original conclusion, is false.
7. Therefore, ‹Every A is not C›, the original conclusion, is true.

This logical proof can be analogously applied to prove the validity of each of the other three valid second-figure moods.

Now let us examine the second of the three proofs for the valid second-figure moods, which is a *proof by conversion* of the major premise, which is valid for the first and third valid moods. In this proof, one converts the major premise, which changes the syllogism into the first figure, proving that the conclusion is valid. The proof can be applied in the first valid mood of the second figure as follows:

1. Assume the minor premise ‹Every A is B› and the major premise ‹Every C is not B›.
2. This results, from the second-figure first valid mood, in ‹Every A is not C›.
3. Convert the major premise, ‹Every C is not B›, which yields ‹Every B is not C›.
4. Now, the minor and major premise together constitute a syllogism that yields ‹Every A is not C›, which is a valid conclusion from the second mood of the first figure.
5. In the first figure, this yields the conclusion ‹Every A is not C›.

This logical proof can be analogously applied to prove the validity of the first and third moods of the second figure.

Finally, let us examine the third proof for the valid second-figure moods, which is a proof by conversion of the minor premise and *reversal of the syllogism's order*, and which is valid only for the second mood. In this proof, one converts the minor premise and then switches the minor premise with the major premise, which results in a first-figure syllogism. Now one converts the conclusion of this new syllogism, and the result is a valid first-figure syllogism that yields the sought conclusion. The proof can be applied in the second valid mood of the second figure as follows:

1. Assume the minor premise ‹Every A is not B› and the major premise ‹Every C is B›.
2. This results, from the second-figure second valid mood, in ‹Every A is not C›, which we want to prove is valid.
3. The converse of the minor premise is ‹Every B is not A›.
4. Switching the major with the minor premise results in the new minor premise ‹Every C is B› and the new major premise ‹Every B is not A›, which by the first figure yields ‹Every C is not A›.
5. The converse of the conclusion is ‹Every A is not C›, which is the sought conclusion. Therefore, the second figure is valid.

In summary, the validity of first and third moods of the second figure can be proven through proof by contradiction and through conversion of the major premise. However, the validity of these moods cannot be proven through the reversal of the syllogism's order because the minor premise would be negative, which does not produce a valid conclusion in the first figure. Also, the reversal would result in the major premise in the third mood being particular, which does not result in a valid conclusion in the first figure. As for the validity of the second mood, this can be proven through the proofs by contradiction and by reversal. However, it cannot be proven through the proof by conversion of the major premise because the conversion would result in a particular affirmative and not a universal affirmative, which is needed as the major premise for the first figure. As for the fourth mood, its validity cannot be proven through the conversion of the major premise, for the same reason, nor through reversal, because the minor premise is a particular negative proposition which cannot be converted. Assuming it could be converted, it would not become the major premise of the first figure. Thus, the fourth mood is proven only through proof by contradiction.

9.1.1.3 The Third Figure

The conditions for the validity of the third figure are that the minor premise be affirmative in quality and actual in modality, and that one of the two premises be universal in quantity.

Quality	Minor premise must be affirmative.
Quantification	One premise must be universally quantified.
Modality	Minor premise must be actual.

Given these requirements, there are six valid moods in the third figure. These six moods, along with the remaining ten invalid moods, are illustrated in the table below.

	Minor Premise	Major Premise	Conclusion	Mood
1	Every A is B.	Every A is C.	Some B is C.	1
2		Every A is not C.	Some B is not C.	4
3		Some A is C.	Some B is C.	3
4		Some A is not C.	Some B is not C.	6
5	Every A is not B.	Every A is C.	-	
6		Every A is not C.	-	
7		Some A is C.	-	
8		Some A is not C.	-	

	Minor Premise	Major Premise	Conclusion	Mood
9	Some A is B.	Every A is C.	Some B is C.	2
10		Every A is not C.	Some B is not C.	5
11		Some A is C.	-	
12		Some A is not C.	-	
13	Some A is not B.	Every A is C.	-	
14		Every A is not C.	-	
15		Some A is C.	-	
16		Some A is not C.	-	

Just like the second figure, the conclusions of the six valid moods of the third figure are *inferentially* known to be valid. And as with the second figure, the valid moods of the third and fourth figures are proven through proof by contradiction, conversion of the major or minor premise, or reversal. In some moods, two or more of these proofs are valid, and in others not.

Let us examine the first of the three proofs, which is a *proof by contradiction*, valid for all six moods:

1. Assume that the minor and major premises are true and that the conclusion is false.
2. Therefore, the contradiction of the conclusion is true.
3. Make the contradiction of the conclusion the major premise of the original syllogism, and make the minor premise the minor premise, since it is affirmative.
4. This will result in a simple syllogism of the first figure whose conclusion is the contradiction of the original major premise.
5. This is an impossible outcome because of the assumption in (*1*) that the original major premise is true.
6. Therefore, the contradiction of the conclusion is false.
7. Therefore, the conclusion is true.

Let us illustrate these steps using Valid Mood 1 in the table above, that is, the syllogism of the form,

Minor Premise: Every A is B.
Major Premise: Every A is C.
Conclusion: Some B is C.

The proof can be applied to this syllogism as follows:

1. Assume that ‹Every A is B› and ‹Every A is C› are true and that ‹Some B is C› is false.
2. Therefore, ‹Every B is not C›, the contradiction of the conclusion, is true.
3. Form a first-figure simple syllogism with this contradiction and the original major premise, as follows:

Minor Premise:	Every A is B.
Major Premise:	Every B is not C.

4. Therefore, ‹Every A is not C›, the conclusion of this valid first-figure syllogism, is true.
5. But ‹Every A is C›, the contradiction of this conclusion, was assumed true.
6. Therefore, ‹Every B is not C›, the contradiction of the original conclusion, is false.
7. Therefore, ‹Some B is C›, the original conclusion, is true.

The second of the three proofs is a *proof by conversion of the minor premise*, valid for Valid Moods 1, 2, 4, and 5. The proof proceeds by conversion of the minor premise, through which the syllogism takes the first figure and results in a valid conclusion. Let us illustrate these steps using Valid Mood 2 in the table above, that is, the syllogism of the form,

Minor Premise:	Some A is B.
Major Premise:	Every A is C.
Conclusion:	Some B is C.

The proof can be applied to this syllogism as follows:

1. Conversion of the minor premise results in ‹Some B is A›.
2. The conversion of the minor premise results in the first-figure syllogism:

Minor Premise:	Some B is A.
Major Premise:	Every A is C.

3. Therefore, ‹Some B is C›, the conclusion of this valid first-figure

syllogism, is true.
4. Therefore, the second figure is valid.

The last of the proofs is a *proof by reversal of the syllogism's order* that includes the conversion of the major premise, and is valid for Valid Moods 1 and 3. One converts the major premise, switches the minor and major premises, and then converts the conclusion. Let us illustrate these steps using Mood 1 in the table above, that is, the syllogism of the form,

Minor Premise: Every A is B.
Major Premise: Every A is C.
Conclusion: Some B is C.

The proof can be applied to this syllogism as follows:

1. Conversion of the major premise results in ‹Some C is A›.
2. Placing the converted major premise, ‹Some C is A›, as the minor premise and placing the minor premise, ‹Some B is C›, as the major premise results in a first-figure syllogism of the third valid mood.
3. This produces the conclusion ‹Some C is B›. When converted, the original conclusion results: ‹Some B is C›.
4. Therefore, the third figure is valid.

9.1.1.4 The Fourth Figure

The conditions for the validity of the fourth figure are that one of two alternative conditions be met with regard to the quality and quantity of the premises. The first of the alternative conditions is that: (*i*) either both the minor and major premise are affirmative and the minor premise is universally quantified, and the second is that (*ii*) the minor and major premise differ in quality and one of the two premises is universally quantified.

Quality & Quantification	(i) Minor and major premises are affirmative; & Minor premise is universal	(ii) Minor and major premises differ; & One of the premises is universal.
Modality	N/A	

Reasoning in the fourth figure is unnatural to the human mind. Thus, it is left to the interested student to construct proofs for the valid moods in this figure. There are five kinds of proof: (1) proof by contradiction, (2) proof by reversal of the syllogism's order then conversion of the conclusion, (3) proof by conversion of both premises, (4) proof through reduction to the second figure by conversion of the minor premise, and (5) proof through reduction to the third figure by conversion of the major premise.

9.1.2 *Complex Syllogisms*

Complex syllogisms are those syllogisms composed of a major complex premise and a minor simple premise. They are of two types: *conditional* and *disjunctive*. There are three conditions for the validity of complex syllogisms, presented in the table below.

<table>
<tr><td>Quality</td><td colspan="2">The major complex premise must be affirmative.</td></tr>
<tr><td>Quantification</td><td>(i) If the complex premise is conditional, then it must have a real connection.</td><td>(ii) If the complex premise is disjunctive, then it must be strongly disjunctive.</td></tr>
<tr><td>Modality</td><td colspan="2">N/A</td></tr>
</table>

A *conditional complex syllogism* is composed of a *conditional complex* major premise and a *simple* minor premise that excludes one of the two parts of the major premise. This exclusion may be done validly in one of the following two ways, meaning that there are two valid forms for conditional complex syllogisms: (*i*) affirmation of the antecedent and (*ii*) negation of the consequent. The affirmation of the antecedent results in the affirmation of the consequent as in:

Major Premise: If A, then B.
Minor Premise: However, A.
Conclusion: B.

Negation of the consequent results in the negation of the antecedent as in:

Major Premise: If A ,then B.
Minor Premise: However, not B.
Conclusion: Not A.

These are the only two valid forms of the conditional complex syllogism. With respect to either form, the reverse is invalid. To affirm the consequent does not conclusively result in the affirmation of the antecedent, since the consequent may be more inclusive than the antecedent and the affirmation of a more inclusive matter does not necessitate the affirmation of the less inclusive matter. Similarly, to negate the antecedent does not conclusively result in the negation of the consequent, since the negation of the less inclusive does not necessarily result in the negation of the more inclusive.

A *disjunctive complex syllogism* is composed of a *disjunctive complex* major premise and a *simple* minor premise. It has three valid forms, corresponding to whether the major premise is a strongly exclusive disjunctive complex proposition, a truth-exclusive disjunctive complex proposition, or a falsity exclusive disjunctive complex proposition. When the major premise is a *strongly exclusive* disjunctive proposition, affirmation of one of the parts of the disjunctive premise results in the negation of the other part. The same rule applies when the major premise is a *truth-exclusive* disjunctive proposition, but not when it is falsity-exclusive.

Major Premise: Either A or B.
Minor Premise: However, A.
Conclusion: Not B.

Additionally, in a strongly exclusive disjunctive proposition, negation of one of the parts results in the affirmation of the other part. The same rule applies when the major premise is a *falsity-exclusive* disjunctive proposition, but not when it is truth-exclusive.

Major Premise: Either A or B.
Minor Premise: However, not A.
Conclusion: B.

A proof by contradiction (*qiyās al-khulf*) is composed of complex premises by which the conclusion of the argument is proven through the demonstration of the falsity of its contradictory opposite. This argument resolves to two complex syllogisms and a simple syllogism. An example of the proof follows, in two parts. First,

Major Premise: If A, then B.
Minor Premise: If B, then C.
Conclusion: If A, then C.

Second,

Major Premise: If A, then C.
Minor Premise: Not C.
Conclusion: Not A.

To illustrate, let us construct a proof by contradiction for the proposition ‹Some animal *actually* is human›. We can start with the following syllogism:

Major Premise: If ‹Some animal actually is human› is not true, then its contradictory opposite, ‹Every animal *always* is not human›, is true.
Minor Premise: If ‹Every animal *always* is not human› is true, then ‹Every human *always* is not human› is true.
Conclusion: If ‹Some animal *actually* is human› is not true, then ‹Every human *always* is not human› is true.

Then we construct the following syllogism, using the conclusion of the previous syllogism as the major premise:

Major Premise: If ‹Some animal *actually* is human› is not true, then ‹Every human *always* is not human› is true.
Minor Premise: However, ‹Every human *always* is not human› is not true.
Conclusion: ‹Some animal *actually* is human› is not not true (i.e., is true).

9.2 Non-Deductive Arguments

The form of a deductive argument conclusively entails its conclusion, meaning that anyone who is certain that its premises are true must also be certain that its conclusion is true. The truth of the premises, in other words, guarantees the truth of the conclusion. The form of a probabilistic argument, on the other hand, does not conclusively entail its conclusion. Someone who is certain that its premises are true will not be certain that the conclusion is true. Rather, they will only have *probabilistic knowledge*, or confidence, that its conclusion is true. The truth of the premises, in other words, gives confidence in the truth of the conclusion, but it does not guarantee its truth.

9.2.1 *Inductive Generalizations*

An *argument by inductive generalization* (*qiyās istiqrā'*) is the partial enumeration of judgments on a universal's instances to evidentially support a judgment on the universal.[12] Whereas deductive syllogisms reason from the general to the more specific, inductive generalizations reason from the specific to the more general. For example, we might examine particular instances of the universal ‹animal› (humans, horses, camels, lions, and so on) and find that the judgment ‹Animal X chews its food by moving its lower jaw› is true. We would then enumerate these judgments to evidentially support the universal judgment that all animals chew their food by moving their lower jaw. This enumeration is an *argument by inductive generalization*. It has the following form:

Premise 1	Instance 1 of ‹X› is Y.	Humans move their lower jaw when chewing.
Premise	Instance 2 of ‹X› is Y.	Horses move their lower jaw when chewing.
...	...	...
Premise	Instance n of ‹X› is Y.	Lions move their lower jaw when chewing.
Conclusion	Every X is Y.	Every animal moves its lower jaw when chewing.

This argument can also be represented in the form of a disjunctive deductive syllogism as follows:

Major Premise	‹X› is either Instance 1, Instance 2...or Instance n.	Animals are either humans, horses,... or lions.
Minor Premise	Instance 1 is Y, Instance 2 is Y...and Instance 25 is Y.	Humans move their lower jaw when chewing, horses move their lower jaw when chewing,...and lions move their lower jaw when chewing.
Conclusion	Every X is Y	Every animal moves its lower jaw when chewing.

12. Some logicians defined an inductive argument as a judgment on a universal that obtains because of the existence of the judgment in most of its instances. This judgment, however, is the conclusion of the inductive argument, not the argument itself. The argument itself consists of multiple individual judgments that bring about this judgment. *TB*, 412.

Representing an inductive generalization in the form of a deductive argument allows us to pinpoint why the argument is merely probabilistic rather than conclusive: the major premise of the disjunctive argument assumes that the instances that have been enumerated are the only ones that matter, and that all other instances will follow suit. This *restriction* (*ḥaṣr*) of the universal to the partial enumeration of its instances (or of its subordinate universals) is an *alleged restriction* (*ḥaṣr iddiʿāʾī*).[13] The basis for alleged restriction is that when we examine a sufficient number of instances[14] then we observe *probabilistic knowledge* within ourselves that the unexamined instances of the universal in question will be the same as the ones examined.

Inductive generalizations only lead to probabilistic knowledge because, no matter how many instances are examined, as long as one's examination (*taṣaffuḥ*) falls short of being comprehensive, the existence of unexamined instances that are different from the examined instances is always possible. To return to the above example, contrary to our initial judgment that all animals chew by moving their lower jaw, we might later discover that crocodiles chew their food by moving their upper jaw.

The fact that the generalized judgment is non-conclusive and that it is possible for it to be false does not negate our knowledge of it; it only negates

13. This is a term the logicians borrowed from the science of Arabic eloquence, where it refers to a figurative restriction that is made by way of hyperbole, in full knowledge of the existence of other instances, emphasizing the importance of the instances that are enumerated and dismissing the importance of those that are not. Scholars of Arabic eloquence express "restriction" with the Arabic word *qasr*, while the logicians prefer *ḥaṣr*. The former illustrate *alleged restriction* (*qaṣr iddiʿāʾī*) with the sentence, "The only scholar in the city is Zayd," as uttered by a speaker who knows that there are in fact other scholars in the city. The speaker's restriction of the city's scholarly population to Zayd is a hyperbole (*mubālagha*) that emphasizes the vastness of Zayd's scholarship; it is as though he has said that Zayd's scholarship is so vast that the scholarship of other scholars disappears in comparison to his. *Alleged restrictions* such as this one are thus figurative and rhetorically forceful. Saʿd al-Dīn Masʿūd b. ʿUmar al-Taftāzānī, Ibn Yaʿqūb al-Maghribī, and Bahāʾ al-Dīn al-Subkī, *Shurūḥ al-Talkhīṣ* (repr., Beirut: Muʾassasat Dār al-Bayān al-ʿArabī, n.d.), 2:174.

14. Most Muslim logicians held that inductive generalizations require the examination of most of a universal's instances in order to afford probabilistic knowledge of the remaining universals. *TB*, 413. The later logicians pointed out, however, that a great many of the important inductive generalizations that Muslim scholars have made (e.g., the great jurist Muḥammad b. Idrīs al-Shāfiʿī's inductive generalization that the maximum duration of a woman's menstrual period is 15 days) are based on what are, relatively speaking, very small subsets of instances, and that it is therefore more accurate to say merely that inductive generalizations require the examination of a number of a given universal's instances such that the examination results in probabilistic knowledge of the generalized judgment. Al-Ṣabbān, *Ḥāshiya*, 118. Modern methods of statistical sampling now help define this number with great precision and are a natural extension of this chapter of logic.

our *conclusive* knowledge of it. Counterexamples do not negate *probabilistic knowledge*, because probabilistic knowledge admits their possibility from the outset. When a counterexample is discovered, as in the example above, the probabilistic judgment is not completely invalidated, but merely rendered *more specific* by subtracting the counterexample from the generalized judgment. After making this modification, we know probabilistically that ‹Every animal *except for crocodiles* moves its lower jaw while chewing›.

When the singular instances are comprehensively surveyed (*istiqrāʾ tāmm*), the restriction of a universal to the examined instances is not *alleged* but rather *real* (*ḥaṣr ḥaqīqī*),[15] and a universal judgment based on such a survey is not *probabilistic* but rather *conclusive*. In fact, a universal judgment that arises from such a survey is not an inductive generalization at all; it is a *disjunctive proposition* that divides the universal into its singular instances or subordinate universals. This disjunctive proposition in turn usually serves as a premise in a *complex syllogism based on division of a universal* (*qiyās muqassim*). For example, the disjunctive proposition ‹Every number is either even or odd› comprehensively surveys all singular instances of the universal ‹number› and serves as a premise in the complex syllogism:

Minor Premise: Every number is either even or odd.
Major Premise: The number five is not even.
Conclusion: The number five is odd.

9.2.2 *Causal Analogies*

An *argument by causal analogy* (*qiyās tamthīl*) begins with a known judgment on a singular instance, the *source*. It then identifies some attribute in the source as the reason, the *analogical cause*, of the judgment. Finally, it transfers the judgment on the source to another singular instance, the *target*, based on the presence of the analogical cause in the target. For example, a jurist may begin with the judgment that drinking wine is unlawful, then identify its quality of being intoxicating as the reason for the judgment, and then transfer the judgment of unlawfulness to beer based on the presence

15. Al-Jurjānī distinguished between inductive generalizations (sg. *istiqrāʾ nāqiṣ*) and universal udgments based on comprehensively surveying their instances (sg. *istiqrāʾ tāmm*) by the fact that the restriction of the universal to its instances in the former case is an alleged restriction whereas in the latter case it is a real restriction. Other logicians, however, disagreed, arguing that inductive generalizations do not comprise an alleged restriction because they would then comprise the claim that their generalization is conclusive, whereas they only claim that it is probabilistic. *TB*, 412.

of the quality of being intoxicating in it. An argument by causal analogy is thus composed of four elements:

1. A source, e.g., wine
2. A judgment on the source, e.g., being unlawful
3. An analogical cause, e.g., being intoxicating
4. A target, e.g., beer.

Formally, an argument by causal analogy is defined as an argument that is composed of premises that describe singular instance A as sharing the cause of a judgment on singular instance B in order to establish that A also shares the judgment on B.

Arguments by causal analogy are most frequently used in the Muslim scholarly tradition by scholars of sacred law to derive the legal rulings of cases that cannot be determined by any explicit revelatory statement. The most detailed theoretical examination of juristic arguments by causal analogy is found in the science of legal theory.[16] The *mutakallimūn*, too, examine such arguments as part of a larger theological question, namely, to what extent the attributes of unseen things that we have not directly experienced (e.g., God, the events of the afterlife, etc.) can be analogically inferred from the things that we do experience in the physical universe (*qiyās al-ghā'ib 'alā al-shāhid*).

9.2.2.1 The Strength of Causal Analogies

The strength of arguments by analogy is normally commensurate to the strength with which one can establish that some property is really an analogical cause. The most common methods for establishing that a quality is an analogical cause are *correlation* (*dawarān*) and *elimination* (*tardīd*). Since each of the methods only probabilistically establishes that a property is an analogical cause, arguments by analogy are probabilistic arguments.

According to Avicenna, arguments by causal analogy are extremely weak arguments, weaker even than inductive generalizations, not even rising to the level of probabilistic arguments. Later logicians, however, unanimously disagreed, arguing that the strength of arguments by causal analogy follows from the strength with which one knows that (1) a particular property is the analogical cause, (2) the analogical cause exists in the target, and (3) the

16. Whereas the Muslim logicians call arguments by causal analogy *qiyās tamthīl* or simply *tamthīl*, the jurists and scholars of legal theory simply call them *qiyās*. Legal theorists examine the theoretical structure of such arguments in the chapter of *qiyās* in manuals of legal theory. See, for example, al-'Aṭṭār, *Ḥāshiyat Jam' al-jawāmi'*, 2:229-382.

analogical cause is transitive, meaning that it brings about the judgment wherever it exists, not merely when it exists in the source-instance (e.g., when the source-instance is a *condition* (*sharṭ*) for the operation of the analogical cause) and not with the exception of when it exists in the target-instance (e.g., when the target-instance is a *preventive* (*māniʿ*) for the operation of the analogical cause).[17] These three things are often known probabilistically and could, theoretically, also be known conclusively, particularly in juristic arguments for questions of sacred law, where revelation can conclusively declare or indicate each of them. This is why jurists sometimes hold that some arguments by analogy are stronger even than *explicit revelatory statements* (sg. *naṣṣ*).[18] This can be illustrated by the fact that an argument by causal analogy can be represented as a deductive syllogism as follows:

Minor Premise:	The target instance possesses the analogical cause that exists in the source.
Major Premise:	Every instance that possesses the analogical cause that exists in the source is also a subject of the source-judgment.
Conclusion:	The target instance is a subject of the source-judgment.

This deductive syllogism is valid and hence *formally conclusive*. That means that if the minor and major premises are *materially conclusive*, then the conclusion of the causal analogy will be conclusive.

The material conclusiveness of the minor premise depends on the conclusive existence of the analogical cause in the target instance. The material conclusiveness of the major premise depends on the conclusiveness of the alleged property being the analogical cause and also on its being transitive. Whenever these three things are known conclusively, the conclusion of an argument by causal analogy will also be conclusive, and whenever they are known probabilistically, the conclusion will be probabilistic. It is, however, extremely difficult to ever know all of these three things conclusively, and so arguments by causal analogy are normally probabilistic.

17. A *cause* (*sabab*) is something whose existence entails the existence of its effect and whose nonexistence entails its nonexistence. A *condition* (*sharṭ*) is something whose nonexistence entails the nonexistence of the thing that it conditions but whose existence does not entail anything. A *preventive* (*māniʿ*) is something whose existence entails the nonexistence of the thing that it prevents but whose nonexistence does not entail anything.

18. An *explicit revelatory statement* (*naṣṣ*) is one that is not open to figurative interpretation. See al-ʿAṭṭār, *Ḥāshiyat Jamʿ al-jawāmiʿ*, 2:87-93.

9.2.2.2 Methods of Determining the Analogical Cause

Both *correlation* (*dawarān*) and *elimination* (*tardīd*), are probabilistic. *Correlation* is for the judgment to exist whenever the posited analogical cause exists and for it to be absent whenever the posited analogical cause is absent. For example, when fermenting grape juice becomes intoxicating, it is unlawful, but when it has not yet become intoxicating, it is not unlawful. This correlation between being intoxicating and unlawfulness indicates that being intoxicating is the cause for grape juice being unlawful. The mere correlation of the *existence* of the posited analogical cause with the *existence* of the judgment is insufficient to establish that it is really the cause. For example, giving a gift correlates with ownership in existence but not in absence, because ownership could arise as a result of something else, such as conducting a sale. In the same way, the mere correlation of its *absence* with the *absence* of the judgment is also insufficient to establish its status as a cause. For example, purification correlates with the validity of prayer in absence but not in existence, because the validity of the prayer requires many other conditions in addition to purification.

Correlation affords only probabilistic evidence that something is an analogical cause because it is possible for the posited analogical cause to only be *part* of the cause, and it is also possible for it to coexist with the cause but not be the cause itself.[19] Just as the complete analogical cause correlates with the judgment, so too do mere parts of the cause and other things that coexist with the cause correlate with the judgment. Correlation hence does not conclusively indicate that the posited analogical cause is indeed the analogical cause.

The second method, *elimination*, is to list the properties of the source that are candidates for being the analogical cause and to then eliminate some of them in order to restrict the analogical cause to the remainder. One might argue, for example, that the cause for the unlawfulness of wine is either intoxication or liquidity, and then eliminate liquidity on the basis that water is liquid and yet not unlawful, leaving intoxication as the analogical cause. Elimination is only probabilistic evidence that something is an analogical cause because it is rarely possible to comprehensively list all the properties of the source. As a result, it is always possible for an unlisted property to be the true analogical cause.

19. In the contemporary metaphysics of causation, *epiphenomena* fall into this category.

Sources

Section	Sources
9 Arguments	*TB*, 363-64; for further reading, see Street, *Najm al-Dīn*, 224-38; Ahmed, *Palimpsests*, 184-190; Tony Street, "An Outline of Avicenna's Syllogistic," *Archiv für Geschichte der Philosophie* 84, no. 2 (2002): 129-60, https://doi.org/10.1515/agph.2002.007
9.1 Deductive Arguments	*TB*, 364-75
9.1.1 Simple Syllogisms	*TB*, 375-407
9.1.1.1 The First Figure	*TB*, 379-83
9.1.1.2 The Second Figure	*TB*, 383-94
9.1.1.3 The Third Figure	*TB*, 394-99
9.1.1.4 The Fourth Figure	*TB*, 399-405
9.1.2 Complex Syllogisms	*TB*, 407-12; for further reading, see Street, *Najm al-Dīn*, 261-64; Ahmed, *Palimpsests*, 190
9.2 Non-Deductive Arguments	TB, 412-16; for further reading, see Street, *Najm al-Dīn*, 266-69; Ahmed, *Palimpsests*, 191-92
9.2.1 Inductive Generalizations	*TB*, 412-13
9.2.2 Causal Analogies	*TB*, 414-16
9.2.2.1 The Strength of Causal Analogies	*TB*, 414
9.2.2.2 Methods of Determining the Analogical Cause	*TB*, 415-16

IV

SUPPLEMENTS

10

THE MATTER OF ARGUMENTS

The goal of Islamic logic is not just to avoid mistakes in the *form* of arguments, but also their *matter*. The difference between form and matter and how they lead to mistakes in reasoning is illustrated by the following two examples of unsound argument:

Minor Premise: Zayd is wise.
Major Premise: Every scholar is content.
Conclusion: Zayd is content

and

Minor Premise: Zayd is wise.
Major Premise: Everyone who is wise can fly.
Conclusion: Zayd can fly.

The conclusion of the first argument is true, but the argument is formally *invalid*: it is true that if Zayd is wise, then he must also be content, but the conclusion does not follow from its premises because there is no middle term to connect the minor and major premises. On the other hand, the conclusion of the second argument is false, but it is formally *valid*: it is not true that Zayd can fly, but the terms of the argument are correctly arranged according to the *first figure* of the simple syllogism. The reason why the conclusion of the second argument is incorrect, then, is not related to its form but to its matter, or the contents of its terms. The major premise is false because it is not the case that wise people can fly.

The previous chapter explained how to avoid *formal mistakes* in inference. The goal of this chapter is to explain how to avoid *material mistakes* in inference.

The method of avoiding material mistakes in inference depends on the goal of one's argument. In the tradition of Aristotle, the *falāsifa* have traditionally listed five goals of argument:

1. To attain certain knowledge (*demonstration*, see 10.1)
2. To convince (*dialectics*, see 10.2)
3. To motivate (*rhetoric*, see 10.3)
4. To influence (*poetics*, see 10.4)
5. To confuse (*fallacy*, see 10.5).

These five kinds of argument are called the *five arts* (*al-ṣināʿāt al-khams*) of *falsafa*. Each of these arts, along with the methods of avoiding material mistakes in it, is described below.

10.1 Demonstration

The goal of *demonstrative argument* (*burhān*) is to bring about *certain knowledge* (*yaqīn*). *Certain knowledge* is (*a*) the belief that something is the case, when (*b*) one also believes that the opposite cannot be the case, (*c*) one's belief is incapable of changing, and (*d*) the belief corresponds to reality. Part (*a*) of the definition excludes *hesitation*, which is not belief; Part (*b*) excludes *probabilistic knowledge*, in which one believes merely that the opposite is unlikely albeit possible; Part (*c*) excludes *belief based on authority* (*taqlīd*), which, unlike belief based on evidence, can be changed by the loss of confidence in the authority; and Part (*d*) excludes *compounded ignorance*, which does not correspond to reality.

The *falāsifa* held a variety of views regarding the relationship between demonstration and certainty. Some held that certain knowledge can only be acquired through demonstrative argument. Others objected that it is not possible to acquire certain knowledge at all through demonstrative arguments because that would lead to an infinite regress of arguments. Yet others objected that demonstrative reasoning is ultimately circular. The later Muslim logicians responded that the last position commits the fallacy of *begging the question*, and that the first two positions are both incorrect because certain knowledge is either acquired through noninferentially certain premises or by demonstrative inference from those premises. These noninferentially certain premises are described next.

10.1.1 *The Matter of Demonstrative Arguments*[1]

A demonstrative argument can only lead to certain knowledge if it ultimately resolves to premises that noninferentially afford certain knowledge. These premises fall into six categories:

1. Self-evident judgments
2. Observational judgments
3. Tested judgments
4. Intuited judgments
5. Mass-testified reports
6. Subconsciously inferred judgments.

Except for Categories 1 and 2, each of these judgments comprises an *implicit argument*. The difference between an *explicit argument* (*qiyās fikrī*) and an *implicit argument* (*qiyās khafī*) is that an explicit argument is the conscious motion of the mind from the knowledge that is sought to its starting points and then through an explicit inference back to the knowledge that is sought (see 1.1.4.2), whereas an implicit argument is a quick and unconscious inference that the mind makes without these motions. Knowledge that is acquired through an explicit argument is inferential, whereas knowledge that is acquired through an implicit argument is noninferential. Judgments of Category 1 are the only judgments that the mind makes by mere conception of the subject and predicate without resorting to anything else. All of the remaining judgments require the mind to resort to something else, such as sensation, experiment, intuition, mass-testimony, or hidden inference.

10.1.1.1 Self-Evident Judgments

Self-evident judgments (*awwaliyyāt*) are judgments that the mind makes by merely conceiving the subject and predicate without any intermediate inference. For example, the perception that one is half of two is a self-evident judgment, because the mind perceives it by the mere conception of ‹one› (the subject) and ‹half of two› (the predicate), without any intermediate inference.

1. The truth of the six kinds of noninferential judgments in this section is based on introspective observation. That means that all of these judgments are tested propositions (see 10.1.1.3) based on repeated observations of our *internal sensations* (see 10.1.1.2) of knowledge and knowledge-acquisition. (Karamali, *Kalām 3.0: The Muslim Manual of Logical Arguments to Show the Truth of Islam in the 21st Century* (Basira Education, 2024), §1.4.)

Other examples of self-evident judgments are the perception that the whole is greater than the part and that every effect has a cause.

Despite the straightforwardness of these judgments, some people fail to make them. This typically happens for one of three reasons. First, they might not properly conceive the meaning of the subject or the predicate. For example, someone may not perceive the self-evident judgment ‹Every contingent thing was made to be the way that it is by something other than itself› on account of not adequately conceiving the subject, ‹contingent›.

The failure to conceive such meanings might be because the *conception* is *inferential*, or, when it is noninferential, it might be because one needs to be *reminded* of it. This illustrates that a particular *judgment* might be noninferential and basic even while the conception of that judgment's subject or predicate is inferential.

The second reason one may fail to make a self-evident judgment is that one's mind may not be fully developed, as with children or simple-minded adults. Such people do not perceive the judgment even when they conceive the subject and predicate because they lack the means (i.e., the mental capacity) to make the judgment.

Finally, one's *natural mental disposition* (*fiṭra*) might be impaired by persistent adherence to incorrect beliefs that conflict with self-evident judgments, especially on the basis of authority. This is often the case with people who lack knowledge. Even when they conceive the subject and predicate, such people will not accept self-evident judgments that conflict with their incorrect beliefs because their natural mental disposition has been impaired. This natural disposition can be repaired by their learning proper inference, provided they are willing to reflect independently instead of continuing to appeal to authority.

10.1.1.2 Observational Judgments

Observational judgments (*mushāhadāt*) are judgments that the mind makes with the help of sensation. There are two kinds of sensation: *external sensation* (*ḥiss ẓāhirī*), i.e., sensation by one of the five senses, and *internal sensation* (*ḥiss bāṭinī*), i.e., *direct knowledge*. An example of an observational judgment by external sensation is the judgment that the sun is shining. An example of an observational judgment by internal sensation is the judgment that one is feeling pain.

Most logicians restrict observational judgments to those that are acquired by external sensation, but some also include internal sensation. Those who restrict observational judgments to external sensation argue that internal sensation cannot be used as the basis of an argument against someone other than the subject because the object of internal sensation is the subject himself, which is different for every observer. The object of external sensation, however, is the extramental universe, which is common to every observer and hence can be used as the basis of an argument against someone other than the subject. Those who include internal sensation respond that even though the object of internal sensation is different for every observer, most of what is observed is nevertheless common to every observer, such as hunger, thirst, love, and hate, and a denial of the knowledge of such commonly observed phenomena is an obstinate denial of something that is obvious.[2]

Observational judgments are always *singular propositions*, never *concept-propositions* or *instance-propositions* (see 6.2), because mere sensation never leads to anything more than a judgment about a singular subject. For example, when we see the sun in the sky, we only perceive that that particular sun is shining, and when we see and feel a particular fire, we only perceive that that particular fire is burning. We never directly sense the universal concepts ‹sun› or ‹fire› because these concepts are mental abstractions from particular extramental objects and hence have no existence in the extramental physical universe. But the singular judgments that arise from sensation can be made universal with the help of empirical testing or intuition. For example, the observational judgment that a particular fire is burning can, through repeated sensation (or empirical testing), be generalized into the universal judgment ‹Every fire burns›.

Mere sensation does not lead to judgment; judgment belongs to the mind. Sensation is a *tool* that the mind uses to make its judgments. This is why we sometimes use our mind to correct our sensations, such as when we judge the sight of water on a hot day to be a mirage. To infer the unreliability of sensation as a source of knowledge from such examples is a mistake because sensation is merely a tool that the mind uses to make its judgments. Just as it sometimes judges sensation to be mistaken, it judges at most times that

---

2. The logicians use observational judgments in their argument for the need for the science of logic. See 1.2. They also provide the epistemological basis for all of the six kinds of non-inferential judgments, which is needed to construct a complete *kalām* epistemology. See: Karamali, *Kalām 3.0: The Muslim Manual of Logical Arguments to Show the Truth of Islam in the 21st Century* (Basira Education, 2024), §1.

sensation is in fact correct. Someone who accepts the mind's judgment that sensation is sometimes mistaken must also accept its judgment that sensation is, at other times, correct.

10.1.1.3 Tested Judgments

Tested judgments (*tajrībiyyāt* or *mujarrabāt*) are judgments that the mind makes with the help of repeated observation, such as the medical judgment that a particular chemical is a laxative. These judgments afford certainty by an implicit syllogism that is composed of the major premise ‹Everything that happens repeatedly in the same way, either always (*dā'iman*) or most of the time (*akthariyyan*), is not a coincidence, but the result of a cause; and whenever the existence of the cause is known, the existence of its effect is known with certainty›. For example, when one observes repeatedly that consuming a particular chemical is always or mostly followed by bowel movements, then the judgment that the chemical is a laxative is the conclusion of the following implicit inference.

Minor Premise:	Whenever one consumes chemical x, bowel movements occur.
Major Premise:	Everything that occurs repeatedly in the same way has a cause.
Conclusion:	Whenever one consumes chemical x, something causes bowel movements.

Note that making a tested judgment does not require knowing what the cause is, only that there is some cause.

Both tested judgments and *inductive generalizations* are universal judgments that are derived from particular observations. But the way that each is derived is different. Whereas tested judgments generalize particular observations through the implicit causal inference described above, inductive generalizations generalize particular observations without any causal inference, but rather by a survey that is *comprehensive* (*ḥaṣr*), either *actually* (*ḥaqīqatan*) or *allegedly* (*iddiʿā'an*). And whereas tested judgments are conclusive, most inductive judgments are probabilistic.

10.1.1.4 Intuited Judgments

Intuited judgments (*ḥadsiyyāt*) are judgments that the mind perceives with the help of things like observation, such as the judgment that the moon does not emit its own light, but that it reflects the light of the sun. The mind perceives (intuits) this when it observes how the moon's phases change with its changing position with respect to the sun. The difference between *intuition* and *inference* is that when the mind *intuits*, it moves involuntarily and instantly from a group of premises (e.g., the observations of the phases of the moon at its different positions with respect to the sun) to a conclusion (e.g., that the moon reflects the light of the sun), whereas when the mind *infers*, it moves purposefully and step-by-step, from the remote conception of the knowledge that is sought to its starting points and then back to the knowledge that is sought.

Both tested and intuited judgments are based on a causal inference. The difference between them is that in tested judgments the cause is unknown, whereas in intuited judgments the cause is known. This is why tested judgments are based on a single implicit syllogism, whereas intuited judgments are based on many implicit syllogisms that are different depending on the cause that is under consideration. Another difference between tested and intuited judgments is that tested judgments are based on repeated observation whereas intuited judgments require neither observation nor repetition because they can be made by merely understanding something with the mind.[3]

10.1.1.5 Mass-Testified Judgments

Mass-testified judgments (*mutawātirāt*) are judgments regarding the truth of mass-testified reports. A report is *mass-transmitted* when such a large number of people independently report having seen or heard something that it is *impossible by regularity* for them to have conspired to lie. Whenever we perceive that a report is mass-testified, we noninferentially acquire certain knowledge of its truth. An example of a mass-testified judgment is the judgment that the Prophet Muḥammad (God bless him and give him peace) made a claim to prophecy and that miracles then appeared at his hands to

3. Simple scientific reasoning that establishes a high-level causal correlation between two natural phenomena (such as between a pharmaceutical drug and its curative effects or its side-effects, or between an advertising technique and customer conversion) leads to the discovery of *tested judgments*. Complex scientific reasoning that establishes scientific laws and theories (such as E = mc2, the Big Bang theory, the theory of evolution, and the atomic theory of matter) leads to the discovery of *intuited propositions*. This latter kind of scientific reasoning is known in modern philosophical literature as *inference to the best explanation*. (Karamali, *Kalām 3.0: The Muslim Manual of Logical Arguments to Show the Truth of Islam in the 21st Century* (Basira Education, 2024), §1.5.)

confirm his claim.[4] Another example is the judgment that the cities of Mecca and Baghdad exist.

Some scholars have said that reports are mass-testified whenever four or more narrators independently report something that they have seen or heard, others have said that they are mass-testified when there are seven or more narrators, and others have given other numbers. But the correct position is that the number of narrators that are required for a report to be mass- testified varies from case to case. The mark that the requisite number of narrators has been reached is that, after considering the circumstances of the event, the narrators, the time, and the place, we noninferentially perceive that it is impossible for that number of narrators to have conspired to lie.

Mass-testimony is an extension of observation: we can either gain certain knowledge of the truth of a singular proposition by observing it ourselves or by having a large number of people independently report that observation to us. Mass-testimony thus only applies to reports of observed truths; it does not apply to reports of inferred truths. If a large number of people independently report that they have all concluded that the doctrine of the trinity is true, for example, this does not lead us to any kind of knowledge regarding the truth of that doctrine.

When an observation is reported through a chain of narrators, it must be mass-testified at every level of the chain in order for the report of its occurrence to be mass-transmitted. That is why reports of Jesus' crucifixion are not mass-testified. On the other hand, reports that the Prophet Muḥammad (God bless him and give him peace) informed us that it is obligatory for us to perform the five daily prayers, that some people are punished in their graves, that God will give some people permission to intercede for others on the Day of Judgment, are, indeed, mass-transmitted.

Muslim logicians treat mass-transmitted judgments as a distinct kind of judgment because the science of *kalām* relies on them to prove the genuineness of the Prophet Muḥammad's claim (God bless him and give him peace) to be a divine messenger and because the central aspects of what the Prophet Muḥammad (God bless him and give him peace) taught us from God are all mass-transmitted.[5]

---

4. For a detailed explanation of why this is mass-testified, see Karamali, *Why Islam is True: Quranic Arguments For God, the Prophet Muhammad, and the Purpose of Life* (Basira Education, 2024), Chapter Eleven).

5. The Indian scholar of *kalām* and hadith from the last century, Anwar Shāh al-Kashmīrī (d. 1933) classified mass-testimony into four categories. His summary has since been widely cited in Muslim scholarly circles. The

10.1.1.6 Subconsciously Inferred Judgments

Subconsciously inferred judgments (*fiṭriyyāt* or *qaḍāyā qiyāsātuhā maʿahā*) are judgments that afford certain knowledge through a hidden inference of which we are not normally conscious such as the judgment that four is an even number. These judgments are in reality inferential, but since their inference is so familiar that we make it subconsciously, the logicians traditionally include them among the judgments that noninferentially lead to certain knowledge.

10.1.2 *Kinds of Demonstrative Arguments*

In every *simple syllogism*, it is the *middle term* that connects the major premise to the minor premise, thereby enabling the inference of the conclusion (i.e., the predication of the minor term to the major term) from the two premises. The middle term is therefore always the cause of the knowledge of the conclusion within the mind. In addition to being the cause of the conclusion in the *mind*, the middle term may or may not be the cause of the conclusion in *reality*. Compare the following syllogisms:

---

following citation of his summary is taken from al-Ghursī, *al-Nukat al-ghurar* (Damascus, Dār al-Qādirī: 2008), p. 52.

(1) **Mass-Testimony by Virtue of Many Chains of Transmission:** This is the kind of mass-testimony with which scholars of hadith concern themselves. The most common example of a mass-transmitted report by virtue of its being reported by a large number of chains of transmission is the hadith, "Whoever falsely ascribes something to me deliberately, let him prepare his seat in the Fire," which Ibn Salāḥ states was reported by 62 Companions.

(2) **Generational Mass-Testimony:** This is when something is reported by an entire generation of people to the following generation, such as the mass-testimony of every generation that the Prophet Muḥammad (God bless him and give him peace) taught the Qur'ān, by the generational teaching of its recitation and memorization, its generational recitation in the daily ritual prayers, and its generational study and citation in books and classes of religious learning.

(3) **Practical Mass-Testimony:** This is when something is practiced in large numbers from one generation to the next, such as the daily performance of the five congregational prayers, the fast of Ramadan, and the annual pilgrimage to Mecca. These actions are mass-testified-to as being from the Prophet Muḥammad (God bless him and give him peace) by virtue of their practice.

(4) **Mass-Testimony of a Common Element:** Reports can either be mass-testimony in wording (*tawātur lafẓī*) or in meaning (*tawātur maʿnawī*). Mass-testimony in meaning is when reports that describe different events all share a common element that they are all effectively reporting, either explicitly or implicitly. Common examples of mass-testimony by meaning are the bravery of the Prophet's (God bless him and give him peace) cousin and son-in-law ʿAlī b. Abī Ṭālib, and the generosity of the pre-Islamic Arab, Ḥātim al-Ṭāʾī. It is also mass-transmitted in meaning that the Prophet (God bless him and give him peace) performed miracles—although the vast majority of the individual hadiths that report his miracles are non-mass-transmitted and report different miracles, when they are taken altogether, they share in common that they are all explicitly reporting that the Prophet (God bless him and give him peace) performed miracles.

Minor Premise: Zayd has an infection.
Major Premise: Everyone who has an infection has a fever.
Conclusion: Zayd has a fever.

and

Minor Premise: Zayd has fever.
Major Premise: Everyone who has a fever has an infection.
Conclusion: Zayd has an infection.

In the first syllogism, the middle term ‹someone who has an infection› is the cause of the conclusion in *reality*, because having an infection causes one to develop a fever. In the second syllogism, the middle term ‹someone who has a fever› is not the cause of the conclusion, because it is the infection that causes the fever, not vice-versa. In the first syllogism, the middle term is the cause of the conclusion not only in the mind but also in reality. Such an argument is termed an *argument from the cause* (*dalīl limmī*), because it infers the effect (e.g., the fever) from the cause (e.g., the infection). In the second syllogism, the middle term is the cause of the conclusion in the *mind*, but not in reality. Such an argument is termed an *argument from the effect* (*dalīl innī*) because it infers the cause (e.g., the infection) from the effect (e.g., the fever).

10.2 Dialectics

The goal of *dialectic argument* (*jadal*) is to convince someone who does not have the aptitude or training to discern certain knowledge from demonstrative arguments. Dialectic arguments must be composed of premises that are either *widely accepted* (*mashhūrāt*) or *accepted by the interlocutor* (*musallamāt*). These premises need not be true since the function of a dialectical argument is merely to convince. As long as they are widespread in society or accepted by the interlocutor, any premises can serve this function. It is not even a requirement that the argument be valid (i.e., that it have a correct form)—as long as the form is accepted by the audience, the argument can achieve the goal of convincing them. Examples of premises that are *widely accepted* are ‹Justice is good› and ‹Oppression is evil›. In most contexts it would not be expected of one to advance a demonstrative argument for the truth of such premises when one uses them to make a point. The reason why widely accepted premises generate belief is that the natures and customs of people play a role in the generation of people's beliefs. Exactly which premises are widely accepted will therefore vary from people to people, from place to place, and from time to time. When natures and customs are corrupted, people may come to believe that something good (e.g., kindness to other people) is bad. Examples of premises that are *accepted by the interlocutor* are the questions of legal theory (*uṣūl al-fiqh*), which are accepted by a given group of scholars and students of sacred law when they debate with each other. Accepted premises are often used for *silencing* (*ilzām*) the opponent in a debate.

10.3 Rhetoric

The goal of *rhetorical argument* (*khaṭāba*) is to motivate people—ideally, to do what benefits them, such as rectifying their character, their livelihood, or their religion. These kinds of arguments are commonly used in sermons. They must either be composed of premises that afford probabilistic knowledge (*maẓnūnāt*) or statements of influential people (*maqbūlāt*), such as religious scholars or saints.[6] Some logicians have mistakenly included prophets and messengers in their list of influential people whose statements are used in rhetorical arguments. This is a grave mistake because the statements of prophets and messengers afford certain knowledge, because (1) they are subconsciously inferred certain propositions (people subconsciously know that prophets and messengers bring evidence to support their claims, which turns their statements into certain premises), (2) they are intuited certain propositions (people can intuit the genuineness of a the Prophet Muḥammad's messengerhood (God bless him and give him peace) by his character and the events of his life, which could only be the case if he was a genuine messenger), or (3) they are demonstratively inferred conclusions of certain propositions (see 5.3.3).

10.4 Poetics

The goal of *poetic argument* (*shiʿr*) is to attract people toward or to repel them away from something. Poetic arguments are not really arguments; they are simply *statements that use emotive imagery* (*mukhayyilāt*) to affect the listener's soul toward or away from something. For example, the statement, "Wine is red liquid rubies," casts the emotive imagery of rubies into the soul of the listener to attract him to wine (which is something bad), and the statement,

6. This reflects the religious nature of traditional Muslim societies. Religious scholars and saints no longer command the influence that they used to. As societies become less religious, they are influenced by other kinds of people. When these people are immoral, the art of rhetoric can have an extremely damaging effect and needs to be constantly checked by the art of demonstration.

"Honey is bee vomit," casts the emotive imagery of vomit into the soul of the listener to repel him from honey (which is something good). These examples illustrate that the truth of the emotive statements is not a requirement for the correctness of poetic arguments. Poetic meter, music, and a beautiful voice all amplify the effect of poetic argument.

10.5 Fallacy

The goal of *fallacious argument* (*mughālaṭa*) is confusion. Fallacious arguments are either composed of *abstract singular judgments* (*wahmiyyāt*) or of *deceptive judgments* (*mushabbahāt*). *Abstract singular judgments* resemble observational judgments; observational judgments comprise the sensation of a particular sensible thing (e.g., ‹This sun is shining›), and abstract singular judgments comprise the perception of an abstract concept that characterizes a particular sensible thing (e.g., ‹This mosque is beautiful›, where beauty is an abstract concept that characterizes the particular sensible mosque that is being pointed at, or ‹This office building is hideous›, where hideousness is an abstract concept that characterizes the particular sensible building that is being pointed at). These kinds of judgments are correct when they are made about particular sensible things, but incorrect when they are generalized to universal concepts, such as when one generalizes from the singular judgment ‹This mosque is beautiful› that ‹Every mosque is beautiful› or from the singular judgment ‹This office building is hideous› that ‹Every office building is hideous›. We are instinctively inclined to make such judgments and need to restrain ourselves from them by using our minds consciously. Another common example of a fallacious premise that arises from the instinctive generalization of abstract singular judgments is ‹Everything that exists has a physical location›. We need to use our minds to restrain the instinct to generalize our perception of specific existent things having locations, for God exists without any physical location. Yet another example is ‹There is unending empty space beyond the limits of universe›. Again, we need to use our minds to restrain the instinct to generalize our perception of empty space, for there is nothing beyond the limits of the universe, not even empty space. The fallacy of materialism—the belief that everything that exists is composed of matter or, equivalently, that nothing that is immaterial exists—arises from this mistaken instinctive generalization.

Deceptive judgments (*mushabbahāt*) are false propositions that resemble true ones either in form or in meaning. An example of a fallacious argument based on a resemblance in form is to say about the sculpted form of a horse:

Minor Premise:	This is a horse.
Major Premise:	Every horse is a neighing animal.
Conclusion:	This is a neighing animal.

This syllogism is formally valid since it is in one of the valid moods of the first figure. However, the minor premise is a false proposition, a *deceptive judgment*, since the form of the horse is not an actual horse.

An example of resemblance in meaning is:

Minor Premise:	Everything that is both human and horse is human.
Major Premise:	Everything that is both human and horse is a horse.
Conclusion:	Some human is a horse.

This syllogism is formally valid since it is in one of the valid moods of the third figure. However, the premises are false since nothing is both human and horse. The meaning of ‹thing that is both human and horse› resembles ‹thing that is both animal and rational›, but the latter exists whereas the former does not.

Other causes of errors in reasoning include scattering the points of an argument such that it is unclear how the conclusion follows, being unnecessarily verbose such that the logical structure of the argument is masked, adding extraneous points, and making trivial, sarcastic, or joking comments in the context of a reasoned discussion or inquiry.

In addendum to the discussion of the types of noninferential premises and the causes of error, the scholars of the Islamic tradition remind the student that to distinguish true noninferential judgments from erroneous ones ultimately requires a sound mind and heart, which are favors from God. To be completely free from errors in thought is contrary to human nature; even brilliant scholars occasionally fall into errors of reasoning. Beyond simply studying the rules of logic, one who wants to be rid of such errors to the extent humanly possible must also strive in the way of spiritual purification and continual remembrance of God—practices learned in the science of Sufism. For, in the Islamic tradition, there is no break between the logical and the spiritual: ultimately there is only a single, unified reality. When one makes oneself open and receptive to that reality, to knowledge of God and His creation, by means of spiritual purification, one arrives at the perception of what the logicians term *subconsciously inferred judgements* and *intuited judgments*, acquiring some or much knowledge (depending on one's state) without the need for deliberate inference.

Sources

Section	Sources
10 The Matter of Arguments	TB, 416-29; for further reading, see Street, *Najm al-Dīn*, 270-82; Ahmed, *Palimpsests*, 192-95
10.1 Demonstration	TB, 417
10.1.1 The Matter of Demonstrative Arguments	TB, 417-21
10.1.1.1 Self-Evident Judgments	TB, 417-18
10.1.1.2 Observational Judgments	TB, 418; Saʿd al-Dīn Masʿūd b. ʿUmar al-Taftāzānī, et al., *Sharḥ al-ʿAqāʾid al-Nasafiyya* (1326H), 24-25
10.1.1.3 Tested Judgments	TB, 418-19
10.1.1.4 Intuited Judgments	TB, 57-58, 419-20
10.1.1.5 Mass-Transmitted Judgments	TB, 420-21
10.1.1.6 Subconsciously Inferred Judgments	TB, 421
10.1.2 Kinds of Demonstrative Arguments	TB, 421-22; for further reading, see Strobinio, "Causal and Noncausal Demonstration," in *Avicenna's Theory*, 217-38
10.2 Dialectics	TB, 422-24
10.3 Rhetoric	TB, 424-25
10.4 Poetics	TB, 425-26; for further reading, see Gregor Schoeler, "The 'Poetic Syllogism' Revisited," *Oriens* 41, no. 1-02 (2013): 1-26, https://doi.org/10.1163/18778372-13410101
10.5 Fallacy	TB, 426-29

11

THE ORGANIZATION OF SCIENCES

The science of logic that has been described in the previous chapters was developed by the scholarly community of the traditional madrasa. This scholarly community inherited this science in a basic form from Aristotle through Avicenna and then extensively refined and developed it in conversation with the other sciences of the traditional madrasa curriculum, such as Arabic grammar, sacred law, rational theology, legal theory, Qur'ānic exegesis, and many others.[1] The science of logic was ancillary to these other sciences—they used the rules of logic described in Chapters 3 and 4 to precisely define their technical terms and the rules of logic described in Chapters 9 and 10 to precisely express their arguments. As a result, logic was a curricular requirement from the earliest stages of the madrasa education.[2] But the science of logic did not merely add precision to the sciences' definitions and arguments; it also added precision to their organization, both the organization of the individual sciences themselves and the organization of their relation to each other. This organizing role of the science of logic is traditionally described at the end of Muslim manuals of logic,[3] and is the subject of this final chapter.

---

1. For a pedagogical description of the traditional madrasa and its curriculum in its social and intellectual context, see Karamali, *Madrasa Curriculum*. The place of the science of logic in this curriculum is described on page 5.

2. For the place of logic in the curricular order of the madrasa sciences, see Karamali, *Madrasa Curriculum*, 27.

3. Such as al-Taftāzānī's *al-Tahdhīb* and Shams al-Dīn al-Kātibī's *al-Shamsiyya*.

11.1 What Is a Science?

The Arabic word for "science" is *ʿilm*. *ʿIlm* is an important word in the science of logic and in its most common usage means *knowledge*. Here, however, it refers to a closely related *set of propositions*. For example, the *science* of sacred law (*ʿilm al-fiqh*) is a set of hundreds of thousands of propositions about the relation of the divine command to the actions of moral agents. These propositions include ‹Fasting the month of Ramadan is obligatory› and ‹Drinking wine is unlawful›. Another example is the *science* of logic (*ʿilm al-manṭiq*), which is a set of propositions about how to acquire new conceptual or propositional knowledge from existing conceptual or propositional knowledge. These propositions include ‹A genus and differentia, when composed in a particular way, constitute a complete essential definition› and ‹A universally quantified affirmative proposition and a singular affirmative proposition that have a common middle term constitute a simple syllogism›.

The propositions that constitute a science are always *inferential*. The goal of studying that science is to *demonstrate* (def: 10.1) the truth of these propositions through inference. In order for this set of propositions to become a science, its study needs to be important in the civilization in which it arises. As a result of this importance, the propositional inferences of the science are revisited by multiple generations of scholars who challenge, refine, confirm, or strengthen them, thereby significantly increasing the number of propositions that belong to that science. This set of closely related propositions that constitute the science thus reflects the direct inferential concerns of the science's key propositions, the interests of the civilization in which the science arose, and the historical trajectory of the cross-generational scholarly debates.[4]

The logicians' organization of sciences is based on the organization of the philosophical sciences, which they inherited from Aristotle through the early *falāsifa*.[5] The goal of these philosophical sciences is to discover the way that all existent things are (*aḥwāl al-ashyāʾ*) as much as is humanly possible (*bi-qadr al-ṭāqa al-bashariyya*). The highest of the philosophical sciences is metaphysics, which studies existent things from the perspective of their existence. The reason why it is the highest science is because it studies things in the most general way possible, namely from the perspective of their mere existence, thus including within its scope all things. This was why it is also

4 For a description of the sciences that were important to traditional Muslim civilizations, how they were refined and developed over centuries, and how they were studied and taught, see Karamali, *Madrasa Curriculum*.

5. For a description of these philosophical sciences, see Karamali, *Madrasa Curriculum*, 6-13.

called "first philosophy" (*al-falsafa al-ūlā*). Below this science is natural science (*al-ʿilm al-ṭabīʿī*), for example, which studies one kind of existent thing, namely the physical object (*jism*).[6] Further below is human medicine, for example, which studies one kind of physical object, namely the human body. And so on. Every philosophical science thus studies a certain kind of existent thing that lies along a hierarchy of genera (*ajnās*) and species (*anwāʿ*), and its relative position within this hierarchy determines its relative positions with respect to other kinds of sciences. The closely related propositions of each science revolve around their common subject, which, when itself precisely defined, in turn precisely defines the kinds of predicates that are predicated of it in the science.

The madrasa scholarly community organized its revelatory sciences in the same way that the ancients organized their philosophical sciences.[7] The highest science in the madrasa is *kalām*, which subsumes the science of metaphysics and adds other Islamically important questions that Aristotelian metaphysics had not historically concerned itself with.[8] Below *kalām* lies a hierarchy of revelatory sciences that rely on revelation but are thoroughly merged with *falsafa*. Like the philosophical sciences, each one of these revelatory science studies a well-defined subject that, together with the well-defined predicates characteristic of the science, constitutes a set of questions. The goal of the science is to demonstrate the truth of these questions. These

6. For an overview of natural science in the context of the traditional madrasa curriculum and a comparison with modern science, see Karamali, *Madrasa Curriculum*, 8-10.

7. Some madrasa sciences were less influenced (or even not influenced at all) by the organization of the philosophical sciences, particularly the sciences of Arabic language and literature. *TB*, 430.

8. The science of metaphysics is particularly suited to being transformed into *kalām*. It divides existent things into those that exist contingently (the universe) and those that exist necessarily (God), then examines those general concept-pairs applied to existent things in general, regardless of whether their existence is necessary or contingent (e.g., the concept-pair of cause and effect and the concept-pair of oneness and multiplicity), and then argues for the existence of a necessary being on which the contingent universe depends. Because of its intimate relation to proving the existence of God, it was also called "the divine science" (*al-ʿilm al-ilāhī*). The *mutakallimūn* transformed this science into *kalām* by developing its arguments for a necessary being into arguments for a single personal deity who is omnipotent, omniscient, alive, created the contingent universe from nothing, and communicated to morally responsible agents through special human beings called messengers. For an overview of metaphysics and *kalām* in the context of the traditional madrasa curriculum, see Karamali, *Madrasa Curriculum*, 10-11, 19-21. For a more technical examination of the relation between Avicennan metaphysics and *kalām*, see Sirāj al-Dīn al-Urmawī, *Risāla fī al-farq bayna nawʿay al-ʿilm al-ilāhī wa-l-kalām*, in *Majmūʿ thalāth rasāʾil*, ed. Muḥammad Akram Abū Ghūsh (Amman: Dār al-Nūr al-Mubīn, 2013).

demonstrations began from certain well-defined inferential starting points. These subjects, predicates, conceptual and propositional inferential starting points, and scientific questions are the subject of this chapter.[9]

The next section (11.2) explains the subjects of sciences, the section after (11.3) explains their questions, and the section after that (11.4) explains the inferential starting points of sciences. Throughout this explanation, running examples are used from the sciences of Arabic grammar, logic, and sacred law. The final section of this chapter (11.5) is like an appendix to the chapter. It gives an overview of each of these sciences and organizes all the running examples, along with some additional examples, with brief explanations. Readers who are unfamiliar with these sciences are advised to familiarize themselves with the contents of the final section before reading the intervening sections and to then return to the final section as they work their way through the rest of this chapter.

11.2 The Subjects of Sciences

Every science studies a well-defined *subject* (*mawḍūʿ al-ʿilm*). For example, the science of Arabic grammar studies Arabic words, the science of logic studies concepts and propositions that lead to new knowledge, the science of sacred law studies the actions of morally responsible agents, and so on. To study a subject means to study its *essential predicates* (*ʿawāriḍ dhātiyya*), meaning those things that are predicated of the subject by virtue of the subject being what it is. For example, the subject of sacred law is the actions of morally responsible agents. To study these actions means to study whether they are obligatory, recommended, permissible, offensive, or unlawful. Obligation, recommendation, permissibility, offensiveness, and unlawfulness are all *essential predicates* of the actions of morally responsible agents because they are predicated to those actions by virtue of their being the actions of morally responsible agents. Something that is not an action of a morally responsible agent (e.g., the movements of non-rational animals) cannot be said to be obligatory, recommended, permissible, offensive, or unlawful.

An example of a *nonessential* predicate of the subject of sacred law (actions of morally responsible agents) is their being created by God. The proposition ‹The actions of morally responsible agents are created by God› is not a

9. Because a science is a collection of propositions, and because those propositions are composed of these elements, traditional manuals of logic call this chapter "The Parts of Sciences" (*ajzāʾ al-ʿulūm*).

question of sacred law.[10] Despite the fact that its subject is the same as the subject of sacred law, its predicate is not predicated to it by virtue of the actions of morally responsible agents being what they are. Rather, it is predicated to those actions by virtue of their being accidents of objects. That is why it is predicated not just of the actions of morally responsible agents, but of all accidents that belong to objects, such as their colors, movements, and locations. The study of this proposition thus belongs to the science that studies existent things from the perspective of their necessity or contingency, namely the science of metaphysics or *kalām*.

The subject of a science is thus that thing whose essential predicates are investigated in that science. The reason why the actions of morally responsible agents are the subjects of the science of sacred law, then, is that the science of sacred law searches for their essential predicates. It seeks to discover, in other words, whether particular actions of morally responsible agents are obligatory, recommended, permissible, offensive, or unlawful. Similarly, the reason why the subjects of logic are concepts and propositions that are means for inferring new knowledge is that the science of logic searches for their essential predicates, namely whether they are a direct or indirect means to conceptual or propositional knowledge.

11.3 The Questions of Sciences

The questions of a science are the *inferential propositions* whose truth the science seeks to *demonstrate*. Like all propositions, the questions of the science are constituted by a subject and a predicate.

11.3.1 *The Subjects of Scientific Questions*

Sometimes, the subjects of these questions are the subject of the science itself, but they might also be a species of the subject, an essential predicate of the subject, a species of the essential predicate, or a *qualifying composition* of the subject (or its species) and one of its essential predicates (or its species). The table below gives various illustrative examples from the science of Arabic grammar with brief explanations. For an explanation of the higher scientific context, see Section 11.5.1.

10. This question is a seminal issue of disagreement between the Sunnis and Mu'tazilīs. The Sunnis argue that divine omnipotence entails that the actions of moral agents be created by God and that this does not conflict with moral agents' freewill. The Mu'tazilīs, on the other hand, argue that God's justice entails that He give moral agents the ability to create their own actions.

Question	Explanation
Arabic words (*kalimāt*) are either inflected (*muʿrab*) or uninflected (*mabnī*).	A question of Arabic grammar whose subject is the subject of the science (i.e., Arabic words).
Past-tense verbs (*fiʿl māḍī*) are uninflected (*mabnī*).	A question of Arabic grammar whose subject is a species of the subject of the science (past-tense verbs are a species of Arabic words).
The non-inflection of nouns is a result of their resembling particles.	A question of Arabic grammar whose subject is an essential predicate of the subject of the science (non-inflection is an essential predicate of Arabic words).
Inflection into the *jazm* state is restricted to verbs.	A question whose subject is a species of an essential predicate of the science (inflection into the *jazm* state is a species of inflection, which is an essential predicate of Arabic words).
Inflected Arabic words either end with an unwritten *nūn* (*munṣarif*) or do not end with an unwritten *nūn* (*ghayr munṣarif*).	A question of Arabic whose subject is a qualifying composition of the subject (Arabic words) and its essential predicate (inflection).

11.3.2 *The Predicates of Scientific Questions*

The predicates of the questions of a science are always essential to their subject. This means that they are predicated to their subject by virtue of the subject being what it is, e.g., the predication of obligation to an action of a morally responsible agent in the science of sacred law. If they were predicated to the subject by virtue of the subject being something else (e.g., the predication of being created by God to an action of a morally responsible agent), then the question would then be studying that other thing rather than the subject of the science and it would properly belong to another science. To illustrate the concept of an essential predicate, the logicians divide predicates into three kinds and then divide the final kind of predicate into a further four sub-kinds, leading to a total of six kinds of predicates. Three of these kinds of predicates are *essential* to their subjects and are hence validly predicated of them as part of their study; the remaining three are *foreign* to their subjects and hence are not validly predicated of them as part of their study. These predicative divisions and their categorization into essential and foreign predications are described below with examples. Readers should keep in mind that the examples of predicates given below are all contrived merely to illustrate the concept of a predicate's *essentialness* or its *foreignness*. Unlike other examples mentioned elsewhere in this chapter, these examples are not actual examples of the predicates of any particular science.

First of all, predicates are divided into the following three types:

> (1) Those predicates that are predicated of their subject by virtue of *all* of what the subject is, i.e., by virtue of its essence in its entirety. Take the predication of amazement to human beings; amazement is predicated of human beings by virtue of what they are, namely rational animals, since someone is only amazed by virtue of being a rational animal.
>
> (2) Those predicates that are predicated of their subject by virtue of *part* of what the subject is, i.e., by virtue of part of its essence. Take the predication of voluntary motion to human beings; voluntary motion is predicated of human beings by virtue of their being animals (human beings are rational animals and animalness is hence only part of what they are), since something only moves voluntarily inasmuch as it is an animal.
>
> (3) Those predicates that are predicated of their subject by virtue of something that lies outside of what the subject is, i.e., by virtue of neither all nor part of its essence.

Predicates of this third type are further divided into:

> (3a) Those predicates that are predicated of their subject by virtue of something that lies outside of what the subject is, but which in turn *relies on* what the subject is. Take the predication of laughing out of amazement to human beings; laughing out of amazement is predicated of human beings by virtue of their being characterized by amazement, which lies outside what human beings are but nevertheless relies on human beings being rational animals.
>
> (3b) Those predicates that are predicated of their subject by virtue of something that lies outside of what the subject is and which is *unconditionally more inclusive* than the subject. Take the predication of motion to ‹something that is white›; motion is predicated of ‹something that is white› by virtue of its being an object, which is more general than

‹something that is white›, because ‹object› encompasses, for example, ‹something that is black›, ‹something that is red›, and many other non-white things.

(3c) Those predicates that are predicated of their subject by virtue of something that lies outside of what the subject is and which is *unconditionally less inclusive* than the subject. Take the predication of laughter to animals; laughter is predicated of animals by virtue of their being humans, and ‹human› is less inclusive than ‹animal› because ‹animal› encompasses, for example, lions, horses, and many other non-human animals.

(3d) Those predicates that are predicated of their subject by virtue of something that lies outside of what the subject is and which is *disjoint* to the subject. Take the predication of heat to water; heat is predicated of water by virtue of its being heated by something hot such as fire, and fire is disjoint to water.

With this division in place, we are in a position to see that the predicates of the questions of a science belong to Divisions 1, 2, and 3a. These three kinds of predicates are called the *essential predicates* of a subject because the basis of their predication is the subject's essence. This is obviously true of Divisions 1 and 2, where the predicate is predicated of the subject by virtue of all or part of its essence. With Division 3a, however, it is less obvious, because the predicate is predicated of the subject by virtue of something (X) that lies outside its essence. But since X is only true of the subject by virtue of what the subject is, Division 3a is effectively essential to the subject because it relies on something that in turn relies on the essence of the subject. Divisions 3b, 3c, and 3d are not valid predicates of the questions of a science because the basis of their predication lies outside of the subject's essence. These three kinds of predicates are called *foreign predicates* (*ʿawāriḍ gharība*).

Note that even though the *basis* of an essential predicate's predication is the subject's essence, the predicate cannot actually be *part* of the subject's essence (as in the predication of ‹rational› to ‹human being›) because its predication would then be obvious and noninferential, whereas the questions of sciences are always inferential. One might object that some of the predicates in the examples above are actually part of their subject's essence, and that would be a valid objection against that predicate from that perspective. The goal of these contrived examples, however, is merely to illustrate the concepts of essentialness and foreignness.[11]

Some have objected that the direct dependence of an essential predicate on its subject's essence necessarily renders its predication noninferential. The logicians respond to this objection by drawing a distinction between actual dependence (*fī nafs al-amr*) and mental dependence. The direct dependence of the essential predicate's predication of its subject is an actual dependence, that is, a dependence with respect to reality. Mentally, however, the predication is indirect, meaning that it requires inference and is not directly entailed by what the subject is. The direct dependence of an essential predicate on its subject's essence hence does not conflict with the predication's status as inferential.

11.4 The Starting Points of Sciences

The *starting points* (*mabādiʾ*) for inference within any science are the collected concepts and propositions on which the demonstration of its questions depends. They consist of two things: a collection of concepts, or *conceptual starting points* (*mabādiʾ taṣawwuriyya*), and a collection of propositions, or *propositional starting points* (*mabādiʾ taṣdīqiyya*). Properly speaking, a science is constituted by its *questions*, and the starting points of its questions fall outside of its scope. However, because the two are so closely connected that it is not possible to infer the truth of the questions without their starting points, the starting points, too, are conventionally considered to be "part" of the science.

11.4.1 *Conceptual Starting Points*

The ability to grasp that a proposition is true presupposes the conception of the proposition's subject and predicate. Grasping the truth of a science's questions thus presupposes that one conceives their subjects and predicates. The *definitions* that bring about these conceptions are the *conceptual starting points* of every science. For example, some of the questions of the science of Arabic grammar predicate ‹inflection› or ‹non-inflection› of Arabic words. But this presupposes conception of what inflection, non-inflection, and Arabic words are. The definitions of all of these concepts are conceptual starting points of Arabic grammar.

11. Note also that the fact that the basis of a predicate's predication is its subject's essence is independent of the predication being inferential or noninferential.

When the essence of the subject of a science is composed of multiple parts, the conceptual starting points of the science will include the definitions of these parts. For example, the definition of ‹the Arabic word› (the subject of the science of Arabic grammar) is ‹an utterance that is linguistically assigned to a non-sentential meaning›. Here, the essence of the concept ‹the Arabic word› is composed of the concepts ‹utterance›, ‹linguistic assignment›, and ‹non-sentential meaning›. Each of these sub-concepts requires a definition. The definitions of these sub-concepts are thus among the conceptual starting points of the science of Arabic grammar.

11.4.2 *Propositional Starting Points*

The purpose of every science is to demonstrate the truth of its questions. These questions all have a well-defined set of subjects that are predicated with a well-defined set of predicates. The demonstration of the truth of the resultant set of propositions, that is, the questions of the science, is the immediate goal of every science. This set of questions constitutes the science. In other words, every science is, properly speaking, nothing more than its set of questions.

For a science to demonstrate the truth of its questions, however, requires inference. The sciences are all ordered in a hierarchy so that the highest science begins its inferences from a set of noninferential propositions and reasons from them to a set of inferential propositions about its subject, namely existent things in general. Lower sciences then build on these questions. Instead of beginning all of their inferences on the same basic set of noninferential propositions that the highest science began with, they take some of its conclusions as starting points for their own inferences. These starting points are then mentioned at the beginning of the lower science and, for the purposes of that science, taken for granted. Students who are interested in learning about how to demonstrate the truth of these starting points must then return to the higher science from which they were taken. For example, the highest of the revelatory sciences is the science of rational theology.[12] The questions of rational theology include propositions such as: ‹God exists›, ‹It is not necessary for God to act in the best interest of human beings›, ‹Muḥammad (God bless him and give him peace) is God's messenger›, and ‹Muḥammad (God bless him and give him peace) conveyed the Qur'ān from God›.

12. The highest of the philosophical sciences is metaphysics. The highest of the revelatory sciences is *kalām*. See Note 197 for the relation between these two sciences.

One of the sciences that lies just below the science of rational theology is legal theory (*uṣūl al-fiqh*). The *subjects* of the science of legal theory are those things that signify the divine address to morally responsible agents. The science of legal theory demonstrates, for example, that the Qur'ān, the Sunna, scholarly consensus (*ijmāʿ*), and analogical inference (*qiyās*) are all means from which we can infer God's address to us—those of His commands that establish obligation, those of His commands that establish recommendation, those of His prohibitions that establish unlawfulness, and those of His prohibitions that establish offensiveness. These demonstrations presuppose the four questions of rational theology stated above—that God exists, that it is not necessary for Him to act in the best interest of human beings (hence the only way to infer His command is to listen to what He says), that Muḥammad (God bless him and give him peace) is His messenger, and that Muḥammad (God bless him and give him peace) conveyed the Qur'ān from Him. These four *questions* of rational theology hence are all *starting points* for the science of legal theory. This relationship between rational theology and legal theory is then reduplicated in the relationship between legal theory and the subordinate science of sacred law (*fiqh*), which takes as its starting points some of the questions of legal theory (e.g., that the Qur'ān, the Sunna, scholarly consensus, and analogical inference all signify God's commands), and then infers what God's actual commands regarding specific human actions are.

11.5 Examples

The following subsections describe the sciences of Arabic grammar, logic, and sacred law, whose questions, subjects, and essential predicates are commonly used as examples to illustrate the rules of this chapter. Whereas students of the traditional madrasa, who studied logic within the traditional madrasa curriculum, studied these sciences and hence understood their purposes and questions, students today outside that context often do not. As a result, whereas the examples that were cited by the logicians in their traditional manuals were appreciated by the students of the traditional madrasa, they are not appreciated by students today. The goal of these subsections is to give an overview of these sciences and their questions to help students appreciate these traditional example and thereby help them appreciate the indispensable role of logic in studying the Islamic sciences.

The logicians distinguish between citing examples (sg. *mithāl*) and citing evidence (*shāhid*): the goal of citing an example is to *illustrate* a principle (*tawḍīḥ*), whereas the goal of citing evidence is to *establish* a principle. A consequence of this distinction is that, whereas it is a requirement of evidence that it be correct and precise, neither correctness nor precision is required of an example. As long as the example *illustrates* the desired principle, it fulfills its goal even if it is incorrect or imprecise. Readers are thus advised to focus on the illustrative goal of the examples that follow rather than examining their correctness or precision.[13]

11.5.1 *The Science of Arabic Grammar*

Arabic is a highly inflected language, meaning that many of its words change depending on their grammatical role in a sentence. The concept of grammatical inflection is difficult for English speakers to understand because in the overwhelming majority of its cases, English is not an inflected language. There are, however, a handful of cases where even English is inflected. Studying these cases can illustrate the concept of inflection and make it easier to understand the science of Arabic. For example, the English first-person pronoun changes depending on its grammatical role in a sentence. When it is the subject of the sentence, it appears as "I," e.g., "I saw him." But when it is the object of the sentence, it appears as "me," e.g., "He saw me." (Note from these examples that the third-person pronoun is similarly inflected.) Whereas in English inflection is restricted to a small number of cases such as personal pronouns, in Arabic the vast majority of nouns and a large number of verbs are inflected. This means that speaking Arabic correctly requires one to be conscious of the grammatical role and corresponding form of the words that one speaks. The goal of the science of Arabic grammar (*naḥw*) is thus to teach those grammatical rules which, when observed, will prevent one from making mistakes in one's speech.

A summary of the science of Arabic grammar is as follows. Arabic words are divided into inflected (*muʿrab*) and uninflected (*mabnī*) words. Inflected words adopt one of four grammatical states—the *rafʿ* state, the *naṣb* state, the *jarr* state, and the *jazm* state. Inflected words are divided into approximately eight categories from the perspective of how they change when they enter into one of these states. The rest of Arabic grammar is an examination of the various grammatical roles that Arabic words can fulfill, and of which grammatical states words enter as a result of fulfilling given grammatical roles. Based on all of this, given any Arabic sentence, one can determine the

13. In the words of al-Khabīṣī, "Ignore the faults in the following examples even if they are incorrect, for one should not argue over examples." *TB*, 432.

grammatical role, grammatical state, kind of word, and proper form of every word in the sentence, thereby avoiding inflection mistakes in one's speech.

The subject of the science of Arabic grammar is the Arabic word. The essential predicates of Arabic words include their being inflected (*muʿrab*) or uninflected (*mabnī*) as well as how to compose a correct Arabic sentence. The following table lists fifteen example questions and starting points from the science of Arabic grammar, along with brief explanations based on the previous sections of this chapter.

	Example	Explanation
1	‹Arabic word (*kalima*)› is ‹utterance composed of Arabic letters that is assigned a non-composite meaning›.	A conceptual starting point (definition of the subject of the science).
2	‹Assignment (waḍʿ)› is ‹to associate a word with a meaning›.	A conceptual starting point (definition of one of the essential parts of the subject of the science).
3	‹Inflection (*iʿrāb*)› is ‹for the ends of words to change because of changing grammatical agents (*ʿawāmil*)›.	A conceptual starting point (definition of an essential predicate of the subject).
4	Arabic words only enter grammatical states by virtue of grammatical agents (*ʿawāmil*) that act upon them.	A propositional starting point.
5	Arabic words (*kalimāt*) are either inflected (*muʿrab*) or uninflected (*mabnī*).	A question whose subject is the subject of the science (i.e., Arabic words).
6	Past-tense verbs (*fiʿl māḍī*) are uninflected (*mabnī*).	A question whose subject is a species of the subject of the science (past-tense verbs are a species of Arabic words).
7	Nouns are in the *rafʿ* state when they are the subject of a verb (*fāʿil*).	A question whose subject is a species of the subject of the science (nouns are a species of Arabic words).

	Example	Explanation
8	Nouns are in the naṣb state when they are the object of a verb (*maf'ūl bihi*).	A question whose subject is a species of the subject of the science (nouns are a species of Arabic words).
9	Present-future tense verbs that are preceded by the particle *lam* are in the *jazm* state.	A question whose subject is a species of the subject of the science (present-future tense verbs are a species of Arabic words).
10	The non-inflection of nouns is a result of their resembling particles.	A question whose subject is an essential predicate of the subject of the science (non-inflection is an essential predicate of Arabic words).
11	Inflection into the *jazm* state is restricted to verbs.	A question whose subject is a species of an essential predicate of the science (inflection into the jazm state is a species of inflection, which is an essential predicate of Arabic words).
12	Inflected Arabic words either end with an unwritten *nūn* (munṣarif) or do not end with an unwritten *nūn* (*ghayr munṣarif*).	A question whose subject is a composition of the subject (Arabic words) and its essential predicate (inflection).
13	Inflected nouns are either inflected through vowels or through letters.	A question whose subject is a composition of a species of the subject (nouns are a species of Arabic words) and the subject's essential predicate (inflection).
14	Present-future tense verbs that end in a weak letter are inflected for the *jazm* state by the omission of the weak letter.	A question whose subject is a species of the subject of the science (present-future tense verbs are a species of Arabic words).
15	Singular nouns in the vocative are uninflectedly fixed (*mabnī*) on a *ḍamma*.	A question whose subject is a species of the subject of the science (singular nouns are a species of Arabic words).

11.5.2 *The Science of Logic*

The logicians have observed that the science of logic is to the mind what the science of Arabic grammar is to the tongue—whereas observing the rules of Arabic grammar protects the tongue from mistakes in the articulation of Arabic words, observing the rules of logic protects the mind from mistakes in rational inference. For an overview of the science of logic, see Chapter 1. A brief summary of that chapter is as follows. Human knowledge is divided into noninferential and inferential knowledge. Most human knowledge is inferential, meaning that it is acquired through correct inference. Humans often make mistakes in these inferences. The goal of the science of logic is thus to teach those rules of inference which, when observed, will prevent one from making mistakes in one's thought.

The subject of the science of logic is conceptual knowledge that leads to new conceptual knowledge (called *definition*) and propositional knowledge that leads to new propositional knowledge (called *argument*). The essential predicates of this conceptual or propositional knowledge are either ‹leads to conceptual knowledge› or ‹leads to propositional knowledge›. Instead of "leads to conceptual knowledge," the logicians normally use the synonymous predicates of either ‹definition›, since definitions directly lead to conceptual knowledge, or of being one of the five universals, since the five universals indirectly lead to conceptual knowledge. And instead of "leads to propositional knowledge," the logicians normally use the synonymous predicates of either ‹syllogism› or ‹argument›, which directly lead to propositional knowledge, or of being a proposition or its subject or predicate, since propositions and their parts indirectly lead to propositional knowledge. The following table lists ten example questions and starting points from the science of logic, along with brief explanations based on the previous sections of this chapter.

	Example	**Explanation**
1	‹Genus› is ‹universal that is predicated of multiple universal concepts that have different essences in response to the question, "What is it?"›	A conceptual starting point (definition of a kind of conceptual knowledge that leads to new knowledge, i.e., a subject of the science).

	Example	Explanation
2	‹Propositional statement› is ‹sentential expression that can be true or false›.	A conceptual starting point (definition of a kind of propositional knowledge that leads to new knowledge, i.e., a subject of the science).
3	The whole is greater than the part.	A propositional starting point (this is a general law of thought that is a propositional inferential starting point of every science but whereas it is a starting point of those sciences remotely, it is a starting point of logic proximately).
4	‹Animal› is a genus of ‹human›.	A question whose subject is an instance of the subject of the science (‹animal› is an instance of conceptual knowledge that indirectly leads to new conceptual knowledge).
5	A genus and differentia, when composed in a particular way, constitute a complete essential definition.	A question whose subject is a species of the subject of the science (genera and differentiae are species of conceptual knowledge that indirectly leads to new conceptual knowledge).
6	‹Rational animal› is a complete essential definition.	A question whose subject is an instance of the subject of the science (‹rational animal› is an instance of conceptual knowledge that directly leads to new conceptual knowledge).
7	‹The universe› is the subject of the proposition ‹The universe began to exist›.	A question whose subject is an instance of the subject of the science (‹The universe› is an instance of a part of propositional knowledge that indirectly leads to new propositional knowledge).

	Example	Explanation
8	A universally quantified affirmative proposition and a singular affirmative proposition that have a common middle term constitute a simple syllogism.	A question whose subject is a species of the subject of the science (universally quantified affirmative propositions and singular affirmative propositions are a species of propositional knowledge that directly leads to new propositional knowledge).
9	‹Everything that begins to exist has a cause› combined with ‹The universe began to exist› is a simple syllogism.	A question whose subject is an instance of the subject of the science (‹Everything that begins to exist has a cause›, and ‹The universe began to exist›, are instances of propositional knowledge that directly leads to new propositional knowledge).
10	Multiple observations that animals move their lower jaw when chewing is an inductive argument.	A question whose subject is an instance of the subject of the science (multiple observations that animals move their lower jaw when chewing constitute an instance of propositional knowledge that directly leads to new propositional knowledge).

11.5.3 *The Science of Sacred Law*

God created morally responsible agents (human beings and jinn)[14] to worship Him. He sent them messengers to convey His divine address to them. This divine address falls into one of five categories: (1) an address that firmly commands them to do an action, as a result of which that action becomes *obligatory* upon them, (2) an address that non-firmly solicits an action from them, as a result of which that action becomes *recommended*, (3) an address that gives them the choice to do an action or to not do it, as a result of which that action becomes *permissible*, (4) an address that non-firmly solicits the non-performance of an action from them, as a result of which that action

14. Jinn are a species of morally responsible beings created out of fire (in distinction to human beings, who are a species of morally responsible beings created out of clay). In their native form, jinn are invisible to human beings, although they can assume the form of living things that human beings can see, such as the form of snakes or the form of human beings.

becomes *offensive* for them, and (5) an address that firmly forbids them from doing an action, as a result of which that action becomes *unlawful* for them. The obligation, recommendation, permissibility, offensiveness, and unlawfulness that arise from the divine address to morally responsible agents are called *rulings of sacred law* (*aḥkām sharʿiyya*). The goal of the science of sacred law (*fiqh*) is to discover the rulings of the sacred law on the actions of morally responsible agents. Its subject is the actions of morally responsible agents. The essential predicates of these actions are the rulings of sacred law. The following table lists seven example questions and starting points from the science of sacred law, along with a brief explanation based on the previous sections of this chapter.

	Example	Explanation
1	‹Morally responsible agent› is ‹adult sane human being who has been reached by a prophetic call›.	A conceptual starting point (definition of part of the subject of the science).
2	‹Obligation› is ‹divine address to a morally responsible agent that firmly asks him to do an action›.	A conceptual starting point (definition of a kind of essential predicate).
3	‹Permissibility› is ‹divine address to a morally responsible agent that gives him the option to do or not to do an action›.	A conceptual starting point (definition of a kind of essential predicate).
4	The Qur'ān is a means of determining the divine address to morally responsible agents.	A propositional starting point (this is taken as a given in the science of sacred law and established as true in the science of legal theory).
5	Praying the afternoon prayer (*ẓuhr*) is obligatory.	A question whose subject is a species of the subject of the science (‹praying the afternoon prayer› is a species of the actions of morally responsible agents).
6	Standing is permissible.	A question whose subject is a species of the subject of the science (‹standing› is a species of the actions of morally responsible agents).

	Example	Explanation
7	Drinking wine is unlawful.	A question whose subject is a species of the subject of the science (‹drinking wine› is a species of the actions of morally responsible agents).

Sources

Section	Sources
11 The Organization of Sciences	For further reading, see Street, *Najm al-Dīn,* 283-86; Strobino, "The Internal Structure of a Science," in *Avicenna's Theory*, 85-112; Strobino, "Division and Hierarchy of the Sciences," in *Avicenna's Theory*, 113-32
11.1 What is a Science?	*TB*, 22, 65-66, 429-30
11.2 The Subjects of Sciences	*TB*, 65-66, 71, 77
11.3 The Questions of Sciences	*TB*, 432-33
11.3.1 The Subjects of Scientific Questions	*TB*, 432
11.3.2 The Predicates of Scientific Questions	al-Rāzī, et al., *Shurūḥ al-shamsiyya*, 154-60; TB, 432-33
11.4 The Starting Points of Sciences	*TB*, 430-31
11.4.1 Conceptual Starting points	*TB*, 430-31
11.4.2 Propositional Starting points	*TB*, 430-31
11.5 Examples	
11.5.1 The Science of Arabic Grammar	*TB*, 431-32
11.5.2 The Science of Logic	al-Ṣabbān, *Ḥāshiya*, 31-33; *TB*, 77-79
11.5.3 The Science of Sacred Law	Abū Bakr 'Uthmān Shaṭā, *I'ānat al-ṭālibīn 'alā ḥall alfāẓ Fatḥ al-Mu'īn* (1997; repr., Beirut: Dār Iḥyā' al-Turāth al-'Arabī, n.d.), 1:13-14

GLOSSARY OF ARABIC TERMS

The following table lists all of the Arabic technical terms in this book along with their English translation, the source of the English translation, brief explanatory notes on why that translation was chosen rather than another one, and a reference to its first occurrence in the book, where it is defined. The translations have been carefully chosen to reverberate with philosophically analogous terms in modern analytic philosophy and logic in order to point the way to a reworking of those concepts in light of the Sunni Muslim theological tradition (*kalām*).

Arabic	English	Notes on Translation	Loc.
aʿamm	more general (definition)		4.4.1
adāt	particle		2.2.3.2
ajlā	clearer (definition)		4.4.2
ajnās	highest genera		3.4.2.1
akhaṣṣ	more restrictive (definition)		4.4.1
ʿaks	conversion; converse		8.2
ʿaks al-naqīḍ	complemented conversion		8.3
ʿaks al-naqīḍ al-mukhālif	contraposition		8.3.2
ʿaks al-naqīḍ al-muwāfiq	negated contraposition	Instead of the original subject, the predication of the proposition as a whole is negated.	8.3.1
ʿalam	proper name		2.2.3.2
ʿalāqa	real		7.1.1
al-kulliyyāt al-khams	the five universals		3.4

Arabic	English	Notes on Translation	Loc.
al-mabādiʾ al-ʿashara	the ten topics of scholarly prolegomena	New	1.4
al-qaḍāyā allatī qiyāsātuhā maʿahā	subconsciously inferred judgments	New	10.2.1.6
al-ṣināʿāt al-khams	the five arts of *falsafa*	Classical logic	10.1
ʿaqīm	invalid argument	Modern logic	
ʿaql	mind	Philosophy of mind	9.1.1
ʿaraḍ (1)	nonessential universal; accident		
ʿaraḍ (2)	property	*Property* is a familiar term to the modern student, and helps disambiguate from the other usage of *ʿaraḍ.*	3.4.3
ʿaraḍ ʿāmm	general accident		3.4.2
ʿaraḍ lāzim	inseparable accident		3.4.3.2
ʿaraḍ mufāriq	separable accident		3.4.3.3
aṣl	source	New	3.4.3.3
ʿawāriḍ dhātiyya	essential predicates	New	9.2.2
ʿawāriḍ gharība	foreign predicates	New	11.3.2
awlawiyya	strength		11.3.2
awwaliyya	precedence		2.2.3.2
awwaliyyāt	self-evident judgments		2.2.3.2
basīṭ	basic		
burhān	demonstration	Classical logic	
burhān innī	demonstration from the effect		10.2
burhān limmī	demonstration from the cause		
buṭlān	falsity		
dāʾima muṭlaqa	extensionally continuous proposition		
dalāla	signification		6.7.2.1

Arabic	English	Notes on Translation	Loc.
dalāla ʿaqliyya	rational signification		2.1
dalāla lafẓiyya	expressional signification		2.1
dalāla ṭabīʿiyya	natural signification		2.1
dalāla waḍʿiyya	conventional signification; linguistic signification		2.1
dalālat al-iltizām	entailed signification		2.1
dalālat al-muṭābaqa	complete signification		2.1.1
dalālat al-taḍammun	partial signification		2.1.1
dalīl	proof; evidence; indicator		2.1.1
dalīl al-khulf	proof by contradiction		
dalīl innī	argument from the effect	New	3.2.2
dalīl limmī	argument from the cause	New	10.2.2
dāll	sign		10.2.2
ḍarūra	necessity	Modal logic	2.1
ḍarūra azaliyya	eternal necessity	New	6.7.1.1; 6.7.2
ḍarūra bi-ḥasab al-waqt	temporal necessity	New	6.7.1.1
ḍarūra bi-sharṭ al-maḥmūl	predicate necessity	New	6.7.1.1
ḍarūra dhātiyya	extensional necessity	Modified from modern modal logic	6.7.1.1
ḍarūra waṣfiyya	intensional necessity	Modified from modern modal logic	6.7.1.1
ḍarūriyya muṭlaqa	extensionally necessary proposition		6.7.1.1
dawām	continuity	New	6.7.2.1
dawām azalī	eternal continuity	New	6.7.1.2; 6.7.2
dawām dhātī	extensional continuity	Modified from modern modal logic	6.7.1.2

Arabic	English	Notes on Translation	Loc.
dawām waṣfī	intensional continuity	Modified from modern modal logic	6.7.1.2
dawarān	correlation	Statistics (cf. the statistical fallacy of equating correlation with causation)	6.7.1.2
dhāt al-mawḍūʿ	subject-referent; extension of the subject		9.2.2.2
farʿ	target	New	6.1
fard (pl. afrād)	instance(s)		9.2.2
faṣl	differentia	Classical logic	4
faṣl baʿīd	remote differentia		3.4.2.3
faṣl qarīb	proximate differentia		3.4.2.3
fiʿl	action	Aristotelian category	3.4.2.3
fiṭriyyāt	subconsciously inferred judgments	New	
ḥadd (1)	essential definition		10.2.1.6
ḥadd (2)	term	Classical logic	4.3
ḥadd akbar	major term	Classical logic	9.1.1
ḥadd aṣghar	minor term	Classical logic	9.1.1
ḥadd awsaṭ	middle term	Classical logic	9.1.1
ḥadd bi-l-ajzāʾ al-khārijiyya	essential definition by extra-mental parts		9.1.1
ḥadd nāqiṣ	incomplete essential definition		4.3.3
ḥadd tāmm	complete essential definition		4.3.1
hadhayān	pointless argument		4.3.1
ḥads	intuition	Procedural inference	9.1
ḥadsiyyāt	intuited judgments		
ḥaml	predication		10.2.1.4
ḥaml awwalī	conceptual predication	New	

Arabic	English	Notes on Translation	Loc.
ḥaml ishtiqāqī	property-predication	New. Taken from the description of this kind of predication as *ḥaml dhū huwa.* Cannot be literally translated because *ishtiqāq* is an Arabic artifact that does not have an English analogue	3.4.1.1
ḥaml muwāṭa'a	identity-predication	New. Taken from the description of this kind of predication as *ḥaml huwa huwa*	3.4.1
ḥaml shā'i'	ordinary predication	New	3.4.1
ḥaqīqa (1)	literal use of an expression		3.4.1.1
ḥaqīqa (2)	essence		2.2.3.2
ḥarakat al-nafs	mental motion	New	3.4.2.1
ḥaṣr	comprehensive survey		1.1.4.2
ḥaṣr ḥaqīqī	actually comprehensive survey	New	9.2.1; 10.2.1.3
ḥaṣr iddi'ā'ī	presumed comprehensive survey	New	9.2.1; 10.2.1.3
hay'a (1)	morphological structure		9.2.1; 10.2.1.3
hay'a (2)	compositional form		2.2.3.2
ḥikāya	description (of what is the case)		9.1
ḥīniyya muṭlaqa lā-dā'ima	non-continuous conceptual-ly actual propositions	New	5.1.1
ḥiss bāṭinī	internal sensation	New	8.2.2.1
ḥiss ẓāhirī	external sensation	New	10.2.1.2
ḥissiyyāt	observational judgments		10.2.1.2
ḥukm (1)	judgment		10.2.1.2

Arabic	English	Notes on Translation	Loc.
ḥukm (2)	predication		1.1.3.1
ḥukm ʿādī	regularity judgment	New. Technical term of *kalām* important for logicians	5.1.1; 7
ḥukm ʿaqlī	metaphysical judgment	New. Technical term of *kalām* important for logicians. See Note 70	5.3.2
ḥukm sharʿī	revelatory judgment	New. Technical term of *kalām* important for logicians	5.3.1
huwiyya	identity		5.3.3
iḍāfa	relation	Aristotelian category	3.1
idrāk	perception		
ikhtirāʿ	imagination		
ʿilla	analogical cause		5.2
ʿilm (1)	knowledge		9.2.2
ʿilm (2)	science		1.1
ʿilm ḍarūrī	noninferential knowledge		11.1
ʿilm ḥuḍūrī	direct knowledge	Epistemology of perception (*direct realism*)	1.1.4
ʿilm ḥuṣūlī	indirect knowledge	Epistemology of perception (*indirect realism*)	1.1.2
ʿilm naẓarī	inferential knowledge		1.1.2
imkān	possibility	Modal logic	1.1.4
ʿinād	real disjunction	New	6.7.2; 6.3; Note 81
infiʿāl	reaction	Aristotelian category	7.2.1
infiṣāl	disjunction		
inshāʾ	non-propositional sentence		7.2

Arabic	English	Notes on Translation	Loc.
intizāʿ	abstraction		2.2.1
ʿaqd al-ḥaml	reference of predication		3.4; 5.2
ʿaqd al-waḍʿ	reference of signification		6.1
ism	noun		6.1
ism jins	common noun		2.2.3.2
istiqrāʾ nāqiṣ	inductive generalization	Statistics. Translating as "induction" is misleading because in modern philosophy, *inductive reasoning* refers to many different kinds of non-deductive argument forms	2.2.3.2
istiqrāʾ tāmm	universal judgment based on comprehensively surveying its instances	Translating as "induction" is misleading because in modern philosophy, *inductive reasoning* refers to many different kinds of non-deductive argument forms	9.2.1
iʿtiqād	belief		9.2.1
iṭlāq	actuality	New	
ittifāq	coincidental connection; coincidental truth-dependence		6.7.2
ittifāqiyya	coincidental connection; coincidental truth-dependence; coincidental disjunction		7.1.1
ittiṣāl	truth-dependence		7.1.1; 7.2.1
ittiṣāl al-salb	truth-dependence of negative sub-propositions		7.1

Arabic	English	Notes on Translation	Loc.
jadal	dialectics		7.1
jāʾiz ʿaqlī	rationally possible		10.3
jāʾiz dhātī	intrinsically possible		5.3.1
jawhar	substance	Aristotelian category	5.3.3
jazm	certainty		
jiha	stated modality	New	1.1.3.3
jins	genus		6.7
jins baʿīd	remote genus		3.4.2.1
jins qarīb	proximate genus		3.4.2.1
juzʾī	singular		3.4.2.1
kadhib	falsity		3.1
kādhib	false		1.1.3.2
kalima	verb		7
kayf (*1*)	quality	Aristotelian category	2.2.3.2
kayf (2)	propositional quality	Classical logic	
kayfiyya	predication-occurrence-quality; modality		7
kayfiyya fī nafs al-amr	real modality	New	6.7
khabar	propositional sentence		6.7
khārij	extramental world; mind-independent world	New	2.2.1
khāṣṣa	special accident		6.6.1
khāṣṣa iḍāfiyya	relative special accident		3.4.3.1
khāṣṣa muṭlaqa	absolute special accident		3.4.3.1
khaṭāba	rhetoric		3.4.3.1
kubrā	major premise	Classical logic	10.4
kullī	universal		9.1.1
kullī ʿaqlī	mental universal		3.1
kullī ʿaraḍī	nonessential universal		3.4
kullī dhātī	essential universal		3.4
kullī farḍī	hypothetical universal	New	3.4.2
kullī manṭiqī	logicians' universal	New	3.1.1

Arabic	English	Notes on Translation	Loc.
kullī ṭabīʿī	natural universal	New	3.5
lā-ḍarūra	negation of extensional necessity		3.5
lā-dawām	negation of extensional continuity		6.7.2.2
lafẓ (pl. *alfāẓ*)	expression(s)		6.7.2.2
lafẓ mufrad	basic expression		2.1
lafẓ muhmal	meaningless expression		2.2
lafẓ murakkab	composite expression		2.1.1; 2.2
lafẓ mustaʿmal	meaningful expression		2.2
lāzim	entailed meaning		2.1.1; 2.2
luzūm (1)	entailment		2.1.2
luzūm (2)	real connection; real truth-dependence		2.1.2
luzūm ʿaqlī	rational entailment		7.1.1
luzūm bayyin	direct entailment		2.1.2
luzūm bayyin bi-l-maʿnā al-aʿamm	collective direct entailment		2.1.2
luzūm bayyin bi-l-maʿnā al-akhaṣṣ	independent direct entailment		2.1.2
luzūm ghayr bayyin	indirect entailment		2.1.2
luzūm qaṭʿī	conclusive entailment		2.1.2
luzūm ʿurfī	conventional entailment		9.1
luzūmiyya	real connection; real truth-dependence		2.1.2
mabādiʾ al-ʿilm	inferential starting points of a science	New	7.1.1
mabādiʾ taṣawwuriyya	conceptual starting points	New	11.4; 1.1.4.2
mabādiʾ taṣdīqiyya	propositional starting points	New	11.4.1; 1.1.4.2

Arabic	English	Notes on Translation	Loc.
mabda'	inferential starting point	New	11.4.2; 1.1.4.2
māddat al-dalīl	the matter of an argument	Classical logic	1.1.4.2
māddat al-qaḍiyya	real modality	New	11
madlūl	significate		6.7
mafhūm	concept	Philosophy of mind (*conceptualism*)	2.1; 4
māhiyya	essence		4
maḥmūl	predicate		3.1; 3.4.2
maḥsūsāt	observational judgments	New	7
majāz	figurative use of an expression		
malzūm	original meaning (of an entailment)		2.2.3.2
ma'nā	meaning		2.1.2
māni'	preventive	Technical term of *kalām* and legal theory	4
māni'at jam'	truth-exclusive disjunctive proposition	New	9.2.2.2
māni'at jam' wa-khulū	strongly exclusive disjunctive proposition	New	7.2
māni'at khulū	falsity-exclusive disjunctive proposition	New	7.2
manqūl	lexcailly shifted expression; a word whose meaning has been shifted		7.2
ma'qūl awwalī	first-order concept	New	2.2.3.2
ma'qūl thānawī (or *thānī*)	second-order concept	New	3.1
al-maqūlāt al-'ashara	the ten basic categories	Classical logic	3.1

Arabic	English	Notes on Translation	Loc.
mā-ṣadaq; miṣdāq	referent	New	Note 27; 3.4.2.2
mas'ala (pl. *masā'il*)			4; 5.1.1
mashrūṭa 'āmma	question (of a science)		11.3
mashrūṭa khāṣṣa	broadly intensionally necessary proposition		6.7.2.1
maṭlab hal	strictly intensionally necessary proposition	New	6.7.2.2
maṭlab mā	is-knowledge	New	4.2.1
mawḍū'	what-knowledge		4.2.1
mu'arraf	subject		7
mu'arrif	definiendum		4.1; 4.3
muḍāf	defining expression; definition		4.1; 4.3
mughālaṭa	correlative		
mughālaṭat al-jadhr al-aṣamm	fallacy		11.6
muhmal	the Liar Paradox		5.1.2
mujarrabāt	meaningless	Translating as "inductive judgments" is inaccurate because the means of judgment is repetition, not induction	2.1.1
mumkina 'āmma	tested judgments	Modal logic	10.2.1.3
mumkina khāṣṣa	broadly possible proposition	Modal logic	6.7.2.1
muntashira	strictly possible proposition	New	6.7.2.2
muntashira muṭlaqa	strictly sometime necessary proposition	New	6.7.2.2
muntij	broadly sometime necessary proposition	Modern logic	6.7.2.1
muqaddam	valid (argument)		9.1.1

Arabic	English	Notes on Translation	Loc.
muqaddima	antecedent	Modern and classical logic	7.1
muqaddima kubrā	premise	Classical logic	9.1
muqaddima ṣughrā	major premise	Classical logic	9.1.1
muqaddimat al-ʿilm	minor premise		9.1.1
muqaddimat al-kitāb	prolegomenon to a science		2
muqassim	introduction of a book		2; Note 9
muqawwim	divisive		3.4.2.3
murakkab	constitutive		3.4.2.3
murakkab nāqiṣ	composite		
murakkab tāmm	phrase		2.2.2
murakkab taqyīdī	sentence		2.2.1
muṣādara ʿalā al-maṭlūb	restrictive phrase		2.2.2
musāwī li-l-naqīḍ	begging the question	New	9.1
mushakkak	effective complement		7.2
mushtarak	a name with varying reference; a varying universal		2.2.3.2
mustaḥīl ʿaqlī	homonym		2.2.3.2
mustaḥīl ʿaraḍī	rationally impossible		5.3.1
mustaḥīl dhātī	extrinsically impossible		5.3.3
mustaḥīl li-ghayrihi	intrinsically impossible		5.3.3
mustaʿmal	extrinsically impossible		5.3.3
muṭābaqa	meaningful		2.1.1
mutawāṭiʾ	correspondence		1.1.3.2; 5.1.1
mutawātirāt	name with nonvarying reference; nonvarying universal	New	2.2.3.2
nafs	mass-transmitted judgments		10.2.1.5

Arabic	English	Notes on Translation	Loc.
nafs al-amr	soul	New	1.1.1; 1.1.4.2
naqīḍ (of *mafhūm*)	the-thing-itself	Set theory	5.2
naṣṣ	complement; actual complement	Technical term in legal theory	3.2.2; 7.2
natīja	explicit revelatory statement		9.2.2.2
nawʿ	conclusion		9.1
nawʿ al-anwāʿ	species		3.4.2.2
nawʿ ḥaqīqī	lowest species		3.4.2.2
nawʿ iḍāfī	essential species		3.4.2.2
naẓar	relative species		3.4.2.2
nisba (1)	inference	Philosophy of language (compositionality)	1.1.4.2
nisba (2)	composition		1.1.3.1
nisba ghayr tāmma	predication		7
nisba iḍāfiyya	qualifying composition		1.1.3.1
nisba inshāʾiyya	possessive composition		1.1.3.1
nisba kalāmiyya	non-predicative composition		1.1.3.1
nisba khabariyya	predication		5.1.1
nisba tāmma	predicative composition		1.1.3.1
nisba taqyīdiyya	sentential composition		1.1.3.1
nisba tawṣīfiyya	qualifying composition		1.1.3.1
qaḍiyya	adjectival composition		1.1.3.1
qaḍiyya ʿaqliyya	proposition		5
qaḍiyya sāliba basīṭa	mental proposition		5
qaḍiyya dhihniyya	uncomplemented negative proposition		6.5
qaḍiyya ḥamliyya	mental proposition		6.6.3
qaḍiyya ḥaqīqiyya	simple proposition		7
qaḍiyya juzʾiyya	common proposition; possible-world proposition		6.6.2

Arabic	English	Notes on Translation	Loc.
qaḍiyya khārijiyya	particularly quantified proposition		6.4; 7.3
qaḍiyya kulliyya	extramental proposition; real-world proposition		6.6.1
qaḍiyya lafẓiyya	universally quantified proposition		6.4; 7.3
qaḍiyya maʿdūla	expressional proposition		5
qaḍiyya maʿdūlat al-maḥmūl	complemented proposition		6.5
qaḍiyya maʿdūlat al-mawḍūʿ	predicate-complemented proposition		6.5
qaḍiyya maḥṣūra	subject-complemented proposition		6.5
qaḍiyya muḥaṣṣila	quantified proposition	Sometimes used to refer generally to uncomplemented propositions regardless whether they be affirmative or negative	6.4; 7.3
qaḍiyya muhmala	uncomplemented affirmative proposition; uncomplemented proposition		6.5
qaḍiyya mūjaba	unquantified proposition		6.4; 7.3
qaḍiyya munfaṣila	affirmative proposition		7
qaḍiyya munfaṣila ḥaqīqiyya	disjunctive complex proposition		7.2
qaḍiyya munfaṣila ʿinādiyya	strongly exclusive disjunctive proposition		7.2
qaḍiyya munfaṣila ittifāqiyya	real disjunctive proposition		7.2.1
qaḍiyya musawwara	coincidental disjunctive proposition		7.2.1
qaḍiyya muttaṣila	quantified proposition		6.4

Arabic	English	Notes on Translation	Loc.
qaḍiyya muttaṣila ittifāqiyya	conditional complex propositions		7.1
qaḍiyya muttaṣila luzūmiyya	coincidental conditional proposition		7.1.1
qaḍiyya rubāʿiyya	real conditional proposition		7.1.1
qaḍiyya sāliba	four-part proposition		7
qaḍiyya shakhṣiyya	negative proposition		7
qaḍiyya sharṭiyya	singular proposition		6.2; 7.3
qaḍiyya ṭabīʿiyya	complex proposition		8
qaḍiyya thulāthiyya	concept-proposition	New	6.2
qaḍiyya thunāʾiyya	three-part proposition	New	7
qaṭʿī (dalīl)	two-part proposition		7
qawl shāriḥ	conclusive (evidence)		1.1.3.4
qiyās	definition; definition-predication; clarifying predication	Sometimes used generally to include deductive and non-deductive forms of argument	4.1
qiyās ʿaqīm	deductive argument; syllogism; argument	Modern logic	9.1
qiyās fikrī	invalid argument	New	9.1.1
qiyās iqtirānī	explicit argument		10.2.1
qiyās iqtirānī ḥamlī	simple syllogism		9.1; 9.1.1
qiyās iqtirānī sharṭī	pure simple syllogism		9.1.1
qiyās istiqrāʾ	impure simple syllogism	Statistics	9.1.1
qiyās istithnāʾī	inductive generalization		9.2.1
qiyās istithnāʾī infiṣālī	complex syllogism		9.1; 9.1.2
qiyās istithnāʾī ittiṣālī	disjunctive complex argument		

Arabic	English	Notes on Translation	Loc.
qiyās khafī	conditional complex argument	New	
qiyās muntij	implicit argument	Modern logic	10.2.1
qiyās muqassim	valid argument	Classical logic	9.1.1
qiyās musāwāh	complex syllogism based on division of a universal	New	9.2.1
qiyās tamthīl	relational syllogism		9.1
quwwa	argument by causal analogy	Aristotelian philosophy	9.2.2
rābiṭ	potentiality	Classical logic	6.3; Note 81
rabṭ ʿādī	copula	New	7
rabṭ ʿaqlī	(non-necessary) regular association	New	5.3.2
rasm	(necessary) rational association		5.3.2
rasm nāqiṣ	nonessential definition		4.3
rasm tāmm	incomplete nonessential definition		4.3.1
sabab	complete nonessential definition	Technical term of *kalām* and legal theory	4.3.1
ṣādiq	cause		9.2.2.2
salb al-ittiṣāl	true		7
shakk	negation of truth-dependence	New	7.1
shakl	uncertainty	Classical logic	1.1.3.3
al-shakl al-awwal	figure (of syllogism)	Classical logic	9.1.1
al-shakl al-rābiʿ	first figure	Classical logic	9.1.1
al-shakl al-thālith	fourth figure	Classical logic	9.1.1
al-shakl al-thānī	third figure	Classical logic	9.1.1

Arabic	English	Notes on Translation	Loc.
sharṭ	second figure	Technical term of kalām and legal theory	9.1.1
shiʿr	condition		9.2.2.2
shurūṭ al-intāj	poetics	Modern logic	10.5
ṣidq	conditions of validity		9.1.1
ṣinf	truth		1.1.3.2
ṣughrā	type	Classical logic	3.4.3.2
sūr	minor premise	Classical and modern logic	9.1.1
ṣūra (1)	quantifier	Epistemology of perception (*representationalism*)	6.4
ṣūra (2)	representation	Aristotelian physics	1.1.2; 1.5
ṣūra (3) (or *ṣūrat al-dalīl*)	hylomorphic form	Classical logic	1.5
tabāyun (of *mafhūm*)	the form of an argument	Set theory	11
tabāyun juzʾī (of *mafhūm*)	disjointedness	Modified from *dis-jointedness*, a term from set theory	3.2
ṭabīʿa	partial disjointedness		3.2.2
taḥaqquq	nature		3.5
tajrībiyyāt (cf. *mujarrabāt*)	realization		
tamthīl	tested judgments		10.2.1.3
tanāquḍ (of *mafhūm*)	argument by causal analogy	Set theory	9.2.2
tanbīh	complementarity	New	3.2.2
taqlīd	reminder		1.1.4
taqsīm	belief based on authority	Classical logic	10.2
taqsīm ʿaraḍī	division	Classical logic	1.1.4.1
taqsīm dhātī	nonessential division	Classical logic	1.1.4.1

Arabic	English	Notes on Translation	Loc.
taqwīm	essential division		1.1.4.1
tardīd	constitution		
taʿrīf	elimination		9.2.2.2
taʿrīf ḥaqīqī (1)	definition	New	4.1
taʿrīf haqīqī (2)	real definition	New	4.2.2
taʿrīf ismī	proper definition	New	4.2.3
taʿrīf lafẓī	hypothetical definition; nominal definition		4.2.2
taṣaffuḥ	lexical definition		4.2.3
tasāwī	examination	Set theory	9.2.1
taṣawwur	equality	Classical logic	3.3; 4.4.1
taṣawwur bi-ḥasab al-ḥaqīqa	conception; conceptual knowledge	New	1.1.3
taṣawwur bi-ḥasab al-ism	real conception	New	4.2.1
taṣdīq	hypothetical conception	Classical logic	4.2.1
taṣdīq bi-thubūt al-shayʾ li-ghayrihi	judgment; propositional knowledge	New	1.1.3
taṣdīq bi-wujūd al-shayʾ fī nafsihi	predicative judgment	New	4.2.1
tashakhkhuṣ	existential judgment	New	4.2.1
ʿumūm wa-khuṣūṣ min wajh	singularization	New	3.1
ʿumūm wa-khuṣūṣ muṭlaq	perspectival inclusiveness	New	3.2
ʿunwān al-maḥmūl	absolute inclusiveness	New	3.2
ʿunwān al-mawḍūʿ	predicate-concept; intension of the predicate	New	6.1
ʿurfiyya ʿāmma	subject-concept; intension of the subject		6.1
ʿurfiyya khāṣṣa	broadly intensionally necessary proposition		6.7.2.1

Arabic	English	Notes on Translation	Loc.
ʿurfiyya lā-dāʾima fī al-baʿḍ	strictly intensionally necessary proposition	New	6.7.2.2
waḍʿ (1)	broadly intensionally continuous propositions that are non-continuous in some cases	New	8.2.2.2
waḍʿ (2) (pl. *awḍāʿ*)	linguistic assignment		2.1.3
waḍʿ nawʿī	state-of-affairs	New	7.3
waḍʿ shakhṣī	assignment of a class of expressions	New	2.1.3
wahm	assignment of an individual expression	New	2.1.3
wājib ʿaqlī	conjecture		1.1.3.3
wājib ʿaraḍī	rationally necessary		5.3.1
wājib dhātī	extrinsically necessary		5.3.3
wājib li-ghayrihi	intrinsically necessary		5.3.3
wāqiʿ	extrinsically necessary		5.3.3
waqtiyya	extra-propositional reality		1.1.3.2; 5.1.1
waqtiyya muṭlaqa	strictly specific-time necessary proposition		6.7.2.2
wasaṭ	broadly specific-time necessary proposition		6.7.2.1
wujūd dhihnī	intermediary premise		2.1.2
wujūd fī nafs al-amr	mental existence	New	5.2
wujūd ikhtirāʿī	existence of a thing in-itself	New	5.2
wujūd intizāʿī	imagined existence	New	5.2
wujūd khārijī	abstracted existence	New	5.2
wujūdiyya lā-dāʾima	extramental existence		5.2
wujūdiyya lā-ḍarūriyya	non-continuous actual proposition		6.7.2.2

Arabic	English	Notes on Translation	Loc.
yaqīn	non-necessary actual proposition		6.7.2.2
ẓann	certain knowledge	New	10.2
ẓannī	probabilistic knowledge		1.1.3.3
yaqīn	probabilistic (evidence)		1.1.3.4
ẓann	probabilistic knowledge	N	1.1
ẓannī	probabilistic (evidence)		1.1

BIBLIOGRAPHY

Arabic Sources and References

al-Anṣārī, Zakariyyā b. Muḥammad and Yāsīn b. Zayn al-Dīn al-ʿĀlimī. *Fatḥ al-Raḥmān sharḥ ʿalā muqaddimat Laqṭat al-ʿajlān wa-ballat al-ẓamʾān wa-bi-hāmishihi ḥāshiyat al-shaykh Yāsīn*. Cairo: Maṭbaʿat Muṣṭafā al-Bābī al-Ḥalabī, 1936.

al-ʿAṭṭār, Ḥasan b. Muḥammad. *Ḥāshiyat al-ʿAṭṭār ʿalā Jamʿ al-jawāmiʿ*. Reprint, Beirut: Dār al-Fikr, n.d.

al-ʿAṭṭār, Ḥasan b. Muḥammad and Muḥammad ʿAlī b. Saʿīd. *Ḥāshiyat al-ʿAṭṭār ʿalā sharḥ al-Khabīṣī wa-bi-hāmishihā ḥāshiyat al-ʿallāma Ibn Saʿīd*. Cairo: ʿĪsā al-Bābī al-Ḥalabī, 1960.

al-Bājūrī, Ibrāhīm. *Ḥāshiyat al-imām al-Bājūrī ʿalā Jawharat al-tawḥīd al-musammāh bi-Tuḥfat al-murīd ʿalā Jawharat al-tawḥīd*. Cairo: Dār al-Salām, 2006.

———. *Ḥāshiyat Ibrāhīm al-Bājūrī ʿalā matn al-Sanūsiyya fī ʿilm al-tawḥīd*. Cairo: Maṭbaʿat Muṣṭafā al-Bābī al-Ḥalabī, 1955.

———. *Ḥāshiyat Ibrāhīm al-Bājūrī ʿalā mukhtaṣar al-Sanūsī fī fann al-manṭiq*. Cairo: Maṭbaʿat al-Taqaddum al-ʿIlmiyya, 1321/1903.

al-Bukhārī, Muḥammad b. Ismāʿīl. *Ṣaḥīḥ al-Bukhārī*, edited by Muṣṭafā Dīb al-Bughā. Damascus: Dār Ibn Kathīr, 1993.

al-Dasūqī, Muḥammad. *Ḥāshiyat al-Dasūqī ʿalā Umm al-barāhīn*. Cairo: Dār Iḥyāʾ al-Kutub al-ʿArabiyya, n.d.

al-Dijwī, Yūsuf. *Khulāṣat ʿilm al-waḍʿ*. Cairo: Maṭbaʿat al-Nahḍa, 1920.

al-Ghursī, Muḥammad Ṣaliḥ. *al-Nukat al-ghurar ʿalā Nuzhat al-naẓar*. Damascus, Dār al-Qa-¯dirī: 2008.

al-Ghazālī, Abū Ḥāmid Muḥammad. *al-Mustaṣfā min ʿilm al-uṣūl*. Beirut: Dār al-Kutub al-ʿIlmiyya, 1993.

al-Khabīṣī, ʿUbaydallāh b. Faḍl, Muḥammad b. Aḥmad al-Dasūqī, and Ḥasan b. Muḥammad al-ʿAṭṭār. *al-Tadhhīb sharḥ ʿalā Tahdhīb al-manṭiq wa-l-kalām wa-ʿalayhi ḥāshiyatān*. Cairo: Maṭbaʿat Muṣṭafā al-Bābī al-Ḥalabī, 1936. [*TB*]

Makhlūf, Muḥammad Ḥasanayn. *al-Ḥāshiya al-thāniya ʿalā al-Jawāhir al-muntaẓamāt fī ʿuqūd al-maqūlāt*. Cairo: Maṭbaʿat Muṣṭafā al-Bābī al-Ḥalabī, 1971.

al-Muẓaffar, Muḥammad Riḍā. *al-Manṭiq*, edited by Ghulām Riḍā al-Fayyāḍī. Qom: Muʾassasat al-Nashr al-Islāmī, 1393/1973.

al-Rāzī, Quṭb al-Dīn, al-Sayyid al-Sharīf al-Jurjānī, ʿAbd al-Ḥakīm al-Siyālkūtī, Jalāl al-Dīn al-Dawānī, al-Dasūqī, and al-Shirbīnī. *Shurūḥ al-Shamsiyya majmūʿat ḥawāshin wa-taʿlīqāt fī al-manṭiq*. Vol. 1. Reprint, Cairo: al-Maktaba al-Azhariyya li-l-Turāth, 2011.

al-Ṣabbān, Muḥammad b. ʿAlī. *Ḥāshiya ʿalā Sharḥ al-Sullam li-l-Mallawī*. Cairo: Maṭbaʿat Muṣṭafā al-Bābī al-Ḥalabī, 1938.

Ṣabrī, Muṣṭafā. *Mawqif al-ʿaql wa-l-ʿilm wa-l-ʿālam min Rabb al-ʿālamīn wa-ʿibādihi al-mursalīn.* Beirut: Dār Iḥyāʾ al-Turāth al-ʿArabī, n.d.

al-Shabrāwī, ʿAbd al-Khāliq. *al-Minḥa al-ilāhiyya fī al-qawāʿid al-waḍʿiyya.* Cairo: Maṭbaʿat al-Saʿāda, n.d.

al-Sharqāwī, ʿAbdallāh b. Ḥijāzī. *Ḥāshiyat al-Sharqāwī ʿalā sharḥ al-Hudhudī ʿalā Umm al-barāhīn.* Cairo: Maṭbaʿat Muṣṭafā al-Bābī al-Ḥalabī, 1955.

Shaṭā, Abū Bakr ʿUthmān. *Iʿānat al-ṭālibīn ʿalā ḥall alfāẓ Fatḥ al-Muʿīn.* Vol. 1. 1997. Reprint, Beirut: Dār Iḥyāʾ al-Turāth al-ʿArabī, n.d.

al-Taftāzānī, Saʿd al-Dīn Masʿūd b. ʿUmar. *Tahdhīb al-manṭiq wa-l-kalām.* Hawalli: Dār al-Ḍiyāʾ, 2017.

al-Taftāzānī, Saʿd al-Dīn Masʿūd b. ʿUmar, Muṣliḥ al-Dīn Muṣṭafā al-Kastalī, Aḥmad b. Mūsā al-Khayālī, and Ramaḍān al-Bahshtī. *Sharḥ al-ʿAqāʾid al-Nasafiyya.* 1326/1908.

al-Taftāzānī, Saʿd al-Dīn Masʿūd b. ʿUmar, Ibn Yaʿqūb al-Maghribī, and Bahāʾ al-Dīn al-Subkī. *Shurūḥ al-Talkhīṣ.* Vol. 2. Reprint, Beirut: Muʾassasat Dār al-Bayān al-ʿArabī, n.d.

al-Tahānawī, Muḥammad ʿAlī. *Kashshāf iṣṭilāḥāt al-funūn wa-l-ʿulūm al-islāmiyya.* Vol. 1. Reprint, Beirut: Dār Ṣādir, n.d.

al-Urmawī, Sirāj al-Dīn. *Risāla fī al-farq bayna nawʿay al-ʿilm al-ilāhī wa-l-kalām.* In *Majmūʿ thalāth rasāʾil,* edited by Muḥammad Akram Abū Ghūsh, 65-79. Amman: Dār al-Nūr al-Mubīn, 2013.

English References

Ahmed, Asad Q. *Palimpsests of Themselves: Logic and Commentary in Postclassical Muslim South Asia.* Oakland: University of California Press, 2022.

———. "Post-Classical Philosophical Commentaries/Glosses: Innovation in the Margins." *Oriens* 41, no. 3-4 (2013): 317-48.

———. "The *Jiha/Tropos-Mādda/Hūlē* Distinction in Arabic Logic and its Significance for Avicenna's Modals." In *The Unity of Science in the Arabic Tradition: Science, Logic, Epistemology and their Interactions*, edited by Shahid Rahman, et al., 229-53. Dordrecht: Springer, 2008.

Ardeshir, Mohammed. "Ibn Sīnā's Philosophy of Mathematics." In *The Unity of Science*, edited by Shahid Rahman, et al., 43-61. Dordrecht: Springer, 2008.

Bäck, Allan. "Islamic Logic?" In *The Unity of Science in the Arabic Tradition: Science, Logic, Epistemology and their Interactions*, edited by Shahid Rahman, et al., 255-79. Dordrecht: Springer, 2008.

Barbour, Ian G. *Religion and Science.* New York: HarperCollins, 1997.

Beall, Jc and Michael Glanzberg. "Liar Paradox." *Stanford Encyclopedia of Philosophy* (Fall 2014), edited by Edward N. Zalta, http://plato.stanford.edu/archives/fall2014/entries/liar-paradox.

Bulliet, Richard. *Conversion to Islam in the Medieval Period: An Essay in Quantitative History.* Cambridge: Harvard University Press, 1979.

El-Rouayheb, Khaled. "Dawānī (d. 1502) and Dashtakī (d. 1498) on Primary (*awwalī*) and Familiar (*mutaʿāraf*) Predication." *Oriens* 51, no. 3-4 (2023): 367-92. https://doi.org/10.1163/18778372-12340031.

———. "Does a Proposition Have Three Parts or Four? A Debate in Later Arabic Logic." *Oriens* 44, no. 3-4 (2016): 301-31. https://doi.org/10.1163/18778372-04403001.

———. *The Development of Arabic Logic (1200-1800).* Basel: Schwabe Verlag, 2019.

———. "The Liar Paradox in Fifteenth-Century Shiraz: The Exchange between Ṣadr al-Dīn al-Dashtakī and Jalāl al-Dīn al-Dawānī." *British Journal for the History of Philosophy* 28, no 2. (2020): 251-75. https://doi.org/10.1080/09608788.2019.1616156.

Fitting, Melvin. "Intensional Logic," *Stanford Encyclopedia of Philosophy* (Summer 2015), edited by Edward N. Zalta, http://plato.stanford.edu/archives/sum2015/entries/logic-intensional.

Gupta, Anil and Stephen Mackereth. "Definitions." *Stanford Encyclopedia of Philosophy* (Fall 2023), edited by Edward N. Zalta and Uri Nodelman, https://plato.stanford.edu/archives/fall2023/entries/definitions.

Horn, Laurence R. "Contradiction." *Stanford Encyclopedia of Philosphy* (Summer 2024), edited by Edward N. Zalta and Uri Nodelman, https://plato.stanford.edu/archives/sum2024/entries/contradiction.

Ichikawa, Jonathan Jenkins and Matthias Steup. "The Analysis of Knowledge." *Stanford Encyclopedia of Philosophy* (Summer 2018), edited by Edward N. Zalta, https://plato.stanford.edu/archives/sum2018/entries/knowledge-analysis.

Karamali, Hamza. *Madrasa Curriculum in Context*. Abu Dhabi: Kalam Research and Media, 2017.

———. *Kalam 3.0: The Muslim Manual of Logical Arguments to Show the Truth of Islam in the 21st Century*. Basira Education, 2024.

———. *Why Islam is True: Quranic Arguments for God, the Prophet Muhammad, and the Purpose of Life*. Basira Education, 2024.

Klima, Gyula. "Medieval Problem of Universals." *Stanford Encyclopedia of Philosophy* (Fall 2013), edited by Edward N. Zalta, http://plato.stanford.edu/archives/fall2013/entries/universals-medieval.

Rezakhany, Hassan John. "Jalāl ad-Dīn ad-Dawānī's Solution to the Liar Paradox and Its Reception in Qāḍī Mubārak and Mullā Mubīn." *Journal of South Asian Intellectual History* 1, no. 2 (2018): 183-220. https://doi.org/10.1163/25425552-12340007.

Schoeler, Gregor. "The 'Poetic Syllogism' Revisited." *Oriens* 41, no. 1-02 (2013): 1-26. https://doi.org/10.1163/18778372-13410101.

Strobino, Riccardo. *Avicenna's Theory of Science: Logic, Metaphysics, Epistemology*. Oakland: University of California Press, 2021.

Street, Tony. "Afḍal al-Dīn al-Khūnajī (d. 1248) on the Conversion of Modal Propositions." *Oriens* 24, no. 3-4 (2014): 454-513.

———. "An Outline of Avicenna's Syllogistic." *Archiv für Geschichte der Philosophie* 84, no. 2 (2002): 129-160. https://doi.org/10.1515/agph.2002.007.

———, Street, Tony, trans. *Najm al-Dīn al-Kātibī's al-Risālah al-shamsiyyah: An Edition and Translation with Commentary*. New York: New York University Press, 2024.

Vaidya, Anand. "Epistemology of Modality." *Stanford Encyclopedia of Philosophy* (Summer 2015), edited by Edward N. Zalta, http://plato.stanford.edu/archives/sum2015/entries/modality-epistemology.

Volumes in the Islamic Philosophy and Theology Series

1. Discerning Religious Truth: A Didactic Exposition of the Logic and Epistemology of the Islamic Sciences.
2. The Logic of al-Fanārī: A study and annotated translation of al-Fanārī's commentary on the *Īsāghūjī*.
3. Occasionalism Revisited: New Essays from the Islamic and Western Traditions.